ALONE

ALSO BY MICHAEL KORDA

Clouds of Glory: The Life and Legend of Robert E. Lee

Hero: The Life and Legend of Lawrence of Arabia

With Wings Like Eagles:
A History of the Battle of Britain

Journey to a Revolution: A Personal Memoir and
History of the Hungarian Revolution of 1956

Horse Housekeeping: Everything You Need to Know to
Keep a Horse at Home (co-author)

Horse People: Scenes from the Riding Life

Marking Time: Collecting Watches and Thinking about Time

Ulysses S. Grant: The Unlikely Hero

Country Matters: The Pleasures and Tribulations of
Moving from a Big City to an Old Country Farmhouse

Making the List: A Cultural History of
the American Bestseller, 1900–1999

Another Life: A Memoir of Other People

Man to Man: Surviving Prostate Cancer

The Fortune

Queenie

Worldly Goods

Charmed Lives

Success!

Power! How to Get It, How to Use It

Male Chauvinism and How It Works at Home and in the Office

Michael Korda

ALONE

Britain, Churchill, and Dunkirk:
Defeat into Victory

LIVERIGHT PUBLISHING CORPORATION

A Division of W. W. Norton & Company

INDEPENDENT PUBLISHERS SINCE 1923

NEW YORK • LONDON

For information about permission to reproduce selections from this book,
write to Permissions, Liveright Publishing Corporation,
a division of W. W. Norton & Company, Inc.,
500 Fifth Avenue, New York, NY 10110

For information about special discounts for bulk purchases, please contact
W. W. Norton Special Sales at specialsales@wwnorton.com or 800-233-4830

Manufacturing by Quad Graphics, Fairfield
Book design by Brooke Koven
Production manager: Anna Oler

Library of Congress Cataloging-in-Publication Data

Names: Korda, Michael, 1933– author.
Title: Alone : Britain, Churchill, and Dunkirk :
defeat into victory / Michael Korda.
Other titles: Britain, Churchill, and Dunkirk, defeat into victory
Description: New York : Liveright Publishing Corporation, a division of
W. W. Norton & Company, [2017] | Includes bibliographical
references and index.
Identifiers: LCCN 2017017244 | ISBN 9781631491320 (hardcover)
Subjects: LCSH: Dunkirk, Battle of, Dunkerque, France, 1940. | World War,
1939–1945—Campaigns—France—Dunkerque. | Korda, Michael, 1933– —
Childhood and youth. | World War, 1939–1945—Great Britain. |
World War, 1939–1945—Personal narratives, English.
Classification: LCC D756.5.D8 K67 2017 | DDC 940.54/21428—dc23
LC record available at https://lccn.loc.gov/2017017244

Liveright Publishing Corporation
500 Fifth Avenue, New York, N.Y. 10110
www.wwnorton.com

W. W. Norton & Company Ltd.
15 Carlisle Street, London W1D 3BS

1 2 3 4 5 6 7 8 9 0

In loving memory of Margaret,
Whose idea it was.

I have myself full confidence that if all do their duty, if nothing is neglected . . . we shall prove ourselves once again able to defend our island home, to ride out the storm of war, and to outlive the menace of tyranny, if necessary for years, if necessary alone.

—WINSTON CHURCHILL,
speaking to the House of Commons, June 4, 1940,
on the completion of the evacuation of Dunkirk

Contents

PART ONE • *The Second Great War*

PART TWO • *The Battle of France*

PART THREE • *Dunkirk*

"The Past Is
a Foreign Country"

*For Europeans the approach to World War Two did not take place as
a sudden event like Pearl Harbor but instead in the form of a numb-
ing series of crises occurring at an increasingly rapid rate, each one
more serious than the last, culminating in catastrophe.*

*As a child these crises did not have much, if any, effect on me until
war finally came and changed my life as it did everyone's, most far
more harshly than mine. All the same, I saw, I remember, and by
now, more than seventy-five years after the events that led to war,
it is possible to know exactly what happened, and why, and to write
about it objectively. All wars occur from a succession of mistakes, usually on both sides, and of no war is that more true than the Second
World War.*

*Mine was a privileged childhood, and for that reason I, like several
thousand other English children, ended up to my surprise in the
United States as a kind of first-class refugee, set comfortably adrift
by the war.*

*I have no complaints. This is not a tale of suffering; it is an
attempt to explain what happened between the halcyon days of the*

summer of 1939, at the end of which war broke out, and the harsh awakening in the summer of 1940. Then we—the British—found ourselves alone, having misjudged the French Army's strength and placed ourselves in a position where what remained of our army was returning from the beaches of Dunkirk in small boats, having abandoned its equipment and its arms, leaving most of Western Europe in German hands.

How we arrived there, on the brink of disaster, is the subject of this book, at once the modest account of my family's dispersal, and a history of the greater events that led to Dunkirk, and to Britain's "finest hour," as Winston Churchill called it.

Memory is not an exact instrument. As we grow older we tend to impose the present on the past, or to remember what we wish had happened rather than what actually did. I was—a phrase that did not then exist—"a movie brat," for everyone in my family either made films or, in the case of the women, acted in them. My uncle Alexander Korda was a famous film director and producer, a "movie mogul" who challenged the Hollywood studio moguls on his own terms. My uncle Zoltan was a famed film director, my father, Vincent, an internationally renowned film art director, my "auntie Merle" Oberon a major movie star, my aunt Joan and my mother respected actresses. Ours was not an ordinary family, but war changes everybody's life, so this is also partly the story of how our lives were reshaped by the events around us, which my uncle Alex and his brothers could perhaps read more clearly than most because they were born in Central Europe, and therefore had no difficulty understanding what Hitler stood for—or what he intended to do.

They had no illusions about Nazi Germany, which is more than can be said for a lot of powerful and respected people on both sides of the Atlantic throughout the 1930s, and even in 1939 and 1940.

It is to those so much less fortunate than myself that I also dedicate this book.

Rule Brittania!
Brittania rule the waves!
Britons never, never, never
Shall be slaves.

—Thomas Arne, 1740

PART ONE

The Second Great War

La Boueé, Plage de la Garoupe, Cap d'Antibes, before the war.

1

To the Brink

Chamberlain, Daladier, Hitler, Mussolini, and Ciano,
Munich Conference, September 1938.

I T IS CURIOUS with what clarity one remembers great events of the past, even from those long-ago days before twenty-four-hour-a-day television and web news became a constant background to daily life.

In the 1930s and throughout the war it was a ritual in many, if not most, households in the United Kingdom to sit down after supper and listen solemnly to the nine o'clock news from the British Broadcasting Corporation. There were no alternative radio channels; however bloodcurdling the events of the day, news was fed out in small doses by the BBC and read in a tone as dry as a sermon. It was no accident that the BBC had originally required those read-

"VERY WELL , ALONE "

ing the news on the radio (or "wireless," as it is called in the United Kingdom) to wear nothing less than formal evening clothes while doing so. Listening to the news then was a secular rite from the most humble home to Buckingham Palace, and although the BBC got much of its news from the government, it was generally trusted. Far from making the news exciting the British and the French governments were to produce calm at all costs and to downplay, or even deny, any crises. Keeping calm was seen as a patriotic duty, even as one crisis after another led inexorably to war—panic was the enemy.

My father, Vincent, a rumpled Bohemian who had followed his brothers into the film business, did not panic easily, if at all, perhaps because he was born in the last years of the Austro-Hungarian Empire, a place where crises were constant, but never taken seriously. The old Viennese joke might have served as the motto for the fading empire: "The situation is desperate—but not serious." Despite threats from Berlin and rumblings of war over Danzig and the Polish Corridor in August 1939, my father did not, as so many other people in England already had, cancel his plans for our summer holiday on what was then still called, as if it were another world, "the Continent." For years he had spent the month of August at the unpretentious Hôtel de la Bouée, on the Plage de la Garoupe on the Cap d'Antibes, owned by his friends the Vials, whose daughter Micheline was the same age as me. Although Micheline and I were only six, it was my father's wish, expressed strongly and frequently in his fluent, inimitably Hungarian-accented French, that we should get married one day, thus assuring him of a permanent nest on the Cap d'Antibes in his old age.

Pleas came from his eldest brother, my uncle Alex, the head of the Korda family and a benevolent though demanding dicta- tor who in the words of one admirer "looked like a Renaissance prince, and spent like one," or from people who were in the know like one of Winston Churchill's loyal friends, the political strate- gist and canny financial adviser Brendan Bracken, to stay put until the crisis was resolved, but my father ignored them. His stately, yearly progress from London to Paris and then on to Antibes, was not something he would give up merely because of threats of war from Hitler. He had survived the First World War, serving in the Austro-Hungarian infantry, as well as the Communist revolution in Budapest that came in the wake of defeat, then the White coun- terrevolution that brought to power Admiral Miklós Horthy, the first Fascist and for a time the leading anti-Semite in Europe. Hav- ing lived through war and the collapse and breakup of an empire, my father treated with indifference seismic geopolitical events that set other people to canceling their reservations. When my mother, a blond, glamorous successful English stage actress, and normally a cheerful and unflappable person, expressed her con- cern, he merely said, "Don't be silly, Gertrude, vat the hell you know about it?"

Winston Churchill and Brendan Bracken.

*　　*　　*

All the same, as Vincent sat beneath a beach umbrella reading a copy of *Le Petit Niçois* in the morning while he dipped a croissant in his café au lait and lit his first cigarette of the day, events that August must have seized his attention—he was not a Central European for nothing.

Less than a year earlier at the height of the Czech crisis in September 1938 the British prime minister, Neville Chamberlain, had addressed the nation on the BBC and remarked, "How horrible, fantastic, incredible it is that we should be digging trenches and trying on gas masks here because of a quarrel in a far-away country between people of whom we know nothing."

But these people were not "far-away" to my father, who had been born when what was now Czechoslovakia had still been part of the Austro-Hungarian Empire, and the southern half of Poland as well. The Czechs, the Poles, and the Austrian Germans were not people about whom my father knew "nothing." They were people who had served as he had in the multinational Imperial and Royal Austro-Hungarian Army.*

What my father read in the papers while my mother slept late and Micheline and I played on the beach under the supervision of my nanny, Nanny Low, caused him and Monsieur Vial, Micheline's father, to chat somberly and at length over more coffee, like doctors discussing a gravely ill patient. Monsieur Vial and my father had both fought in the Great War, as it was still then known, although on different sides, and both of them could recognize from experience the warning signs of war.

It is perhaps significant that the popular song one heard played everywhere in France that summer on the radio or the gramophone was "Tout va très bien, Madame la Marquise," that French comic classic about an aristocratic lady on vacation calling home to see how things are going in her absence only to be told by her servants of one disaster after another, each described as "a little incident, a nothing," culminating in the suicide of her husband and the burning down of her château, every horrific step to ruin celebrated by the cheerful refrain

> *Mais à part ça, Madame la Marquise,*
> *Tout va très bien, tout va très bien.*

---

* The emperor Franz Joseph was emperor of Austria and king of Hungary, so all national institutions, including himself, were "*kaiserlich und königlich*," that is, "imperial and royal."

(But apart from that, Madame la Marquise, everything is going just fine.)

My mother, whose French was fluent and perfect thanks to a childhood in a French convent school, took to singing this constantly, like the whole French nation as it tumbled step by step toward exactly the catastrophe everyone feared most.

The French premier Edouard Daladier, known to his supporters as "the bull of the Vaucluse" after his birthplace, more because of his stocky, portly build than from any bull-like degree of fierceness, seemed dazed by the steadily mounting threats from Berlin against Poland. Daladier had represented France at the Munich Conference in 1938, when the British and the French had forced France's ally Czechoslovakia, in a triumph for Hitler, to give up the Sudetenland (and with it the Czech line of defenses) to Nazi Germany. As his aircraft approached Le Bourget on his return, Daladier was

Chamberlain, French foreign minister Georges Bonnet, and Daladier.

alarmed to see below him an immense crowd, the largest since Lindbergh had landed there in 1927, and drew the conclusion that he was going to be lynched by his angry countrymen for abandoning the Czechs. When the aircraft landed and the door was opened, Daladier was momentarily shocked speechless to discover that they were there to cheer him for bringing back peace. Turning to an aide he whispered in savage contempt, "Mais quels cons!" (A close English equivalent would be "What assholes!") Daladier might not live up to his nickname, but at least he was a realist who knew that he had caved in shamelessly to Hitler.

In the nine-hundred-year-old tradition of mistrust between France and England the person Daladier blamed for this was Neville Chamberlain, not Hitler. Ironically Chamberlain has passed into history as the ultimate appeaser, his tightly rolled umbrella the symbol of spineless surrender, but in fact he was a man of far greater will power, energy, determination, and moral authority than Daladier, a tough-minded politician with a firm grasp on his party, a solid majority in the House of Commons, and the full support of the king and queen. His flaw was not pusillanimity; it was a lethal combination of vanity and pig-headedness.

NEVILLE CHAMBERLAIN

When Graham Stewart wrote his splendid book about the relationship between Churchill and Chamberlain, he called it *Burying Caesar*, and it was an insightful title. Between May 1937 and May 1940 Chamberlain bestrode the British political world like a colossus. He was "masterful, confident, and ruled by an instinct for order . . . but his mind, once made up [was] hard to change." Like Caesar he seemed beyond challenge, even beyond criticism, master of all he surveyed. Majestic, calm, determined, he did not listen to criticism, or encourage it from those around him—he had entire confidence in his own judgment and, more important, in the rightness of his cause, and always presumed he stood on the moral high ground. Coupled with his dislike of foreigners—he was contemptuous of Frenchmen, Russians, and Americans, not just Germans—Chamberlain had dragged a reluctant Daladier into the betrayal of Czechoslovakia, but unlike the French premier he was proud of what he had done.

When Chamberlain waved the Anglo-German declaration above his head to those who greeted him at Heston Aerodrome in September 1938, and declared to the crowd in front of 10 Downing Street, "I have returned from Germany with peace for our time," he felt supremely confident—indeed except for a small group of naysayers consisting mostly of Churchill and his few supporters, Chamberlain was hailed not only in Britain, but around the world as a statesman-hero. The *New York Times* spoke for most of the world the day after Chamberlain's return: "Let no man say that too high a price has been paid for peace . . . until he has searched his soul and found himself willing to risk in war the lives of those who are nearest and dearest to him."

It was not that Chamberlain *liked* Hitler—in fact, he had described him as "the commonest little dog"* after their first meeting—but he had looked Hitler in the eye and decided he could trust his word. He had seen in Hitler an ordinary man who had made good, much like Chamberlain himself, neither a smooth, supercilious diplomat

* For his part, the Führer was bored and annoyed by Chamberlain's attempts to break the ice between them with small talk on the subject of dry-fly fishing, something about which Hitler knew nothing and cared less, and which led him to dismiss Chamberlain and his advisers as "worms." This had unfortunate consequences in August 1939—Hitler believed that Chamberlain would not intervene if he attacked Poland, and he turned out to be wrong. Foreign Secretary Lord Halifax did worse, however—at *his* first meeting with Hitler he almost handed the Führer his overcoat and hat under the impression that he was a footman.

nor an aristocrat. Chamberlain himself was the grandson of a man who had labored as a shoemaker as a child in Victorian England like Dickens in his "blacking factory," and the son of a man who had made his fortune manufacturing screws in industrial Birmingham, yet who almost succeeded in winning the prime ministership. Joseph Chamberlain's second son, Neville,* was a tough negotiator and a gifted politician, but he had the successful businessman's conviction that he could tell at a glance whether a man's word was his bond or not.

When it turned out that Hitler's was not, even when accompanied by his signature—the Führer occupied the rest of Czechoslovakia with a brutal show of force in March 1939—Chamberlain finally had to face the fact that Hitler could not be trusted. He moved at once to respond to Germany's aggression with a hasty and incautious guarantee to come to Poland's support in case it was attacked by Germany, and dragged an ever more reluctant Daladier along with him, thus placing France and Britain in the direct path of Hitler's next foreign policy move.

German diplomacy moved immediately into the familiar ascending Wagnerian chorus of threats, saber rattling, arbitrary deadlines, and shrill lies, alternating with assurances of good behavior in the future if the Führer got what he wanted at once. These tactics had set European nerves on edge from 1936 to the early months of 1939, securing for Germany the Rhineland, Austria, the Sudetenland, and now the rest of Czechoslovakia without a shot fired. This time there were two obstacles in the way, however. The first was the Poles themselves, who stubbornly, and as it turned out self-destructively, refused to negotiate even small issues with the Germans. The second was Neville Chamberlain, who could neither forget nor forgive that Hitler had broken his word.

Daladier might respond to Hitler's duplicity with a weary, Gallic shrug, but Chamberlain was *personally* affronted. Nonetheless,

---

* Neville Chamberlain's older half brother, Austen, was the more glamorous of the two; he became a respected foreign secretary and a Knight of the Garter who was awarded the Nobel Peace Prize in 1925.

he did very little to speed up the glacial pace of British rearmament, and he hesitated to take the one step that might have made sense—for Britain and France to secure an alliance with Soviet Russia, which would have confronted Hitler and his generals with the dreaded "war on two fronts" that had eventually undermined Germany in the Great War. Step by step he and Daladier stood by helplessly as events swirled out of their control.

Chamberlain's political archenemy former Prime Minister David Lloyd George might contemptuously dismiss the prime minister as "a good Lord Mayor of Birmingham in a lean year," but Chamberlain was more than that—he was a man so convinced of his own strength, wisdom, and virtue that he failed to understand the degree to which his cautious diplomacy had ensured just the war he had sought so hard to avoid.

Thus matters stood in those first, sunny weeks of August 1939 as we, like most families, took our holiday, since France then virtually closed down in August, as it still does. Monsieur Vial was not an ardent supporter of Daladier, who had accepted a cabinet post during Léon Blum's Front Populaire in 1936, and was therefore a little too radical* for his taste, though Daladier was hardly "a man of the left." My father, partly influenced by his eldest brother, Alex, and by Brendan Bracken, was a supporter of Churchill rather than Chamberlain, insofar as he took any interest at all in British politics. Vincent, unlike Brendan and Alex, was a man of leftish sympathies, and for that reason Alex had made him responsible for dealing with the film unions at the London Films studio in Denham.

In the ordinary course of things Churchill would have been too far to the right about social issues to appeal to my father, but

---

* It should be explained that the word "radical" in French politics does not connote, as it does in the UK and the US, wild-eyed, bomb-throwing anarchists, but describes instead members of the well-respected Radical Party, essentially bourgeois, republican, anticlerical defenders of the status quo. Daladier was suspect to small businessmen like M. Vial because he had favored the forty-hour week and other mild social reforms.

Admiral Horthy enters Budapest, 1919.

at the same time he admired Churchill's firm stand against Hitler, and understood far better than most Britons did at that time how evil and dangerous the Nazis were. His experience of living under Horthy's Fascist regime in Hungary in 1919 and 1920 had given him a clear understanding of just how brutal the Nazi regime was in Germany. Besides, from 1933 to 1939 he was in constant touch with old friends, film people, and artists fleeing from Austria, from Germany, and from Czechoslovakia because they were Jewish, or on the left, or both.

He and my uncle Alex strove mightily to get their old friend and trusted doctor Henry Lax and his family out of Vienna in 1938, and at dinnertime in our house on Well Walk, near Hampstead Heath in London, there was a constant stream of polyglot arrivals from the Continent on their way to New York or Los Angeles thanks to the Korda brothers, men and women with odd accents like my father's who preferred to speak Hungarian or German with him and French to my mother. They had the haunted look of people who have just witnessed a bad accident, people with aggressive charm and formal manners who had grown up with the Kordas in Túrkeve, or had been to university in Budapest with Alex, or loaned him money, or worked with my father on film sets in Vienna, Paris, or Berlin. Most of them were relieved to be in England, but still determined to put the Atlantic between themselves and Hitler if possible, not just the English Channel.

My father hardly needed the newspapers to tell him about what was going on in Europe: old ladies in Vienna after the Anschluss forced to get down on their knees and scrub the pavement in front of their apartment building with their toothbrush while Brownshirts—and often enough their own neighbors—jeered and kicked them, Jews and men of the left disappearing into concentration camps throughout Germany, life savings expropriated, businesses taken over and "Aryanized," apartments, artwork, jew-

Jews being forced to scrub the pavement, Vienna, 1938.

elry confiscated, synagogues and books burned, shop windows shattered. It was already a long trail of suffering, humiliation, and cruelty about which nobody wanted to hear, and that neither the British nor the American government wanted to address for fear of having to accept hundreds of thousands of Jews who were *not* world famous doctors and scientists like Sigmund Freud and Albert Einstein, or film stars like Louise Rainer, or successful playwrights like Ferenc Molnár, or nuclear physicists, or the kind of people who could get a job of some kind at any movie studio in Hollywood.

The Korda brothers never bothered to mention that they were Jewish to their wives or children—no doubt as Hungarians they were already exotic enough when they arrived in England in 1932 without adding another layer—but that is not to say that they ignored what was going on, or what was likely to come.* Apart from his friendship with Churchill, who worked for London Films in the thirties, Alex was also a friend of Major-General Sir Stuart "Jock" Menzies, KCB, KCMG, DSO, MC, chief of MI6, known in government circles as "C,"† and used his innumerable European contacts to procure information for British intelligence, as well as giving jobs in the London Films offices overseas to covert MI6 agents. In New York City he rented much more expensive office space than he needed for London Films in Rockefeller Center to give "cover" to a number of well-dressed men and young women whose knowledge of the film industry was insubstantial. There were secrets that the three brothers kept from their wives, and many secrets that Alex kept from his investors, but there were no secrets among the brothers themselves.

Vincent can therefore have had no doubt about the meaning of the headlines on August 24 announcing the bombshell signature

---

* I did not learn it until 1961, when my uncle Zoltan died, having asked for a rabbi to attend his funeral. My mother went to her grave at the age of ninety-four still convinced that this was another of my father's practical jokes.

† The head of MI6 (or SIS, as it is also called) is always known as "C," after the last name of its first director. Ian Fleming changed it to "M" for his Bond novels.

of a nonaggression pact between Germany and the Soviet Union, negotiated in secret while the Anglo-French delegation was still meeting in a leisurely way with Soviet officials in Moscow. It says everything about this failed and halfhearted attempt to secure a last-minute alliance with the Soviet Union that the head of the British delegation was the aristocratic Admiral the Hon. Sir Reginald Aylmer Ranfurly Plunkett-Ernle-Erle-Drax, KCB, DSO, JP, scarcely a name likely to appeal to the proletarian sympathies of officials in Stalinist Russia. The appointment of Sir Reginald was symptomatic of the lack of enthusiasm on the part of the British and the French governments for any sort of formal alliance with the USSR. In France those on the right told each other, sotto voce, "Mieux vaut Hitler que Staline" (better Hitler than Stalin), and even in Britain there were people of the same opinion, though less likely to say so aloud. In the end any possibility of an agreement with the Soviet Union to defend Poland was doomed in advance by the Poles' refusal to allow Soviet troops to cross the border in case of German aggression, and by Chamberlain's dislike of the idea of Stalin as a partner: "I must confess to the most profound distrust of Russia," he wrote frankly.

This doubt communicated itself to Stalin, who responded by dismissing Maxim Litvinov as people's commissar for foreign affairs, replacing him with Vyacheslav M. Molotov. Although a Bolshevik, Litvinov was urbane, charming, worldly and had a good sense of humor. He had lived in England, was married to an Englishwoman, and counted H. G. Wells and George Bernard Shaw among his friends. He was also a Jew, as was his wife, Ivy, so the Germans would have found it difficult, if not impossible, to negotiate with him. Molotov was not only a famously tough bargainer, without a trace of charm or humor, but a gentile.

This sudden change should have come as a warning to everyone that Stalin was preparing to make an agreement with Hitler, but it did not. Soviet politics was a mystery even to experienced politicians, "a riddle wrapped in a mystery inside an enigma," as Churchill put it. Hundreds of thousands of people had been swept away to execution or the Gulag in waves of "purges" over what seemed like minor points of Marxist doctrine or because of Stalin's paranoid suspicion, with the result that even quite significant changes in the Soviet government seemed arbitrary and whimsical to outsiders, a game of "musical chairs" on a vast scale in which the losers were shot. In Berlin, however, the signal was not missed—it takes one dictator to recognize a subtle message sent by another—and the replacement of Litvinov by Molotov was seen at once by Hitler as an invitation to negotiate the hitherto unthinkable, an alliance between Nazi Germany and Soviet Russia.

On August 23 Reich Foreign Minister Joachim von Ribbentrop and Molotov signed this bombshell of an agreement in Moscow, with a beaming Stalin looking on as if he were about to give away the bride. When the news broke the next day, along with the Soviet decision to end negotiations with Britain and France while their negotiators were still in Moscow, almost everybody but the most dogged of appeasers realized that war would break out soon. It would begin when the harvest was in, my father told Monsieur Vial,

August 27, 1939, the signing of the nonaggression pact between
Germany and the USSR (far left, Ribbentrop; center, Stalin;
right, Molotov).

RENDEZVOUS

and Monsieur Vial did not disagree. This was old-fashioned folk wisdom in every European country.

Vincent booked us on the "Blue Train" home, for once giving up the chance to break his journey and spend a few days in Paris, and made his farewells to old friends on the Riviera like Marcel Pagnol, the playwright, whose hit play *Marius* my uncle Alex had made into a film in 1931. Until then Vincent had been living peacefully as a painter in Golfe-Juan, a little seaside town near Vallauris, but Alex had not been happy with the set designs for *Marius*, which had been borrowed from those of the play. On the grounds that my father at least knew what the Old Port in Marseille looked like, he sent for him (in the Korda family Alex's wishes were commands) to design something more suitable, thus setting Vincent on the path to a new career.

Like everyone else Pagnol was depressed at the idea of having to fight the Germans all over again only twenty-one years after they had been defeated at the cost of 1,350,000 French lives. Like most of the French he hoped without much confidence that things could be "arranged" at the last minute, just as they had been at Munich, without descending into total war. If the politicians were unable to do so—a lift of the eyebrows, a shrug—then France would merely have to retire behind the Maginot Line and wait to see what happened.

Even as a boy of six, I observed that everybody in France talked about *la ligne Maginot* reverentially as if it were a holy object, some older ladies even making a discreet sign of the cross when it was mentioned. It was explained to me that it was a line of underground fortresses designed to protect France from invasion, which I already knew because far from being secret, the Maginot Line, which had cost France over three billion francs to build and stretched almost five hundred miles from the Swiss border to Luxembourg, was widely publicized. Lavish photo displays of it had appeared in such magazines as *Life* in the United States, *Picture Post* and the *Illustrated London News* in the United Kingdom, and the equivalents all over the world. For a child who liked to play with toy soldiers and castles, there was something irresistibly fascinating about underground fortresses connected by electric railway lines buried deep in the earth,

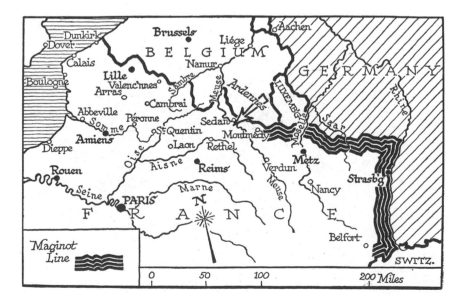

and armored steel turrets that rose from apparently peaceful meadows and hills like gigantic mushrooms at the push of a button.

My father even had big enlargements of photographs of the Maginot Line stacked in the clutter of his studio at home—he had based some of his designs on them for *Things to Come*, Alex's film of the futuristic H. G. Wells novel—and they were very impressive, with guns of every size raised and lowered by gleaming pneumatic tubes and aimed by telescopic periscopes, like that in a submarine. The silent underground electric trains, the ammunition hoists, the water filtration plants and the state-of-the-art air-conditioning, the network of telephone lines linking every part of it together—it was all decades ahead of its time, a modernist triumph equal in its own way to the German autobahns.

The more publicity the Maginot Line received, the happier the French were—they even ran tours of it, and those who took the tour were given a small stamped silver medal, as if they had visited a shrine like Lourdes—for its purpose, after all, was to *deter* invasion. The whole object of all this concrete, steel, and technology was to *prevent* a war, not to win one. Left unsaid was the fact

An underground electric train delivers the soup, Maginot Line, 1939.

that the shape of the French frontier with Germany created what amounted to "a salient," with its base stretching from Metz to Strasbourg and its tip pointing toward Karlsruhe, of exactly the kind that had cost the lives of hundreds of thousands of men in the Great War but on a much larger scale, and the more important reality that the line of interconnected forts, pillboxes, and antitank ditches ended south of the Belgian frontier.

The French did not want to seal themselves off from neutral Belgium, even though attacking France through Belgium had been the heart and soul of the famous Schlieffen Plan in 1914, which very nearly succeeded. More dangerous still, the Maginot Line did not protect the Ardennes Forest, which, for reasons of economy and disputes between rival French strategists, was left undefended on the grounds that it could not easily be crossed by a modern, mobile army because of the rough terrain, dense woods, narrow secondary roads, steep valleys, and numerous rivers and streams that cut through it. Marshal Pétain himself had said so, and who would argue with the man who had held Verdun in the most costly battle of the Great War?

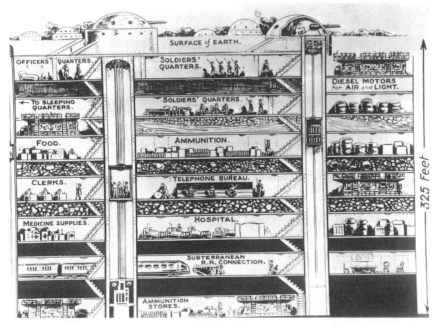

Cross-section of a Maginot Line fort.

Considering that the Ardennes Forest had originally been named by the Romans, who had fought many battles there against the German tribes, and that it has been fought over ever since then in every century, this proved to be an illusion, and the French, of all people, should have known better. If the Romans could hack their way through the Ardennes nearly two millennia earlier, so presumably could the Germans, but such fears were pooh-poohed by the French general staff, and the British, whose initial contribution to the defense of France would only consist of two infantry divisions, were in no position to dispute it, even had they cared to. What concerned the British more was that they could not move forward to take up defensive positions in Belgium until or unless the Germans breached Belgium's neutrality.

Vincent's sense of urgency was relative, and by the time we boarded the Blue Train at Cannes with our mountain of luggage it was the last week of August, and events were already moving more swiftly than he knew. The Blue Train in those days was still one of the

First-class dining car, 1939.

great *trains de luxe* of Europe, the sleeping compartments elegantly furnished, the food and the service impeccable. My father and mother had one compartment, Nanny Low and I the adjoining one, with a connecting door between them. Even to this day I can recall with pleasure the sheer perfection of the sheets once the beds had been lowered and made up, the linen of a smoothness that could only be found traveling first class on wagons-lits and ocean liners. The train was full, mostly of wealthy British people who like us were trying to get home in case the crisis turned into a war. There was no sense of panic, merely a certain guilt at having waited to the last moment to leave the south of France, and a degree of camaraderie that strangers—particularly well-dressed British strangers of a certain class—don't typically exhibit. The train was longer than usual—third-class carriages had been added to it, and as it made its stops at Marseille and Lyon during the night, they filled up with men wearing the khaki uniform of the French Army.

At every station we passed there were more of them, waiting for trains that would take them to the depot of their regiment. From time to time they wandered through the sleeping cars and restaurant car, no doubt out of curiosity to see how the rich traveled, many of them smoking a pungent, unmistakably French cigarette, a Gauloise or a Gitane. The soldiers seemed resigned and glum rather than enthusiastic, and did not present the spit-and-polish appearance, social deference, and disciplined behavior of British regulars—their long, baggy overcoats were unbuttoned, most of them had left the collar of their tunic unfastened, their boots and brass were dull, and some were poorly shaved. Every so often one of the wagon-lit porters would shoo them back to their carriages, and they left with undisguised resentment. It was not just *class* resentment but also a hint of strong French resentment toward their ally.

The French felt—many, perhaps most—that they had been dragged by Britain, still as always in French minds *l'Albion perfide*, first into the Czech crisis and now the Polish crisis, and that if war came they would be left to fight it while the British sheltered behind their fleet and took their own sweet time to arrive on the battlefield in any significant number. The French Army, once fully mobilized,

Anti-British posters, France, 1939. "Dead for Whom? For England!"

would consist of 86 divisions in France alone, over three and a half million men, one of the largest in the world (the German Army consisted of 116 divisions). By contrast, the British had only two regular divisions to send to France on the outbreak of war, to be reinforced by two more divisions about a month thereafter, and then formed into two corps, a formidably professional army, but tiny by Continental standards.

The French reminded themselves constantly that they had no other significant ally—pushed by the British they had consented to the loss of Czechoslovakia and turned away from an alliance with Soviet Russia. The United States was three thousand miles away, still recovering from the Great Depression, lost in the fog of isolationism and determined not to be dragged into another war in Europe, Poland was neither a democracy nor in any position to help France, while Italy was frankly hostile—Mussolini made no secret of his desire to annex French territory—and therefore successive French governments between the wars were obliged to do their best to please the British.

There were plenty of linguists in the British regular Army, and in the days of the empire no shortage of officers who spoke Urdu,

Pashtu, Hindustani, Arabic, or Swahili, but in the 1914–1918 war young Captain Edward Spears had been made liaison officer to the French high command because of his rare gift of fluent French, and in World War Two he would be recalled at a much higher rank[*] to the same duty, so rare was it for a British officer to speak flawless French—indeed so uncommon that in France it was generally believed by the French generals that Spears must be Jewish.

In those days being on a *train de luxe* was like being cut off for a time from all news. My father and my mother ate a long and elaborate meal in the dining car—the food on the great trains was at the level of at least a one-star restaurant, with superb service and a long wine list—while Nanny Low and I were served dinner in our compartment before the attendant made up our beds for the night.

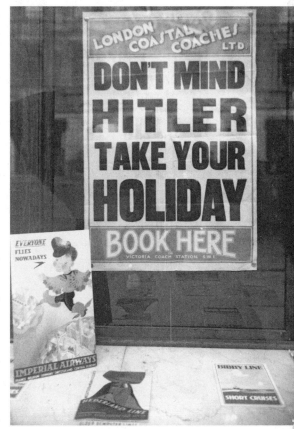

The next day the train shunted around the dreary outskirts of Paris, shedding the extra carriages and the soldiers for the next stage of the journey to Calais and the cross-Channel ferry. I remember my mother's pointing out to me the bold red posters that were already being put up on walls of the Gare Maritime at Calais showing a map of the French empire with the slogan "Nous vaincrons parce que nous sommes les plus forts," (We shall win because we are the stron-

---

[*] He rose to become Major-General Sir Edward Spears, KBE, MC, CB, and to win the grudging praise of Charles de Gaulle.

gest), but otherwise I remember very little of that day, which seemed endless to a child of six—meals, the coming and going of officials, inexplicable delays, then at last the appearance of British customs officers and the overwhelming presence of England surrounding us, the sea air, so much saltier, cooler, and moister than that of the Mediterranean, the slightly brackish smell of tidal waters at Dover, and the comforting sound of English being spoken all around us. The waiters and porters were English now, and familiar things were available: tea, of course, Marmite, Colman's mustard, toast in a silver toast rack covered with a cozy to keep it warm, English butter that for some reason was never as nice as French butter. Outside the train newspaper vendors had their signs put up, one of them with the simple, scrawled headline in big, black letters: "**WAR?**"

Nanny said as she sighed with relief, "It's so nice to be home."

2

The Failure of Diplomacy

Neville Chamberlain, with the famous umbrella.

A T HOME PREPARATIONS for war had been going on since the German seizure of Prague in March 1939. Trenches had been dug close to our house on Hampstead Heath, for what purpose it was not clear. Instructions had been given to every householder on how to prepare "blackout" curtains in case war came. We had been issued gas masks that had to be carried at all times—mine came in a small, square brown canvas-covered cardboard box, with a flimsy string so that it could be slung over the shoulder. (A special one like a rubberized canvas sack with a transparent face shield was even available for babies.)

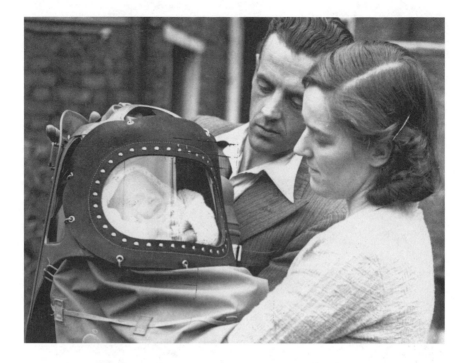

It was, in those last few days of peace, firmly believed that if war came it would begin with a massive bombing raid that would destroy London. This belief had been stated by former Prime Minister Stanley Baldwin, who summed it up in the House of Commons as "The bomber will always get through," a phrase borrowed from the Italian theorist of air warfare Giulio Douhet in his influential book *Command of the Air*—strange reading for Baldwin, who usually napped through discussions of foreign policy and military planning at the cabinet ("Wake me when this is over," he would say to anyone sitting beside him) and whose usual reading was Thackeray or Trollope. It became the strategic policy of the Royal Air Force, not that RAF Bomber Command in 1939 had the aircraft or the technology with which to destroy targets in Germany—nor would the British or the French government have allowed them to do so, since it was feared that whoever first killed "women and children" by bombing would bring about a devastating retaliation by the Luftwaffe on London and Paris. French governments were especially determined not to risk

German bombing of Paris, and therefore not to give Hitler any excuse to bomb it.

The fear that war would begin with a huge aerial attack using high explosive and poison gas to kill large numbers of civilians was pervasive, and it helps to explain the reluctance of the British and French governments to challenge Hitler. The British government was not only issuing gas masks and instructions for blackout curtains but, unbeknownst to the public, was also selecting sites for mass graves and ordering thousands of cheap, mass-made cardboard coffins.

Quite inadvertently my father, Vincent, had been partly responsible for the widespread belief that the war would begin with a massive assault from the air. My uncle Alex's film *Things to Come*, perhaps the most ambitious science-fiction motion picture of the era, began with a long, immensely convincing sequence of London (named Everytown in the film, but with the ruins of St. Paul's

One of Vincent Korda's sets for *Things to Come*.

Cathedral and Covent Garden clearly identifiable) being destroyed from the air in a surprise attack, followed by Armageddon as the survivors flee from the city's ruins and civilization collapses.

So striking were my father's designs for this scene of mass destruction (he was helped in creating it by his Hampstead neighbor and fellow countryman the constructivist visionary and futurist László Moholy-Nagy) that it imprinted itself on the mind of many people, including two prime ministers, Stanley Baldwin and Neville Chamberlain, and the editor of the *Times* Geoffrey Dawson, as well as the general public. It even impressed Hitler when the film was screened for him in Berlin. Audiences everywhere were stunned as the sky was darkened by masses of bombers like huge flocks of black, predatory birds, saturating Everytown with high explosives and poison gases, against eerie background music by the distinguished composer Sir Arthur Bliss.

This vision of instant mass destruction—soon enough to become commonplace throughout Europe—prompted otherwise comparatively sane civil servants to prepare for the worst. Plans were laid to "evacuate" more than a million children from major cities. Operation Pied Piper, as it was called (somebody in the Home Office must have had a sense of humor), would eventually evacuate almost three and a half million people, most of them to "reception zones" in the country, some of them, including myself, overseas to British Dominions or the USA. In keeping with its belief in the efficacy of the bomber, the Air Ministry estimated in 1938 that there would be at least sixty-five thousand civilian casualties in the first week of war and a million in the first month, while at least three million refugees from the destroyed cities would flee to the countryside, causing "total chaos and panic" and creating social disorder and disease. Responding to these wildly alarmist estimates from the Air Ministry, the Home Office had over a million emergency death certificates printed and distributed in advance to local authorities.

When we arrived home in London nothing seemed to have changed, except that we were reunited with our gas masks, but outside our blackened brick garden walls in Hampstead events were moving at a rapid pace. Since March 1939 Hitler had been agitating about the return of the Baltic port city of Danzig to Germany and a solution to the so-called Polish Corridor, separating East Prussia from the rest of Germany. The Treaty of Versailles (1919) had created this "corridor" linking Poland to the Baltic Sea, thus separating East Prussia from West Prussia, and placed the "Free City of Danzig," with a majority of Germans, under League of Nations rule to award the Poles a seaport. Danzig even had its own currency, its own postage stamps (prized by collectors today), a national anthem, and its own "League of Nations High Commissioner," a Swiss diplomat who attempted to govern a city in which even the smallest, most everyday matters were a subject of fierce dispute between German and Polish residents. Danzig and the corridor represented a grievance to *all* Germans, even those who were anti-Nazi, and there were few people in Britain or France who would or could defend it.

Hitler's original demand had been for an "extraterritorial" highway across the corridor, linking East and West Prussia— Germans crossing the corridor complained of being singled out for unreasonable and intrusive searches and delays by Polish customs officers and police—and for the return of the city of Danzig to German rule. A negotiated settlement along these lines might well have succeeded, except for the fact that Polish Minister of Foreign Affairs Józef Beck, a slippery character at best, was unwilling to negotiate. He had only to look at what had happened to Czechoslovakia the year before—first the Czechs lost the Sudetenland, and with it their defense line against the Germans, then what remained of their country was taken from them by brute force, now they were ruled by a Nazi "Reich Protector of Bohemia and Moravia" in Prague, backed up by the SS and the Gestapo. Poland, like Hungary, had shared in the spoils, annexing parts of Czechoslovakia that adjoined Poland, so Beck was no stranger to the process of divvying up a small country in Eastern Europe, or to the Nazis, with whom he shared a strong degree of anti-Semitism and a preference for autocratic rule as opposed to democracy.

Hitler and Polish foreign minister Józef Beck.

Beck did not create a good impression on anyone. Hitler despised him—there is a revealing photograph of Hitler and Beck meeting over tea in the Reich Chancellery that shows the Führer sitting stiffly and staring at the camera in sullen rage while Beck lounges beside him gracefully, a diplomat's smile on his face as if he and Hitler were best friends. In London, Beck's stubborn refusal to listen to the advice of his allies, and his serene confidence that he was in control of events, strained the patience of both Chamberlain and Foreign Secretary Lord Halifax. In Paris, the dawning realization that French foreign policy was now, thanks to Britain, a hostage to Beck's skill as a negotiator, filled everyone in the government with a curious mixture of horror and fatalism, like people being swept inexorably toward Niagara Falls in a canoe without a paddle.

On a visit to London early in 1939 Beck blithely reassured Chamberlain that he doubted "whether there was 'any serious danger' of German aggression," and downplayed the importance of Danzig and the corridor, asserting that the whole matter was "not in itself a grave one." Beck did not explain why Poland had been so eager to obtain a guarantee from Britain and France if there was no grave threat from Germany, nor did he reveal that Józef Lipski, the Polish ambassador to Germany, had already been treated to an icy and "violent" demand from German Foreign Minister von Ribbentrop for the immediate return of Danzig and a German road across the corridor. Beck told Chamberlain and Halifax what they wanted to hear—that there was no threat to Poland, and therefore no likelihood that Britain and France would be called upon to fulfill their guarantee to defend it. For their part they were more concerned to persuade the Poles not to provoke Hitler than to come up with any reasonable strategy for defending them.

Despite his demand for Danzig and the corridor and the intense diplomacy taking place over it, Hitler had already made up his mind to attack and annihilate Poland. We now know that as early as April 3, 1939, he had issued "War Directive No. 1," stating that his intention was "to settle the account for good" and "to smash the Polish armed forces." The operation was code-named *Fall Weiss* (Case White) and opens with this brisk statement: "Since the situation on Germany's Eastern frontier has become intolerable . . . I have decided upon a solution by force." The military was ordered to complete full preparations for an attack that was to be launched on September 1, 1939. At the same time "the conversion of the entire German economy to a war basis [was] now decreed." In the meantime, the British and the French worked hard to persuade the Poles to undertake negotiations with Germany for the peaceful return of Danzig and a road across the corridor, causing the British ambassador to Poland to complain, "If we are not careful [the Poles] may think we are getting cold feet."

The Poles, however, resisted stubbornly, while at the same time playing down the seriousness of the crisis. They rejected Chamberlain's proposal for an alliance of the smaller East European countries (Hungary and Romania), afraid that any such attempt would trigger a violent German reaction. They refused to cooperate with British and French negotiations for an alliance with Soviet Russia, since from the Polish point of view Russia was an even more dangerous enemy than Germany. Besides, the Poles had no great opinion of the Red Army, which they had defeated at the gates of Warsaw only eighteen years previously, and even Chamberlain had to admit that he had "no belief in [Russia's] ability to maintain an effective offensive even if she wanted to," hardly an opinion calculated to persuade the Poles to allow their powerful neighbor to the east to cross the Russo-Polish frontier in the case of a German attack on them.

Nor did the French and the British make any sensible provision for military aid to the Poles. Neither of their countries had any way of reaching Poland by land. In the case of war the French Army would be deployed defensively behind the Maginot Line, which would hardly be of much help to the Poles. As for the British, they were in no position to provide modern fighter aircraft to the Poles, besides which the British government was in any case hoping to be "the honest broker" of a peaceful international negotiation to solve the problem, rather than encouraging the Poles to fight. Even negotiations for a British loan that would enable the Poles to buy British arms was allowed to bog down because of the Treasury's pessimism about the value of the zloty and the ability of Poland to repay it.

Hopes that Mussolini would repeat his role as a peacemaker during the Munich crisis by persuading Hitler to accept another negotiation with Britain and France intended to impose a settlement on the Poles flickered throughout the early summer of 1939. It was a role that Mussolini was eager enough to play, especially since he knew better than anyone else that, given the state of Italy's armed forces, he would have to disappoint Hitler by not going to war beside him, but this time Hitler did not want to settle for a mere slice of the pie; he wanted the whole thing, and by seeking an alliance with Stalin he knew he was going to get it.

Mussolini's smooth, but realistic, foreign minister and son-in-law, Count Galeazzo Ciano, who was trying to produce a diplomatic solution to the problem, learned from his German counterpart Joachim von Ribbentrop that there was no hope of a peaceful solu-

Ciano and Ribbentrop.

tion. Walking with him before dinner in Salzburg, Ciano asked, "Well, what do you want, Ribbentrop? The Corridor or Danzig?"

" 'Not that anymore,' Ribbentrop said, "gazing at me [Ciano] with his cold, metallic eyes. *'We want war!'* "

There has been a tendency among historians to doubt Ciano's account of this conversation, since it was written shortly before his execution by a firing squad on the orders of his own father-in-law in December 1943, but there seems no reason why a doomed man would necessarily invent words; on the contrary, it seems more likely that he would record the truth. Certainly it *sounds* like Ribbentrop, who was notorious for coldly repeating his master's voice, as well as for his lamentable gaffes as a diplomat, such as giving the Nazi salute when he was presented to a startled King George VI as German ambassador to the Court of St. James, and complaining afterwards because the king did not return it. Even Ribbentrop's fellow Nazis complained about the snobbery, ignorance, and slavish sycophancy of the ex-champagne salesman turned expert on foreign affairs whom Hitler constantly praised as "a second Bismarck." When Hermann Göring complained to Hitler about him, the Führer rather weakly defended Ribbentrop on the grounds that he knew the English. "Perhaps," Göring replied skeptically, "but the problem is that they know *him*."

No one factor is sufficient to account for the outbreak of World War Two—great events inevitably have many causes—but there is no doubt that Ribbentrop's misreading of the English, and Hitler's misplaced confidence in his obsequious foreign minister's opinions, played a major part. Hitler's own knowledge of the English was limited to Chamberlain and Halifax, and to the succession of visitors who came to pay homage to him in the thirties like the Marquess of Londonderry, David Lloyd George, and the Duke and Duchess of Windsor, all of whom were eager to reach a mutual "understanding" between Great Britain and Germany, and therefore unlikely to argue with Hitler, or tell him what he did not want to hear. As for Ribbentrop, his knowledge of the English was limited to the wealthy, upper-class appeasers he admired, and was so superficial that he reported home that the abdication of King Edward VIII was the result of a plot by Jews and Freemasons, two of the major bêtes noires in the Nazi mind.

Neither Hitler nor Ribbentrop appreciated the degree to which Chamberlain felt *personally* betrayed by the seizure of the rest of Czechoslovakia in March 1939, nor the subtle shift in the opinions of all but the most determined of British appeasers as Hitler began to annex or threaten areas that did *not* contain a majority of ethnic Germans. The British were not ready for war, and certainly not eager for it, but even in the Conservative Party there were rumblings of discontent amid the apprehension. It was still mostly from the few "glamour boys" around Anthony Eden, or "the Gangsters," as Churchill's small circle of admirers was known within the party, based on the dislike among the rank and file for such "flashy" friends of Churchill's as Brendan Bracken and the wealthy newspaper tycoon Lord Beaverbrook (caricatured as "Lord Copper" in Evelyn Waugh's novel *Scoop*), but there was also

Hitler greets HRH the Duke of Windsor and the Duchess,
October 1937.

a growing feeling of uneasiness in the party about the possibility
of repeating the Munich settlement of 1938 in Poland. Despite
this Chamberlain's majority in the House of Commons was huge,
over two hundred, and secure, the bulk of Conservative members
of Parliament were loyal to him—their loyalty kept fiercely in line
by the formidable chief whip, Captain David Margesson—and
he retained an immense authority and personal popularity, in

politics, in the media and among the public, as well as with the royal family.

Although Chamberlain has been criticized for doing "too little, too late," as the end of August approached, preparations were made to mobilize the fleet and the Royal Air Force, to recall army reservists and Territorials, and to make final preparations for a blackout—quiet, but unmistakable, warnings to the Germans that the invasion of Poland might have serious consequences.

These warnings Hitler ignored—or more likely he did not take them seriously. The German Army and the Luftwaffe were fully mobilized along the border with Poland, nobody could mistake these preparations for peacetime maneuvers, while German diplomacy marched beside the army, becoming daily more threatening toward Poland. On August 25, in response to numerous British and French "peace feelers," both through their ambassadors in Berlin and to Mussolini, Hitler confided to the British ambassador Sir Nevile Henderson "that he accepts the British Empire and is willing to pledge himself to its continued existence," provided that Germany's former colonies were returned and that the "German-Polish question" was resolved.

Sir Nevile, a longstanding and determined appeaser, whom many accused of groveling to Hitler, flew to London at once to communicate this offer to the government and seek a reply to bring to Hitler, but Chamberlain and Halifax were

Sir Nevile Henderson and Göring.

taken aback by Hitler's grandiose offer to guarantee the existence of the British Empire, however conditionally. To even the most stalwart of appeasers this had the ring of hubris.

It proved more difficult to obtain a reply to Hitler's offer than Henderson had presumed. The first draft seemed to some members of the cabinet "fulsome, obsequious and deferential," quite apart from skating lightly over Britain's obligation to defend Poland *including* Danzig and the corridor. In order to prevent a revolt within the cabinet the draft was revised several times, but it still seemed a weak response to Hitler's threat to go to war with Poland if he did not get what he wanted.

By the last week of August, the situation had been further complicated by the appearance on the scene of Birger Dahlerus, a well-connected Swedish businessman who traveled back and forth between Berlin and London bearing messages to and from Field Marshal Göring in a last-minute effort to inform the British government of exactly what Hitler would (and more important would not) accept in their reply to his "offer."

The intrusion of Dahlerus as a kind of Swedish deus ex machina is an indication of just how determined Chamberlain and Halifax were to preserve peace at the expense of Poland, and of their own misreading of German politics, if the word "politics" can be applied to government by a dictator. It suited Chamberlain and Halifax to believe that Göring was a mollifying influence on Hitler, even that Göring was a possible alternative to him, a delusion that Sir Nevile constantly reinforced from Berlin.

Göring's expansive, bluff charm, his supposed Anglophilia, his passion for upper-class blood sports, and his lavish, self-indulgent life style all combined to make him seem like a more approachable figure than the remote, abstemious, vegetarian Führer, with his sudden rages and bullying negotiating style. Halifax had described Göring in admiring English upper-class terms that make him sound like a character in a Nancy Mitford novel: "a great schoolboy . . . a composite personality—film star, great landowner interested in his estate, Prime Minister, party manager, head game-keeper at Chatsworth."*

Whereas Chamberlain and Halifax supposed that Göring was the "good" face of Nazism and overlooked his record of brutali-

Göring and the Führer.

ties, the truth was that Göring was slavishly devoted to the Führer, and never dared to argue with him. Like so many less important Germans, Göring too went "weak at the knees" at one gaze from those glaucous, hypnotic blue eyes. In fact Göring's involvement in the Anglo-German crisis was carefully stage-managed by Hitler himself, an illusion intended to distract the British leaders and give them the impression that there existed a "moderate" element in the Nazi government. No such moderate element existed, of course, from the Nazi regime's beginning to its sordid end.

Dahlerus has come in for a good deal of criticism for his part in this deception, but he seems to have believed sincerely, even desperately in his role as a peacemaker and, more important, in Göring's supposed desire for peace and ability to restrain Hitler. Had the British investigated the supposedly neutral Dahlerus, they would have discovered that he was pro-Nazi, married to a German woman, and a useful tool for Göring since 1934, but clutching at straws, they took him at his own self-inflated importance.

By August 28 Chamberlain and Halifax, without consulting the cabinet, had already passed on to Dahlerus Britain's willingness to persuade the Poles to give up Danzig and the corridor, and heard back that they would also have to persuade the Polish government

---

* Chatsworth House is the seat of the immensely rich Duke of Devonshire. Think *Downton Abbey*, but vastly bigger and more elegant.

to send a negotiator, presumably Colonel Beck, to Berlin at once. This was a role that Beck refused to play.

Through August 29 and 30 the Germans turned up the heat, demanding that Poland initiate "direct discussion" immediately with the German government. Hitler now openly spoke of "annihilating Poland," going far beyond his previous demand for Danzig and the corridor, and even the mild-mannered Henderson, whose sympathies predictably lay with the Germans rather than the Poles, found himself in a shouting match with Hitler, telling the Führer that "if he wanted war . . . he would have it." Unusual as it was for a British ambassador to lose his temper at the head of state to whom he had been accredited, it was followed by twenty-four hours more of extraordinary attempts to bully the Poles into sending a major figure of the Polish government to Berlin without any preconditions in order to learn the full extent of the German demands to which the Poles would have to agree in advance.

Only a year before, during the Sudetenland crisis, Halifax had expressed to another German amateur diplomat that he hoped

Lord Halifax and Göring.

to see "as the culmination of his work, the Führer entering London, at the side of the English King, amid the acclamation of the English people." Whether Halifax actually used those exact words as they were reported to Berlin is hard to know, but if so they reveal an altogether unexpected gift for fantasy in the normally neat and cautious mind of the British foreign secretary. In any case, this hope was by now rapidly receding into the province of daydreams. The British government was informed that Hitler was drawing up a list of his demands on Poland, and that the Poles must send a representative to receive them immediately, but by the time the sixteen demands were finally produced in written form the deadline had passed. In any event, Hitler had already decided on war, and refused to receive the Polish ambassador or to accept Mussolini's offer to call for an international conference to take place in Italy on September 5.

An "incident," however, was still needed to justify the German attack, and orders to produce one had already been given to *SS Gruppenführer* Reinhard Heydrich, the dreaded chief of the Sicherheitsdienst, who had orchestrated the Kristallnacht program in November 1938 and the roundup of the Austrian Jews after the Anschluss, and who would soon be called upon to organize the death camps and the killing squads. Heydrich had, along with a gift for organization and consummate, cold-blooded brutality, a vivid imagination and a knack for propaganda. He arranged a carefully staged attack on a German radio station at Gleiwitz, in Upper Silesia near the Polish border. In order to make it look more convincing, he had several prisoners from Dachau concentration camp dressed in Polish uniform and shot so that it would look as if they had been killed during an "attack" on the station. The prisoners, in the merciless tradition of the SS, were cynically code-named Canned Goods for the purposes of the operation, and their bodies were exhibited to the neutral press as proof of a serious Polish provocation.

*   *   *

This and several other bogus border "incidents" were preludes to the full-scale attack on Poland that began at 4 a.m. on September 1. The Germans attacked with two armies, comprising sixty divisions, nine thousand guns, nearly three thousand tanks, and over two thousand aircraft. It was an overwhelming force, over twice the size of the Polish Army, which was not as yet fully mobilized and which was markedly, but not surprisingly, deficient in tanks and aircraft. Perhaps to demonstrate Hitler's contempt for the Poles and his intention to wipe their country off the map of Europe, the attack was not preceded by a declaration of war—indeed it took place while the Polish ambassador in Berlin was still struggling to convey Hitler's sixteen demands by telephone to his government in Warsaw.

The Poles fought valiantly, but inevitably they were pushed back. It did not improve their morale that their British and French allies not only did nothing to support them but delayed declaring war on Germany for over forty-eight hours. The indefatigable Dahlerus was on the telephone from Berlin, offering to fly to London immediately and passing on Göring's lame assurance that only military targets would be bombed, even though three major Polish cities had already been attacked by the Luftwaffe, with considerable civilian casualties.

To the dismay of the Poles the British still hoped for a negotiated solution, and prepared a carefully drafted note "warning" that if the Germans did not suspend their invasion of Poland and agree to withdraw their troops His Majesty's Government might be compelled to fulfill their obligations to Poland. As if to rub salt deeper into Polish wounds, Halifax specifically requested the British ambassador in Berlin to make it clear that the note was only a warning, not an ultimatum. Henderson presented the note to Ribbentrop at 9:30 p.m. in a meeting that he later described as "courteous and polite" for a change. He asked for an "immediate" reply, but Ribbentrop said he could not give one until he had consulted with the Führer, who was in no hurry to read it.

By the morning of Saturday, September 2, the full violence of modern war had spread far and wide across western Poland while its allies struggled to avoid declaring war. Frantic telephone calls between Halifax and Georges Bonnet, his French counterpart, led to a succession of failed attempts to get Hitler to agree to a negotiation, but in the meantime two new factors surfaced. The first was that of public opinion in Britain—little as the British wanted war they, unlike their government, had no difficulty in recognizing German aggression when it took place. Even within the ranks of the Conservative Party there was some discomfort at the government's failure to support the Poles. The second, and more remarkable, factor was Neville Chamberlain's growing conviction—a historical fact long since forgotten—that before any conference could take place German troops must be withdrawn from Poland.

The prime minister had always possessed a firm and unshakable sense of right and wrong, which was at the heart of his intense dislike of Lloyd George, whose standard of personal and political morality was notoriously low, and once a moral imperative had entered that austere and logical mind, there was no hope of removing or softening it. Chamberlain was still anxious for a conference and hopeful that the Poles could be persuaded to give Hitler what he said he wanted, but he was determined that German troops must leave Poland first. The French had already gone behind the back of their British ally to renew their appeal to Mussolini to get Hitler to the conference table, but as Ciano pointed out to them, the British demand that German troops withdraw first was unrealistic.

The French had by this time reached the same conclusion themselves. The Germans were advancing. German bombs were falling on Warsaw. Nobody could imagine that Hitler would end a war he could already sense he was going to win, or humiliate his generals by ordering them to withdraw. The German generals had been aghast when he proposed to remilitarize the Rhineland in 1936, and they had been reluctant at the prospect of fighting in Austria and against the Czechs in 1938, but each crisis had proved them wrong. They had all been *Blumenkriege,* "flower wars," triumphant victories in which no blood was shed. Now they were fighting a real war. Their enthusiasm was higher and their confidence in the

Führer, though never complete given the aristocratic background of many of his generals, was also greater. Hitler could not afford to lose their confidence by giving in to the British demand, even had he been so inclined.

The fact that the British and French had not yet declared war seemed to him proof that he would be able to eliminate Poland without a war in the west.

3

"Speak for England!"

Winston Churchill arrives for his first full day back as first lord of
the Admiralty.

ALL THAT WAS about to change. At 7:30 p.m. on Saturday,
September 2, the House of Commons met. The House was
packed, and tension was extraordinarily high—the members on
both sides of the House, even those who had been loyal appeas-

ers until now, were expecting Chamberlain to announce an ultimatum.

It was a moment for firmness and an inspiring, historic speech. Instead, Chamberlain explained in a low key that the government was still trying to arrange for "a discussion" between Germany and Poland. "If the German Government should agree to withdraw their forces," the prime minister said to a surprised and hostile House, "then His Majesty's Government would be willing to regard the position as being the same as it was before the German forces crossed the Polish frontier."

These words, spoken while Warsaw was being bombed, had the worst possible effect on the House. Chamberlain himself had an almost superhuman ability to control his own emotions, and a sublime objectivity—without which he could hardly have sat through three grueling meetings with Hitler—but as a consequence he failed at this crucial moment to understand his audience, which by and large reflected the view of the British people. Chamberlain's goal was peace for Britain, and he knew that peace could not be obtained without satisfying Germany's demands for the revocation of the terms of the Versailles peace treaty. What mattered to him was to keep that goal in mind, no matter what difficulties arose. He would not be provoked, he would not give way to emotion rather than reason, he would, if necessary, turn the other cheek. He put the position plainly to the House and expected that all but the firebrands would accept it, as most of them had accepted (and rejoiced over) the settlement he had brought home from Munich a year earlier. But 1939 was not 1938. "The house was aghast," wrote one Conservative member. Chamberlain's speech was followed not by cheers but by an appalled silence.

When Arthur Greenwood rose to speak for the Labour opposition (the Labour leader Clement Attlee was sick), Leo Amery, an old friend and Harrow schoolmate of Churchill's, shouted out from the Conservative back benches, "*Speak for England!*"

Greenwood was no spellbinding orator; he was a stiff-collared and colorless socialist theoretician, whose chief claim to fame was that he combined being the author of a book on "public owner-

Right: Clement Attlee
and Arthur Greenwood.
Below: Attlee.

ship of the liquor trade" in favor of national-
ization and prohibition with a reputation for
heavy drinking. In his fumbling way Greenwood attempted to warn that every minute's
delay could only lead "to more loss of life,"
and imperil "our national interests."

From the Conservative back benches Robert Boothby, another friend of Churchill's,
shouted out, "*Honor*," so Greenwood went on to
add, "Let me finish my sentence. I was about
to say—imperiling the foundations of our
national honor."

The word resonated in the hushed chamber. Greenwood, perhaps not the most likely
spokesman for old-fashioned patriotism, had
expressed not only what the House was feeling but what the whole country had been
coming, with whatever reluctance, to feel over

Robert Boothby.

the past two days—that Britain's *honor*, not just its "national interests," was at stake. For better or for worse Britain had made itself
an ally of Poland, and Poland was under attack—there could be no
further delay in declaring war on Germany, whatever the French
decided to do.

Chamberlain sat white-faced as the debate proceeded, and
when it was over he retired to his room in the House of Commons
to face the anger of most of his own cabinet. The House could
not be held, he was told even by his own closest supporters—the
government might fall unless the prime minister could announce
that a firm ultimatum had been sent before the House met again
on Sunday. After an evening of soul-searching interrupted by
anguished telephone calls from Warsaw for help, and from Paris
for more delay, Chamberlain made the only decision that could
save his government—an ultimatum would be delivered to the German government at 9 a.m. the next morning, to expire at 11 a.m.

Sir Nevile Henderson in Berlin was instructed late Saturday
night to ask for an appointment to meet with Ribbentrop at 9 a.m.

on Sunday morning, September 3, followed by the text in code of the ultimatum he was to present. The French, aghast, would lag two hours behind the British, after making yet another feeble attempt to persuade Mussolini to intervene, the text of which Ciano threw into his wastepaper basket contemptuously "without informing the Duce."

In the event, Ribbentrop, once he had been informed of Sir Nevile's request, decided not to meet with him personally, and delegated Paul Schmidt, the German Foreign Office interpreter, to stand in for him. Fortunately Schmidt knew Henderson well and made a record of the meeting.

> Henderson was announced as the hour struck. He came in looking very serious, shook hands, but declined my invitation to be seated, remaining solemnly standing in the middle of the room.
>
> "I regret that on the instructions of my Government I have to hand you an ultimatum for the German Government," he said with deep emotion, and then, both of us still standing up, he read out the British ultimatum. "More than twenty-four hours have elapsed since an immediate reply was requested to the warning of September 1st, and since then the attacks on Poland have been intensified. If His Majesty's Government has not received satisfactory assurances of the cessation of all aggressive action against Poland, and the withdrawal of German troops from that country, by 11 o'clock British Summer Time, from that time a state of war will exist between Great Britain and Germany." . . .
>
> I then took the ultimatum to the Chancellery, where everybody was anxiously awaiting me. Most of the members of the Cabinet and the leading men of the Party were collected in the room next to Hitler's office. . . .
>
> When I entered the next room Hitler was sitting at his desk and Ribbentrop stood by the window. . . . I stopped at

some distance from Hitler's desk, and then slowly translated the British Government's ultimatum. When I finished, there was complete silence.

Hitler sat immobile, gazing before him. He was not at a loss, as was afterwards stated, nor did he rage as others allege. He sat completely silent and unmoving.

After an interval which seemed an age, he turned to Ribbentrop, who had remained standing by the window. "What now?" Hitler asked with a savage look, as though implying that his Foreign Minister had misled him about England's probable reaction.

Ribbentrop answered quietly: "I assume that the French will hand in a similar ultimatum within the hour."

. . . In the anteroom, too, this news was followed by complete silence.

[Then] Göring turned to me and said: "If we lose this war, then God have mercy on us."

Americans of an advanced age can usually remember exactly where they were and what they were doing when the news of the Japanese bombing of Pearl Harbor was announced on the radio. I am one of a fast-diminishing number of Britons who also heard Neville Chamberlain's announcement that we were at war with Germany.

The only radio in the house was in the kitchen—an admiring visitor from Hollywood had brought it as a gift to my father, in the days when a portable radio was still an American marvel, something one saw in American films and magazines, a radio you could take to the beach with you, or to the swimming pool. I think it was a Zenith, a big, heavy black leather-covered box with a brushed stainless-steel handle and lots of shiny chrome. My father had exiled it to the kitchen since he hated noise of any kind, and it was only played while he was away at work. With some ceremony it was brought into the dining room, placed on the table, and turned on while we sat around it as if it were some mysterious object of worship, its rectangular tuning dial glowing fluorescently, the hint of much technology to come, most of which my father would resist having in his home—this despite the fact that we had all been taken to Alexandra Palace one rainy afternoon to watch my mother appear singing and dancing on the tiny screen of the BBC's experimental television program in a room half filled with mysterious circuitry like something out of an H. G. Wells novel.

My father sat quietly, eyes closed as if in pain. I sat next to my mother, who was incapable of not looking cheerful and glamorous, whatever the occasion. Nanny Low and the Hungarian cook in her white apron stood behind the radio, perhaps because they were the only people in the house who knew how to turn it on. My father's wirehaired fox terrier Jani (an affectionate diminutive of the Hungarian name János, or Johnny), who accompanied him to the studio every day, lay beside him, apparently attuned to some kind of drama. Beyond the French windows was the small garden and the brick wall that separated the house from the street—a neat, tidy world about to be disrupted. The solemnity of the occasion, and my father's expression kept me from fidgeting or asking questions—silence was clearly called for.

At exactly 11:15 a.m. the somber voice of the prime minister speaking for the first time from the Cabinet Room in 10 Downing Street came on after a brief announcement: "This morning the British Ambassador in Berlin," Chamberlain said, "handed the German Government a note stating that unless we heard from them by 11 o'clock that they were prepared at once to withdraw their troops from Poland a state of war would exist between us. I have to tell you that no such undertaking has been received, and that consequently this country is at war with Germany."

He went on, "It is evil things that we shall be fighting against—brute force, bad faith, injustice, oppression and persecution—and against them I am certain that right will prevail."

For some reason, Chamberlain has never been given his due as a speaker—he had a deep, sonorous voice, a natural gravity that made even me, as a child, aware of the importance of the occasion.

It is true that Churchill was the better speaker; he had wonderful ability to change the tone of his voice from grave to humorous, and an actor's gift for the long, pregnant pause that made you wonder whether he was going to finish the sentence at all (Laurence Olivier and Ralph Richardson employed the same trick on the stage to keep the audience in suspense), and of course he had an energy, the gift of Shakespearean eloquence, and a taste for historical allusions that came close to poetry, sweeping his listeners along with him as the tide carries away a small boat, even those who did not agree with him politically.

All the same, Neville Chamberlain's voice, if not his words, remains etched in my memory seventy-five years later. Chamberlain has been accused of self-pity in his speech telling us that we were at war, but I cannot find that, reading it or listening to it again. On the contrary it seems to me moving and dignified. One might wish for a hint of anger, a touch of fire, but those are just the qualities that Chamberlain himself lacked; he had none of Churchill's theatricality and hid his emotions rather than displaying them. Quietly and briefly, he told us the facts, but did not disguise his sadness or his personal disappointment.

As if in a play the prime minister's speech was followed almost immediately by a moment of high drama as air raid sirens began to wail all over London. With reluctance we trooped down to the basement, carrying our gas masks, and sat down on a bench in front of shelves piled high with my father's bottles of wine. Nanny held my hand tightly, the dog lay at our feet, my mother chatted away cheerfully. The Hungarian cook kneaded her handkerchief, or perhaps her rosary, poor woman—there was a faint possibility that she might become "an enemy alien," in which case she would be interned for the duration of the war or deported home, but luckily for her Hungary did not join the war until December 1941, by which time my father had duly arranged, no doubt through Brendan Bracken, to somehow get her British papers. How she managed to communicate with Nanny and my mother or they with her was a mystery, but given the ingredients of a dish, however foreign it might be to her, she could cook it.

I do not remember being particularly afraid, since for children excitement often cancels out fear, but in any event nothing happened—the cataclysm predicted by H. G. Wells failed to take place. After a few minutes the all clear sounded—it emerged, as I discovered many years later, that the alarm had been set off not by German bombers but by a private light plane carrying a few wealthy golfers home from a weekend in Le Touquet—and we went back upstairs for lunch.

"Well, that wasn't too bad, darling," my mother said.

To which my father answered darkly, "You will see how wrong you are."

4

The Phoney War

General Gamelin and General Lord Gort.

Although nobody could have known it at the time, the next eight months would become known as "the phoney war," a phrase coined by Senator William Borah of Idaho, characterized by timidity, inaction, and lethargy on the part of the Allies, and a puzzling hesitation on the part of the Germans. "Is Hitler trying to bore us into peace?" quipped the American-born Henry "Chips" Channon, member of Parliament, wit, social climber *extraordinaire*, and, as acknowledged after his death, infamous diarist. Of course it was not "phoney" for the Poles, who were defeated in an eight-week campaign that gave birth to the term "blitzkrieg," a lightning war of movement spearheaded by a few elite "panzer divisions" consisting of tanks, motorized infantry, and artillery, backed up by the ubiquitous Ju 87 "Stuka" dive-bombers and followed by the slower-moving mass of regular infantry divisions. These tactics were novel and controversial in the German Army (as well as stoutly resisted by the more conservative German generals), and virtually ignored by the French and British armies.

In other respects too, the war was anything but "phoney" for Poland, which was brutally divided between Germany and its ally the Soviet Union, and altogether eliminated as a state. In the eastern part, seized by the Red Army, Soviet rule would be marked by such events as the notorious Katyn Forest Massacre, in the course of which over twenty thousand Polish officers, lawyers, landowners, and priests were executed by the NKVD (the acronym then for what later became known as the KGB). In the western part, Nazi political control was added to the rule of the German Army, which was already harsh. Poles were stripped of all rights; forced labor, expropriation, the execution of Polish intellectual and political leaders, and draconic "security measures" were undertaken immediately, following the policy foreordained by Hitler as early as 1923 when he wrote *Mein Kampf,* in which Poland was to be depopulated and turned into a German agricultural colony, farmed by slave labor. In no other occupied country save those parts of the Soviet Union that fell under German rule between 1941 and 1944 were the precepts of what the British historian Hugh Trevor-Roper later described with acid precision as "bestial Nordic nonsense" carried out with such thoroughness and severity.

For the three and a half million Polish Jews a far worse fate was envisaged. From the moment the SS crossed the frontier in the wake of the army, they carried out against Jews summary executions, random murders, and massacres, a policy of terror and repression soon to be followed by the more systematic operations of the *Einsatzgruppen,* or mobile killing squads, then "ghettoization" and the "Final Solution" of "extermination camps."

For all practical purposes, Poland simply ceased to exist, just as Hitler had promised.

*   *   *

None of this was revealed to the public in Britain or France, though some of it seeped out thanks to the trickle of Polish soldiers, airmen, and sailors who had miraculously made their way to Paris and London in the wake of defeat (eventually over 200,000 Poles would fight in the British armed services). My father knew more about it than most people, since a stray Polish antiaircraft battery was sited near the London Films studio at Denham, and many Poles from the southern part of the country had a smattering of German—since that had been the common language of the old Austro-Hungarian Empire. My father spoke what was known as *Miklosdeutsch,* basic German with a strong Hungarian accent, which was enough for him to communicate with the Polish antiaircraft gunners, who were lonely out in the English countryside and at this point in the war had no German aircraft to shoot at. At the time Vincent was preparing the sketches for two of London Films' most ambitious and expensive projects, *The Thief of Baghdad** and *Jungle Book*, on both of which he was the art director, and from time to time he took a break from his work by walking over to visit the Polish gunners, who, whatever their problems, were not pressing him for set designs and production estimates. For the most part he sat next to their gun, sharing his Player's Navy Cut cigarettes with them. Vincent had no special interest in Poland, but at least the gunners were familiar: Central Europeans, rather than the incomprehensible English, with their strange accents, their incomprehensible class differences, and their fondness for tea with milk and sugar at all hours of the day and night, like my mother and her parents.

Denham was about to play a larger role in our lives, since Alex, who took being "head of the family" very seriously and felt responsible for all of us, had decided to lease a nearby country house and

---

* He would win an Academy Award in 1940 for the art direction of *The Thief of Baghdad.*

move the whole Korda family there, still apparently convinced by his friend H. G. Wells's belief that Hitler's first move against Britain would be a colossal air attack on London. This move was stoutly opposed by my mother, a working stage actress who had no taste for country living, and by my uncle Zoltan's wife, Joan, also an actress— each had met her future husband while playing small parts in Alex's breakthrough English film, *The Private Life of Henry VIII*—in 1932. But Alex's wishes were the equivalent of a command to his brothers. News of the impending move even percolated down to my six-year-old level, or rather made its way upstairs to "the nursery" where Nanny and I lived, and was the subject of many hushed, serious talks between Nanny Low and Nanny Parker, my cousin David's nanny, as well as of frequent arguments between my father and mother.

Looking back on it with the hindsight of three-quarters of a century, it seems likely to me that Alex took the threat of what might happen more seriously than his brothers or their English wives— *his* name was on the Gestapo's then secret list of those prominent British anti-Nazi political, financial, and cultural figures who were to be arrested and killed once the Germans occupied Britain, the so-called Black Book, or *Sonderfahndungsliste-G.B.*, a tidy printed handbook like the pocket *Guide Michelin*, with the address of those listed neatly and carefully printed next to each name. It included not only Alex but such friends as H. G. Wells, Winston Churchill, Noël Coward, and the cartoonist David Low. ("My dear—the people one should have been seen dead with," Rebecca West, who was also on the list, would telegraph Noël Coward, once the war was over and the list made public.) Others on this curiously selected list included Churchill's son-in-law, the formerly Austrian-Jewish comedian and singer Vic Oliver, and the novelist Virginia Woolf, who would be dead by her own hand the following year. Already a famous movie director and producer, Alex had been in Budapest when Admiral Horthy's Fascist troops took the city in 1919, and knew what to expect—he had only escaped from being executed in the White Terror that followed the overthrow of Béla Kun's Communist regime by the energetic intervention of his first wife, the silent film star Maria Corda, and his brothers. However brutal Horthy's actions had been when he seized power, German efficiency and Nazi zeal could certainly be counted on to make things much worse if the Germans invaded Britain. Harold Nicolson and his wife, Vita Sackville-West, were not the only couple to have obtained poison pills from their doctor just in case, "the bare bodkin,"* as they referred to them in their letters to each other.

In the meantime, the gardens, with their peacocks and topiary, and the luxurious furnishing of the manor house in Denham, which looked rather like one of my father's film sets, were not making this enforced family exile more tolerable. At dinner the three brothers sat at one end of the dining room table arguing in Hungarian, while my auntie Merle (Oberon), just back from Hollywood, where she had been playing Cathy in *Wuthering Heights*, my mother, and my auntie Joan sat in silence at the other end. There was no love lost between Merle and her sisters-in-law, both of whom resented her rapid rise to stardom and her marriage to Alex. As for Auntie Merle herself, she was anxious to return to California as soon as possible, since *Wuthering Heights* had made her an international star. Every night my mother looked with longing toward London, expecting to see the fiery glow from H. G. Wells's anticipated attack on London, and seeing nothing once again she moaned one night, "Oh, where *is* that wretched Göring!"

At one point, the atmosphere became so poisonous that my mother peed in her chair—the dining room chairs were upholstered in expensive moiré silver silk—and was too ashamed to get up after dinner. Alex, more sensitive than his brothers, noticed that she was still sitting there after the butler had cleared the table and everybody else had gone into the sitting room, and gently asked her what the matter was. Her answer did not *shock* Alex, nothing

---

*   *For who would bear the whips and scorns of time,*
     The oppressor's wrong, the proud man's contumely . . .
     When he himself might his quietus make
     With a bare bodkin?
     —WILLIAM SHAKESPEARE, *Hamlet, act 3, scene 1*

could do that, but it did apparently convince him that he had made a mistake. Within days Merle was on her way back to California by air, and the rest of us were on our way back to our homes.

The feeling of helplessness and confusion that briefly overcame the Korda family at Denham in the seven months of the phoney war was not unlike that which gripped almost everybody in the wake of the rapid German conquest of Poland, with the possible exception of the Germans themselves. Neville Chamberlain had been shamed into declaring war against Germany by the unexpected resolve of the House of Commons, and the French were bullied into following suit, but the old instinct of appeasement, the urge to negotiate an end to the war rather than fight it to the bitter end, had not yet been laid to rest, and soon resurfaced in Paris and London. The French, acting momentarily out of guilt, fulfilled their obligation to Poland by advancing a few miles into Germany around Saar, then returned to their lines, having achieved nothing except a few propaganda photographs of French soldiers standing underneath German street signs. RAF Bomber Command

Sir Howard Kingsley Wood.

was strictly limited to dropping bundles of propaganda leaflets over Germany.

The spirit of appeasement lived on. In Britain, when it was suggested to Sir Howard Kingsley Wood, the secretary of state for air, that the Royal Air Force should drop incendiary bombs on the Black Forest and set it on fire (the Black Forest was then believed to contain a large number of hidden ammunition dumps), he protested indignantly, "Are you aware that is private property? The next thing, you will be asking me to bomb Essen!"

In fact the most warlike decision that Chamberlain made—and the one that would have the most drastic effect on the war—was to invite Winston Churchill to join the War Cabinet, and also to serve once again, as he had from 1911 to 1915, as first lord of the Admiralty (the civilian head of the Royal Navy, roughly equivalent to the American secretary of the navy). Chamberlain's War Cabinet consisted of nine men, including the prime minister—probably too many, Lloyd George's War Cabinet in World War One had only consisted of five—and placing Churchill in it was tantamount to putting a hawk in a cage full of doves.

It may or may not have been true that when Chamberlain offered Churchill the Admiralty the message was transmitted to all the Royal Navy's ships, "WINSTON IS BACK." The dean of all Churchill biographers and researchers, the late Sir Martin Gilbert, was unable to find the original signal, but felt that even if it was not true, it ought to have been, and so included it in volume one of *The Churchill War Papers*—like so much else about Churchill, fact and myth are superimposed and inseparable. It is not just that Churchill was a "bigger than life" personality even as a youth; he was also an indefatigable, prolific, and gifted writer, with a flair for the dramatic. When in an argument about the delay of "the Second Front" at the Tehran summit meeting in 1943, he was goaded by an angry Stalin, who said icily, "History will be the judge of this," Churchill replied, "History will judge me kindly, for I intend to write it."

That has proved to be true. Much of what we assume we know

about the history of World War Two in fact derives from the six volumes of Churchill's *The Second World War*, at once a history and a memoir, which not only won him the Nobel Prize in Literature in 1953, but stamped his view of what took place indelibly on what we know, or think we know, about the events, the people, and their motives during the period. Churchill achieved exactly what he set out to do—in the English-speaking world we still see that war largely through his eyes, particularly since his opponents Hitler and Mussolini did not live to write their memoirs, nor, among the Allies, did Roosevelt, while Stalin chose not to.

Churchill paints a dramatic scene of his return to the Admiralty in volume one of *The Second World War*:

> So it was that I came again to the room I had quitted in pain and sorrow almost exactly a quarter of a century before, when Lord Fisher's resignation had led to my removal from my post as First Lord and ruined irretrievably, as it proved, the important conception of forcing the Dardanelles. A few feet behind me, as I sat in my old chair, was the wooden map-case I had had fixed in 1911, and inside it still remained the chart of the North Sea on which each day . . . I had made the Naval Intelligence Branch record the movements and dispositions of the German High Seas Fleet. . . . Once again! So be it.

He rolled up the carpet, sent for his old octagonal table, gave orders to have a map room set up and staffed for him so that he could follow every naval development as signals came in, then got down to work. In his history of the war he makes the fact that Chamberlain offered him a place in both the War Cabinet and the Admiralty seem like a decision he welcomed, but in fact both his enemies, which then still included the majority of Conservative members of Parliament, as well as his closest supporters all thought that this had been an adroit political move of Chamberlain's intended to keep Churchill so busy with naval affairs that he would not have time to make trouble in the War Cabinet.

If so, this was a battle lost before it even began. Churchill's experience of war, his phenomenal energy, his curiosity, his remarkable memory, his ability to stay up until the small hours of the morning sipping whiskey while he dictated immensely long and well-informed papers on every aspect of the war all combined, together with his personality and his gift for what we would now call "public relations," to make him the dominant member of the War Cabinet, overshadowing everyone, including the prime minister. Unlike other members of the War Cabinet, he brought with him his own corps of advisers and specialists, including his supremely self-confident and abrasive friend and scientific adviser Professor Frederick Lindemann of Oxford, referred to not necessarily with affection by those around Churchill as "the Prof." As a result Churchill often seemed better informed than the other service ministers, or even than the prime minister himself, whose interest in military affairs was in any case limited.

The undercurrent of hostility toward Churchill was fierce, strongest of all in his own party, hence the rumor that the first thing he did when he reached his desk at the Admiralty was to send for a bottle of whiskey, although that is contradicted by the accounts of everyone who was present. Rumors that Churchill was a drunk had been around for many years (appearing nowhere more frequently than in the Nazi press in Germany), but in fact he was that rarest of men, a well-functioning, even *hyper*-functioning alcoholic. He drank a weak whiskey and soda (without ice, of course) at frequent moments during the day when most other people would have asked for a cup of tea or coffee, while his meals were accompanied by vintage Pol Roger champagne and followed by brandy. Churchill would shock Eleanor Roosevelt during his first stay at the White House when she learned that he had told the White House butler to make sure he received a large glass of sherry every morning on his breakfast tray, but he was never seen to be actually drunk— he simply needed a certain amount of alcohol to keep him going through his long days and longer nights, and was a good judge of how much he needed and when to stop. As he would one day in old age put it himself, "I have taken more out of alcohol than alcohol has taken out of me."

A man more different from the abstemious and stiff Neville Chamberlain would be hard to find than the half-American grandson of a duke, a colorful military adventurer who had participated in the last great cavalry charge of the British Army at the Battle of Omdurman in 1898, and who wrote of his experience under fire in Cuba, "Nothing in life is so exhilarating as to be shot at without results."

Churchill's feelings about Chamberlain were ambivalent. On the one hand Churchill respected him as the leader of the Conservative Party and as a shrewd politician; on the other he had been fighting vigorously against Chamberlain's policy of appeasement since 1933, both in and out of Parliament. Once, when a cabinet minister was speaking about a murderous riot between Arabs and Jews, and ended his speech by expressing his solemn regret that this incident should have occurred of all places "in Bethlehem, birthplace of the Prince of Peace," Churchill could be heard throughout the chamber asking the member sitting beside him in a stage whisper, "But have we not always been given to understand that Neville was born in Birmingham?"

Making fun of Chamberlain was easy enough, for he had no discernible sense of humor himself, and was a perfect target, with his lean scarecrow figure and solemn face—although he was actually a ruthless and unforgiving politician, with complete control over his own party. Harold Nicolson, the diarist and at that time member of Parliament, described him unforgettably as looking like "the Secretary of a firm of undertakers reading the minutes of the last meeting," but Churchill's speeches against appeasement and in favor of rearmament had drawn blood over the years. They were brilliant, well informed, deeply wounding to Chamberlain and unrelenting. Of the Munich agreement Churchill said, "£1 was demanded at the pistol's point. When it was given, £2 were demanded at the pistol's point. Finally, the dictator agreed to take £1 17s. 6d, and the rest in promises of good will for the future. . . ." The fact that Churchill had been proved right in the end did nothing to endear him to most of his fellow Conservatives.

None of that is to say that Churchill was *always* right. A lifelong Francophile, he gravely overrated the French Army, and therefore failed to appreciate the degree to which it had become a mere façade, weakened by the political and class divisions in France between the wars, hollowed by the enormous sacrifices France had made in World War One, and led by senior officers who distrusted their own politicians and clung to outdated strategies. Although more than three million men strong in France alone,* the French Army was in reality a shadow of its former self, but that shadow was still softened by the glory of its past.

Luckily for Churchill, the Royal Navy in 1939 was still the world's largest and most powerful—here, at least, was an area in which Germany could not compete on equal terms, and the war on the sea began at once, albeit at a fairly low level, and not without mishaps. Whatever the deficiencies and doubts of the other services, the Royal Navy at least was ready for war. "By the 27th September the Royal Navy . . . had moved to France, without the loss of a single life, 152,031 army personnel, 9,392 air force personnel, 21,424 army vehicles [and] 36,000 tons of ammunition," the first installment of "the British Expeditionary Force," without any interference from German surface ships, submarines, or mines, a remarkable testament to the Royal Navy's professionalism, skill at improvisation, and control of the sea. When the British thought of their strength, the one thing in which they reposed trust was "the great, gray ships" of the Royal Navy, and in 1939 they were not wrong.

Churchill spoke for that strength, and from the very first min-

---

* It must be kept in mind that France was then still a worldwide empire. There was a French commander in the Levant (Syria and Lebanon), another in North Africa (Algeria and Morocco), and yet another in the Far East (French Indochina), not to speak of other, sub-Saharan African colonies, and Pacific and Caribbean islands. All of them reported to the commander in chief General Maurice Gamelin in Paris.

ute that he took office on September 3, 1939, he devoted himself to the navy's needs in detail, with the easy grace of an opera
singer taking on a familiar role from his past repertoire. On his
first day in office the famous crisp Churchillian notes began to
go out at once, signifying that he was back in charge, and causing necks bearing gold-braided caps to snap to attention all over
the world—

> TO DIRECTOR OF NAVAL INTELLIGENCE:
> 3 September 1939
> Let me have a statement of the German U-boat force,
> actual and prospective, for the next five months. Please
> distinguish between ocean-going and small-size U-boats.
> Give the estimated radius of action in days and miles in
> each case.

> TO THE FOURTH SEA LORD:
> 3 September 1939
> Please let me know the number of rifles in the posses-
> sion of the Navy both afloat and ashore. . . .

> TO THE DEPUTY CHIEF OF THE NAVAL STAFF:
> 3 September 1939
> Kindly let me know the escorts for the big convoy to the
> Mediterranean (a) from England to Gibraltar, and (b)
> through the Mediterranean. I understand these escorts
> are only against U-boat attack.

Officers at every level scrambled to answer the first lord's questions, and assemble the reams of information that he required, and
also learned that delay or imprecision would be instantly rebuked.
No item was too small or too large in scope to escape Churchill's
attention.

Meanwhile, a torrent of congratulatory letters and telegrams
flooded in from HRH the Duke of Windsor to Lady Blood, the
wife of Churchill's old commander in the Malakand Field Force,

in which Churchill had served as a second lieutenant in 1897, and he struggled to answer them all.

The most important of them was a letter from President Roosevelt, congratulating "My dear Churchill" on having completed the fourth and final volume of his biography of the Duke of Marlborough, his great ancestor, before the war broke out, and inviting him to "keep me in touch personally," thus beginning the longest, the most intimate, and surely the most productive secret correspondence in history, consisting of over seventeen hundred letters between them, almost one a day until Roosevelt's death, dealing with every aspect of the war.

Neither the prime minister himself—whose speeches in the House of Commons were "as dull as ditchwater," in the words of Harold Nicolson—nor Foreign Secretary Lord Halifax could match the first lord's zeal for combat, persistence, oratorical skill, or formidable powers of argument. He dominated the other members of the War Cabinet, including the other service minsters. Sir Kingsley Wood, secretary of state for air, had been a successful and innovative postmaster general, described unkindly but accurately by Roy Jenkins as "the legal panjandrum of industrial insurance," and Leslie Hore-Belisha, secretary of state for war, was a former minister of transport, in which office he had created a national speed limit, and instituted the familiar "Belisha beacons" and "Zebra crossings" that have protected pedestrians in the United Kingdom as they cross the road ever since.

Hore-Belisha, who had been in charge of the army since 1937 when Chamberlain appointed him to reorganize and modernize the British Army—always referred to as "the Cinderella of the Armed Services," since the bulk of defense spending went to the Royal Navy and the Royal Air Force—might have been a rival to Churchill, but he was instead a good example of Chamberlain's blind confidence in his own judgment over other people's advice. Hore-Belisha loved publicity and got lots of it, he was flashy, impatient, obsequious to those above him and rude to those below, and he was also, in an age when that still mattered a great deal more to many people, a Jew. No choice for secretary of state for war could have been better calculated to enrage the senior officers of the British Army, who, despite their differences, clung to a man to exactly those things that Hore-Belisha wanted to change or reform, the abolition of the cross strap on the Sam Browne belt for officers and warrant officers being one of the most deeply resented.

In addition to Hore-Belisha's other problems with his generals, he had the further disadvantage of possessing an éminence grise in the person of Captain B. H. Liddell Hart, the *Times* military correspondent and controversial author of at least twenty-five books on warfare. Liddell Hart was a proselytizer for what he called "indirect warfare," by which he meant that the British Army should avoid the frontal attacks that had made the 1914–1918 war so costly in lives. He also believed strongly that Britain should never again field "a Continental army," as it had in the last war—that its contribution to its Continental allies should consist of a strong navy and air force, leaving land warfare to others. This coincided with Chamberlain's own view on the subject—nobody in his right mind wanted to repeat the 1914–1918 war—but as Hitler rearmed Germany and stripped away one French ally after another, it became apparent that Britain could not expect the French to take on the whole burden of land warfare, and that the British Army would have to be drastically enlarged and reequipped in haste if it was to be of any help to France.

Liddell Hart was one of the small band of visionaries who saw the tank as opening up a new kind of warfare, in which fast-moving columns of armored vehicles would range far behind the enemy front line wreaking havoc on his lines of communications. In this respect he was a prophet without honor in his own country, like Major-General J. F. C. Fuller, CB, CBE, DSO, and Colonel Charles de Gaulle in France, whose book on armored warfare, *Vers l'Armée de Métier,* sold fewer than seven hundred copies in France (it was either ignored or ridiculed by his superior officers), but over seven *thousand* in Germany, where it became the bible of almost every one of the future German panzer generals and was read aloud in German to Hitler.

Although the tank had been invented in Britain early in World War One—it was designed to cross *over* enemy trenches, hence the curious elongated and rhomboid shape of early tanks—the British Army did not follow up on it with any energy, partly for lack of funds, partly because if the government's policy was to avoid at all costs "a Continental war" it would not *need* tanks. All three of these visionaries developed their theory of armored warfare *before* the appropriate vehicles to carry it out had been produced—they had to imagine not only the tactics but also the tanks.

In the event, British tank development was not only "too little, too late," but gave the British Army two different kinds of tank, neither of which was appropriate to Liddell Hart's ideas, first a heavy, slow-moving "infantry tank," intended to support infantry, then a "cruiser tank," which was faster, but too lightly armored and armed, and mechanically unreliable. The French Army did much better— it had, in fact, more and better tanks than the Germans in 1939, let alone the British, but they were organized to support infantry attacks, rather than to play the role Liddell Hart, J. F. C. Fuller, and de Gaulle had envisaged.

The early models of German tanks were small and lightly armed, but Germany had several advantages over its enemies. In the first place, German tanks had been tried out in combat during the Spanish Civil War only three years before and important lessons had been learned there. In the second, Hitler was susceptible to new and radical ideas and had a special interest in motor vehicles of all kinds, hence his enthusiasm for Dr. Ferdinand Porsche's prototype air-cooled *Kraft durch Freude Wagen*, intended to be sold on the installment plan to members of the Nazi Party's "Strength through Joy" organization,* which eventually became known as

---

* Not all of Dr. Porsche's creations were as pacific in intention as the Volkswagen. A favorite of Hitler's, Porsche was deeply involved in the design of later German tanks, including the Panther and the Tiger (the latter arguably the most formidable tank of World War Two), and after the German defeat spent some time in prison accused of being a war criminal.

the Volkswagen, and then as the beloved postwar "Beetle." Finally, the younger German generals who had taken the writings of Hart, Fuller, and de Gaulle more seriously than they were taken in their own country evolved from them a strategy that would become known, for the most part outside Germany, as blitzkrieg, or lightning war.

The man who pulled all these theories together into practical form was Major General Heinz Guderian, who also distilled them into a book, *Achtung—Panzer!*, which attracted the attention of Hitler, though regrettably not that of anybody in France or Britain. In it the new German method of attack was clearly described, had anyone outside Germany cared to read it.

Something of *une chapelle*, the French term for a group of officers drawing inspiration from their common belief in the theories of one charismatic, innovative, visionary officer, like that which formed around Ferdinand Foch in the French War College in 1911, had also formed around Guderian as early as 1927. Guderian had been trained as a signals officer rather than a cavalryman, and therefore approached the development of tanks from a different, more practical point of view than was the case in the postwar French or British Army. He did not assume that the tank was "merely an armoured, mechanical horse," in the words of one British military manual.

First of all he understood at once that the tank commander must be able to communicate with his crew despite the noise of battle (not to speak of the ever-present mechanical noise of the engine) by means of an intercom system, and that each tank must also have a radio and a trained radio operator so that the tanks could communicate with each other, receive orders, and report artillery coordinates.

Guderian, whose personality was described by his fellow generals as "bull-like" (they meant that in praise), set out from the very beginning with the idea that each armored division should be like a miniature army and consist of at least two brigades of heavy and medium tanks, as well as two brigades of motorized infantry—tanks could *take* ground, he realized, but they could not *hold* it; therefore they must work in tandem with infantry that could follow them in armored vehicles (or "armored personnel carriers," as they are now called), and these troops must be specially trained to work closely with "armored fighting vehicles."

What is more, the armored division Guderian had in mind must be self-supporting, which meant it must also include motor-drawn artillery and antiaircraft guns, a unit of armored, fast-moving reconnaissance vehicles, pioneers (or engineers) in armored half-tracks who could repair or build bridges and demolish antitank obstacles on the spot, and a motorized repair unit with heavy vehicles that could tow damaged tanks or tanks with a serious mechanical failure out of the way.

The critical factor was to keep the tanks moving forward at all costs, never to let them be halted, which would transform them into targets for enemy artillery or aircraft. Radio communications would have to be sophisticated enough to let tank commanders call in artillery fire when and where it was needed (and eventually to call in support from dive-bombers, which Guderian's imagination thought up before they existed) to destroy or demoralize enemy forces that might hold up or slow down the tanks—the vital element was speed. His model was the great Thomas J. "Stonewall" Jackson, whose Shenandoah Valley Campaign in 1862 provided the inspiration for German armored warfare tacticians.

It should not be imagined that all this came about quickly or without determined opposition on the part of senior generals of "the old school," few of whom were admirers of Stonewall Jackson or students of the Battle of Port Republic in 1862. Guderian had no previous experience with tanks, but when he was transferred as a staff officer in 1922 to the "Motor Transport Troops," itself then a small and unglamorous cog in the Truppenamt, the shadow general staff of the tiny German Army of 100,000 men, which was all Germany was allowed under the terms of the Treaty of Versailles, Guderian immediately looked beyond the humdrum task of transporting troops by motor vehicles to the battlefield to the development of a secret armored force. The early German tanks were tested in the Soviet Union—the two "outcast" nations, Germany and Bolshevik Russia, found it expedient to collaborate on military experiments out of the sight of Allied observers—but it wasn't until 1927 that Guderian actually got to sit in a real tank and drive it, while on a visit to Sweden. Most of his "exercises" were carried out with dummy tanks, trucks, and motorcycles, and it wasn't until 1934 that his concept received the unequivocal blessing of the new *Reichskanzler*, Adolf Hitler, who witnessed "a demonstration of motorized troops" at Kummersdorf "and exclaimed, 'That's what I need, that's what I want to have!'"

This enthusiasm was not shared by most of the senior generals of the German Army. Like their opposite numbers in the British and French armies, they were reluctant to accept radical new ideas. In the British and French armies this view was of course strengthened by the fact that they had won the last war, admittedly by the narrowest of margins, so there seemed no good reason to reinvent what had worked. In the German Army, the view of the most senior generals was that they had almost won the last war at the time of the Ludendorff offensive in March 1918 only to be "stabbed in the back" by Socialists, Communists, and Jews on the home front. What was needed was diplomacy that would limit a future war to one front, a firm hand at home against the left and the trades unions, and renewed conscription that would build the German Army back to its former strength rather than faddish and expensive new ideas about how to wage war.

There were exceptions, one of the most important being the brilliantly talented Erich von Manstein, nephew of Field Marshal and

President von Hindenburg, who was at once by birth and marriage a well-connected member of the army's social elite and an admirer of Hitler's (though both he and Guderian would eventually fall out of favor with him). The idea of armored warfare also attracted a significant number of field rank officers, among them such famous future panzer generals as Erwin Rommel and Hasso von Manteuffel, but controversy about the importance and the use of tanks would continue to bedevil the German Army until the very end of the war.

In 1935 Guderian was made commander of the new 2nd Panzer Division, one of three newly created panzer divisions, and began to put into practice his theories about armored warfare, at the heart of which was his pithy comment "Nicht kleckern, sondern klotzen!" (Smash them, don't spatter them!), which became so well known that Hitler adopted it for his own use, and which Guderian expanded later into a compact, but complete, description of armored warfare: "Man schlägt jemanden mit der Faust und nicht mit gespreitzen Fingern." (You hit somebody with your fist, not with your fingers spread.) In other words, tanks must not be spread about in "penny packets," in the words of future Field Marshal Montgomery, but concentrated in a single, powerful thrust. To this he added his three indispensible requirements for successful tank combat: "Suitable terrain, surprise, and mass attack in the necessary breadth and depth."

Promoted to lieutenant general, Guderian commanded the XIX Corps in the attack on Poland, and demonstrated the correctness of his theories in combat, but although neutral (mostly American) journalists called the war in Poland a blitzkrieg, conjuring up pictures of masses of fast-moving tanks against cavalry, the German Army in fact achieved victory in Poland by superior numbers (over 1,500,000 men against 950,000) and vastly superior weapons, and fought a relatively conventional war against an enemy that was not yet fully mobilized. The panzer divisions were largely used in support of the German infantry—just the opposite of how Guderian believed they should be used—and although the presence of tank

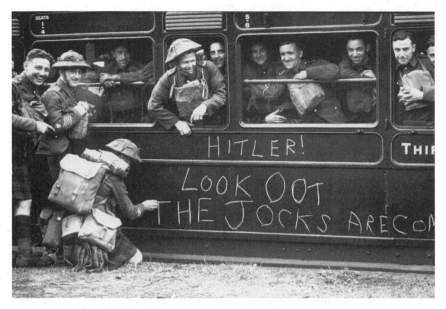

Highland troops on their way to France, 1939.

formations impressed neutral journalists, they accomplished nothing decisive.

All the same, the abilities of the tank to travel substantial distances at a relatively high speed and to influence the outcome of a battle were both proved—as was the ability to keep the tanks supplied with fuel and to repair them in the field, as well as the use of the Ju 87 Stuka dive-bomber in the role of "flying artillery to support the tanks." The number of panzer divisions was increased to ten for the attack against France and the Low Countries, which was planned for October 1939, only a month after the Polish surrender.

5

Operation Pied Piper

Children being evacuated, 1939 (note gas masks).

At our home in Hampstead it almost seemed as if we were still at peace in the spring of 1940. The lilac tree at the far end of the garden was in full bloom, my father went off to the London Films studio at Denham early every morning, chauffeured, much to his dislike, since my uncle Alex had no confidence in his driving ability,* and my mother was in a play in the West End, and slept until late in the morning and seldom got home before midnight. On

---

* Like many people born in the age of the horse, neither of my father's brothers learned how to drive. My father *did*, in midlife, and remained an enthusiastic but terrible driver well into old age, going straight down the middle of the road slowly and in low gear to the fury of other drivers, and signaling for a turn a mile before he reached it.

Sir Alexander Korda and his wife Merle Oberon, after receiving
his knighthood at Buckingham Palace.

the rare occasions when their paths collided, they quarreled. At the
time I had no idea why, but seventy-six years later it is clear enough
to me—Alex had lost control of the London Films studio at Denham, the largest and most ambitious in Europe, after his financial
backer the Prudential Insurance Company lost nearly three million

pounds, and he was also trying to gain control of United Artists in Los Angeles, in which he was a partner. At the same time he was working on the three very expensive pictures, *The Thief of Baghdad*, *Jungle Book*, and *That Hamilton Woman*, the last a carefully disguised propaganda film that Alex had promised Winston Churchill he would make. Alex was near the height of his career, but he was also deeply mired in debt, his marriage to Merle Oberon was fragile, and he was faced with the fact that in wartime England there was little or no hope that these three ambitious productions, two of them in Technicolor, at that time a hugely complicated and expensive procedure, could be completed. It was clear to him—and was soon made clear to his brothers, Zoltan (usually called Zoli) and Vincent—that the entire family might have to be uprooted and moved to Hollywood, all the more so since two of the most "bankable" stars under contract to London Films, Laurence Olivier and Vivien Leigh, whom he would need to play Admiral Nelson and Lady Hamilton, were already there. That is not to say that my mother and my aunt Joan, Zoli's wife, were reconciled to being moved suddenly five thousand miles away—and in my mother's case away from a successful London stage career. Alex, Merle, and Zoli, on the other hand, were in that rare class of people in those days who already moved effortlessly back and forth between London, New York, and Los Angeles, either making the Atlantic crossing on one of the great liners or, in Alex's case, flying from London to Lisbon to take the Pan American "Clipper" flying boat to New York, then crossing the United States in a TWA DC-3, in those days a trip of eighteen hours, with refueling stops in Chicago, Kansas City, and Albuquerque. At one point Alex flew from London to Los Angeles and back twice in three weeks for United Artists board meetings, a feat something on the order of Jules Verne's *Around the World in Eighty Days* in 1940.

What Alex did *not* tell his sisters-in-law was that the move to California had the blessing of MI6 and Churchill, or that the British government was clandestinely helping to finance the move. Albeit at the most privileged and luxurious level, we were about to become refugees like so many others set adrift by the war, but without much in the way of discomfort or real danger.

*   *   *

Seen from the United Kingdom and France, the autumn and winter of 1939–1940 was indeed a "phoney war." The anticipated bombing of London did not take place, and the RAF was still strictly limited to dropping propaganda leaflets over Germany by night. Hitler's broadcast "peace offers" were ignored or ridiculed in public, but behind the scenes in the War Cabinet and the Foreign Office (and the French equivalents) they were examined rather more seriously. The small irritations of rationing and government regulations constituted the principal proof that we were at war.

The familiar British reply to "How are you?," which is "Mustn't grumble," was falling into disuse. Everybody had something to grumble about, and did. People grumbled about rationing, which though it was not as draconic as it was soon to become, included everything from tobacco and "sweets" to meat and eggs. They grumbled about the many inconveniences of "the blackout" as urban crime, prostitution, and accidents soared in the darkness of the streets, and about "petrol rationing," which soon took almost every car off the road except those owned by doctors, farmers, and other special categories. The poor grumbled that the rich still ate at their club or at expensive restaurants where, at a price, food remained plentiful, while the rich grumbled about taxes.

Outside the big cities, the poor and the rich *both* grumbled about the evacuation of "slum" children to the countryside, under Operation Pied Piper, the ambitious prewar plan (improbably concocted by the Conservatives) intended to protect them from being bombed, and which went forward inexorably, despite protests from villagers and country dwellers throughout England. There was almost as much protest from the families of the urban poor at having their lives disrupted by what was perceived as a vast—and possibly half-baked—social experiment. Evelyn Waugh wrote a whole satiric novel about it, *Put Out More Flags*, and the normally urbane

Above: Operation Pied Piper
in action, 1939.
Right: Harold Nicolson and
Vita Sackville-West.

Harold Nicolson commented in his diary, "Many of the children are verminous and have disgusting habits. . . . Much ill feeling has been caused."

In the end almost three and a half million would be evacuated, most of them before the bombing started, in a scheme that seemed more in keeping with social planning in the Soviet Union than in Great Britain. In practice the urban poor were sent to the English countryside, where people naturally attempted to procure the more attractive and docile of the children by fair means or foul, while much smaller numbers of upper-class and middle-class children were evacuated to Canada or the United States, often sponsored by well-meaning organizations and individuals, and parked there for the duration of the war.* Anna Freud, the daughter of Sigmund Freud, later studied the effects of evacuation in 1941 and reached the unsurprising conclusion that "separation from their parents is a worse shock for children than a bombing."

All this grumbling would cease when the phoney war was over and the fighting and bombing began in earnest, a reflection of the British people's peculiar ability to draw together when under direct threat, and to lower the level of class warfare—the normal preoccupation of the nation—at least briefly, when faced with real danger. The German belief that *Schrecklichkeit*—the application of frightfulness on a large scale, long the default position of Germany in dealing with the rest of the world—would shatter the British will was a serious misreading of the national character. Instead, it would momentarily unite us all by giving us something to hate more than those who were richer or poorer on the social scale, or who spoke with a different accent.

---

* Among those evacuated to the United States by way of Canada were my friends Martin Gilbert, the future official biographer of Winston Churchill, Alistair Horne, who was sent to the Millbrook School, in Millbrook, NY (where his roommate was William F. Buckley), and who would go on to become Sir Alistair Horne, CBE, the respected historian, and myself.

The evacuation of children was hard to avoid then, given the determination with which the bureaucracy enforced it, and London railway stations soon became the chaotic scenes of tearful partings between parents and children, rather than the tearful farewells to those going off to war, as had been the case in 1914. It was as if the British government and the civil service had decided to put their major war efforts into the disruption of British home life, rather than creating the divisions that would be needed in France. If they could not create well-armed new divisions of troops, they could at least shuffle children around the country in huge quantities according to a complex scheme that was unclear even to those who were administering it.

In my case, being among the socially priviledged, I was for the time being kept out of the hands of officialdom, first sent to live up north with Nanny Low's family on a windswept farm in Yorkshire, of which I remember only pigs, driving rain, and a local accent so pronounced that I would not have understood a word that was said to me had my maternal grandfather, a prosperous dentist in suburban London, not been "from the North" himself. From there I was eventually moved in a journey of unthinkable length and seemingly infinite changes of train to a red-brick boarding school on the Isle of Wight, along with a batch of other middle- and upper-class London evacuees of my age, all clad in identical gray flannel shorts, jackets, and caps, and all desperately homesick. This was a curious place to have sent evacuated children, since if the Germans ever attempted to invade England the Isle of Wight would surely have been high on the list of places where they could be expected to land.

Apart from acquiring a lifelong dislike of the smell of cabbage being boiled, I remember little about this episode except seeing barbed wire unrolled on the beaches, which were guarded at intervals by soldiers, many of them sitting on the peacetime canvas deck chairs holding their rifle and looking out to sea. One or two of them, I still recall, sensibly held an umbrella in the other hand to shield them from the rain.

As it gradually became apparent that Armageddon was not about to pour down out of the skies on London for the moment, despite H. G. Wells's prediction, the long arm of the Korda family eventually reached out and placed me back in our home in Hampstead, none the worse for wear, except for a strong dislike of English boarding schools.

6

Case Yellow

General von Manstein and the Führer.

S O FAR AS France and England were concerned, the war was being conducted in the most soporific way, as if both countries were waiting for Hitler to make the first move and still anxious not to give him a reason for attacking. Behind the scenes, however, a whole first act of a fatal drama was being played out—indeed the major players, many of them more or less unsuitable for their role, were already in place.

At the very beginning of the war Secretary of State for War Hore-Belisha, with Chamberlain's consent, had chosen the then chief of the Imperial General Staff, General the Viscount Gort, to command the British Expeditionary Force in France and General Sir Edmund Ironside to replace him as CIGS. Ironside had expected to be given command of the BEF himself and was dis-

Leslie Hore-Belisha visits the troops, 1939.

mayed on September 3 when it went to Gort instead, who he judged had already been promoted far beyond his capabilities.

It was the reverse of what everybody in the army had assumed would happen when war came. Ironside was enormously tall and physically impressive (hence, following British military tradition, his nickname was Tiny), he spoke French well (and also German), and he had attended prewar German Army maneuvers as an observer and met not only the senior German commanders but even Göring and Hitler. He seemed ideal to command the BEF.

Gort was an aristocrat (John Standish Surtees Prendergast Ver-eker, 6th Viscount Gort) and outstandingly brave, one of the most decorated officers in the British Army, having won the Victoria Cross, Britain's highest award for valor, three Distinguished Service Orders, and the Military Cross in the 1914–1918 war, but he had neither the brains nor the temperament for high command; he fussed over details like a sergeant-major and had no discernible gift for seeing "the big picture." As CIGS he had been essentially a fig-urehead, and he particularly disliked dealing with politicians—not a good recommendation for the commander in chief of the BEF, who needed to be at once a strategist, a politician, and a diplomat.

Lord Gort was a popular choice to command the BEF outside the circle of his fellow generals. He was exactly the kind of Englishman the French profess to admire: heroic, modest, and profoundly unin-tellectual. His title and his Victoria Cross won him the respect of the British press, and although the notion of "public relations" would have been repugnant to Gort, he, unlike his predecessors in World War One, made an effort to fraternize with British war correspon-dents, and even invited them to lunch in his mess. Gort was particu-larly forthcoming with the dashing, witty, and well-informed young *Times* war correspondent to the BEF, Harold "Kim" Philby. Naturally, for Lord Gort, as for most Englishmen of his class, the *Times* was a cut above any other newspaper, so he could talk more frankly with Philby than with most reporters. What he did not, of course, know was that Philby had been a spy for the Soviet Union since his Cambridge days, and passed on every scrap of information from Lord Gort to Moscow, via his Soviet contact in Paris. Since Soviet Russia was then an ally

of Nazi Germany, that information was no doubt passed on immediately to Berlin. There would be no surprises about the plans and
the strength of the BEF when the Germans finally attacked, thanks
to Philby, who went on to decades of further betrayal when he was
recruited away from the *Times* by MI6 later in 1940.

It may well be that Chamberlain should have quietly sought further
advice before allowing Hore-Belisha to give command of the BEF
to Gort, but the prime minister's lack of interest in military affairs

General Gamelin contemplates the map of Europe—
and apparently, the English Channel.

was notorious. He should certainly also have given more thought to the role of the BEF itself. Although the BEF would eventually grow to over 300,000 men (including its RAF Air Component), it was dwarfed by the French Army, which was over 5,000,000 men strong, 3,500,000 of them in Metropolitan France alone. In view of this huge disparity in numbers the Chamberlain government had agreed from the beginning that the BEF should take a place in the "line of battle" of the French Army, and that the commander in chief of the BEF should come under the orders of the French commander in chief, General Maurice Gamelin. The commander in chief of the BEF would retain the right to appeal to his own government in case he disagreed with the orders he received, but except under extraordinary circumstances it was hard to imagine that Gort was the right man to do this. His natural disposition was to obey his orders, not to argue about them, and by the time he finally made use of this right it was almost too late. Gort's own chief of staff, the acerbic Lieutenant-General Henry Pownall, was of the opinion that Gort was better suited to a "regimental" command (that is, a lieutenant-colonel's job) than as the British commander in chief in France.

Lieutenant-General Pownall.

During the First World War the British Expeditionary Force had not been placed under French command until the crisis of March 1918 when Germany's last great offensive, Ludendorff's *Kaiserschlacht*, threatened to overwhelm the French, British, and American armies. In the emergency the Allies reluctantly agreed to accept General Ferdinand Foch as *Généralissime*, or Allied Supreme Commander. Gort's BEF received its orders from France's Grand Quartier Général, filtered down through several levels of command, and took its place between two French armies facing Belgium, to its north the French Seventh Army, to its south the French First Army.

As they had in the previous war, the French insisted on keeping a French army between the BEF and the Channel ports, just in case the British got cold feet. The role the BEF was to play when the Germans finally attacked was subordinated to Gamelin's strategic vision, and also to the surreal confidence of the Belgian government in its policy of strict neutrality.

Gamelin's plan was known as Plan D because it involved an advance to the Dyle River in Belgium, perhaps unfortunately because in the French Army "le système D" stands for "débrouillez-vous," or more rudely "démerdez-vous," the equivalent of "sort it out for yourself" when things go wrong. Gamelin assumed that the main German attack would come through neutral Belgium, as it had in the First World War, and that Germans might attack the Netherlands as well this time, a neutral country they had avoided in 1914. He did not think the Germans would dare to attack the Maginot Line in major force, and like almost everybody else he assumed that the Ardennes Forest—that is, the southernmost spur of Belgium and Luxembourg that extends from Namur in Belgium to Montmédy in France, where the Maginot Line ended—would be inappropriate for a major attack because of its hilly, heavily wooded terrain, which contained too many small streams and too few major roads. Besides, the Meuse River would present a major natural obstacle for the German armored forces as they emerged from the Ardennes. In Gamelin's opinion, the Maginot Line could hold the Germans indefinitely and it would take them at least two weeks to cross the Ardennes in force, therefore the first and major blow would come in the north through Holland and Belgium, with their flat terrain and excellent roads, hence good tank country. It was there that the Germans must be met, Gamelin believed, and counterattacked boldly and with maximum force.

*   *   *

This had in fact been the original German plan, and it presented the Allied armies with an unanswerable question: What would Belgium do? Belgium's neutrality was a sacred cause—the German breach of Belgian neutrality in August 1914 had been the deciding factor in bringing the United Kingdom into the war. The British government did not go to war to support France in its hour of need, the British went for "plucky little Belgium," to defend its neutrality, which Britain was bound by treaty to support. Of all the many mistakes made by the Kaiser's Germany, the most serious (and the earliest) was the decision to ignore what the Kaiser notoriously dismissed as "a scrap of paper" and invade Belgium, since by doing so he would automatically bring Britain and the British Empire into the war against him.

Nobody doubted that Hitler would not hesitate to breach Belgium's neutrality, and Holland's too if it suited him, but the French and the British could not. Thus the advance to the Dyle River, which was at the heart of Gamelin's plan, could not take place unless the Belgium government invited them to, or until the Germans had crossed the Belgian border, which effectively placed the timing of the Allied attack entirely in the hands of the Germans, or those of the king of the Belgians. This fact did not escape General Alphonse Georges, commander of the northeast front, who had no faith in Plan D and disliked General Gamelin.

Churchill and General Georges.

*   *   *

The feeling was mutual. From the beginning of the war General Gamelin had placed his headquarters—the Grand Quartier Général—in the gloomy Château de Vincennes in the suburbs of Paris, determined not to be influenced by politicians or by General Georges, while Georges moved his headquarters as commander of the northeast front as far away as he could from General Gamelin.

General de Gaulle and the king.

The Château de Vincennes was a curious choice—it was the scene of many historical tragedies going back to the fourteenth century, and its former moat had been used for executions by firing squad in the past, and would be used again for that grim purpose by the Germans from 1940 to 1944.

In order to avoid having to meet face-to-face, Gamelin and Georges communicated by courier or, more rarely, by telephone, although there was no guarantee that the telephone lines were secure. Oddly, there was no radio at the GQG, both because Gamelin feared the Germans would intercept and decode messages, but also because he did not want messages from General Georges disturbing the Olympian calm of his planning for grand strategy, or upsetting his sacred routine. Gamelin was not only physically remote and protected by his devoted staff from outside influence within the sprawling confines of the Château de Vincennes, a kind of military Dalai Lama; his was in any case a somewhat withdrawn personality, "smooth, secretive, non-committal." Georges, on the other hand, was of a more outgoing nature—he had a good deal of that charm and taste for good living that the British find reassuring in a Frenchman.

Just before the beginning of the war the ubiquitous Spears had brought his friends Churchill and Georges together for a lunch at a fashionable restaurant in the Bois de Boulogne, and by the end of the long lunch, over "wood strawberries soaked in white wine," the two men found themselves of one mind. Churchill warned Georges about the mistake of thinking that "the Ardennes were impassible to strong forces," as both Marshal Pétain and General Gamelin believed, while Georges made clear his opinion that King Leopold III of Belgium "was reputed to be much under German influence," and intended to hold the Allies "at arms length." These two concerns would be at the root of the problems facing the Allies in 1939 rather than the relative

King Leopold III
of Belgium

The assassination of King Alexander of Yugoslavia, in which
General Georges was badly wounded.

strength of the Allied and German armies, or German superiority
in ground attack aircraft.

Owing to the intricacies of the French command system, General Gamelin gave direct orders to all the French Army commanders worldwide *except* General Georges, who had direct command of
the Allied armies facing the Germans. On the other hand, since
Gamelin was commander in chief, he controlled the flow of troops
and supplies and had the power to promote generals, who in the
northeast therefore looked to Georges for their orders, but toward
Gamelin at the Château de Vincennes for their future.

The British liked Georges more than the unapproachable
Gamelin—Georges seems to have won over General Lord Gort
easily enough, no small achievement given the uneasy relationship
between British commanders of the BEF and French generals in
World War One—but some questioned whether Georges had recovered completely from the life-threatening wound he had received
during the assassination of King Alexander of Yugoslavia at Marseille in 1934. Was he the same man he had been before the inci-

dent? It was the length of his recovery, together with Daladier's fears that Georges was too far to the right politically, that had led to making Gamelin the commander in chief in 1935 instead of Georges, who was merely made Gamelin's deputy and "eventual successor" instead, much to his chagrin.

In the meantime it was unclear to both the British and the French whether Lord Gort would receive his orders from Gamelin or from Georges. Not even Tiny Ironside, who was as bold and as blunt as he was tall and broad-shouldered, was able to ascertain this vital point from Gamelin, who was theoretically his counterpart. This was only one ingredient, but an important one, in a recipe for disaster.

The Belgian problem was insoluble. Neutral Belgium and the Netherlands were like the proverbial deer caught in the headlights of a huge truck speeding toward them, driven by Hitler. In order to protect their neutrality they could not enter into formal staff talks with the French and the British; on the other hand they both expected that the Allies would come to their rescue immediately if they *were* attacked. Since Gamelin assumed that they *would* be attacked, he blithely added their military strength to his own: twenty-two Belgian divisions and ten Dutch, the equivalent of 400,000 Dutch troops and 650,000 Belgian, *if* they could be mobilized in time. But neither the Belgians nor the Dutch were in any way equipped to fight a modern war, being deficient in everything from artillery to airplanes, in addition to which they could not begin to mobilize their armies until the Germans attacked them, since Hitler would regard that as a provocation. Gamelin's plan assumed that it would take several weeks for the Germans to reach the Dyle River, whereas when the time came they would reach it in four days. His view was at once cynical and fatally optimistic: "The Allied advance would be so rapid," he told Edward Spears, "that the Belgians, even on the most unfavorable hypothesis, would not have time to give way."

Left unspoken was the fact that after their experience in the

First World War the underlying rationale for Plan D was French determination to fight the next war, if it had to be fought at all, beyond the French frontier. The Belgian king and his countrymen were certainly afraid of being invaded by the Germans, but that did not reconcile them to the prospect of France, Britain, and Germany fighting out the war on Belgian soil. The Dutch plan was to flood the dikes and stage a fighting retreat to "Fortress Holland," the area around Rotterdam, Amsterdam, and The Hague, until the French could link up with them. This too would prove to be a chimera.

The lack of trust in the king of the Belgians in 1939 was sharpened by the shining example of his father, Albert I, who had been the preeminent hero of the First World War, and whose character was that of a *preux chevalier*, like the legendary "knight in shining armor" in an otherwise sordid tale. When he learned from the Kaiser of Germany's plan to attack France by crossing Belgium in the event of war, and of the Kaiser's hope that Belgium would permit the German Army to do so, Albert replied with the courage and dignity he would show throughout his reign: "Belgium is a nation, not a road."

King Albert I of Belgium.

Small as its army was—less than a tenth the size of the German Army—Belgium had declared war on Germany in 1914 when her territory was infringed, and slowed down the German advance at great cost for over three weeks, making possible the French victory at the Battle of the Marne. The king of the Belgians became an international hero, all the more so since the German occupation of Belgium was by the standards of the time exceptionally cruel; it included such "war crimes," to use a modern term, as the shooting of over five thousand randomly selected male and female civilian hostages and the wanton destruction of Belgian historical and cultural sites, the most famous of which was the deliberate burning of the great library of the University of Louvain, with its priceless collection of medieval manuscripts and books.

Leopold III lacked his father's firmness of character, as well as Albert's ability to govern a small, but volatile and divided, country and win the respect of both the Walloon and the Flemish populations, still today a difficult task. Leopold III was deficient too in many of the qualities demanded of a constitutional monarch, and apt to make sudden and rash decisions on his own.

Some of this unsteadiness communicated itself to the British and the French—Belgium expected them to come to its assistance if it was attacked by the Germans, but in the meantime they were kept in ignorance of the defenses the Belgians were preparing, to such an extent that it was not until March 1940 that a French staff officer was allowed to see them, and then only on the condition that he wore civilian clothes and did not leave his vehicle (the little he *did* see left him unimpressed). Nevertheless, Gamelin's Plan D remained the only strategy for the Allies, who persistently overrated Belgian and Dutch powers of resistance.

A more intransigent British commander than Lord Gort might have voiced doubts about Plan D to his own government if not to Gamelin, but this was not part of Gort's nature. He had won the Victoria Cross not by questioning his orders but by obeying them gallantly despite wounds that would have incapacitated almost any other man.* Gort had his doubts about the ability of the BEF to advance rapidly to the river Dyle, or possibly beyond it to the Albert Canal, in the absence of any knowledge of the Belgian defenses, but he suppressed them gamely in the interests of Allied solidarity.

*　　*　　*

---

* The Victoria Cross is so rarely given that only 1,358 have been awarded since it was instituted by Queen Victoria in 1856.

The phoney war was not a deliberate stratagem on the part of the Germans—Hitler was infuriated by the maddeningly long delay between his victory over Poland and the attack on France and the Low Countries in May 1940; indeed he had intended to turn on France in 1939 as soon as possible after defeating the Poles. His problem was that he did not like the initial plan for the attack drawn up by the Oberkommando des Heeres (OKH, Army High Command).

Hitler has come in for great criticism as an amateur strategist, some of it deserved, but not all. In the first place, he was not without military experience; he had served as a soldier on the western front through some of the worst battles of that, or any other, war and been awarded the Iron Cross First Class for bravery, a decoration rarely awarded to mere lance corporals; in the second, he had a kind of *Fingerspitzengefühl*, or second sense, about military matters, which at first seemed to demonstrate the truth of Napoleon's famous remark that "in war, as in prostitution, the amateur is often better than the professional."

In this case the amateur's instincts were correct. When Chief of the General Staff of the Army Franz Halder presented to him the first version of *Fall Gelb* (Case Yellow), the invasion of the Low Countries, it seemed to Hitler merely a less ambitious rehash of the Schlieffen Plan, which had guided the German Army in August 1914, and which led to four years of costly stalemate. The end result, so far as he could see, would very likely lead to another battle on the Somme River, the graveyard of hundreds of thousands of Allied and German sol-

General Franz Halder.

diers, where Lance-Corporal Hitler had fought in the mud and barbed wire entanglements of the Great War. A military plan of this size, scope, and complexity, drawn up by the most professional and clear-minded general staff in the world, was not something that was easy to dismiss out of hand, but Hitler felt intuitively that it was wrong and sent Halder "back to the drawing board," as the saying goes.

Halder's personality was dry and professorial, emphasized by his pince-nez, and that perhaps influenced Hitler as well—he had a horror of being "talked down to" by experts. Halder's second version of Case Yellow did not please Hitler much either, since it retained the idea of a main attack through Belgium, adding to it secondary attacks to the north and the south, thereby sacrificing the all-important principle of concentration of forces. By now it was October, a full month after the outbreak of war, and the weather had become an issue. The longer the Germans waited, the greater the danger that they would be committed to a winter offensive, and the more time the Allies would have to build up their strength. All the same, Hitler waited, by no means patiently, but at any rate determined not to accept a plan about which he felt to his fingertips uncomfortable, whatever his generals thought. His military instincts had not yet been clouded by too many victories, a taste for gigantism, and the tendency to interfere in tactical battlefield decisions.

He was not alone in disliking the various iterations of Case Yellow. General Erich von Manstein, the most prominent convert to General Guderian's ideas about armored warfare, had been moved to the post of chief of staff to the commander of Army Group A, Colonel General Gerd von Rundstedt, whose steely professionalism and forbidding appearance made him perhaps the most respected of the older German generals. Rundstedt too thought that the traditional German strategy going back to the time of Frederick the Great—the swift encirclement of the enemy—was being sacrificed in favor of a frontal attack through northern Belgium and Holland by Army Group B, and that the main attack should be made instead farther to the south, toward Sedan, by Army Group A.

A chance meeting with Guderian led to Manstein's preparing a series of radically different approaches to Case Yellow, in which not only the main weight of the attack but the bulk of the panzer forces would be aimed at Sedan, and move directly west from there to the English Channel ports, cutting the British and French armies in Belgium off completely. He elaborated this in "a series of memoranda," which he sent off one after the other to OKH, but even when endorsed with a covering note from Rundstedt they were studiously ignored. His two main points were that "the *main weight* of our attack must lie with Army Group A, not B," and that "*a surprise attack through the Ardennes* . . . was the only possible means of destroying the enemy's entire northern wing in Belgium preparatory to winning a final victory in France" (Manstein's italics).

General Gamelin's belief that the Ardennes were impassable to tanks was contradicted by the observations of many German officers who had spent their leave hiking through the Ardennes with binoculars and Leicas. Manstein's demands for a complete revision of Case Yellow were outrageously bold, but he persisted. He had anticipated furious resistance from most of the senior German generals, particularly Halder, and he was right.

A further delay was caused by the crash landing in Belgium on January 10, 1940, of a Luftwaffe light aircraft that had gone astray in bad weather carrying a courier with the latest version of Case Yellow. This officer was taken into custody by Belgian policemen before he had a chance to burn the documents completely. Although the charred pages did not contain the actual date of the attack, enough remained legible to cause alarm, somewhat tempered by initial disbelief, in Brussels. From other sources, however, the Belgians heard that the attack was to take place on or around January 14 (the actual date was supposed to be January 17), and they sent a transcript of the material on to Paris.

This incident has become so encrusted with legend that it is hard to sort out fact from fiction. French intelligence suspected that it was a *ruse de guerre* intended to mislead the Allies about the timing and direction of the German attack, but there is no evidence that this was so—in any case, it was taken seriously by General Gamelin, who hoped that it would encourage the Belgians to open their frontier to the Allied armies, and by the king of the Belgians, who passed a coded warning on to Queen Wilhelmina of the Netherlands by telephone, and to Winston Churchill via their mutual friend Admiral of the Fleet Sir Roger Keyes.

In the event, after much anxiety in London, Paris, Brussels, and The Hague, nothing happened. A heavy snowstorm made the attack unlikely, and as the various dates passed with no sign that the German Army was about to invade the Low Countries, apprehension gave way to the previous nervous inaction. The Belgian chief of staff, who had rashly ordered the barriers on the Franco-Belgian frontier to be removed, was severely reprimanded, and the king's determination to keep Belgium strictly neutral (and his hope of riding out the storm without provoking either side) was rekindled.

In Berlin Hitler's reaction was at first explosive. General Alfred Jodl, chief of staff of the OKW (Oberkommando der Wehrmacht), was understandably reluctant to inform the Führer that the plans for *Fall Gelb* had fallen into the hands of the enemy only a week before the attack was supposed to begin. "Situation catastrophic," Jodl noted in his diary, surely an understatement, but once Hitler's initial rage had cooled down a bit, clearer, calmer military minds took over, and it was decided to proceed with the attack as planned.

"What material did they get?" General Halder asks himself sensibly in his diary entry for January 11. "Fueher has reserved decision. Should location of Hq. be changed? What has been divulged: location of Hq., number of armored units, Hq. of 7th Air Division, airfields of Air Group 2?" These are not the questions of a panic-stricken man. In the days to come Halder's diary merely reflects

an orderly reassessment of the attack, and eventually a postpone-
ment because of bad weather—the winter of 1939–1940 would be
the coldest and harshest in many years, so bad that it would later
be seen as an important element in the decline of morale in the
French Army.

By January 20, as Halder noted to himself after the day's Führer
conference, Hitler has already accepted a much longer postpone-
ment, even to Easter perhaps, and the "Off with his head!" tone
of his first reaction gave way to a reasonable enough demand for
greater security to prevent an incident like this from occurring
again. As the days went by, the capture of the plans no longer
seems to have been regarded as catastrophic; indeed for Hitler it
may have become a blessing in disguise. He had never liked the
plan for Case Yellow, and now he had a good excuse for altering it
dramatically.

In the meantime, in order to keep General von Manstein from
further tinkering with *Fall Gelb*, General Halder appointed him
to command an army corps in Prussia, the order to take effect on
February 9, and accompanied by a promotion that was intended to
disguise Halder's annoyance with him. However, Manstein's loyal
staff—he was already developing a cult following—managed to
leak his proposals for changes in the plan to bring them to Hitler's
attention, an "end run" around Halder that succeeded.

Hitler liked what he heard, and invited Manstein to attend a
meeting with him on February 17. The Führer had been interested
for some time in the idea of making Sedan the *Schwerpunkt* of the
attack, against the advice of his senior generals, who thought this
was too risky. Now he was presented with a plan that would put the
bulk of his forces in what later came to be called a *Sichelschnitt*, or
"sickel cut," advancing through the Ardennes, crossing the Meuse,
then driving straight on to the English Channel. The attack on
the Low Countries would be retained as a kind of huge deception
plan, intended to lure the main force of the French Army and the
BEF deep into Belgium, where they would be isolated, exposed,

and outflanked by the attack on their right, which would swiftly cut them off from the rest of the French Army.

The fact that the Allies already had in their hands the plan for the attack on Belgium and Holland would now work to the advantage of the Germans, a fortuitous example of turning a lemon into lemonade. The Allies would be expecting the German Army to attack the Low Countries, and when it did they would not be looking toward the Ardennes, where the real blow would come. Almost as important, the tanks would be used the way Guderian (and Liddell Hart) thought they should be used: punching holes in the enemy line through which the slower-moving infantry would march.

Fall Gelb was ambitious and conceived on an enormous scale, involving nearly three and a half million men, over three thousand tanks and three thousand aircraft. In the aftermath, it would be described as a blitzkrieg, and the German victory attributed to superior mechanization, but this is a false picture of what was to come. The bulk of the German infantry marched on foot just as it had in 1914, and there were still over half a million horses in the German Army in 1940. Most of the artillery was horse drawn, company commanders rode ahead of their men, while farriers and cobblers, mainly in horse-drawn wagons, moved behind the troops to keep men and horses shod. By comparison, the British Army, though small and poorly provided with tanks, was almost completely motorized. Of course neither the French nor the British (still less the Belgians and Dutch) were equipped or prepared for long marches, since from the beginning they had intended to fight a defensive battle. The Germans, on the other hand, would have long distances to cover, and commanders worried, not without reason, about the gap that would open up between the fast-moving panzer divisions and the much slower infantry divisions behind them.

At first Halder did his best to sabotage Manstein's plan by surreptitiously detaching armored divisions from Army Group A, but he eventually came around to the Manstein plan, partly because it was a daring gamble that promised decisive results, whereas what he feared most was that a longer, slower "conventional" campaign might fail, or bog down into static warfare like the previous war. His diaries reflect the immense complexities of the plan, as well as Hitler's growing obsession with the details, and his tendency to ask for the transfer of whole corps and armies without giving any thought to the logistics involved, the mark of an amateur.

Over lunch Manstein found Hitler "surprisingly quick to grasp the points which our Army Group had been advocating for many months past." Even more to his surprise, Hitler approved the new plan, and it was put into immediate effect, though without Manstein, who had been deftly shifted to the sidelines by his superiors. Manstein concluded that "Hitler had a certain instinct for operational problems, but lacked the thorough training of a military commander," a portent of things to come, but in the meantime, the plan that Manstein and Guderian had worked out in such detail would emerge as the final version of Case Yellow, while the Allies still clung to the belief that the main focus of the coming attack would be in Belgium, on the Dyle River, and that their best chance for victory was to get there in full strength before the Germans did.

7

"Gad, Gentlemen, Here's to Our Greatest Victory of the War"

Gracie Fields visits the troops, 1939.

Tⁿᴴᴱ ᴹᴼˢᵀ ᶜᴼᴺˢᴾᴵᶜᵁᴼᵁˢ Allied casualty of the phoney war was the secretary of state for war, the Rt. Hon. Leslie Hore-Belisha. Hore-Belisha had failed to gauge correctly the dislike in which he was held by his own generals, and fell into a trap of his own making. Having announced that he wished to visit the British Expeditionary Force, he was asked by General Ironside, the CIGS, whether he wanted "to concentrate on seeing the men or the defenses," and replied that he wished to see the men.

This was the wrong answer. Both Ironside and Lord Gort, like most senior British officers, disliked the whole idea of a politician chitchatting with the "Other Ranks," as enlisted men are called in Britain, and did not in any case like or trust Hore-Belisha. There is a photograph of Lord Gort and Hore-Belisha that tells the whole story: Hore-Belisha is on the left, slouched, slightly disheveled, chain-smoking, and argumentative; on the right Gort sits bolt upright, almost sitting at attention, his expression that of a man who is sternly resisting a sales pitch, or who has just been told a vulgar joke that he resents. It is altogether apparent that Gort is uncomfortable and disapproving and that Hore-Belisha either doesn't care or more likely doesn't notice.

Once Hore-Belisha was in France he was subjected by Lord Gort, who possessed what even his devoted biographer calls "a schoolboy sense of humor," to a remarkable degree of snide and contemptuous ragging (or "hazing," as it is called in the United States) by Gort and his staff. Had Hore-Belisha attended Harrow like Lord Gort, instead of Polack's House, the "Jewish wing" of Clifton School, Bristol, he might have understood that he was being bullied and made to look foolish by upper-class experts on the subject, but he seems to have thought, or at any rate pretended, that it was all in good fun. "Gort took pleasure in subjecting Hore Belisha to every form of climactic and gastronomic discomfort which the Flanders climate and Gort's spartan régime could provide." This included "picnics" in the pouring rain with "bully-beef" sandwiches (the British Army's much reviled version of canned corned beef), accompanied by a good deal of chaffing about Hore-Belisha's allegedly self-indulgent life style at home. All this seems to have been intended to keep the secretary of state for war busy and uncomfortable and, perhaps more important, to prevent him from having any heart-to-heart chats with the troops.

It did not, however, prevent him from deciding that "pillboxes" (a pillbox is a concrete fortification intended to hold one or two soldiers, with a concrete roof to protect them from grenades and firing slots, or "loopholes" for a rifle or a light machine gun) were not being built at the rate he expected. On his way home he paused to pay his respects to General Gamelin, who told him—or so Hore-Belisha understood—that the French Army needed only three days in which to build a concrete pillbox. Once he was back at his desk in Whitehall, Hore-Belisha wrote what he no doubt supposed was a helpful letter to General Lord Gort about the superiority of the French method of building a pillbox, suggesting that Gort send some officers to observe this.

Hardly anything could have been better calculated to infuriate Gort and his staff. The British had in fact been building pillboxes at a much faster rate than the French (French soldiers, rather like Confederate soldiers in the Civil War, bitterly resented spadework as beneath their dignity), and had even been building them *for* the French, and it turned out, after the whole affair had grown into a huge public embarrassment, that what Gamelin had really meant was it required only three days *after* the excavation had been dug and the concrete poured—it actually took the French three *weeks* to produce a pillbox from start to finish.

Hore-Belisha shared his concern with everybody from the prime minister to the Dominion ministers who happened to be in London at the time, no doubt in a well-meaning effort to improve the BEF defenses, but also to show that he was "on top of things." Instead, he succeeded in starting a row much bigger than he can have possibly imagined. Even King George VI heard all about the pillbox controversy from General Ironside, went out to Flanders to see for himself what was going on, and also got an earful about Hore-Belisha from Gort while he was there. The king, who took very seriously the fact that this was *his* army and these were *his* generals—he was always very conscious of his right to be consulted over the appointment or promotion of general officers—prodded his prime minister into making a fact-finding trip to Flanders for himself.

That Hore-Belisha had been wrong about the speed and rate with which pillboxes were being built, and that he had shared all this with the French commander in chief, made Gort's resentment even stronger. Not only class consciousness (and some degree of anti-Semitism) but national pride was now involved—the British Army had nothing to learn about building fortifications from the French!

It soon began to dawn on Chamberlain, always a shrewd politician, that Hore-Belisha had by now managed to infuriate the king, the chief of the Imperial General Staff, and the commander in chief of the British Expeditionary Force—too powerful a combination of upper-class Englishmen to ignore. Even General Ironside warned Hore-Belisha that "he must be careful how he deals with his C.-in-C. He was put in by the King and must not be monkeyed about with."

By this time it was too late. Chamberlain had already decided to replace Hore-Belisha, hoping to shift him skillfully to another office. Given Hore-Belisha's undeniable knack for getting newspaper publicity for himself, Chamberlain thought that the Ministry of Information might be the right place for him, but Lord Halifax, the foreign secretary, objected that this might have "a bad effect on the neutrals both because Hore-Belisha was a Jew and because his methods would let down British prestige," an interesting comment on the level of anti-Semitism present even in such an otherwise respected member of the establishment.

In the end Hore-Belisha was "summoned" by the prime minister, told that there was "prejudice" against him at the War Office and offered the presidency of the Board of Trade. This was a shock to Hore-Belisha, since it was a considerable demotion. He called Churchill, who was in Paris and advised Hore-Belisha to accept the Board of Trade, with the wisdom of a man who had experienced over half a century of political ups and downs, had filled almost every cabinet post over the years except that of prime minister and foreign secretary, and had long since learned that it was always better to be in the cabinet than on the back benches of the House of Commons.

Hore-Belisha was replaced in January 1940 by Oliver Stanley,

Oliver Stanley.

a sound man who was unlikely to upset the king or the generals: "Oliver Stanley," the prime minister wrote, "will do well at
the W. O. though of course he is of a retiring nature." This was
just the reverse of Hore-Belisha, who was the least "retiring" of
men, and just as Churchill had predicted, after he turned down
the Board of Trade his political career was effectively ended.
Needless to say, even though the pillboxes, however many of
them were built, would be of no earthly use to the army when it
advanced into Belgium, leaving them behind was never considered by anyone.

Hore-Belisha's resignation sparked off brief, but intense, media
attention, including a famous cartoon by David Low in the *Evening Standard* showing a banquet of "Colonel Blimps," Low's trademark symbol for the backwardness, reactionary thinking, and class
prejudice of the senior officer class, celebrating the event with a
toast in vintage port while the prime minister dressed as a waiter

Evening Standard, Wednesday, January 10, 1940   11

GAD, GENTLEMEN, HERE'S TO OUR GREATEST VICTORY OF THE WAR *(Copyright in All Countries.)*

looks on, lugubriously standing next to a portrait of Hore-Belisha pierced by sabers. The caption reads, "Gad, gentlemen, here's to our greatest victory of the war."

Sadly, the sacking of Hore-Belisha was the *only* victory that the British Army could claim in the winter of 1939–1940. The BEF grew as Territorial divisions (roughly the equivalent of the state National Guards in this country) arrived. They were much less well equipped than the regular divisions, and still comparatively untrained, and a huge effort was made over the winter to get them up to standard, with mixed results. By 1940 the BEF was, at least on paper, a fairly powerful force of over 300,000 men, comprising ten divisions of infantry split into three corps, a brigade of tanks, and a division of the Royal Artillery. The weakness in tanks was only too apparent, considering that the BEF was up against an enemy that could field three thousand of them, most of them faster and more reliable, but there was no possibility of quickly remedying the deficiencies of the 1930s in the design and production of British tanks.

Apart from tanks, the greatest weakness of the BEF was in air support. From its difficult birth as a separate service in 1918, the RAF had stoutly resisted the role of supporting the army, and even more strongly any suggestion of putting its aircraft at the beck and call of generals. So far as was possible, the RAF intended to fight the war its own way. German tank commanders could summon up Stuka dive-bombers as "flying artillery" when they needed it, but the RAF maintained its prickly independence, and in any case had no aircraft suitable for dive-bombing, nor pilots trained for it.

The British Air Forces in France comprised the "Air Component," which accompanied the BEF, and the "Advanced Air Striking Forces," which consisted of ten bomber squadrons intended to attack Germany if the political decision to do so was ever reached, plus two squadrons of Hurricanes intended as their escort. The Air Component consisted of five squadrons of Westland Lysanders, a hopelessly outdated and feeble type, four squadrons of Bristol Blenheim light bombers and four squadrons of Hurricanes, intended to act as their air cover. These two separate forces were placed under the command of Air Marshal A. S. Barratt in January 1940, who seems to have had little or no communication with the French high command or the French Air Force, and as little as possible with General Lord Gort and his staff. Lieutenant-General Pownall, Gort's chief of general staff, a sharp observer, bewailed the situation in his diary: "It all comes from allowing the Air Force to have too free a hand—and in their theory and practice of air warfare all experience to date shows they have been consistently wrong."

There was a curious ambivalence toward their French ally in the BEF, leaving aside the normal British derision of "Frogs." On the one hand, particularly among the senior commanders, the French

Army was admired for its size, its glorious past, and the intellectual brilliance of its staff officers. On the other hand, those who
came into direct contact with the French Army could hardly fail
to notice the slovenly appearance of the troops, their slapdash
approach to the beloved "spit and polish" of the British regular
army, their apparent lack of enthusiasm for the war, and their
indifference toward sanitation, always a sore point when British
troops took over a portion of the French lines. A British private in
the Royal Engineers, ordered as punishment to clean up a school
in which French soldiers had been billeted, remembered with disgust that it was "absolutely filthy. . . . The French army had been
sleeping in it, and there was about two foot of straw in every room.
And there was excreta all over the place. The French had obviously wiped their backsides with their hands and wiped it down
the wall."

In both the Allied armies, as the winter of 1940 went on with
mind-numbing cold—it was the coldest on record in over a hundred years—the most challenging task was to keep the men's
morale up. This played no part in the German plans, but unin-
tentionally the phoney war worked to their advantage—nothing is

Troops clearing snow in the brutal winter of 1939–1940.

more harmful to the morale and spirit of a large army than seven months without fighting, particularly a conscript army like that of France with millions of men sitting idle in uniform, knowing that their family and loved ones were only a day or two away by train. (Since the German Army was intending to attack, their soldiers were kept busy training for exactly the role they would play, rather than manning useless fortifications in the freezing cold.)

Curiously, although the British Army of the time was regarded as hopelessly "class-ridden," there seems to have been a closer relationship between officers and other ranks than in the republican French Army, and certainly more regard for the men's welfare. British officers sought to encourage sports, and "each battalion was allocated eight hundredweight of sports equipment which included twenty-four hockey sticks, fifty pairs of football boots, and clothing sufficient to kit out six teams," testifying to the British upper-class belief in sports as a morale and character builder, while major efforts were made to provide entertainment, including variety shows, a few with such major stars as Gracie Fields, and mobile cinema units. NAAFI (Navy, Army, and Air Force Institutes, the rough equivalent of the American PX, known to the troops as "No Ambition and Fuckall Interest") were set up on as ambitious a scale as possible, and ENSA (The Entertainments National Service Association, known to the troops as "Every Night Something Awful")* took on the task of providing popular entertainment. British troops were in most ways better looked after and better paid than the French, which gave rise to a certain amount of bad feeling toward the "Tommies."

Boredom, discomfort, and inaction led, among other things, to a rapidly rising VD rate—every French town and larger village in those days had one or more brothels, and none was disguised, illegal, or hard to find, an "eye opener" for British troops coming from a much more straitlaced society to one in which the attitude

---

* I am indebted to my friend Peter Metcalfe, formerly of the Intelligence Corps, for both of the army elaborations on NAAFI and ENSA.

Above: Major-General Bernard Montgomery on the left, Lieutenant-General Alan Brooke, center, 1940.
Right: General Alan Brooke.

toward sex was famously open and unjudgmental. In fact, Major-General B. L. Montgomery (the future field marshal), commander of the Third Division of II Corps, commanded by Lieutenant-General Alan Francis Brooke (another future field marshal) got himself into hot water by writing an outspoken and frankly worded order on the matter to his division, insisting "that the subject of sex and disease was not [to be] buried under a blanket of sanctimoniousness" in the division, and ordering that condoms be on sale in the NAAFI canteen and the men instructed on how to use them, and also taught the French word for them so they could buy condoms in shops and insist on them in brothels.

This brought down on his head the indignation of the senior Church of England and Roman Catholic chaplains of the BEF, who demanded that Lord Gort sack him, but after a huge controversy—the first of many for Montgomery—all he got was a strong talking down to (or "bollocking," as it is known in the British Army) from his corps commander Lieutenant-General Brooke, who impressed upon him "the magnitude of his blunder" and attempted to discourage him "from a mad desire to talk or write nonsense." Of course Montgomery was right, and in the absence of his sensible reforms the VD rate in the BEF and among the RAF in France continued to soar.

The word "army" inevitably suggests sameness and uniformity, but the BEF was nothing like that. Its regular battalions were very different from its Territorial battalions, which mostly consisted of young men who had "joined up" for part-time soldiering, and had received only the most rudimentary military training. At one extreme were the battalions of the Foot Guards, perhaps the most polished, best trained, and physically perfect professional soldiers in the world, at the other extreme units of Pioneers, brought over to perform the rough labor of digging trenches and ditches. In the words of one soldier, the Pioneers were "a tough crowd. . . . A lot of them had been in prison, and released on the understanding that they went to France. They had a sergeant major with them, a huge man . . . and he used to carry a stick with a big ball on the end, and he used to whack them with it when they got out of hand." Not only were the Pioneers not trained soldiers; most were not even equipped with a rifle.

In Joshua Levine's *Forgotten Voices of Dunkirk*, a fascinating collection of the memories of men who served in the BEF, there comes across a kind of touching innocence, as well as the unmistakable insularity of a generation far removed from today, when television, the Internet, and cheap, easy travel have familiarized most people in Britain with the rest of Europe, at least to some degree. Travel was still then largely for the wealthy and privileged, France and Belgium were deeply "foreign," and the only communication with home was in clumsily censored letters.

The voices of the Territorials are a far cry from those of Kipling's Tommies—they are mostly young, middle-class, shy and homesick, tempted by the sight of sex for sale, but too nervous or embarrassed to give it a go, disparaging of French cooking, more apt to drink beer than to try wine or spirits, and only too conscious of the fact that most of their officers don't know anything more about war than they do.

In most places BEF soldiers were billeted in various degrees of discomfort on local civilians in everything from barns and farmhouses to abandoned schools, and they soon learned all "the old

Dartboards for the troops, 1939.

soldier's" tricks of improving their situation: one photograph of British soldiers billeted in a barn shows that they have all made up neat paillasses of straw for bedding, put up makeshift shelving for their kit and a hook for their clothing, and fixed a dartboard to a pile of hay bales at the right height. A few men did not get along well with the French, but most worked out a friendly relationship of sorts, some even acquired a French girlfriend and were as good as adopted by her family. It was very much as it had been in 1914–1918, but on a smaller scale, and of course so far without the fighting.

8

Hitler "Missed the Bus"

German troops cross a fjord, Norway, 1940.

THE QUESTION OF when the fighting would begin, and how, remained unanswered. Frequent false alarms of a German attack on Belgium or Holland kept the Allies on their toes, but never amounted to anything. As winter gave way to spring, attention moved instead from the Low Countries to Scandinavia, of all unlikely places.

The background to this was the Soviet attack on Finland that began in November of 1939, intended by Stalin to secure a broad swath of territory to the north of Leningrad and reduce Finland, which had declared its independence from Russia in 1918, to a vassal state. The war was a costly and humiliating disaster for the

Soviet Union. Although outnumbered three to one by the Russians, and even more so in terms of arms—the Finnish Army had twenty-four tanks while the Red Army deployed several thousand—the Finns resisted heroically and effectively, helped by the arctic winter conditions, the paucity of roads, and the inefficiency of the Red Army, the senior officers of which had been decimated in Stalin's great purge of their ranks in 1937.

The temptation to come to Finland's aid was felt strongly in London and Paris, but apart from small quantities of supplies and arms it was difficult to find any way to *reach* Finland. Continuing and heroic resistance there, however, focused attention on Scandinavia, particularly that of the first lord of the Admiralty.

Winston Churchill had been drawing the War Cabinet's attention for some time to the fact that nearly half of Germany's iron ore came from the mines at Luleå, in Sweden, much of it transported by railway to the Norwegian port of Narvik and thence by sea to Germany down the coast of Norway behind the long chain of islands and fjords known as the Leads, so that the freighters were always in neutral Norwegian territorial waters. Churchill described this as a "sheltered" or "covered" way, within the Norwegian three-mile limit. This, surely, was a naval matter, he argued. Seizing Narvik would enable the Allies to support the Finns against the Russians, and at the same time cut off shipments of iron ore to Germany.

The fact that Norway and Sweden were both neutral countries and terrified of German reprisal did not slow down speculation on this project in London and Paris. Surprisingly, the French were intrigued enough to offer troops for the operation—the Chasseurs Alpins (French mountain troops), the Foreign Legion, Polish forces—for the French government was moved by two contradictory impulses, the first being the fear that if it continued to do nothing it would be thrown out of office, and the second that if the war was going to be fought at all, the farther away the fighting was from France, the better—if it was a naval or amphibious war in which the British predominated, better still.

Serious preparations were made in strictest (but unavailing) secrecy for winter warfare in Finland. Hurricanes were experimentally fitted with skis so that they could operate from snowy airfields, officers who could claim skiing experience from glamorous winter holidays in Davos or St. Moritz were withdrawn from their regiments and sent to northern Scotland to train troops in "winter warfare," all of it captured brilliantly by Evelyn Waugh in *Put Out More Flags* when Peter Pastmaster turns up at the bar in "Bratt's" (Waugh's pseudonym for White's) in the battledress of a different regiment than his own:

> "Hullo. Why on earth are you dressed like that?"
> Peter smirked as only a soldier can when he knows a secret. "Oh, no particular reason." . . .
> "You're the sixth chap I've seen in disguise this morning."
> "That's the idea—security, you know." . . .
> They went to the bar.
> "Good morning, my lord," said MacDougal, the barman. "I see you're off to Finland too. Quite a number of our gentlemen are going to-night."

In the end nobody did go to Finland. David forced Goliath to a costly stalemate (the Finns lost 25,000 men, the Soviet Union nearly 150,000), Finland accepted terms less generous than it might have had from Stalin without fighting, but received admiration from neutrals and from both belligerent sides for exposing the greed, incompetence, and cynicism of the Soviet Union.

In the meantime, the idea of seizing the remote and unprepossessing port of Narvik remained in Churchill's mind, another bee in that capacious bonnet, and he sent the prime minister a series of long papers describing the benefits that would follow from it. One might have thought that memory of the failure of Churchill's cherished plan to breach the Dardanelles with warships in 1915 and drive Turkey out of the war would have set off alarm bells in the minds of other members of the War Cabinet, but apparently it did not. Once again a combined naval and military expedition with enormous risks was being proposed, the previous one having cost Churchill his career for a time, as well as the lives of nearly a quarter of a million men for no gain, but possibly Churchill's energy and powers of persuasion were too strong to resist. More likely it was simply that he was the only member of the War Cabinet who wanted a fight, a hawk in the dovecote.

Churchill had already begun pressing his case as early as September 19, 1939, only sixteen days after the beginning of the war, but the War Cabinet's initial interest soon gave way to caution at the prospect of infringing the neutrality of two countries. Churchill reluctantly reduced his plan to "mining the Leads" to prevent ore traffic to Germany, but this too dragged on, in the absence of Norwegian permission to allow it.

Unfortunately, Churchill was not the only person whose eye was set on Norway. As early as October 3, 1939, the Führer had taken the first steps toward what would become code-named *Unternehmen Weserübung*, the invasion of Denmark and Norway. By December

German Ju 52 transport aircraft over Copenhagen, 1940.

General von Falkenhorst (left), commander of the invasion
of Norway.

14 he had made up his mind, and by February 20, 1940, he had
appointed a commander, General von Falkenhorst, who had fought
in Finland briefly in 1918 and therefore had some experience of the
Scandinavian terrain. This was in sharp contrast to Britain, where
War Cabinet discussion of what was tentatively called Operation Wilfred dragged on for months and ended with a mishmash of a plan,
in which the main part of the operation was naval, in addition to
which "a British brigade and a French contingent" might be landed
by the navy to seize Narvik, then advance to the Swedish frontier.

The opinion of professional soldiers was tartly expressed by
Lieutenant-General Pownall in his diary: "I understand that it
is the plan of those master strategists Winston and Ironside. . . .
Of all the harebrained projects I have heard this is the most
foolish—its inception smacks too alarmingly of Gallipoli.* . . .

* The focal point of the disastrous Allied attack to force the Dardanelles and
take Constantinople in 1915, of which Churchill was the most outspoken
supporter.

Sideshows again—Winston Churchill is no longer held in check by a C.I.G.S. of the type of Robertson [Field Marshal Sir William Robertson, CIGS from 1916 to 1918] but encouraged in his broad sweeping ideas by an Ironside whose basic military knowledge is nil and has never studied strategy in its broad sense. . . ." Pownall was concerned that any operation in Scandinavia would inevitably draw troop strength away from the BEF in France at just the moment when the Germans could be expected to attack.

A change in the premiership in France—the cautious M. Daladier was replaced by the slightly less cautious M. Paul Reynaud, the latter having been against the Munich settlement, the former a shame-faced but unrepentant participant in the dismemberment of Czechoslovakia—led the Supreme War Council to agree to launch Operation Wilfred on April 9, although the military side of the plan still called for that traditional harbinger of disaster, the landing of what General Montgomery would refer to disparagingly later in the war as "penny packets" of troops at widely separated places on the Norwegian coast, without a commander in chief or a plan for a single decisive blow. As has so often been the case in

Paul Reynaud.

English history, the fact that the Royal Navy was involved on a large scale led members of the War Cabinet to overlook the obvious risks on the ground—the age-old British trust in anything that depends on the navy.

Confidence in the operation was high, so much so that the prime minister, jauntily assured his audience in a speech to the Central Council of the National Union of Conservatives and Unionist Associations on April 5, "one thing is certain, [Hitler] missed the bus."

Winston Churchill, many years later, would write with commendable restraint, "This proved an ill-judged utterance," and truer words were never written. At about the same time as Chamberlain was speaking, the German Navy was landing troops at Bergen, Trondheim, and Narvik in neutral Norway.* Neutral Denmark as well was invaded and the king of Denmark surrounded in his own palace. The Germans seized the major ports and cities while the British struggled to hold the rugged, snow swept, underpopulated terrain of northern Norway. "Within forty-eight hours all the main ports of Norway were in the German grip," Churchill wrote. "Surprise, ruthlessness and precision were the characteristics of the onslaught upon innocent and naked Norway."

The Allied response was muddled. Clearly, as Churchill admitted, Britain and France had been "forestalled, surprised . . . and outwitted," but at sea the Royal Navy prevailed, although Hitler

Hitler with Vidkun Quisling.

---

* Neutrality is not a sacred cause or a permanent state, except perhaps to the Swiss; it merely describes a country that by diplomatic skill or fortunate geography, or both, is able to stay out of the war and hopes to do business with both sides. In World War Two this included Switzerland, Sweden, Spain, Portugal, and, until December 7, 1941, the United States.

did not have the same interest in his navy that he had in his army, so naval matters were never his first concern. A photograph of Hitler in a naval cutter inspecting the fleet before the war shows the Führer with wind-tousled hair and the uneasy expression of a land-lubber fighting seasickness. When the navy suggested naming its new 50,000-ton super-battleship after him, Hitler declined on the grounds that it would damage German morale if a ship named after him were sunk, so it was named *Bismarck* instead. (Hitler's premonition was sound: the *Bismarck* was sunk on May 27, 1941, after a long chase during which she sank the pride of the British fleet, the battlecruiser HMS *Hood.*)

The Norwegian campaign cost the German Navy three cruisers and ten destroyers, and together with those warships that had been heavily damaged Hitler's navy would be in no position to carry out an invasion of England in the summer of 1940. On the land, however, the German Army gained yet another quick victory. By the first week of June all of Norway was in German hands, the king and his family were on the way to Britain in a British cruiser, and a pro-German government had been set up under Major Vidkun Quisling, a Fascist politician whose name would be used to describe every collaborationist leader ever since.

9

"In the Name of God, Go"

David Lloyd George and Leo Amery.

ALREADY BY MID-APRIL of 1940 it was apparent to many people—certainly to members of the House of Commons— that the battle for Norway had gone badly wrong. British naval successes, though considerable, could not disguise the fact that

Hitler had taken the Allies, by surprise with a well-planned, swift, and ruthless attack, and that there appeared to be no Allied strategy in place for victory. Initial euphoria that Britain was at last in action gave way to "a general feeling of apprehension," and to questions in the House even from loyal Conservatives. It was clear, to those in the know at least, that a major political crisis could only be prevented by news of a victory in Norway. It was not yet a political earthquake, merely a tremor, but it set off alarms and rumors.

Even Churchill, speaking to the House on the fighting in Norway, failed to strike the right note. Harold Nicolson, a friend and admirer, notes in his diary, "To the House. It is packed. Winston comes in. . . . When he rises to speak it is obvious that he is very tired. He starts off by giving an imitation of himself making a speech. . . . I have seldom seen him to less advantage." Others noted that Prime Minister Chamberlain seemed to betray a certain satisfaction at Churchill's poor performance. There was speculation that Churchill was "too old" for the post of first lord of the Admiralty (he was sixty-six at the time, five years younger than Chamberlain), and even talk that former Prime Minister David Lloyd George, Chamberlain's nemesis, might be a better choice for prime minister than either of them, although he was seventy-seven,* and would very likely not have been acceptable to the king.

Even at his least effective, Churchill's speeches to the House contrasted sharply with the short and funereal statements of the prime minister. Brendan Bracken referred to Chamberlain as "the Coroner," and Harold Nicolson vividly drew the contrast between the prime minister and the first lord of the Admiralty seated side by side together on the front bench, one "dressed [as if] in deep mourning," the other "looking like the Chinese god of plenty."

Never forgetting that Churchill was a potential rival, or perhaps under the illusion that the best way to control him was to keep him in sight, Chamberlain took him to a meeting of the Supreme War Council in Paris presided over by Paul Reynaud, the new French

---

* To put this in perspective, President Roosevelt was only fifty-eight in 1940, Hitler fifty-one.

premier, with results that disappointed them both. The French did not disguise their reluctance to launch "Royal Marine," Churchill's plan to place mines in the Rhine and float them downstream to disrupt German river traffic; moreover, still concerned about Paris, they continued to oppose bombing the Ruhr, or anywhere else for that matter. Even at this late date Belgium continued to follow a policy not unlike that of the ostrich that sticks its head in the sand when confronted by danger, so a preemptive move forward into Belgium was still ruled out. Though rather late in the day, the French proposed that neither of the Allies should seek peace terms without the consent of the other, something that one would have thought had been implicit from the beginning.

Neither Chamberlain nor Churchill appears to have been aware of something that *le tout Paris* had known for ages—the feud between Edouard Daladier, the former prime minister and now defense minister, and Paul Reynaud was not just a question of policy but also *une histoire de femme.* Daladier's mistress the Marquise de Crussol,* a daughter of the wealthy owner of France's most important sardine cannery, was the rival and mortal enemy of Reynaud's mistress the Comtesse de Portes, daughter of a family of shipowners, both of them *bourgeoises* who had married into the nobility, and both forceful personalities whom it was unwise to cross. The two ladies fought out their rivalry not only in terms of fashion and haute couture but also in politics. Churchill came quickly to think of Reynaud as a kindred spirit, certainly preferable to Daladier, but had no idea that Hélène de Portes was bitterly Anglophobic and opposed to the war, if indeed he even knew of her existence. It was due to the influence of Mme de Portes that Reynaud had just reshuffled his cabinet to get rid of the more determined members in favor of those who saw no gain in France's fighting England's

---

* Major-General Sir Edward Spears relates that in society those who did not like Mme de Crussole described her as "la sardine qui s'est crue sole" (the sardine who thinks she's a sole), but the translation of course misses the pun on her name.

war. These were deeper waters than Chamberlain, Halifax, and Churchill knew—none of them was what one might describe as "a lady's man," and it would surely have surprised them to know that France's defense minister and its premier were each receiving political advice from their respective mistress, or revealing military secrets as pillow talk.

In any case, nothing the French could do at that point would save Norway. By the first week of May it was evident that the south of Norway was lost, and that it would be difficult, if not impossible, to hold on to the northern part in view of German control of the air. What little was known to the member of the House of Commons was a story of muddle, individual heroism, poor planning, and lack of even the most basic military equipment. Although the prime minister had asked Churchill, as the senior service minister, to preside over the "Military Coordination Committee," nothing could disguise the confusion and lack of leadership at the top. Churchill himself aptly complained about "the formlessness of our system," which resulted in there being "six Chiefs [and Deputy Chiefs] of the Staff, three Ministers, and General Ismay, who all have a voice in Norwegian operations," with nobody able to impose his will upon these layers of authority except the prime minister himself, who neither wished nor was able to. Churchill, hard pressed by the demands of the navy, found himself obliged to ask the prime minister to take over "the day-to-day management of the Military Coordination Committee," and it was not until May 1 that Churchill was finally given control over the chiefs of staff and in effect, if not in title, made minister of defence.

Little blame for what had gone wrong in Norway was aimed at Churchill, if only because the navy had performed brilliantly, and because the person who had tried the hardest to produce a more rational system was Churchill. Blame attached itself instead, however reluctantly among many members, to Chamberlain himself and to those closest to him, particularly the arch appeasers Sir

Sir Horace Wilson and Chamberlain.

Samuel Hoare, the lord privy seal, Sir John Simon, the chancellor of the exchequer, and Chamberlain's adviser and backstairs strategist Sir Horace Wilson,* the most unrepentant appeaser of them all. Chamberlain, hitherto a supremely confident politician, seems to have had no forewarning of what was in store for him—after all, he had always managed to master the House of Commons, and he had a majority of over two hundred, making his position as prime minister virtually unassailable.

---

* Sir Horace Wilson was the head of the Home Civil Service, normally an important but innocuous bureaucratic post, which did not involve giving advice on foreign policy or military affairs.

*   *   *

Nobody expected that the rumblings of discontent would turn into a roar on May 7. The opposition had asked for a debate on the Norwegian situation, but as soon as the prime minister rose to speak there were catcalls and shouts of "Missed the bus!" and it was clear that the mood of the House was angry, hostile, and confused over events in Norway. In the face of it, Chamberlain made a "feeble" speech, followed by several more from both sides of the aisle that failed to draw blood, but the session might have ended without much damage to Chamberlain had it not been for the intervention of Admiral of the Fleet Sir Roger Keyes, Conservative member for Portsmouth North since 1934, a friend of Winston Churchill's, and a controversial naval hero of the First World War. Keyes commanded instant attention by appearing in his uniform as an admiral of the fleet, with six rows of medal ribbons glittering on his chest, in a rage about what he took as an insult

Admiral Roger Keyes, center.

to the Royal Navy by a Labour member, J. C. Wedgewood, something of a war hero himself. However, Keyes had a more important and personal ax to grind—he had proposed to lead a fleet of
superannuated battleships into the Trondheim Fjord to recapture
the city and prevent the Germans from taking central Norway,
but the chiefs of staff had declined to accept his offer, a decision
against which Keyes had protested with a series of long, angry
letters of protest, all of which Churchill had tactfully deflected
with what was for him unusual patience. Churchill's own caution about Keyes's scheme was understandable, since on paper it
looked very much like the Dardanelles, in which Keyes had played
a vigorous part. Keyes went on to give the House his side of that
story and from there to make a long, slashing, well-informed, and
"absolutely devastating" attack on the government.

Although not a great speaker, Keyes rose to the occasion—he
had sought the help of Harold Macmillan, a future Conservative prime minister, in preparing his speech and his blunt, forceful delivery and naval expertise caught the mood of the House.
There was a "great gasp of astonishment" at his frank assessment
of the muddle at the top (exonerating Churchill), ending with
a damning statement, "One hundred and forty years ago, Nelson said, 'I am of the opinion that the boldest measures are the
safest,' and that still holds good today." Keyes sat down to "thunderous applause" from both sides of the House. (It is almost
impossible to go wrong by quoting Admiral Nelson in Parliament
in time of war.)

He was followed by Leo Amery, one of only four Conservative
members who had remained seated in protest when Chamberlain
announced that he was flying to Munich to meet with Hitler at the
height of the Czech crisis in 1938,* and who despite a diminutive
stature had a formidable mind. Half Hungarian-Jewish, he spoke
seven languages fluently, and had served as first lord of the Admiralty and as colonial secretary—even to die-hard supporters of the
prime minister he commanded respect. Amery too was normally

---

* The others were Winston Churchill, Harold Nicolson, and Anthony Eden.

The king and queen; on the right, Herbert Morrison.

by no means a great orator, but on this occasion "his implacable sentences gave the impression of volleys fired into sandbags," in the words of Edward Spears, speaking "as if he were hurling stones as large as himself" to a "still, strained House," and rising to one of the most damning perorations in the history of British politics:

> Somehow or other we must get into this Government men who can match our enemies in fighting spirit, in daring, in resolution and in thirst for victory. . . . We are fighting today for our life, for our liberty, for our all; we cannot go on being led as we are. I have quoted certain words of Oliver Cromwell. I will quote certain other words. I do it with great reluctance, because I am speaking of those who are old friends and associates of mine, but they are words which, I think, are applicable to the present situation. This is what Cromwell said to the Long Parliament when he thought it was no longer fit to conduct the affairs of the nation. "You have sat

too long here for any good you have been doing. Depart, I say, and let us have done with you. In the name of God, go."

Even as David Margesson, the chief whip, sought to rally the party faithful to support the prime minister, the impact of these words seemed to wound Chamberlain physically, as if the words had indeed been stones hurled at him. Chamberlain's greatest failing was his vanity—vanity that had been ratified by a long record of success and a brief, though intense, period of adulation and increased by his insatiable appetite for flattery—but it must by now have been clear to him that he could no longer dominate the House, or even his own party, that he had been fatally damaged, not by the opposition—after all, as Winston Churchill once said, "The business of His Majesty's Opposition is to oppose"—but by members of his own party. By the end of the first day of the debate, as members drifted off to dinner, it was apparent to almost everyone that the government was doomed

Captain David Margesson.

without a major reconstruction. A mere "reshuffle" of ministers would not save it, and Chamberlain seems to have reached that conclusion himself.

The debate the next day, on May 8, got off to a rocky start for the government, even the normally supportive newspapers like the *Times* were critical of Chamberlain's speech, while the tabloids and left-wing newspapers were staunchly critical. For a man who had always had a good press, it was a rude awakening. Worse was to follow.

Herbert Morrison, speaking for Labour, in Clement Attlee's absence owing to illness, rose to make it brutally clear that the debate must be followed by a vote of censure. "I cannot forget," Morrison said, speaking of the prime minister, the chancellor of the exchequer, and the secretary of state for air, "that in relation to the conduct of British foreign policy between 1931 and 1939, they were consistently and persistently wrong. . . . I have the genuine apprehension that if these men remain in office, we run a grave risk of losing this war." This was an attack aimed directly at Chamberlain, and more important a warning that Labour might not serve under him if he should call for a coalition or "national" government, as some were beginning to suggest.

Chamberlain now made the mistake that would cost him his office. Rather than standing on his dignity, he let his feelings show. Smarting from this personal attack, he rose to welcome a division for a vote of confidence, and then added, "I do not seek to evade criticism, but I say this to my friends in the House—and I *have* friends in the House—no Government can prosecute a war efficiently unless it has public and Parliamentary support. . . . I call on my friends to support me tonight."

Harold Nicolson noted that Chamberlain spoke the word "friends" with "a leer of triumph," but in fact he could hardly have made a worse mistake than by emphasizing his anger about the personal attack on him in the middle of a debate about the conduct of the war, a fatal error of wounded vanity that shocked even the prime minister's own supporters. Chamberlain might as well have put his own head on the block to be chopped off.

Lloyd George had been Chamberlain's bitterest enemy since they had clashed during World War One, and when he rose to speak the House fell silent, as if they were about to watch an execution. With his lion-like mane of white hair and his piercing eyes, "the Welsh Wizard" Lloyd George had dominated British politics for nearly five decades. He was old now, and somewhat discredited by the greed and unscrupulous political dexterity with which he had clung to power after the First World War, by such scandals as the sale of titles for contributions, and by his reputation for relentless womanizing, but he had served as one of the most formidable war leaders in British history, as well as the innovator of much of the modern British welfare state—perhaps no one man was ever responsible for so much social legislation and so many radical changes in British life, or made such daring and far-reaching decisions in war and at the peace table after it. Perhaps no man before or since has ever had such absolute command of Parliament—even so great a speaker as Churchill was in awe of Lloyd George's speeches.

The old man had been waiting for many years to take his revenge on Chamberlain, but with the skill of a master politician and spellbinding orator he took his time about it, carefully mentioning every failure of the government with the precision of a man who had been a great wartime prime minister himself, then, ignoring interruptions, he gave the coup de grâce in his soft Welsh voice* as he made the case for Chamberlain to resign:

> I was not here when the Right Honorable Gentleman made the observation, but he definitely appealed on a question which is a great national, Imperial and world issue. He said, "I have got my friends." It is not a question of who are the Prime Minister's friends. It is a far bigger issue. The Prime Minister must remember that he has met this formidable foe

---

* Lloyd George was the first and last British prime minister for whom English was not his or her first language.

of ours in peace and in war. He has always been worsted. He is not in a position to appeal on the ground of friendship. He has appealed for sacrifice. The nation is prepared for every sacrifice so long as it has leadership, so long as the Government show clearly what they are aiming at and so long as the nation is confident that those who are leading it are doing their best. I say solemnly that the Prime Minister should give an example of sacrifice, because there is nothing which can contribute more to victory in this war than that he should sacrifice the seals of office.

Churchill concluded the debate, after attacks on Chamberlain from both sides of the House, with a long and ferocious defense of Chamberlain. Churchill was honor bound as a member of the government to do so, but his mastery of the House, despite constant catcalls and interruptions, made it clear how much better he was suited to the prime ministership than was Chamberlain. After a tense and angry division—Spears remembers the expression of "implacable resentment" on the face of Government Chief Whip David Margesson as he noted which Conservative members were voting against the government or abstaining—the government won by eighty-one votes, to shouts of "Resign! Resign!" and "Go! Go!"

To win by only eighty-one votes with a majority of over two hundred was tantamount to defeat—certainly it was a stinging indictment of the government's conduct of the war. Chips Channon, a faithful supporter of the prime minister, caught sight of Mrs. Chamberlain in the speaker's gallery: "She was in black—black hat—black coat—black gloves—with only a bunch of violets in her coat. She looked infinitely sad as she peered down into the arena where the lions were out for her husband's blood." Spears noted Chamberlain's expression as he rose to his feet, of "cold aloofness, even disdain." Chamberlain "turned, picking his way over the protruding feet of his colleagues, as he always had to do from the Treasury Box to the Speaker's Chair, but before he got there, whilst still in view of the House, he seemed to grow even slighter than usual, and his erect figure bent. He walked out of the House and through the lobby with heavy feet, a truly sad and pathetic figure . . . solitary, following in the wake of all his dead hopes and fruitless efforts." There were no crowds to cheer him now. As Chips Channon wrote, he was now "only a solitary little man who had done his best for England."

Gracie Fields's famous 1932 music hall song "He's Dead But He Won't Lie Down" best describes Chamberlain's position on the night of May 8. "Solitary" he might be, but he still cherished hope, however faint, that he could form a "national" government, that is, a coalition of the major parties. To the extent that he did, such hope evaporated almost completely the next day. Brendan Bracken, Churchill's ubiquitous political "fixer," had already sounded out Attlee about whether Labour would serve in a government led by Chamberlain, and came away with the impression that Labour would not, but might agree to serve in a coalition government led by Lord Halifax or, with rather less enthusiasm, by Churchill.

Within the Conservative Party sentiment for Halifax as Chamberlain's replacement was growing. Halifax was trusted, reliable, respected, and respectable, a friend of the king and queen,* both of whom hoped that he would replace Chamberlain if a change proved to be necessary. Indeed the royal couple liked Halifax so much that they had given him his own key to the Buckingham Palace gardens, so he could walk through them on his way to the Foreign Office every morning. Churchill was, as the saying goes, "damaged goods"—the queen had not yet forgiven him for his noisy support in favor of the marriage of King Edward VIII and Mrs. Simpson, when Churchill had let his heart, his sympathy for the king, and his instinctive royalism overcome his caution. Churchill, whose greatest fault was a blindness to other people's feelings—he always assumed he had won over anybody he talked to—was happily unaware of any lingering hostility toward him

---

* Future beloved "Queen Mum," mother of Queen Elizabeth II.

on the part of the king and queen. He failed to gauge the king's "natural shyness" and the extent to which, as Channon noted, "an inferiority complex towards his eldest brother made him on the defensive," or the degree to which he "was almost entirely dependent on the Queen whom he worshipped." It would take Churchill some time to win over the royal couple, not to mention his own party. Many in the Conservative Party still decried him as "a half-breed American," "a wild man" who loved war for its own sake and who was responsible for a whole roster of things that ordinary Conservatives disliked, from Mrs. Simpson to Gallipoli.

Small groups of those anti-appeasers who supported Churchill huddled together on the morning of May 9. Duff Cooper, Leo Amery, Edward Spears, and Harold Nicolson all attest to an intense "huggermugger" intended to persuade Chamberlain that he must resign and name Churchill as his successor, while in 10 Downing

Duff Cooper.

Street the prime minister, with the help of David Margesson, who was the most accurate gauge of the state of mind of the Conservative Party, saw a stream of backbenchers and tested out the possibility that throwing Simon and Hoare overboard might be enough to satisfy the less extreme malcontents. In *The Holy Fox*, his masterly biography of Lord Halifax, Andrew Roberts suggests that Chamberlain even went so far as to offer Leo Amery a choice of "either the Chancellorship of the Exchequer or the Foreign Office," although the latter would have meant sacrificing Halifax. Chamberlain remained a shrewd and ruthless politician and might have thought it worthwhile to divide his opponents within the party by enlisting one of his most outspoken critics in an office so high that he could not reject it. Since the source for this is Labour MP Hugh Dalton, who would only have heard it secondhand, it may not be true, but if the offer was actually made, or even suggested, it indicates that Chamberlain was determined not to go down without a fight on the morning of May 9, and still felt he had a few good cards left in his hand. Perhaps like any professional politician he was just trying to keep his options open.

In any event, by midday Margesson's soundings among the party had made it clear to him that Chamberlain must go. Margesson was the ruthless party disciplinarian, the dispenser of patronage, the Tory Party's equivalent of Ko-Ko the Lord High Executioner in *The Mikado*.* He had been a devoted and fierce supporter of Chamberlain, feared and loathed by the appeasers, but his primary loyalty was to the *party*, not to the prime minister, and once it was evident to him that the party was too badly shaken by the two days of debate about Norway to rally behind Chamberlain, Margesson firmly and frankly gave him the bad news.

Chamberlain understood at once—if the chief whip reported that the party and the mood in the constituencies was disturbed by the controversy, then it was time to resign and secure the prime

---

* Following this analogy, it would be amusing—and perhaps instructive—to think of Lord Halifax as the Tory Party's equivalent of Pooh-Bah the Lord High Everything Else.

ministership for Halifax before it was too late. Halifax remained the undisputed choice of the party, of the royal family, and of Chamberlain himself.

Early in the afternoon Chamberlain, Churchill, Halifax, and Margesson met with the two most prominent Labour leaders, Clement Attlee and Arthur Greenwood, in the Cabinet Room at 10 Downing Street, the four Conservatives on one side of the big table, the two Labourites facing them. There was no drama, and no rhetoric, it was all very polite and English, but Attlee and Greenwood made it clear that they did not believe Labour would agree to join a national government under Chamberlain, although the final decision would have to be made at the Labour Party's annual conference at the seaside resort of Bournemouth. They did not express a preference for Churchill or Halifax—that too would have to be discussed in Bournemouth, which was about to take place. They left quietly, and there was a moment of silence as the four Conservatives contemplated what now seemed like an inevitable decision.

There was no animosity between Churchill and Halifax—after the departure of the two Labour leaders they left the prime minister for a time and quietly shared a pot of tea in the garden of 10 Downing Street in the "bright, sunny afternoon," which, if it is true, must be one of the few times that Churchill ever accepted a cup of tea as a refreshment instead of a weak whiskey soda.

At some point in the afternoon—accounts differ about the time—they gathered again in the Cabinet Room, Chamberlain, Halifax, Churchill, and Margesson, and Chamberlain asked whom he should appoint as his successor. Churchill's friends Bracken and Beaverbrook had foreseen this moment, and urged him to remain silent—no easy task for a man who was by nature a great talker, argumentative, emotional, and impulsive. Churchill's own account of the critical moment is dramatic, but not entirely accurate, since he gets the date wrong and omits the presence of Margesson, who was a key player. Chamberlain made it clear that he preferred Halifax as his successor, and Halifax did not apparently think it necessary to mention his hope that the war could still be brought to an end by careful diplomacy—the ultimate triumph of appeasement.

At the same time, Halifax appears to have had doubts that he was the right man, or perhaps more important that he could control and influence Churchill from the House of Lords as "his number two." As Andrew Roberts puts it, Halifax might be "in a more powerful position behind the throne than sitting on it." Certainly Halifax thought it was his duty to restrain and advise Churchill, though he did not say so at the time. Instead, he once again brought up, after a long silence, his doubt that he could lead the country effectively from the House of Lords.

This was not, in fact, as difficult a problem as Churchill makes it out to be. Given the national crisis, a way could have been found to seat Halifax in the House of Commons. The king would later— too late by a day, as it happened—suggest that Halifax's peerage could have been placed "in abeyance" for the duration of the war. However, Halifax's doubt that he could be an effective leader if he wasn't "in charge of the war" or able to lead in the House hung in the air for what seemed to Churchill "a very long pause," one that seemed to him to go on longer "than the two minutes [of silence] which one observes in the commemorations of Armistice Day," during which Churchill got up and stared out the window, his broad back turned to the other three men.

Silence, as Bracken and Beaverbrook had advised, was his best answer. It validated the doubts Halifax had expressed about becoming prime minister himself, and confirmed Churchill's belief that in the circumstances he was the right man—the *only* man—for the job. This has been interpreted as a moment of self-sacrifice and "self-abnegation" on the part of Halifax, and so it may have been: after all, he was an ambitious man, a former viceroy of India, and in no doubt that he could *do* the job, indeed he may even have *wanted* it—but at the critical moment he did not, or perhaps *would* not, say so. Possibly it was out of pride, or a lifelong unwillingness to admit to his own ambition. In Halifax's life, honors had presented themselves to him, and would continue to do so, without his ever appearing to seek them out—the viceroyalty, the Garter, the chancellorship of Oxford University—though in his quiet way he was more Machiavellian in pursuit of what he wanted than he seemed to be. He may indeed even have supposed that Churchill would fail and that he would be the one who would pick up the pieces and bring an end to the war. In any case, Halifax did not speak out, and Churchill took his silence for consent. As he put it, he decided that "the duty would fall upon me—had in fact fallen upon me."

In the face of a bolder and stronger personality, Halifax and Chamberlain had given way, and Margesson, always the supreme political realist, decided to switch sides, confident that he could persuade the Conservative members of the House to accept Churchill, with whatever doubts and reservations they might have, instead of the man they wanted. After all, if Margesson, the man in charge of party discipline, could change sides, who were they to disagree?

Churchill broke the silence by saying that he would have "no communication with either of the Opposition parties [Labour and the much smaller Liberal Party] until [he] had the King's commission to form a Government," having in effect, like Napoleon at his coronation, placed the crown on his own head.* He went back to the Admiralty and let events take their course, or so he says—it seems more likely that he spent the night communicating to his friends and supporters. Certainly, he dined that night with Anthony Eden, whom he told that Chamberlain "would advise King to send for him" the next day, and to whom he offered the post of Secretary of State for War. Eden described Churchill as "quiet and calm." Churchill spoke by telephone to his son, Randolph, and told him, "I think I shall be Prime Minister tomorrow."

At five in the morning of May 10 the news came that Germany had attacked Holland, Belgium, and France, the long-awaited attack on

---

* Although Napoleon brought the pope to Paris in 1804 to crown him emperor of the French in Notre Dame Cathedral, he took the crown from the pope and crowned himself in a dramatic gesture at the last moment, an act of supreme power that was lost on no one.

the west. Luxembourg too had been invaded—the first sign, had anyone been aware of the danger and looking in that direction, of Manstein's plan to send the panzer divisions through the Ardennes toward Sedan, instead of through Belgium toward the Somme River. Churchill was woken in his apartment at the Admiralty and convened the other two service ministers, the secretary of state for war and the secretary of state for air, to meet with him at once. As a sign of things to come, he ate a hearty breakfast as the bad news poured in. "We had had little or no sleep, and the news could not have been worse," Sir Samuel Hoare wrote later. "Yet there he was, smoking his large cigar and eating fried eggs and bacon, as if he had just returned from an early morning ride."

Reports came in of heavy bombings of cities in Holland and the dropping of German parachute troops, then a novelty, in both Holland and Belgium; more important were accounts that the British and French armies had begun their advance into Belgium—Gamelin's famous Plan D was taking place as intended. The French were so overwhelmed by the news of the German attack that they at last agreed to let Churchill's scheme for mining the Rhine proceed.

In 10 Downing Street the news brought about an unwelcome change of heart in Neville Chamberlain, who now thought it was his duty to remain prime minister until "the French battle" was finished. Sir Kingsley Wood, hitherto a faithful supporter, talked Chamberlain out of this calamitous illusion by ten in the morning.

Throughout the day in matters great and small one can sense, in every account, the presence of Winston Churchill taking over the reins of government, although he was not yet prime minister. He brought his scientific adviser Frederick Lindemann, the Prof, with him to an early-morning War Cabinet to demonstrate a new homing (or proximity) fuse for antiaircraft shells, provoking General Ironside to ask, "Do you think this is the time for showing off toys?" He suggested that the Foreign Office offer sanctuary in Britain to the eighty-one-year-old Kaiser Wilhelm II, who had been living in exile in Holland since 1918.* He asked the War Cabinet to send Admiral of the Fleet Sir Roger Keyes to Brussels "to offer his counsel and support to the King of the Belgians, with whom he was on terms of close personal friendship," thus establishing what we would now call a separate "back channel" to the Belgian king. He ordered the Royal Navy to remove the Dutch gold reserves before they fell into German hands. Before the day was out the Dutch ministers, "haggard and worn," had flown to London to say that the Germans had attacked them without any warning or pretext, that cities had been bombed and large numbers of civilians killed, and that Holland had already opened the dikes to flood large stretches of land and slow down the German advance.

By the late afternoon the word that Churchill was to become the prime minister had begun to spread, though not yet to the newspapers. John Colville, the handsome and engaging young assistant private secretary to the prime minister, and therefore "in the know," noted in his diary the reaction of most Conservatives to the news:

> At about 4:45 Attlee rang up to say that they would agree to join a Government provided Neville Chamberlain was not PM. . . . Provided the PM and Halifax remain in the War Cabinet there will at least be some restraint on our new War Lord. He may, of course, be the man of drive and energy the country believes him to be . . . but it is a terrible risk, it involves the danger of rash and spectacular exploits. . . . Nothing can stop him having his way—because of his powers of blackmail—unless the King makes full use of his prerogative and sends for another man; unfortunately there is only

---

* This was done, but after two days in which to think it over, the Kaiser politely declined the offer and remained in Holland, provided with an honor guard of German troops until his death in June 1941.

one other, the unpersuadable Halifax. Everybody here is in despair at the prospect.

To be fair, Colville would soon change his mind, and become devoted to Churchill, but on May 10 his was the prevailing opinion. Mrs. Churchill was out of London attending her brother-in-law's funeral, but Churchill called her and asked her to return as soon as possible. Chamberlain finally sought an audience with the king, who saw him "after tea." Chamberlain told him that he wished to resign, and the king, deeply perturbed, told him "how grossly unfairly" he thought Chamberlain had been treated and added that he "was terribly sorry all this controversy had happened." The king reluctantly accepted Chamberlain's resignation, suggested that Halifax was "the obvious man" to replace him, and was taken aback to learn that Halifax had ruled himself out. "Then I knew," the king wrote, "that there was only one person whom I could send for to form a Government who had the confidence of the country, & that was Winston."

Churchill with his bodyguard, Inspector W. H. Thompson of Scotland Yard.

A messenger summoned Churchill to Buckingham Palace at six o'clock. Mrs. Churchill had arrived back by then and accompanied her husband to the palace, where Churchill was taken directly to see the king. The king asked him to sit, and said, "I suppose you don't know why I have sent for you?" Churchill replied with a wry grin, "Sir, I simply could not imagine why," and the king promptly asked him to form a government. Churchill said he would do so, then drove back to the Admiralty.

It was only a two-minute drive from the palace to the Admiralty, and when Churchill got out of his car he turned to his bodyguard, Inspector W. H. Thompson,* and said, "You know why I have been to Buckingham Palace, Thompson?" Thompson said he did and congratulated him on his "enormous task." Churchill paused, then said, "God alone knows how great it is. All I hope is that it is not too late. I am very much afraid it is. We can only do our best."

"Tears came into his eyes," Thompson related. "As he turned away he muttered something to himself. Then he set his jaw, and with a look of determination, mastering all emotion, he began to climb the stairs."

---

* Thompson had been Churchill's bodyguard since 1921, when he was assigned by Scotland Yard because of threats to Churchill's life from the IRA.

PART TWO

The Battle of France

"The Thin Red Line"—4th Battalion, Border Regiment holding the line.

10

"The Top of the Greasy Pole"

I T HAD TAKEN Churchill forty-one years in politics to "climb to the top of the greasy pole," in Disraeli's famous words. The office of prime minister had eluded his father, Lord Randolph Churchill, and until May 9, 1940, seemed likely to elude the son. Nobody ever came to that high office with a heavier baggage of lost causes, political misjudgments, and missed opportunities, but his accession to power was notably free from political vindictiveness. The only person to suffer was Sir Horace Wilson, Chamberlain's high priest of appeasement, perhaps the most influential éminence grise in British political life since Cardinal Wolseley. Sir Horace arrived in his office next to that of the prime minister at 10 Downing Street on the morning of May 11 to find Lord Beaverbrook and Brendan Bracken waiting for him grimly as he hung up his umbrella and hat. He quietly packed the few personal belongings from his desk into his briefcase and left to return to the humdrum job of overseeing the civil service and promoting the purchase of savings certificates. His office was taken over immediately by Bracken in his new role as the prime minister's parliamentary private secretary.

ALL BEHIND YOU, WINSTON

Churchill was that rarest of politicians—he never forgot a friend or a supporter. Anthony Eden became secretary of state for war, Duff Cooper, who had resigned his place in the cabinet in protest over Munich, became minister of information, Harold Nicolson became parliamentary secretary to the Ministry of Information (in effect, Cooper's number two). Brendan Bracken and Lord Beaverbrook were made privy councilors over the strong objection of the king. Churchill's generosity of spirit even impelled him to let Mr. and Mrs. Chamberlain continue living in 10 Downing Street until they had time to move out while the Churchills continued to live in the more cramped but gilded splendor of the first lord's flat in the Admiralty. He retained Chamberlain in the War Cabinet as lord president of the council (an ancient, but by now honorific office) and more important as leader of the Conservative Party, and Lord Halifax as foreign secretary.

He did not forget my uncle Alex, either. Alex was one of that small group of wealthy loyalists who had helped keep the Churchill ship afloat during the years when he was out of office (these included the South African financier Sir Henry Strakosch and Lord Beaverbrook) and was one of the few strong critics of Nazi Germany and the policy of appeasement. Alex cannot have hoped to reap any benefit from Churchill in 1934 when he hired him to serve as an adviser on historical films at £4,000 a year, no small sum at the time.* Churchill was then in the political wilderness, with few prospects of escaping from it, and saddled with a life style that soared well beyond his income. No doubt Alex admired his historical knowledge, but that alone would not explain his commissioning Churchill to write a screen treatment for a life of King George V for the then astronomical sum of £10,000, or his purchase of the screen rights of several of Churchill's books for inflated sums.

In any event the two men acquired a respect for each other that

---

* That was the equivalent then of $20,000 a year, with the purchasing power of at least $300,000 today, allowing for inflation.

went beyond a much needed source of income for Churchill. When Alex acquired the film rights to T. E. Lawrence's *Revolt in the Desert* (Lawrence described Alex as "unexpectedly sensitive," and surprisingly sympathetic to Lawrence's desire that no film be made about him during his lifetime), Churchill was diligent in making suggestions about the screenplay, and even wrote dialogue for it that found its way into the script of David Lean's *Lawrence of Arabia* twenty-five years later, as well as for *That Hamilton Woman* in 1941, in which several of the patriotic passages in the screenplay have the unmistakable ring of Churchill's prose. Alex also provided those in the shadowy world of the British intelligence services who shared Churchill's view of Nazi Germany with contacts throughout Europe, and in the United States—he would even hire two of Churchill's daughters, Diana and Sara, to work for London Films and would probably have hired Churchill's rambunctious son too had Randolph been employable. Through whatever chemistry, the two men liked each other. Alex never forgot that Churchill's was the first, the strongest, and the most consistent voice against Hitler; Churchill never forgot Alex's generous (and supremely tactful) support.

They shared a tolerant view of the world and a lack of prejudice—Churchill himself, after all, was half American, Strakosch was born an Austrian Jew, Beaverbrook was a Canadian, Bracken an Irishman masquerading as English or Australian according to his whim, Alex an anglicized Hungarian Jew—as well as a love of fine food, good cigars, champagne, brandy, and the south of France, and a taste for the luxurious life whether they could afford it or not. They also had in common a belief that Hitler and Nazi Germany were evil and must be defeated long before most other people had begun to come to that conclusion.

In May 1940 that was still being resisted by many people, including that apostle of appeasement and last-ditch Chamberlain loyalist, the United States ambassador to the Court of Saint James, Joseph P. Kennedy, father of President John F. Kennedy, who noted pessimistically in his diary on May 10 the "definite undercurrent of despair" in England, his concern that Churchill was a drunk, his belief that "the affairs of Great Britain might be in the hands of the most dynamic individual in Great Britain, but certainly not in the hands of the best judgment in Great Britain," and predicted in a letter to his wife, Rose, "a dictated peace with Hitler probably getting the British Navy."

Alex had already made Britain's first full-length feature propaganda film, *The Lion Has Wings*, at Churchill's request, with Ralph Richardson playing an RAF wing commander[*] and Auntie Merle his wife (Merle Oberon was not particularly convincing in the

Merle Oberon and Ralph Richardson in *The Lion Has Wings*.

---

[*] Richardson was an enthusiastic amateur pilot, and joined the Royal Navy's Fleet Air Arm as a pilot, as Olivier would also do until Churchill urged them to leave the Royal Navy and resume acting.

role of an RAF officer's wife, but Alex needed a star for the film at once). It had been necessary to halt work on Alex's other film projects to make *The Lion Has Wings* quickly, but both Alex and Churchill recognized that in the long run overt propaganda like this was not going to dismay the Germans or impress the United States and other neutral countries. The vital element was to produce ambitious British films that could succeed on their own in America, beating the Hollywood studios at their own game, and demonstrating that the British film industry, like Britain herself, was still alive and kicking. The aim was to convince people not that the morale of British bomber squadrons was high, as *The Lion Has Wings* tried to do on the cheap, but that Britain, and the British way of life, was worth defending and had many things in common with the United States—unlike Nazi Germany, whose propaganda films were boastful and militaristic, and never played in American movie theaters, not because they were banned but because nobody wanted to watch them. The best thing Alex could do for Britain was to complete *The Thief of Baghdad* and *Jungle Book*, and make *That Hamilton Woman* even if it meant making them in Hollywood with the connivance and support of the British government.

The Korda family being the kind of top-to-bottom authoritarian structure it was, none of this was revealed to us at the time. In any case, even at my age I was aware that much bigger events were taking place at the time that absorbed everybody's attention.

The news that the long-anticipated German attack on the west had begun on May 10 was doggedly optimistic, and in retrospect clearly filtered through layers of censorship and the Ministry of Information. The *Times* reported with exceptional restraint the laconic communiqué from Gamelin's Grand Quartier Général that fighting was taking place "on a large front, and the enemy was everywhere repulsed."

This piece of wishful thinking was followed shortly by the

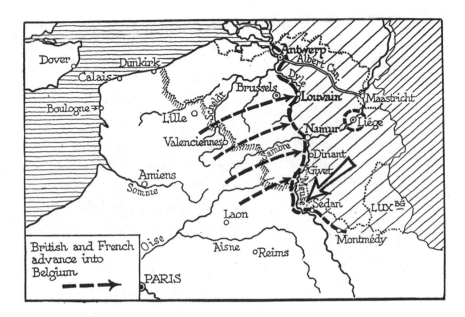

news that the Belgians had—at last—"opened the red and white poles spanning the roads near the Belgian Customs houses" and appealed for the assistance of the French Army and the BEF. In keeping with Hitler's usual ruthlessness the Dutch, the Belgians, and the Luxembourgers had been attacked without any warning or declaration of war—they were woken before dawn by the sound of bombing, artillery fire, tank engines, and aircraft dropping parachute troops. British soldiers entering Belgium were greeted "with an enthusiastic reception from the population" who decorated their vehicles and guns with flowers. Girls kissed the British soldiers, men handed them bottles of beer, snacks, and chocolates, "wherever we went through a village our welcome was rapturous," recalled an officer of the East Surrey Regiment.

By all accounts General Gamelin was calm and content; Plan D was being carried out exactly as he had conceived it. French armies and the BEF were advancing into Belgium on schedule. At the sharp end of the stick there was slightly more concern. "News at present is sketchy," wrote Lieutenant-General Pownall, Lord Gort's chief of staff on May 10, "but we know that Holland, Belgium and

Luxembourg are attacked. . . ." He concluded with a trace of philosophy unusual for a general, "A lovely May day. To think the human race should spend it in this folly."

The British 12th Lancers, unhorsed and transformed into an armored car regiment, were first across the Belgian frontier and crossed without difficulty the Escaut and the Dendre rivers, the bridges of which General Pownall had supposed would be blown up by saboteurs or parachutists. The 12th Lancers reached the Dyle River in central Belgium, on the evening of May 10, their advance slowed down only by the crowds of civilians lining the roads to cheer them.

The Dyle River, once the British reached it, turned out to be something of a disappointment, "little more than a wide stream," as the British *Official Military History of the Second World War* puts it, and disconcertingly shallow, certainly not to all appearances a seri-

German sappers building a bridge across the Meuse, May 1940.

Fort Eben-Emael and the Albert Canal.

ous obstacle for the German Army. By the evening of May 10 news was already coming in that caused more concern at General Gort's headquarters, which was being moved east from village to village as he followed his army.

In a daring move, a dawn attack by German gliders and parachute troops had succeeded in securing two vital bridges over the Meuse at Maastricht, in southern Holland, which the Belgians were supposed to have destroyed, as well the enormous fort of Eben Emael, Belgium's equivalent to the Maginot Line, which was supposed to guard both the bridges over the Meuse and those over the nearby Albert Canal, and which was to have been Belgium's first line of defense. German armor was "pouring through the hole," and the Belgian Army, which was still in the process of mobilizing, was already in retreat. "Trust the Belgians to bog it,"* General Pownall commented sourly, less philosophical now.

An altogether different mood reigned at the Felsennest, Hitler's forward headquarters in the Eifel Mountains, near the Belgian border, where the Führer had gone to observe the battle. As the day ended, Hitler breathed a sigh of relief, despite a sleepless night and a good deal of anxiety. He would later exclaim, "I could have wept for joy; they'd fallen into the trap!"

His generals were more cautious—"Very good marching achievements," was the most Halder would concede for the day— but Hitler was right. He had gambled that the French and British would advance as deeply and as quickly as possible into central Belgium and Holland with their strongest units, while to the south of them General von Kleist's panzer divisions were driving west at top speed toward the Meuse, under the canopy of the Ardennes Forest.

The next day it was beautiful weather again. Hitler paused to enjoy the birds singing all around him in the woods at the Felsennest, but farther to the west there was a mood of sharply increasing anxiety among the Allies. To the north, the Dutch Army, still in the process of mobilization, was unable to slow the German advance, most of the aircraft of the Belgian and Dutch air forces had been destroyed on the ground by the initial German air attacks, and now the roads were beginning to fill with terrified civilian refugees fleeing the fighting, and slowing down the advance of the French and British armies to their lines.

The Luftwaffe attacked the refugees mercilessly to increase the confusion on the ground. A British private of the 2nd Battalion, Royal Norfolk Regiment, would later write,

---

* This is the polite British equivalent of "fuck it up."

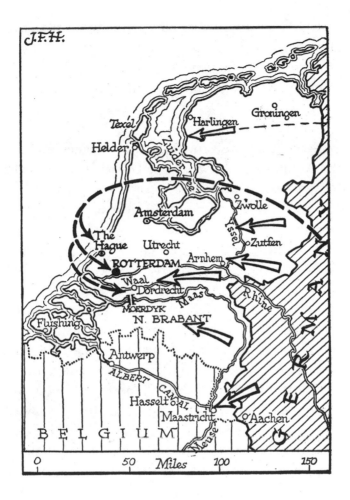

As we were moving forward, there were thousands of refugees around. I remember going down this long straight road
with fields on either side. [It] was filled with children, old
people, horses and carts, prams, wheelbarrows, donkeys, anything that would carry a load. We had to take to the fields on
either side. The bombers came along and bombed this column of refugees, and the Messerschmitts came behind and
machine-gunned them. We were all right because we were
in the flanks in the field—but at that time they didn't bother
about us. . . . We saw people and horses and carts blown sky
high. It was terrible. I remember seeing people mutilated,
blown to pieces. . . . We could do something about the ani-

mals. We saw a horse that had its guts blown open, and we could shoot it. But there was nothing we could do about the human beings. We couldn't stop and give first aid. . . . It was just murder. . . . I still dream about it.

A more threatening problem than the refugees was a request from the Belgian government for the BEF to stop using the roads through the suburbs of Brussels for the passage of British troops at once, since the king had just declared it an "open city" to prevent its being bombed or fought over. Undoubtedly the king was alarmed by the news of heavy German bombing of Dutch towns, and was just as anxious to spare Brussels as the French government was to spare Paris, but it was not a good start to an alliance. The king's decision led to a high-level conference at the Château Casteau the next day to straighten out the misunderstandings between the French, British, and Belgian armies. Unfortunately, General Lord Gort missed the conference—as usual, he wanted to be up front with his troops, rather than in his headquarters—so Lieutenant-General Pownall substituted for him, which was probably just as well since Pownall was a particularly sharp and accurate observer. This was a kind of "summit meeting," to use the modern phrase, attended by His Majesty the King of the Belgians, M. Daladier, now the French war minister, General Georges, commander of the northeast front, General Gaston Billotte, commander of the French 1st Army Group, and a full cast of lesser generals and aides. King Leopold III was accompanied by his military adviser General van Overstraeten, whose influence on the king everybody agreed was unfortunate, since Van Overstraeten was servile, militarily incompetent, and defeatist. "A little too suave, glib and specious . . . more of a courtier than a soldier," Pownall commented.

Although the king had been educated at Eton, he did not make a good impression on the British. He was slender, handsome, and coldly polite, but his face exhibited none of his father's strength, and in photographs he looks spoiled and impatient rather than regal. To Pownall he also seemed "pretty dazed," and it was left to

Van Overstraeten to explain the loss of the Meuse bridges at Maastricht, the Belgian attempt to hold a position east of the Dyle River instead of linking up with the BEF and the French First and Seventh Armies and the king's decision to declare Brussels an open city without consulting his allies. General Georges seems to have been his usual charming self, but distracted, perhaps because as the man in command of the entire French front from Switzerland to the Channel he was already aware that German armored forces in unprecedented numbers were making their way through the supposedly impassible Ardennes with little or no opposition.

Georges had never had any faith in Gamelin or his ideas, and now his worst fears about Plan D were coming true. In any event, he brought the conference to a close with two conclusions, the first of which was to recur again and again over the next six weeks: that the Royal Air Force should provide more fighter squadrons immediately—lack of British fighter aircraft would shortly become the French (and Belgian) explanation for every failure on the ground.

The second was General Georges's admission that he could no longer hope to coordinate three separate national armies in battle from his own headquarters at La Ferté—doubtless Georges was already beginning to sense that the decisive battle would not be fought here in Belgium, but farther south at Sedan when the Germans emerged from the Ardennes. His attention would be required there, so he proposed that General Billotte undertake the task of coordinating the three armies in Belgium on his behalf.

This was a fatal mistake. Billotte was sixty-four years old, already overwhelmed by the responsibility of commanding 1st Army Group, and by no stretch of the imagination an inspired or inspiring leader for a coalition—when he returned to his headquarters he is said to have burst into tears in front of his own staff at the immensity of the task and his incapacity to perform it. Even the normally unshockable General Gamelin was surprised by this decision when news of it reached Vincennes—he referred to it as "an abdication" on General Georges's part.

In any case, everybody at the conference agreed to the proposal, including General Pownall on behalf of the absent Lord Gort, although it meant that the BEF would now be receiving its orders passed from Gamelin's GQG in Vincennes to Georges's HQ at La Ferté, and from there to Billotte's HQ. As if this were not already complicated enough, in a further attempt to isolate himself from General Georges, General Gamelin had set up at Montry, half-way between Vincennes and La Ferté, a headquarters to act as a kind of way station between himself and Georges. Given the fact that there was no radio at Vincennes, and that the telephone system in Holland and Belgium was swiftly collapsing as the Germans advanced (the crowds of refugees on the road doubtless contained any number of switchboard operators and linesmen), it is difficult to estimate how long it might take for an order to reach the hapless Billotte as his headquarters moved from place to place in the ebb and flow of battle, or how long it would take for him to contact General Gort or the king of the Belgians, even if he tried.

There was a further problem that haunted General Georges. General Gamelin had long ago insisted that a French army should be placed in the north to hold Antwerp and advance to Breda in support of the Dutch the moment the battle began. General Henri Giraud's powerful Seventh Army was poised to do this, despite vigorous protests from Georges and Giraud from the very beginning. Gamelin might be uncommunicative and his GQG as hard to make contact with as the Forbidden City in Beijing (Paul Reynaud said Gamelin would have made a better bishop than a soldier), but he was still commander in chief, and he clung stubbornly to the idea of keeping an army in the north; indeed it was a vital element of Plan D.

Left unsaid was the fact that General Giraud's Seventh Army also comprised the French Army's strategic reserve. If the Germans *did* succeed in piercing the Allied line, it would be up to the Seventh Army "to plug the gap," although how it was to get there from Antwerp while under attack was unclear to everyone except Gamelin and his staff, which specialized in just such ambitious and closely detailed *projets*, or what might be called in English "speculative plans."

Plan D was in any case built on a certain degree of speculation—nobody had guessed how quickly the Germans could move, or had learned the lessons of the German attack on Poland. General Gort, for example, thought it would take the Germans two or three weeks to reach the Dyle River, whereas they did it in four days, and General Gamelin assumed that if the Germans were foolish enough to advance through the Ardennes it would take them weeks to cross it. In fact, the Germans would reach Sedan in two days, and by the evening of May 12 they were already in sight of the Meuse River.

By the thirteenth General Pownall was complaining that the king of the Belgians was in a panic ("seems completely to have lost his head") and was ordering bridges destroyed before French troops had crossed them. "What an ally!" Pownall confided to his diary.

But the next day was to produce a crisis bigger than anyone could have imagined, one that would seal the fate not only of the BEF but of France.

11

Rommel Crosses the Meuse

Major General Erwin Rommel, center, with his staff,
after crossing the Meuse.

"**D**EAREST LU," Major General Erwin Rommel wrote his wife
on May 9. "You'll get all of the news for the next few days
from the papers. Don't worry yourself. Everything will go all right."

Rommel was an infantryman, who had only taken command
of the 7th Panzer Division on the Rhine in February 1940. The
author of a respected and bestselling book on infantry tactics,
Infanterie greift an (*Infantry Attacks* when it was eventually published
in English), that sold over half a million copies in Germany, and
attracted Hitler's attention, Rommel had no previous experience
with tanks.

Hitler's appreciation of the book led to Rommel's appointment
in 1938 as the commander of Hitler's military bodyguard battal-

Top: Rommel.
Bottom: Baldur von Schirach, center, leader of the Hitler Youth,
with the Führer.

ion, a largely ceremonial army unit—the serious work of protecting the Führer was carried out by the hardened professionals of
the SS Reichssicherheitsdienst. The army bodyguard battalion was
spit-and-polish soldiering instead of the real thing, and although
it eventually won Rommel promotion from the rank of lieutenant

colonel to that of major general, he was not happy among the overbearing Nazi politicians in Hitler's entourage: he clashed at once
with Baldur von Schirach, leader of the Hitler Youth, and quickly
earned the enmity of Hitler's powerful personal secretary Martin
Bormann. Politics had in any case played no part in his selection:
Rommel was not a Nazi, he was a superbly trained professional
soldier, a war hero—as a lieutenant in World War One he won the
Pour le Mérite, the Imperial German Army's equivalent of Britain's
Victoria Cross or America's Medal of Honor when awarded to a
junior officer—and perhaps more important he was not a Prussian,
did not bear a "von" in front of his name or wear a monocle; it was
thought that the Führer might therefore get along well with him,
and so it proved. It did not hurt that he was actually slightly shorter
than the Führer.

Rommel, however, got no chance to see combat in Poland,
where he was basically a combination of spectator and military
tour guide for the Führer, but afterwards he asked Hitler to give
him command of a panzer division so that he could get back into
action again. Hitler liked and respected Rommel as a soldier, and
agreed with some reluctance to let him go, thus setting Rommel
on the path to a military career that would place him among the
world's great captains.

The 7th Panzer was still in the process of transforming itself
from a "light division"* into an armored division when Rommel
took command—it had fewer tank battalions and more motorized infantry battalions than the older panzer divisions, and was
equipped with a mix of tanks, almost half of which were Czech
38(t) tanks taken over by the German Army after Hitler seized
Czechoslovakia.

Rommel seems to have understood instantly that what was
needed was to apply to tanks the same tactics that had worked
so well for him as an infantry leader: a combination of boldness,

---

* These were basically motorized infantry divisions, beefed up with armored
cars and a few light tanks, which had not proved a satisfactory mix during
the Polish campaign.

speed, and the aggressive use of firepower. Swift raids, the element of surprise, and long, unexpected flank attacks were his specialties; indeed his generalship resembled in many ways that of Stonewall Jackson, and like Jackson Rommel "led from the front," setting an example of indifference to danger for his men at every opportunity. He was a natural leader, one of those rare individuals who remain perfectly cool under fire and always seem to know what to do in the confusion of battle—it is hard to think of any general on either side in World War Two in whom his men had more absolute confidence.

Rommel's 7th Panzer Division was part of Lieutenant General Hermann Hoth's XV Panzer Corps, intended to protect the right flank of the main attack by Guderian's much more powerful XIX Panzer Corps toward Sedan—it would have been essentially a sideshow, had it not been for the astonishing speed of Rommel's advance. His division motored peacefully through Luxembourg, then separated into two columns and plunged into the Ardennes Forest only to find that the Belgian Chasseurs Ardennais had already barricaded forest tracks and blown up the roads to slow down the German

A German military policeman guides traffic toward Sedan,
May 1940.

advance. Most of the lightly armed Chasseurs Ardennais had then been withdrawn over the Meuse or were ordered north to reinforce the forces defending the Belgian heartland, and Rommel simply blew away those who remained.

Nobody understood better than Rommel B. H. Liddell Hart's admonition that an undefended obstacle is quickly overcome. Faced with an obstruction he moved his tanks off the roads into the fields and woods, drove his combat engineers on to perform miracles of road repair and bridging, and kept up the swift pace of his advance, shouting to everyone, "Tempo, tempo, tempo!" (Perhaps best translated as "Get on with it!" or "Hurry up!")

French armored and horsed cavalry, intended to make contact with the enemy, was slow coming up, hampered partly by the demolition work of those same Chasseurs Ardennais, and was unprepared for Rommel's boldness, which would soon become legendary. His columns were led not by horsemen, like the French, but by motorcyclists riding at high speed over rough ground with a machine gunner in the sidecar who opened fire at the first sight of the enemy. His troops were taught never to halt and take cover, but to keep moving at all costs and "spray" fire at the enemy, in keeping with Rommel's belief that "the day goes to the side that is the first to plaster its opponent with fire. . . . It is fundamentally wrong to simply halt and look for cover without opening fire," he wrote, "or to wait for more forces to come up and take part in the action."

He himself set a perfect example of the German principle of *Auftragstaktik*, setting a goal for his units rather than issuing binding step-by-step orders, thus leaving it for junior officers and even NCOs to devise their own means of accomplishing their goal, and relying on the lavish use of superior German firepower to force the enemy back.

The French reconnaissance forces, an unwieldy and outdated mix of light armor and horsed cavalry, were overwhelmed and forced back into what Rommel described as a "hasty" retreat. "I've come up for breath for the first time today," he wrote to his wife, Lucia, on May 11. "Everything wonderful so far. Am way ahead of my neighbors. I'm completely hoarse from orders and shouting.

Had a bare three hours sleep and an occasional meal. . . . Make do with this, please, I'm too tired for more."

What it was like to be faced with a German panzer division on May 11 was described by a French officer as the remains of his division emerged from the woods near the Meuse: "Towards midday, groups of unsaddled horses returned, followed on foot by several wounded cavalrymen who had been bandaged as well as possible; others held themselves in the saddle by a miracle for the honour of being cavalrymen. The saddles and the harnesses were all covered with blood. Most of the animals limped; others, badly wounded, just got as far as us in order to die, at the end of their strength; others had to be shot to bring an end to their sufferings. . . ."

By 4 p.m. on May 12, only two days after the beginning of *Fall Gelb*, what remained of the French defenders of the Ardennes had crossed to the west bank of the Meuse, then destroyed the bridges behind them, just in time. The Meuse is about 120 yards wide at this point, a landscape suitable for a painting by Monet, but a formidable military obstacle. Rommel reached it between Dinant and Houx just as the last bridge in front of him was blown up, but late that night his men discovered "an ancient weir" connecting the east bank of the Meuse at Houx to a small, heavily wooded island midstream. In the dark some of his dismounted motorcyclists managed to tiptoe precariously across the slippery stones to the narrow island.* On its far side they found a rusty lock gate that enabled them to cross to the west bank of the Meuse one by one, and establish a small, beleaguered bridgehead there, slightly covered by a road and the railroad that ran along the west bank of the river.

---

* General Corap, commander of the French Ninth Army, has been criticized for not having destroyed the weir and the lock, but as Sir Alistair Horne points out sensibly in *To Lose a Battle* (and which is confirmed by looking at the river at this point), doing so might have lowered the level of the Meuse upstream sufficiently to provide the Germans with several places at which it could be forded. All war is a question of hard choices, and each choice has unforeseen consequences.

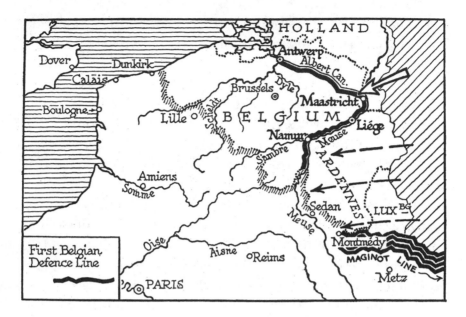

First Belgian Defence Line

By dawn on May 13 the unthinkable had happened, German panzer troops had not only traversed the supposedly "*impénétrable*" Ardennes in fifty-six hours but had crossed the Meuse River, the major "natural obstacle" between there and Paris—or the English Channel.

Guderian's panzer divisions, the main blow, were already approaching Sedan, but Rommel was the first to cross the Meuse, as he must surely have hoped for from the start.

Rommel spent the day of May 13 in constant action. The French had at last woken up to what was happening, and Rommel's attempts to get his men across the Meuse at several points in inflatable rubber boats were met with fierce small arms fire and constant artillery shelling. A smoke screen might have been useful, but he had no smoke unit, so as a substitute he ordered his men to set fire to the houses nearest the river, the normally placid surface of which was whipped into a white froth by rifle and machine-gun fire. A German soldier described it as looking like the head in a stein of beer; a French soldier described it, not surprisingly, as looking like the froth in a glass of champagne. Rommel saw "a damaged rubber boat [come] drifting down to us with a badly wounded man clinging to it, shouting and screaming for help—the poor fellow near to drowning," but there was nothing to be done for him. Rommel's casualties were mounting up rapidly, and many of the rubber boats were damaged or sunk. A few of Rommel's tanks had come up by then, so he ordered them to drive up and down the east bank firing directly across the river at the French emplacements on the west bank. Rommel at this point took over command of one of his own rifle battalions, got the river crossing going again under intense fire, crossed over to the opposite bank in the first boat, "and organized the fresh effort, in which he himself took the lead." Then he went back across the river and drove north to supervise another fiercely contested crossing, found a company of engineers trying to build a bridge across the Meuse with 8-ton pontoons, "stopped them and told them to build the 16-ton type," and as soon as the bridge was ready he was the first over it in his "8-wheeled signal vehicle" despite heavy shelling. In Rommel's own words, the situation "was looking decidedly unhealthy" on the west bank, where a strong French counterattack was taking place. The commander of the 7th Motorcycle Battalion and his adjutant had both been killed, so Rommel took over personally, organized the remaining troops to resist it—like that of all great generals, his display of courage, calm, and optimism was infectious—then left his vehicle where it was and returned once more to the east bank on foot to give orders for ferrying a few of his tanks across that night. He had established a small, insecure bridgehead, but a bridgehead all the same.

Even without his tanks, however, the news of Rommel's river crossing on May 13 caused consternation all the way up the Allied chain of command.

Sluggish and poorly planned communications prevented the news of Rommel's crossing of the Meuse from reaching General Gamelin in his ivory tower at Vincennes until lunchtime on May

13. First reports produced "a lively emotion" even in those hushed surroundings where the luncheon hour was sacred, and Gamelin actually roused himself to place two calls to the chief of staff of the Ninth Army, who replied calmly that everything was under control and that "the incident at Houx was in hand."

Gamelin and his staff were busy dealing with what must have seemed more serious problems. The Dutch were on the brink of surrendering, the king of the Belgians was in a panic, the full force of the German attack toward the Dyle River was beginning to be felt; it was not until half past nine that night that General Georges, for once placing a direct call to General Gamelin despite their scarcely being on speaking terms, revealed that there had been "*un pépin assez sérieux*" (a rather serious pinprick) on the Meuse.

This was putting it mildly. While Rommel was consolidating his bridgehead, about thirty-eight miles upstream as the crow flies General Guderian's XIX Panzer Corps was launching the body blow that Manstein's revision of *Fall Gelb* had called for. One of the mysteries of the war is how Guderian managed to get over 60,000 men, 22,000 vehicles, and nearly 800 tanks through the Ardennes without being observed by British or French reconnaissance air-craft. His passage through the forest was not without problems—despite intense and meticulous planning there were countless traffic jams on the narrow roads and trails—and he was woefully short of artillery for a force of this size, less than 150 guns; still his advance units reached Sedan by the evening of May 12, to find the town deserted, except for the dead horses that littered its streets.

What followed was an extraordinary feat of war, and the confirma-tion in practice of all Guderian's controversial and revolutionary theories about waging war, which he had written about so concisely in *Achtung—Panzer!* in 1937. The French before him across the river not only held the high ground, much of it fortified (though not as well as it should have been—they had not used their time well during the long winter), but had superior numbers of men and artillery, as well as more and better tanks, but from battalion commanders all the way up to the commander in chief they still thought of warfare in the terms of the western front from 1914 to 1918—their preoccupation was to form and hold a line, whether it was on the Meuse or farther north on the Dyle.

Guderian had no interest in lines or in making sacrificial frontal attacks against one; his mantra was movement. Each of his panzer divisions was a self-contained army in miniature, intended to break through the enemy's line and keep going, without concern for its flanks, or even for its supplies. German fuel tankers struggled to keep pace with the tanks, and where necessary Guderian's tankers raided enemy supply dumps for fuel, or occasionally stopped and refueled at civilian gas stations along the way. His early training as a radio officer not only kept him in constant communication with his tanks but enabled his tank commanders to call down dive-bombers, "airborne artillery," to destroy any concentration of the enemy that threatened to halt or slow down their advance.

He was not only ahead of his time but ahead of his own superiors, and turned "a blind eye," like Admiral Nelson, to orders he did not like. His immediate commander, Colonel General Ewald von Kleist, had ordered a single massive bombing of the French positions overlooking Sedan on the west bank of the river. Guderian disapproved—he wanted "carpet bombing," as it came to be called, in which successive waves of bombers attacked immediately in front of his advancing troops, a much more demanding tactic both on the ground and in the air.

Not for the last time Kleist ordered Guderian to do as he had been told, but Guderian, in collusion with Luftwaffe

General Ewald von Kleist.

Lieutenant General Bruno Loerzer, managed to ensure that Kleist's order did not reach the pilots of Fliergerkorps II in time, and as a result got exactly the air attack he wanted. It was certainly the most efficient use of air power in direct support of ground operations to date—indeed, perhaps until D-day in 1944—consisting of over fifteen hundred warplanes methodically attacking the French defenses one by one with such thoroughness that by three in the afternoon, partly concealed by immense clouds of smoke drifting from the explosions on the west bank, Guderian's infantry began to cross the Meuse in rubber boats.

By late afternoon his engineers had completed a bridge that could bear the weight of his tanks, and by nightfall the French line had already begun to disintegrate into shattered fragments. Their dependence on telephone lines rather than radio cost the French dear as bombs cut the lines everywhere, leaving units unable to receive orders or find out how neighboring infantry or artillery units were faring. As a result the appearance of only a few German troops—and very shortly German tanks—*behind* fragmented French defenders led to panic as artillerymen abandoned their guns and whole regiments of infantry retreated in a confused *pêle-mêle* "of unimaginable chaos," which quickly infected rear echelon units, preventing an effective counterattack. For an army that is taught to believe in the importance of forming and holding a line before all other things, the breaking of that line is a catastrophe. The number of troops and tanks Guderian had actually managed to get across the Meuse by midnight on May 13 was comparatively small, as was the size of his bridgehead, but its effect on the French Second Army was to sap the soldiers' confidence in their commanders and in themselves, which once lost, like time, can never be regained.

In the confusion and mayhem of defeat it escaped everybody's attention in the French chain of command that Rommel's breakout to the north of Sedan was not, as everybody expected toward the southwest, in the direction of Paris, but directly west, toward the English Channel. It was not Paris that was suddenly in danger—always the French nightmare—but the Anglo-French alliance itself.

12

"We Are Beaten;
We Have Lost the Battle"

Belgian refugees and retreating soldiers block the roads, May 1940.

THE DEBACLE AT Sedan grew worse on May 14, despite sacrificial French and British air attacks that failed to destroy the German engineers' hastily built bridges over the Meuse. Guderian's bridgehead expanded rapidly, while Rommel forged ahead relentlessly, his lead tanks almost fifteen miles to the west of the Meuse by the end of the day.

Fighting was severe at first—Rommel, in the lead as usual, was lightly wounded when the tank he was in was hit, and had to abandon it in the middle of a fierce artillery barrage. In Belgium, where the French Seventh and First Armies, the BEF, and the Belgian Army were clashing with the Germans before the Dyle River line and in front of Brussels, General Pownall heard the news of what was happening farther south with restrained alarm: "Bad news from down south. The Germans, inexplicably, have got across the Meuse in the neighborhood of Sedan and Mézières, a big hole twelve miles wide and ten deep, or more. . . . Gort was away for

General Lord Gort.

eight hours today—too long at difficult times, but he did well in heartening Corps Commanders and, especially the King of the Belgians who like the rest of his army is in a complete state of wind up."* Gort's preference for being up front with his troops tended to make him unreachable, given the chaotic communications between himself and his headquarters.

That night General Corap made the fatal mistake of withdrawing his French Ninth Army from the Meuse and trying to form a line farther west. The withdrawal quickly turned into "a helplessly confused retreat," which soon became a rout as the five German

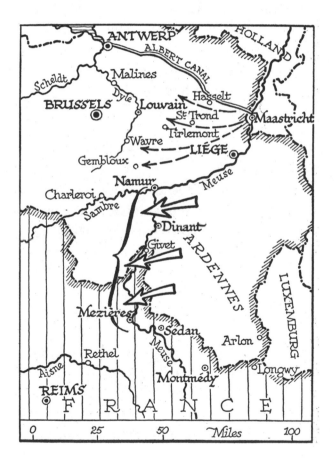

---

* The nearest American equivalent to getting one's "wind up" is "scared shitless." It derives from the fact that horses often get frightened when a strong wind is blowing from directly behind them.

armored divisions broke through scattered resistance into open country. Around half-past seven in the morning of May 15, Winston Churchill was woken in his flat at the Admiralty with the news that "M. Reynaud was on the telephone at my bedside." In Churchill's words, "He spoke in English, and evidently under stress. 'We have been defeated.' As I did not immediately respond he said again: 'We are beaten; we have lost the battle.'"

Reynaud may or may not have said that the road to Paris was open, but it was certainly what he *thought*. It would naturally be the first thought of any Frenchman in the circumstances, and demonstrates that the real goal of Guderian's armored divisions was not yet clear to General Gamelin at GQG. The French habit of assuming that Paris was at the center of the world made even experienced military leaders like Gamelin and Georges misread the situation. The Germans had made a dash toward Paris in 1870, and they had tried it once again in 1914, so it was difficult to believe they would not do so once more in 1940—after all, they were now only 130 miles away from Paris, with no shortage of excellent roads. Where else would they be going?

The burning question at GQG was no longer whether the Allies could prevent the Germans from taking Brussels, but whether the French government might have to abandon Paris in haste. The next day General Gamelin went so far as to tell Reynaud and Daladier that "he could no longer take responsibility for the safety of the capital after midnight," a moment of high drama that astonished both politicians, but his pessimism about the safety of the capital— and his helplessness at the speed of the German breakthrough— had already been remarked on the day before. That did not prevent him and General Georges from trying to reassure the British prime minister. General Gamelin informed Churchill that "he viewed the situation with calm," a wonderfully soothing French phrase, and General Georges, to whom Churchill placed a call, was reported to be "cool," by which Churchill meant that Georges expressed himself as neither excited nor concerned by events at Sedan.

Clare Boothe, author of *The Women* and wife of Henry Luce, co-founder of *Time* magazine, was touring Europe that spring to report on the war; an intermittently astute observer of the social and political scene, she remarked correctly that "the English didn't really like or trust the French any more than the French liked or trusted the English," so it is perhaps not surprising that both French generals tried to mislead the British about the seriousness of the situation—after all, nothing could be more humiliating for a French general than to have to tell an Englishman that he had been beaten by the Germans and that German tanks were expected to be in Paris shortly.

Clare Boothe Luce.

Paris being Paris, the rumor that the Germans were on the way spread quickly, and became more dire with each telling. Reynaud no doubt told his mistress the Comtesse de Portes, Daladier told *his* mistress the Marquise de Crussol, they in turn told their friends, their friends called others. Even on May 15 people in the know, that is in or close to the government, were already advising friends to prepare to leave Paris, and people who were Jewish to leave at once. To all appearances Paris in mid-May was as beautiful and gay as ever, in perfect spring weather. Clare Boothe, usually clear-eyed, rhapsodized over "the gardens of the Luxembourg and the Bois," over "the gilded corridors of the Ritz," the crowded, noisy streets, the clink of ice at the polished marble café tables on the Champs-Elysées, the elegant women and well-dressed men—"Paris sera toujours Paris," as the great French entertainer Maurice Chevalier sang—but "the drawing rooms of Paris . . . became a hotbed of rumors that flew from lip to lip so fast that a few hours later *tout Paris* knew them." Behind the façade of elegance and nonchalance there was a growing sense of terror and fear of defeat. Already waves of refugees were thronging the railway stations and filling the roads, not only Belgians now, but French fleeing the fighting before it engulfed them, an eventuality that nobody in Paris had anticipated or prepared for.

*   *   *

None of this was reflected in the British newspapers, or on the BBC news. General Gamelin despised and feared the press, whether French or foreign, so bulletins from the GQG were kept brief and positive. The war correspondents attached to the BEF were also kept on a tight leash. The easygoing familiarity with which General Lord Gort had treated Kim Philby of the *Times* during the phoney war had been replaced by the stiff upper lip, strict censorship, and encouraging "human interest" stories.

My father, who read all the newspapers intently every day and disliked being interrupted while he was doing so, dropped them on the floor after reading them with a deep sigh and said to nobody in particular, "Lies." Nanny Low, who picked them up to take the more "popular" ones like the *Daily Express* and the *Daily Mail* up to the nursery, read them with greater faith. Those headlines that caught her attention she read aloud to me. Of course in every war "truth is the first casualty," a remark that goes all the way back to Aeschylus in the fifth century BC and possibly further, and reading the British popular press (and even the *Times*) seventy-five years later confirms his wisdom.

Some pieces of bad news were impossible to stifle. Holland surrendered on May 15, causing General Pownall to note caustically, "There was no chance that [Holland] would hold out for long, but five days is a little short," and sending Belgian morale, which was already sinking, into a tailspin. To be fair to the Dutch, their resistance was finally broken by the brutal bombing of Rotterdam, in which 900 civilians were killed, nearly 90,000 made homeless and the center of the city totally destroyed by a firestorm that ignited medieval buildings, an act that caused almost as much worldwide condemnation as the bombing of Guernica in 1937. Still, the tone of the papers in Britain remained strikingly upbeat during the first week of the battle. "ALLIES ADVANCING ON FRONT OF 200 MILES," ran a banner headline in the *Daily Mail* on May 10 and "B.E.F. SWINGS INTO ACTION," three days later. On the same day the newspaper reported that the Belgian Army in the Ardennes was—in that beloved military cliché for headlong flight—pursuing "a strategic retreat to new and more strongly fortified positions," and that the situation in Holland was "improving," this just forty-eight hours before the Dutch surrendered.

As would often be the case throughout the war, Royal Air Force figures of German aircraft shot down were delusory, and reports of heavy British and French air raids on German cities at this stage of the war hugely exaggerated. Even the normally sedate *Times* reported on May 15 that German troops were "falling back" in confusion under "a seemingly endless torrent of [French] bombs," a complete reversal of actual events, while in Paris the equally respected and respectable *Le Temps* reported that French tanks and fighter aircraft had proved themselves technically superior to those of the enemy.

Unfortunately most of this was not true. A courageous attempt on the part of the obsolete French bombing force to destroy the bridges built by German combat engineers over the Meuse led to the loss of nearly three-quarters of the French bombers engaged, with no damage to the bridges. An attack by 109 British Blenheim and Battle bombers of the Advanced Air Striking Force led to the loss of forty-five aircraft (and the award of two posthumous Victoria crosses), without inflicting damage to any of the bridges. The RAF effort on May 14 made it clear that daylight bombing in the face of heavy German antiaircraft fire was sacrificial, and helped to further undermine the morale of French troops, since most of the bombs that *were* dropped by the RAF fell short on them, rather than on the enemy.

May 15 was the last day on which we at home could bask in the belief that things were going well, or at least were under control, and that France's reputation as the world's preeminent military power was secure. Possibly my uncle Alex already knew better—friends of his had better sources of information than the newspapers, after all. One of his closest friends was Sir Robert Vansittart, the fiercely anti-appeasement permanent undersecretary at the

Sir Robert Vansittart.

Foreign Office in the 1930s and head of the "German desk," now sidelined as the government's chief diplomatic adviser. Vansittart had been a powerful and well-informed dissenting voice from deep within "the Establishment" against Germany and Hitler's plans during the governments of Stanley Baldwin and Neville Chamberlain, and a loyal Churchillian. Indeed Vansittart was *plus royaliste que le roi*; his dislike of Germany seemed to many people more deeply ingrained than Churchill's, and helps to explain why his warnings were ignored by those above him. He was also a man of many talents—he had not only helped Alex to finance London Films through his contacts in "the City," but as a gifted amateur playwright and songwriter had written lyrics for *The Thief of Baghdad* in between sifting through every intelligence source from Berlin.

The end of the phoney war did nothing to slow down Alex's trips back and forth to Los Angeles, with stops in New York, Lisbon, and Tangiers, and it was already clear both to him and to my father that there was no hope of completing *The Thief of Baghdad* in the United Kingdom. For once it was not money that was lacking—Alex could always whistle that up out of thin air—but the skilled workmen needed for such a complicated and ambitious project. Every day my father went to the studio to find more of his men "called up," or shifted to jobs in the armaments business. No matter how late he stayed at the studio, the film languished, having already absorbed some £400,000 ($2,000,000 at the time, at least $24,000,000 in today's values).* As Alex was so fond of saying,

---

* This is about the same as the cost of *The Wizard of Oz*, and a little more than half the cost of *Gone with the Wind*.

with a disarming shrug, "A lot of money—other people's money, of course, but still a lot."

At some point my father may have gone to Paris briefly—my mother certainly said so in her old age—and it is possible. Although he had never mentioned the fact to her, he had a family in Paris, his former mistress and two children, from the days before Alex had called him from his life as a painter to a film career, and it may be that he wanted to make sure they were securely provided for before the Germans reached Paris. My father was not especially secretive; he simply tended to draw a curtain down between one episode of his life and the next, as did his brothers. All three brothers were masters at putting the past behind them, especially when it came to their English spouses, who could scarcely be expected to understand the many convolutions and changes of fortune that had brought them so unexpectedly to England in 1932.

Another possible explanation for the sudden trip to Paris may be that Alex had chosen my father to carry out some last-minute transfers of money. Alex was, after all, the supreme realist—the war would eventually end, like all wars. Unless the Germans won, people would resume going to the movies, the London Films offices in Paris, Berlin, and Vienna would reopen, the European studios now producing Nazi propaganda films would return to producing more normal fare, the copyrights to Alex's old films would be as valuable as ever, perhaps more so, and in the meantime the more money that could be placed safely out of harm's way in Swiss and American banks, the better. Nobody could have been better shaped to play this last-minute role than my father, an artist with shabby clothes, a battered hat, and a cigarette adhering to his lower lip in the French manner, whose friends included almost every painter, sculptor, and filmmaker of note in France, multilingual (all the languages he knew spoken with a Hungarian accent of course), and gifted most improbably with a genuine British passport and impeccable visas, thanks no doubt to Sir Robert Vansittart. It would have been hard to find a figure less likely to arouse the suspicion of the authorities in France than my father, or with better credentials and more friends.

Vincent would no doubt have been happy to escape from the problems of *The Thief of Baghdad* for a few days. It was in any case a truly international film. Its first director (there would be several) was Ludwig Berger, a German Jew and a friend of Alex's from his filmmaking days at the UFA studios in Berlin in the 1920s, one of the screenwriters was Alex's old friend from his student days in Budapest Lajos Bíró, and the music score was being composed by my father's old friend Miklós Rózsa, who had also composed the score for *The Four Feathers.* The cinematographer was another old friend from my father's days as a painter in Paris Georges Perinal, and the two major male stars were an anti-Nazi German refugee, Conrad Veit, and an Indian, Sabu, the young *mahout* whom my Uncle Zoli had "discovered" in India while making *Elephant Boy.* Only my uncle Alex could have collected all these people together in the expectation that they would produce a successful English-language motion picture, and it may well have been that it was not only my father who had matters to wind up in Paris before the Germans arrived there, but many of the people connected with the film. In any case, he was home before May 15, his suitcase stuffed with tins of foie gras from Fauchon, the great purveyor of gourmet foods in the Place de la Madeleine, which he would not revisit until 1945, and for my mother a beautiful gold brooch from Cartier on the rue de la Paix in the shape of a rose mounted with diamonds, each petal articulated by tiny gold springs so that it could be changed from bud to an open flower. My father was as interested in jewelry design as in any other form of art, and had old friends in the Cartier design studio. This was not so much a piece of jewelry as a unique work of art. Ever the forgetful artist, Vincent was apt to overlook birthdays and anniversaries, but instead had moments of what sometimes seemed like spontaneous and outrageous generosity. In this case, it was something in the nature of a preemptive strike, since he was about to make my mother do the last thing she wanted to do. The Cartier rose was at once a gift offering and an apology in advance.

*　*　*

The bulk of the BEF had moved forward to the Dyle River in Belgium, the beauty of which one English officer compared to the Thames Valley, so efficiently that its GHQ was left behind, struggling to keep up. By May 16, after a few clashes in which the Germans learned, as their fathers had in 1914 at Ypres and Mons, just how effective the massed rifle fire of well-trained British regulars was, it was becoming obvious that a line on the Dyle, the heart and soul of General Gamelin's Plan D, would be difficult to hold. The Belgian Army to the north of the BEF was at best shaky, the First French Army to the south had advanced much more slowly than the British and was beginning to give up ground under pressure, and a withdrawal to the next defensible line, the Senne Canal, seemed the obvious move.

The rivers and canals in central Belgium all run more or less parallel, and the next few days would see the Allied armies moving back from one river or canal to another. If the BEF's neighbors to its north and south gave way, the British risked being left in a salient with wide-open flanks, but each withdrawal would expose more of Belgium to the enemy. Retreat to the Senne would almost certainly mean the loss of Louvain; a retreat to the Escault River (or the Scheldt, as it is known in Belgium), which many people in the French and British armies thought would have been a better place at which to form a line than the Dyle in the first place (the Dyle is hardly more than a shallow stream, the Escaut is a major river), would mean abandoning Brussels, and thus undermine any reason for the Belgian Army to continue fighting. Any retreat farther west to the Lys River would bring the Allied armies back to the French frontier where they had started from, and also risk the loss of Antwerp, the major port of northern Europe and a permanent British strategic interest on the Continent.

That General Georges had delegated the "coordination" of the three armies to General Billotte was already becoming a difficult problem. "Coordination" is not the same thing as supreme command. Billotte's tears at the prospect were justified—his was not a dominating personality, the British and the Belgians received no orders from him; indeed he seemed barely able to animate the

French First Army, which he commanded. It was his decision to withdraw to the Senne, a huge "bound" to the rear for the BEF, with four divisions to disengage, and nearly ten thousand vehicles to move. The news so surprised the BEF that General Pownall sent a liaison officer to emphasize they needed a clearer sense of "policy and timing," but none was forthcoming.

The fact that the main German attack was taking place seventy miles farther south, let alone that Premier Reynaud and General Gamelin already thought that the war had been lost, had not yet penetrated to the Allied armies fighting on the plains of Belgium any more than it had to the French or British public.

13

"The Mortal Gravity of the Hour"

A German Ju 87 Stuka dive-bombing.

A MORE IMPORTANT VISITOR than my father arrived in Paris late in the afternoon of May 16, having flown from London to see for himself what the situation was. Winston Churchill had spent the past two days with his chiefs of staff and the War Cabinet considering Premier Reynaud's alarming early-morning telephone call on May 14, and repeated messages since then warning of disaster and appealing for more British fighter squadrons. Even more alarming was a guarded telephone call from General Lord Gort to General Sir John Dill, until recently one of Gort's corps commanders and now vice-chief of the Imperial General Staff, to say that the French were thinking of withdrawing from Belgium altogether owing to the "deep penetration" of German armored forces toward Paris "from the direction of Mézières." This is a reference to Rommel's 7th Panzer division, which was already in Avesnes, which he took on May 16, and after which Rommel wrote, "The way to the

Churchill, General Sir John Dill, Attlee, and Reynaud at a meeting of the Supreme War Council, Paris.

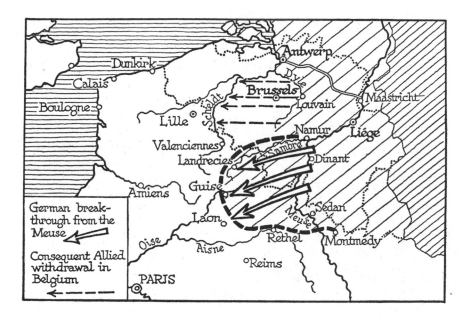

west is now open." His tanks would shortly be advancing up to fifty miles a day.

Among the prime minister's attributes was a well-developed nose for disaster, as well as a gamecock's fighting instincts. Nobody had greater, or more varied, experience of military and naval disasters over many decades from the reign of Queen Victoria to that of her great-grandson George VI than the prime minister. Few people had stronger nerves, or a more deeply ingrained belief that attack is the best form of defense too, but Churchill came to the Supreme War Council determined to listen. His respect for the French Army remained unshaken, and although the War Cabinet was cautious about any undertaking to send more RAF fighter squadrons to France, the prime minister, always a Francophile, was inclined to be sympathetic toward Reynaud's appeal on the subject, and had sent four more fighter squadrons to France in the morning.

Unfortunately neither Premier Reynaud nor General Gamelin understood that the British fighters were a part of an intricate and complex defense system—admittedly the most visible and glamorous part, but not intrinsically more important than the radar towers along the southern coast of England, or the young women of the WAAF* who plotted incoming attacks at Fighter Command Headquarters and watched the radar screens, or the repair facilities scattered throughout southern England that could take a damaged Hurricane or Spitfire and restore it to fighting trim, sometimes overnight (and often returned to the fighter squadrons by young civilian women ferry pilots), all of it linked together by hundreds of telephone and telex lines buried deep underground and armored in concrete to withstand even a direct hit by a bomb.

The king and Air Chief Marshal Sir Hugh Dowding, commander in chief of Fighter Command.

Churchill himself did not yet appreciate or understand the complexity of Fighter Command, or the degree to which the precious fighters and their pilots would be wasted operating from makeshift airfields in France without the organization that Air Chief Marshal Sir Hugh Dowding, commander in chief of Fighter Command, had been building up painstakingly since 1936. Sending more Hurricanes to France—there was no thought of sending the more sophisticated Spitfire, which was more difficult to manufacture and whose narrow undercarriage track made it unsuitable for rough fields—was, in Dowding's mind, "turning on a tap" that no politician would have the courage to turn off, and that risked leaving England defenseless when the Luftwaffe attacked.

* Women's Auxiliary Air Force.

The meeting took place in Reynaud's "study" on the Quai d'Orsay, and Major-General Hastings Ismay, Churchill's military adviser, thought as he looked at the faces of Reynaud, Daladier, and Gamelin, "The French High Command are beaten already." The meeting was not made more cheerful by the sight through the windows of clouds of smoke and pieces of charred paper rising from bonfires in the gardens as "venerable officials [pushed] wheelbarrows of archives onto them," a sign that the French government was already planning to leave Paris. "Utter dejection was written on every face," Churchill wrote, remarkably for someone who did not normally pay much attention to other people's feelings. Everybody was standing—there was no big conference table. General Gamelin stood beside what Churchill described as "a student's easel" with a map that showed "a small but sinister bulge at Sedan." In a flat and unemotional voice Gamelin explained the military situation. The Germans had broken through and were advancing "with unheard-of speed towards Amiens and Arras, with the intention, apparently, of reaching the coast at Abbeville or thereabouts. Alternatively they might make for Paris." It still does not seem to have dawned on Gamelin that Abbeville loomed larger in the Germans' minds than Paris.

Gamelin talked for several minutes, after which there was, understandably, a long and uncomfortable silence. At last, the prime minister asked where the strategic reserve was? "Breaking into French, which I use indifferently (in every sense)," he recalled, he asked, "*Où est la masse de manoeuvre?*" General Gamelin shrugged and said, "*Aucune.*" (There is none.)

Churchill was "dumbfounded," he later confessed, although whether he was quite as surprised as he claimed in his memoirs to have been is open to doubt. After all, he had flown from London with Generals Ismay and Dill. Ismay had never had any faith in Gamelin's Plan D or the idea of fighting the Germans in central Belgium, and Dill had served in France under Lord Gort and had had every opportunity to observe the flaws in the French Army at close range. As for Gamelin's somber *tour d'horizon*, he passed over the fact that he *had* a powerful mobile strategic reserve, but had placed it in northern France to advance into Holland and support the Dutch when the battle began. With the collapse of resistance in Holland what remained of General Giraud's Seventh Army should have been moved south immediately to reinforce the flagging Ninth Army before Sedan. It was not that there was *no* mobile strategic reserve—Giraud had not only some of the French Army's best infantry divisions but three armored corps with heavier and better armed tanks than the Germans—it was simply in the wrong place.

Churchill hit on this immediately, but Gamelin explained smoothly that he had not been able to effectuate this movement because the Belgian railway workers were on strike. "Shoot the strikers," Churchill replied,* sharply changing the tone of the meeting. It is possible, even probable that Churchill merely wished to light a fuse under Gamelin, rather than to suggest that the French Army start executing Belgian railwaymen. Certainly he was annoyed that the French commander in chief had spent five minutes talking about his woes without proposing any solution to them. What Churchill saw when he looked at the map was a long, narrow German salient created by armored divisions that were moving much faster than the infantry divisions marching far behind them on foot—a perfect opportunity for a counterattack on the exposed German flanks, which was exactly what Hitler and his senior generals feared would happen.

But Gamelin would have none of it. The French troops, he insisted, had been prevented from counterattacking by German bombing—he needed fighter aircraft to protect the infantry, and also the railway lines over which reinforcements would have to be brought up. This was at last something on which all the French present could agree—lack of British fighter aircraft was responsible for the German breakthrough, and it could only be halted by more British fighter squadrons, which were required immediately. As M. Daladier put it, perhaps giving away more of the truth

* Churchill later denied saying this, but his words were confirmed by General Ismay.

than Gamelin would have wanted to, "If the French infantry could feel that the fighters were above protecting them, they would be given confidence and would not be taking cover when the tanks came along."

This was the first admission that the real problem was the *morale* of French soldiers, who were unable to hold their ground when attacked by Ju 87 Stuka dive-bombers, even though dive-bombing produced far fewer casualties than a well-organized artillery barrage, or when they saw German tanks approaching in the distance. The fact was that the French were fleeing from even the *rumor* that German tanks were near, and that their nerve was broken by the howl of the Stukas as they dived—the Germans had cleverly attached a siren under each wing of the Stuka, "Jericho Trumpets" as they were called, which gave off a howling, piercing, banshee screech that froze men's blood. It was a classic case of the bark being worse than the bite.

If Gamelin was reading the messages on his desk, he must have known how badly things were going. A staff officer he sent to see for himself what was happening on General Corap's front facing Sedan reported back, "This Army is in an indescribable disorder, troops are falling back on all sides, Army H. Q. have lost their heads, they do not even know where their divisions are. The situation is worse than anything we could have imagined." This was a rout that could hardly be stopped by more fighter aircraft, and Gamelin knew it, despite his carefully maintained façade of eerie, calm self-satisfaction.

Churchill could see well enough that the demand for more fighters was merely a convenient way of ignoring the fact that the French divisions at Sedan had performed very poorly, and at the same of shifting the blame for the French Army's failure to stop the Germans from their own shoulders to those of the British, and did his best to explain in rational military terms why this was not the case. Tanks, he pointed out, could not be stopped by fighter aircraft armed with .303-caliber machine guns, the bullets of which would simply bounce off their armor. "It was not reasonable that the British aircraft should be required to take on German armoured fighting vehicles. This should be done by ground action," he pointed out.

The French had ample numbers of seventy-five-millimeter cannon, the famous "French seventy-fives," and fired over open sights these could destroy any tank the Germans had with one shot. As for bridges, they were notoriously difficult targets for bombers,* and the Germans had plenty of antiaircraft guns with which to defend them—losses would be crippling. These reasonable arguments accomplished nothing. Whatever their other differences, and there were many, Gamelin (who feared for his job), Daladier (whose protégé Gamelin was), and Reynaud (who wanted to get rid of them both) all agreed that only the prompt arrival of British fighter squadrons could prevent the German armies from continuing their advance toward Paris. If the Germans reached Paris, Daladier said, the war would be lost.

Churchill could already see where all this was leading, and although he kept it to himself for the moment it was clear enough to him that the war would *not* be lost if the Germans reached Paris—the French Army was still big enough to hold a line somewhere in France and fight it out, and if it could not, then Great Britain would have to carry on the war alone if necessary, in which case the fighter squadrons would be essential for its survival.

As the meeting dragged on disputatiously—Gamelin remained silent, as if he had no place among all these civilians and foreigners and was anxious to be back at Vincennes, where nobody could ask him inconvenient questions—Churchill finally offered to add six more squadrons to the four that had been promised that morning, subject to the approval of the War Cabinet. Although there was no particular magic in the total of ten fighter squadrons except that it was a round number, it seemed to satisfy the French. By Churchill's reckoning this would represent one-quarter of the number

---

* With the aircraft then available for the task, Battles and Blenheims carrying 250-pound bombs, it was indeed an impossible task. Later in the war it would be calculated that a minimum of 250 *tons* of bombs were required to guarantee the destruction of a bridge.

of squadrons that would be needed to defend Britain, a figure he seems to have made up by himself—in fact Air Chief Marshal Dowding had stated that he needed *fifty* squadrons of fighters only the day before in a charged confrontation at the War Cabinet—but it was no doubt intended to impress the French, or at least to shut them up for the moment, and in that it succeeded.

Churchill went back to the ornate calm of the British Embassy on the rue du Faubourg St. Honoré and composed a careful message to the War Cabinet asking it to agree to send six more fighter squadrons at once. His message makes it clear that his recommendation to send them is not basically a *military* decision but a *political* one. "It would not be good historically if their requests were denied and their ruin resulted," he wrote, prompting one of his secretaries to say, "He is still thinking of his books," although it may be that the prime minister was already thinking of the judgment of history, and that it would not look good if Britain failed its only ally at this crucial point in the war. He emphasized, in another powerful phrase, "the mortal gravity of the hour," and the importance of giving the French Army "the last chance . . . to rally its bravery and strength," and ended by asking for the reply to be telephoned to General Ismay "at Embassy in Hindustani," Ismay having previously worked out that two British officers communicating in Hindustani would be safe from any Frenchman (or German) who was listening in on the line.

At 11:30 that night Ismay received a call from London. The answer was "*haan*," or yes.* He informed the prime minister immediately, who was so pleased that he decided to break the good news to M. Reynaud personally, and bundled General Ismay into an embassy car to drive to the premier's apartment at once.

---

* As Ismay points out, this was not a new or original idea. Prime Minister David Lloyd George did the same thing at crucial moments during the Versailles peace conference, except that in his case he arranged for a Welsh speaker to be present in London.

Reynaud had already retired for the night, much to Churchill's surprise since he was himself an indefatigable night owl, so the two Englishmen were obliged to wait in the darkened living room while the premier was woken. Not being a ladies' man the prime minister failed to notice a fur coat and several items of intimate female clothing strewn about the room, so when Reynaud at last emerged in his dressing gown to hear the good news, Churchill could have no notion that the Comtesse de Portes, Reynaud's mistress, was listening from behind the door to the bedroom. Many difficulties over the next three weeks might have been solved had Churchill known of the degree to which Reynaud was subject to the wishes and opinions of his mistress, whose outspoken Anglophobia and disapproval of the war was one more factor in the rapid deterioration of the alliance.

14

May 20, 1940:
"A Pretty Fair Pig of a Day"

General Weygand.

S UCH NEWS AS was printed in the United Kingdom did not of course reflect the dramatic visit of the prime minister to Paris, or the real state of the French Army. The *Times*, usually cautious and accurate but still under the spell of GQG's communiqués, hailed "the vigorous counter-attack" of the French at Sedan, and the "powerful" bombing attacks of the RAF against the German pontoon bridges over the Meuse. On May 17 the *Times* described the German attack through the Ardennes as "small in scope compared with the momentous battles farther north," the exact opposite of the truth, and referring to General Corap's troops, hailed "the gay spirits of these lean, wiry young men who in an hour or two were to go back into the lines," when in fact they were retreating in disorder, having abandoned their guns.

In Well Walk, Hampstead, the *Times* did not appear in the nursery. Nanny Low read the *Daily Express* and the *Daily Mail*, which ran stories of the "magnificent" French Army, of the Belgians and Dutch driving back the Germans, and of titanic air victories. These Nanny perused carefully through her thick reading glasses, and carefully clipped out stories like that of the four Battle bomber crews, the only ones of their squadron to have returned from an attack on the bridges over the Meuse, who bravely volunteered to go back and try again. None of them returned, but "the bridge was destroyed." Several different versions of this story ran in all the "popular" press, and Nanny not only read it aloud to me but tucked it in the corner of one of her framed photographs of other children she had cared for—she had a nephew who was an air gunner in the RAF, so she had a particular interest in stories of RAF heroism, of which there were plenty at the time, perhaps because the RAF was better at what is now called "public relations" than the other two services. Needless to say, the press did not run stories about the fact that the RAF raids on the Meuse bridges had produced the highest rate of loss in RAF history without seriously inconveniencing the Germans.

British eyes were still fixed on the battle in central Belgium, not on the collapse of the French Ninth Army at Sedan, about which even those much better informed than the average newspaper reader remained ignorant. It was the BEF fighting successfully against the odds that held the public's attention. Not only were they "our boys" but many of the names of places they passed through on the way to the Dyle River were engraved in the memory of the previous generation: Mons, Ypres, Passchendaele, familiar landmarks of the great battles in Flanders that had cost the lives of hundreds of thousands of Britons only twenty-six years ago. The names of the regiments involved were recognized all over the United Kingdom, since each regiment had strong local roots: the Cheshire Regiment, the Middlesex Regiment, the Gordon Highlanders, the Argyll and Sutherland Highlanders, the Royal Scots Fusiliers, the Royal Norfolk Regiment, the South Staffordshire Regiment, the West Yorkshire Regiment, the Sherwood Foresters, the Lancashire Fusiliers, the North Staffordshire Regiment, the Royal Welch Fusiliers, the Duke of Cornwall's Light Infantry, the Black Watch, the Buffs, the Green Howards, the Queen's Own Royal West Kent Regiment, the Gloucestershire Regiment, the Oxfordshire and Buckinghamshire Light Infantry, the list goes on and on of battalions from almost every one of the famous regiments of the British Army, each with its own traditions, peculiarities of dress, numerous battle honors won in every corner of the globe, and turreted and mullioned home depot in its county seat, and that is without counting the five regiments of the Foot Guards (the Grenadier Guards, the Coldstream Guards, the Scots Guards, the Irish Guards, and the Welsh Guards) or storied cavalry regiments now converted to tanks or armored cars like the King's Royal Hussars, the Fife and Forfar Yeomanry, the Royal Inniskilling Dragoon Guards, the 12th Royal Lancers, the Queen's Bays, the 10th Royal Hussars, name after name familiar in British history.

There can have been few people in the United Kingdom who did not have a relative who had served or was now serving in one of these regiments, no county or big city throughout the United Kingdom that did not pride itself on its local regiment and its history, from the Tyneside Scottish to the Durham Light Infantry. Of course there were specialist services too, the Royal Artillery, the Royal Engineers, the Royal Army Service Corps, and so on, not to speak of the Royal Air Force, but this was still an army of nearly 400,000 men whose territorial and local roots remained relatively strong, and most of whose units retained fierce regimental loyalty and local pride.

A number of its officers were noblemen, including the 9th Duke of Northumberland, a lieutenant in the 3rd Battalion the Grenadier Guards, the 10th Viscount Downe who commanded the 69th Brigade, and of course the 6th Viscount Gort, the commander in chief. Despite the intermingling of Territorial battalions, the BEF still reflected the older British Army, in which musketry, discipline, and regimental esprit de corps were all-important, and the bayonet charge remained the final arbiter of battle.

This was the army that had advanced to the Dyle River on the orders of General Gamelin, and had already been ordered to fall back by stages to the Escaut (or Scheldt) River, since the Belgian Army to its north was withdrawing and the French First Army to its south was "shaken," as General Pownall tactfully described it. Pownall already foresaw that Brussels was a goner, and complained that General Billotte, to whom General Georges had delegated the "coordination" of the three northern armies, was unable or unwilling to do so, with the result that nobody was effectively in command—a very dangerous situation against a well-trained, more numerous, and better-armed foe. An army is never in greater danger than when it is in retreat, and there was a real possibility that the entire Allied line from north of Brussels to the Ardennes might simply disintegrate—already there were reports of Belgian soldiers fleeing in large numbers without their rifles, hopelessly mingled with hordes of desperate civilian refugees who blocked the roads, the beginning of a huge exodus of misery that would soon involve millions of people. In these circumstances it was something of a miracle that the BEF managed to withdraw in relatively good order despite some heavy fighting, first to the Senne River, then to the Dendre, and finally to the Escaut, where the BEF was firmly established by midnight of May 19.

The BEF had advanced to the Dyle River in three days and it took it three days to march back again, reminding more than one participant of the old nursery rhyme commemorating the futile maneuvering of HRH Prince Frederick, the Duke of York, second son of King George III, in the Flanders campaign of 1793–1794 against the French:

> *Oh, the grand old Duke of York,*
> *He had ten thousand men;*
> *He marched them up to the top of the hill,*
> *And he marched them down again.*

This was, surely not accidentally, the last time a member of the British royal family had personally commanded troops in the field.* In May 1940, of course, the BEF was obeying the orders, or perhaps more accurately the vaguely expressed misgivings of General Billotte. British casualties were still considered "light," mostly from German dive-bombing of the roads, and few vehicles were lost except for the heavy "I" tanks—slow, cumbersome, and poorly armed—which the striking Belgian railwaymen refused to load onto flatcars, so the BEF returned to the Escaut more or less intact.

Disappointingly, even the Escaut turned out not to be as formidable a military obstacle as General Billotte had supposed from looking at the map. Nobody seems to have informed him that the water level had dropped several feet because of "a long spell of dry weather" and the closing of the sluices farther upstream, so there were places where it would not be difficult for German infantry to cross. Falling back to the Escaut carried with it other problems—the loss of Brussels and Antwerp, thus making it increasingly difficult for many Belgians to see any good reason for continuing to fight, and eliminating one of the major strategic reasons for the BEF to be in northern France in the first place.

Even more alarming was the fate of what remained of the

---

* To be fair to the Duke of York, he later served for thirty-two years as commander in chief of the British Army, and was an effective, if occasionally corrupt, administrator, though his strongest interests were women and gambling for high stakes.

French Seventh Army, which was in the process of disintegrating as it attempted to move behind the BEF to reinforce the collapsing Ninth Army farther south—its commander, General Giraud, one of the more energetic and competent French generals, who would go on to become briefly a rival of de Gaulle's, was captured by the Germans in his command car as he tried to rally the rest of his army. Thus what remained of the best-equipped French army was fed into the battle piecemeal, instead of being concentrated for a single powerful counterattack—another major tactical error on the part of General Georges.

Gort's line on the Escaut was badly stretched, for he had only seven divisions with which to hold a front thirty miles long, and on one of his rare visits to Gort's headquarters the hapless General Billotte held out little hope that the gap farther south could be filled in, which meant that short of a miracle Guderian's armored divisions would shortly advance straight across the BEF's tenuous lines of communication with the major ports of Le Havre, Brest, and Cherbourg, and leave it stranded in Flanders—cut off and desperately short of supplies and ammunition. The spearhead of Guderian's panzer forces, Billotte confided, was already close to Cambrai, and he had nothing with which to slow down or stop this rapid mechanized march to the sea—the Germans would very shortly be closer to the English Channel than the BEF was.

If what Billotte intended was to put in Gort's mind the idea of moving the BEF south to join the shattered fragments of the French Ninth and Seventh Armies in forming a line on the Somme, he failed. On the contrary, his "gloomy" visit to Gort at midnight on May 19 seems to have been the point at which it first dawned on the British commander that the only way to save the BEF might be to carry out a fighting retreat to Dunkirk and evacuate it altogether. Gort was the bravest of generals, and the least "political"— that and his nickname in the British Army, "Fat Boy,"* may have

---

* Judging from photographs Lord Gort was not so much fat as stocky, tall, and broad-shouldered. He exercised furiously and ate abstemiously in a life-long effort to control his waistline.

led the French high command to underrate his intelligence—but he had not forgotten that his orders gave him the right to make a direct appeal to his own government if he thought that the BEF was in danger, and that preserving the BEF was his responsibility, and not that of the French chain of command.

It was all very well for Premier Reynaud to complain to British Ambassador Sir Ronald Campbell "that British generals always made for harbors in an emergency," but Gort was of all British generals the one whose first instinct was to stay and fight. He had loyally obeyed the few orders he had received from General Billotte over the last nine days, but Billotte now seemed to have no idea what to do, and assuming his information was correct Gort might soon have German armored divisions *behind* him as well as on his flanks.

In "guarded language" General Pownall, Gort's chief of staff, conveyed his commander in chief's concerns to the director of military operations (DMO) in London, whose reaction Pownall described as "singularly stupid and unhelpful," and who wanted to know why the BEF couldn't "make for Boulogne," revealing that it had not yet occurred to anybody at home that the Germans would almost certainly reach Boulogne before the BEF could get there, and that by moving his army to the northwest Gort would be exposing his right flank to the German armored divisions.

The next day ("A pretty fair pig of a day," noted Pownall) began with the arrival of the chief of the Imperial General Staff himself, Tiny Ironside, bearing an order that the BEF retire *southwest*, toward Arras—a reflection of Churchill's belief that if the BEF could move south and the French First Army could move north, they could meet and squeeze off the German "bulge." Pownall described this as "a scandalous (i.e. Winstonian) thing to do and in fact quite impossible to carry out," and he was right.

The BEF was only just beginning to consolidate its position on the Escaut facing west against a vastly superior force, and was now being asked to abandon that position before they were even dug in. Very fortunately, the news that Arras was already under attack by German armor made the order academic. From Arras, it must have occurred to everyone, it is only ninety miles by good roads to Calais and the English Channel.

General Ironside.

Ironside was a professional soldier, which is to say a realist. "At this moment it looks like the greatest military disaster in all history," he confided to his diary before leaving to visit Lord Gort's headquarters at Wahagnies, close to the Franco-Belgian border. By the time he arrived there a major French political crisis was in full swing. Premier Reynaud had reshuffled his cabinet, taking over Daladier's place as minister of national defense—Daladier was moved, reluctantly, sideways to the Ministry of Foreign Affairs—while Reynaud retained his own place as *Président du Conseil*. Daladier had fiercely defended his protégé General Gamelin, despite ample evidence that Gamelin had no idea what to do after his Plan D failed, but Reynaud sent him unceremoniously into retirement and replaced him with General Maxime Weygand, who was recalled from Beirut immediately to become commander in chief.

Weygand was reputed to be spry and lively, certainly a big change from Gamelin, but he was seventy-three years old, and his chief claim to fame (apart from rumors that he was the illegitimate son of King Leopold II of Belgium) was that he had served Marshal Foch loyally as his chief of staff for years, the supremely tactful spokesman for a man who spoke as few words as possible himself. As if these changes were not enough, Reynaud also protected himself politically from his enemies on the right by bringing the eighty-four-year-old (and some said senile) hero of Verdun, Mar-

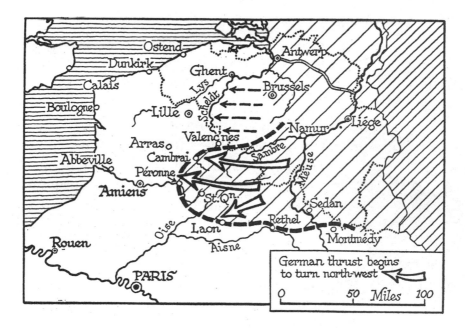

shal Pétain,* back from Spain, where he had been serving as French ambassador, to serve in his cabinet as deputy prime minister, a fateful decision for France.

All but the most fervent of the marshal's admirers thought he was too old, and those in the know believed he was also tired, pessimistic, and deeply Anglophobic.

---

* Marshal Philippe Pétain was an immensely popular figure, both for his victory at Verdun in 1916 and for his firm, but relatively humane, suppression of the mutinies in the French Army after General Nivelle's failed offensive on the Chemin des Dames in 1917. Pétain's reputation as an indefatigable womanizer did him no harm among the French, either. At one point during World War One, an aide, unable to find him in an emergency, went up and down the corridors of a Paris hotel until he saw the general's massive boots placed outside a door next to a tiny, elegant pair of women's high-heeled shoes.

Marshal Philippe Pétain.

Admiral Darlan.

Minister of the Interior Georges Mandel, Clemenceau's fierce right-hand man, described him as "barely alive—and what there is left is pure vanity." Nevertheless, Pétain's belief that France had been drawn into an unnecessary war with a poorly prepared army (thanks in his view to Socialist and Jewish politicians in the thirties) to serve the purposes of the perfidious British, who would let the French do all the fighting and dying, was widely shared, and not just by reactionaries or admirers of Hitler— the commander of the French Navy, Admiral of the Fleet François Darlan, never ceased to remind people that his great-grandfather had been killed by the English at the Battle of Trafalgar.

"Belief" is the correct word—for distrust of Great Britain was part of an ingrained system of belief, beyond mere politics, in which France was always the innocent victim. The Germans, after all, had only made their appearance as France's enemy in 1870, whereas the English had been fighting France for over nine hundred years. There was no child in France who did not begin to learn French history by hearing the story of Joan of Arc, whom the English had caused to be burned at the stake in 1431.

For a man of his age General Weygand made a remarkable journey in stages from Beirut to Paris seated in a rickety garden chair placed in the fuselage beneath the midships gun turret of a Glenn Martin bomber, which crash-landed on arrival. Weygand had to be "extricated" with some difficulty from the wrecked aircraft, and proceeded at once to pay his respects to the major political and military figures he would have to deal with. He had no immediate strategic solution to the problems facing the Allied armies; indeed when he was shown the position of the armies on a map, Weygand is said to have remarked, "If I had known the situation was so bad I would not have come," perhaps a sign that

already "he was thinking of his reputation" more than of victory.

There was no sympathy lost between
Weygand and Premier Reynaud, quite
the contrary. Weygand was an unapologetic reactionary, a "political general"
rather than a fighting one. Reynaud
had picked him, as he had Pétain, in
the hopes of disarming his political
enemies on the right, and because
Weygand had been so close to Foch,
perhaps expecting that some of Foch's
fighting spirit might have rubbed off
on Weygand, at least in the eyes of the
public. If so, he was mistaken.

General Ironside, perhaps embarrassed that he had been sent by the
War Cabinet to make Lord Gort attack
to the south only to find that he agreed
with Gort's decision not to do so, was
astonished to realize how detached

Joan of Arc.

General Billotte was from the battle—Gort had received no orders
from him in over a week. Taking General Pownall with him, Ironside set off toward Béthune in the hope of finding the elusive commander in chief of the armies in the north, and was swiftly caught
up in the chaos of defeat. "The road's an indescribable mass of
refugees," he wrote, "both Belgian and French, moving down in
every kind of conveyance. Poor women pushing perambulators,
horsed wagons with all the family and its goods in it. Belgian units
all going along aimlessly. Poor devils. It was a horrible sight and
it blocked the roads." He eventually found Generals Billotte and
Blanchard at Lens, near the old Vimy Ridge battlefield of the previous war, "in a state of complete depression. No plan, no thought

of a plan. Ready to be slaughtered. Defeated at the head without casualties. *Très fatigués* and nothing doing."

Ironside lost his temper, shouted at the emotionally exhausted Billotte, and shook him by a button of his tunic to emphasize his points. He must have made an impressive and threatening sight, broad shouldered, nearly six and a half feet tall and powerfully built, as he towered over the two French generals, both of them shouting indignantly back at him, but in the end it produced nothing, and neither did a call to General Weygand, the new commander in chief of the Allied armies, although he promised to come and straighten matters out himself the next day—more than Gamelin had ever done. Ironside returned to London via Calais, where his room at the Hotel Excelsior was struck by a German bomb as he slept, blowing him out of his bed.

15

"The Fatal Slope"

General de Gaulle.

"**T**HE WHOLE ART of war consists in getting at what lies on the other side of the hill." The Duke of Wellington's famous remark held as true in May 1940 as it had before Waterloo. Merely because the French were in a state of panic at the speed and impact of the German advance did not necessarily signify that the German Army and its Führer were happy and confident. On the Allied side, Winston Churchill still remained mistakenly convinced that the German panzer divisions would eventually run out of fuel or enthusiasm, and that the mass of the infantry divisions was a long way behind them, and exhausted, offering a ripe target for a vigorous counterattack.

This opinion was shared "on the other side of the hill" by the more cautious, and for the most part more senior, German generals, as well as intermittently by Hitler himself. Like a gambler whose first bets at the table have been successful, he was torn between caution and going for broke. In September 1939, when he had staked everything on his intuition that Chamberlain would not declare war over Poland, Hitler told Göring that he had decided to play "*va banque*" (a French phrase used in playing baccarat, which passed into German as the equivalent of "going for broke"), to which Göring replied, "But have we not always played *va banque, mein Führer?*"

This was true enough, Hitler's nerve had never failed him in the past, but it is important to bear in mind that he, like the rest of the world, still had an exaggerated respect for the French Army, and for France's position as a world power. Isolating and defeating the BEF, which was a tenth the size of the French Army, did not seem to him as important as defeating France and securing Germany's revenge for the humiliating surrender of November 11, 1918. Still influenced by Ribbentrop's conviction that once "the right people" came to power in London the British would see reason and agree to German peace terms, the fate of the BEF did not loom large in his mind the way it did for the British—or for some of his own generals.

As early as May 12 and 13 the rapid breakthrough of Guderian's panzer divisions was already beginning to cause concern higher up the German chain of command. General Ewald von Kleist, commander of Panzergruppe von Kleist and Guderian's immediate superior, attempted to rein Guderian in, both in expectation of a French counterattack from the reserves behind the Maginot

Line—the Germans estimated that "thirty to forty divisions" were available there for this purpose—and in order to give the infantry time to catch up with the tanks. Unfortunately for the Allies, no such idea crossed General Weygand's mind. Guderian argued that Kleist was "giving away the German victory to the French," strong words even for him. Their disagreement became so heated that Guderian threatened to resign if he was not allowed to continue, then made its way all the way up to Colonel General von Rundstedt, commander of Army Group B, and from there to the OKH, the Army High Command, and to Hitler himself.

Eventually Guderian managed to regain control of his fiery temper, and a face-saving compromise was reached—he was allowed to push forward "a reconnaissance in force" toward the west, which quickly gathered strength and speed just as he had intended, only under another name. However, twenty-four hours had been wasted, and as Napoleon pointed out, "Space we can recover, but time never."

Fierce fighting throughout the breakthrough area on May 14 and 15, combined with reports of heavy German casualties and lack of food, water, ammunition, and fuel, made the problem reappear almost at once. On the night of May 15–16 OKH, apparently suffering from cold feet again, ordered Kleist to "suspend all westward movements," igniting another furious outburst from Guderian, who sensed that his advance was "rapidly developing into a pursuit" and that it was by now too late for the French to bring up fresh divisions for a major counterattack in force. This time Kleist backed his willful subordinate, and on May 16 the panzer columns were freed to "advance westwards unimpeded."

By now the German tank crews were no longer bothering to take prisoners. They passed long columns of retreating French infantry on the road and simply disarmed them, sometimes ordering them to pile their weapons by the side of the road, then running over them with a tank to destroy them. There was no time to round up prisoners of war, or for the niceties of accepting their surrender; Guderian's goal was to reach the Channel as quickly as possible before the French or OKH had a chance to stop him.

*   *   *

Although Rommel's division was not part of Panzergruppe von Kleist—he was advancing ahead of Guderian's panzer divisions, on their right flank, as if it were a race to the sea—like Guderian, Rommel dealt with orders to halt or slow down by simply ignoring them, plunging forward in a plume of dust along roads packed with refugees and French military personnel fleeing toward the west, and benefiting from breakdowns in radio communication to keep his tanks going at all costs. When enemy tanks appeared he put them out of action without stopping and moved on, and wherever he found the way forward blocked by French military vehicles intermingled with the cars, trucks, and carts and horses of refugees, he simply took to the fields with his tanks and bypassed them. His account of one incident during May 17 gives a picture of what all the panzer divisions were experiencing as General Corap's army collapsed.

> Hundreds upon hundreds of French troops, with their officers, surrendered at our arrival. At some points they had to be fetched out of vehicles driving along beside us.
>
> Particularly irate over this sudden disturbance was a French lieutenant-colonel whom we overtook with his car jammed in the press of vehicles. I asked him for his rank and appointment. His eyes glowed hate and impotent fury and he gave the impression of being a thoroughly fanatical type. There being every likelihood, with so much traffic on the road, that our column would get split up from time to time, I decided on second thoughts to take him along with us. He was already fifty yards away to the east when he was fetched back to Colonel Rothenburg, who signed to him to get in his tank. But he curtly refused to come with us, so, after summoning him three times to get in, there was nothing for it but to shoot him.

This is a description of the horrors of war worthy of Hemingway (or perhaps Goya) in its matter-of-fact portrayal of a small incident with its brutal surprise ending,* typical of so many others as the German panzer divisions passed through towns and villages on their way to the Channel. It was not for lack of brave officers and soldiers that the French Army was collapsing; it was more because of fatal strategic misjudgment, paralysis of will, helpless pessimism, and political intrigue at the top, combined with certain areas in which the French armed forces were poorly equipped for a modern war, especially an inadequate and obsolete air force.

Over the years French investment in aircraft had been spread over too many different (and inferior) types, without a strong direction or strategy for their use—even a last-minute splurge on buying modern aircraft from the United States could not provide France with a first-rate air force. As for tanks, the French had more of them than the Germans and their newer types were heavier, better armored, and better armed, but they suffered from weak tracks, awkward refueling in the field, and lack of a well-organized system of radio communications. They had been designed in fact, like almost everything else in the French armed forces, for supporting the infantry, not for traveling long distances—the French, after all, had never intended to attack anybody. From the building of the Maginot Line to the formation of the air force, the dominating philosophy of French defense policy was to *avoid* a war, not to fight one. When that cautious policy failed, it could not be replaced overnight by a sudden return to Foch's attack à l'outrance of 1914—furious bayonet charges would not stop tanks or dive-bombers.

The truth is that neither on the left nor on the right over the last twenty years had there ever been a desire to wage war—indeed on the extreme right there were those who admired Hitler and the "new" Germany, on the extreme left those who still could not believe that the Soviet Union would behave with the same callous selfishness as any other great power and support Nazi Germany.

---

* Perhaps even more surprising is a German officer describing a French one as "fanatical." Fanaticism is possibly in the eye of the beholder, rather than a national or ethnic characteristic.

Nobody in France needed to be reminded that last time it had required France, Britain, Italy, Russia, and the United States to defeat Germany—and even then by only the narrowest of margins. Hardly anybody believed that France could win a war against Germany with Britain as its only ally, while Russia and the United States remained neutral and Italy threatened to join Germany.

Commitment to the defensive inevitably sapped France of its will, and ultimately its potential to attack, like a boxer who stands in the middle of the ring and allows his opponent to hit him without striking back. During the first week of the German attack, in the words of then Colonel Charles de Gaulle, "Our fate was sealed. Down the fatal slope to which a fatal error had long committed us, the Army, the state, France were now spinning at a giddy speed."

By a supreme irony, de Gaulle was called upon, now that it was too late, to take command of a last-minute attempt to slow down the rush of the German armored divisions. Immensely tall, austere, but with a scalding, sardonic sense of humor that does not translate easily into English, a devout Catholic in an army in which clericalism was controversial, at once an aloof intellectual and a fierce warrior, de Gaulle had fought heroically in the First World War—he was seriously wounded, gassed, and taken prisoner during the Battle of Verdun, that epic ten-month conflict in which the Germans attempted "to bleed the French army to death," but which ended in a stalemate that cost over 750,000* casualties to both sides—perhaps the bloodiest battle in history. An aide and protégé of Marshal Pétain, the victor of Verdun, de Gaulle's belief that mechanized warfare would transform the battlefield, boldly outlined in a book that was greeted with skepticism and outright ridicule in France, had slowed his promotion, and rendered him anathema to many of his own chiefs. De Gaulle had prophesied that relatively small numbers of fast-moving tanks would pierce

---

* Some estimates put the number of casualties at Verdun closer to a million. The remains of bodies are still being dug up today, with no end in sight.

even the best-planned and strongest of defensive lines ("the fixed and continuous front," as de Gaulle described it with contempt) and swiftly paralyze an army by disrupting its lines of communication, thus dismissing at one stroke both French strategy and the Maginot Line. Guderian proved the validity of de Gaulle's thesis in less than a week.

De Gaulle's admiration for his former *grand chef* Marshal Pétain was also ironical, and curiously self-revealing. He recognized the older man's contempt for people of less intelligence and courage than himself, his colossal vanity that could never be satisfied by "the bitter caresses" of mere military glory, his tendency to identify himself with France as if they were one and the same. De Gaulle's description of Pétain's character is a perceptive, and perhaps also an unconscious, self-portrait: "Too proud for intrigue, too forceful for mediocrity, too ambitious to be a mere time-server, he nourished in his solitude a passion for domination. . . ."

The day after the German attack on the west on May 10 de Gaulle was ordered to take command of the 4th Armored Division, which did not yet exist, but was being cobbled together out of bits and pieces of other units, and to assemble it as rapidly as possible at Laon. Treated with a certain, but predictable, coldness at the GQG in Vincennes, he was greeted with slightly greater, if patronizing, warmth by General Georges at his headquarters on May 15. "There, de Gaulle! For you, who have so long held the ideas which the enemy is putting into practice, here is the chance to act."

De Gaulle set up his headquarters at Bruyère, south of Laon, and perceived at once that the enemy was moving directly west, with his flank on the Serre River. His reconnaissance was slowed by "miserable processions of refugees" and by soldiers who had been told to surrender their weapon and "make off to the south so as not to clutter up the roads." The spectacle moved de Gaulle powerfully: "At the sight of those bewildered people and of those soldiers in rout, at the tale, too, of that contemptuous piece of insolence of the enemy's, I felt myself bourne up by a limitless fury. Ah! It's too stupid! The war is beginning as badly as it could. Therefore it must go on. For that the world is wide. If I live, I will fight, wherever I must, as long as I must, until the enemy is defeated and the national stain washed clean. All I have managed to do since was resolved upon that day."

De Gaulle was a natural leader of men. Not only did he tower over them in height; he dominated them by his cold courage, his forceful mind, and his contempt for those who did not live up to his standards—or to the country's, for de Gaulle believed, and would always believe, that "France cannot be France without greatness."

He put his ramshackle, improvised, and untrained armored division into action by dawn on May 17, sweeping twelve miles forward toward Montcornet, on the Serre River, under constant attack from German dive-bombers. By nightfall he had taken 130 German prisoners, and given a rude shock to German troops of the 1st Panzer Division who had crossed the Serre.

On the nineteenth he regrouped and attacked again, this time to the north of Laon, but without air support and woefully short of infantry he was unable to cross the Serre, and was ordered by General Georges to break off the attack. De Gaulle has been criticized by even so eminent, fair-minded, and Francophile a military historian as Sir Alistair Horne for transforming this comparatively small and ineffective engagement into an element of his own myth, but while there is some truth to that (it did not slow down Guderian, who did not even bother to report the incident to Kleist), for de Gaulle it had a whole other significance. In the vast military chaos that stretched from the Maginot Line to the English Channel, he had attacked, inflicted casualties, taken prisoners, his men had fought aggressively and well, he was not wrong to believe that if four or five similar French armored divisions had been available to attack the left wing of the German panzer thrust, history might have been dramatically altered. He could not help "imagining what the mechanized army of which [he] had so long dreamed could have done," and he was right. But it did not exist.

*　　*　　*

De Gaulle would repeat his feat at Abbeville, moving his division one hundred fifty-five miles west in five days, itself no mean accomplishment, to form part of a last-ditch Anglo-French attack intended to cut off and destroy the German bridgehead over the Somme. This too failed, with heavy losses on both sides, but the three-day battle would reverberate up the German chain of command with serious consequences, and would give de Gaulle a reputation that would bring him to the French cabinet as under-secretary of state for national defense, and, at last, to the rank of brigadier general, which he would hold for life—even as president of the Fifth Republic he would almost always be referred to by everyone as "General de Gaulle," or as "*le général,*" as if no other identification was necessary.

16

"Hard and Heavy Tidings"

UNFORTUNATELY DE GAULLE'S attack passed almost unnoticed in Britain. The *Times* reported that the BEF had been withdrawn from Brussels (bad news for Belgium, but not seen as so serious from London) and that a "readjustment of the front" was taking place, a masterly phrase—one senses Brendan Bracken's hand at work here—to cover a widespread retreat. The Air Ministry, never at a loss for producing good news from disaster, boasted shooting down over 1,000 German aircraft in a week—in fact the Luftwaffe lost only 1,266 aircraft during the *entire* campaign, nearly 300 of them as a result of accidents. The more popular papers reported that German attacks were being "repulsed," although even the tabloid papers had at last woken up to the fact that the French and British armies had effectively broken off any attempt to hold a line in Belgium, and that the main thrust of the German Army was no longer there, but across the Meuse and directly toward the English Channel. It did not require any great degree of strategic knowledge to look at the maps on the front page of the newspapers and see that once the Germans reached the sea the BEF, at least one French army, and the entire Belgian Army would be cut off from the bulk of the French Army and effectively surrounded, with their backs to the sea.

My father, who was good at reading maps, glanced at the morning newspapers and silently shook his head in dismay, then went off to the studio to wrestle with the problems of producing *The Thief of Baghdad*, the sets for which now took up most of the soundstages at Denham, and to begin the rough sketches for the sets for *That Hamilton Woman*. That the film was to be about Admiral Nelson had not been explained to him—the script had not been completed and he had somehow been given to suppose it was to be about the Duke of Wellington and the Battle of Waterloo, and he had painted several views of an elaborate ballroom for the famous

Vivien Leigh and Laurence Olivier in *That Hamilton Woman*.

ball in Brussels that preceded the battle. When he showed them to my uncle Alex he shook his head in annoyance and said, "No, no, Vincikém,* it's about the bloody admiral, not the bloody general— tear it all up and draw me a bedroom in a palace in Naples, for God's sake!"

As for my mother, she went off to work at the theater every night, apparently determined not to let the news diminish her normal high spirits, and by lucky chance I was so far spared the disruptions taking place on what was becoming referred to, no longer altogether facetiously, as "the home front." Clare Boothe, yet another friend of my uncle Alex's of course, noted that the government "continued to agitate (rather uselessly) for Londoners again to evacuate their children, who had been drifting back to London all winter and spring," but in fact the pressures on families to evacuate their children were much more powerful than she supposed.

Operation Pied Piper, once it was set in motion, ground on remorselessly like any other civil service project—slum clearance, say, or tax collection. By keeping me moving between Hampstead, Denham, Yorkshire, and the Isle of Wight, my father had managed for the moment to outwit the authorities, who were busy moving millions of urban children to places where they were not wanted and had no desire to be. As Clare Boothe rightly predicted, the worse things got, the more people wanted to have their children with them, as opposed to being placed in the care of total strangers by the state.

The great events taking place in France did not prevent Churchill from keeping track of even the most minor matters of government, or even for thinking ahead to the future and imagining how to win the war. On the day of de Gaulle's attack on Guderian's flank— which would have given Churchill a good deal of pleasure had he known about it—his son, Randolph, on leave from his regiment, visited his father at Admiralty House, where he was still living owing to his reluctance to evict the Chamberlains from 10 Downing Street.

---

* This is the affectionate diminutive of my father's name in Hungarian. Vince, Vincikém; Zoltan, Zolikám, etc.

Randolph Churchill, Coco Chanel, and Winston Churchill at a
boar hunt on the Duke of Westminster's estate in France.

Randolph recalled the conversation.

I went up to my father's bedroom. He was standing in front
of his basin and was shaving with his old fashioned Valet
razor. He had a tough beard, and as usual was hacking away.

WSC: *"Sit down, dear boy, and read the papers while I finish
shaving." I did as told. After two or three minutes of hacking away,
WSC half turned and said, "I think I see my way through." He
resumed his shaving. RSC was astounded, and said: "Do you mean
we can avoid defeat?" (which seemed credible) "or beat the bastards"
(which seemed incredible).*

WSC *flung his Valet razor in to the basin, swung around and
said:—"Of course I mean we can beat them."*

RSC: *"Well, I'm all for it, but I don't see how you can do it."*

By this time WSC had dried and sponged his face and
turning round to RSC, said with great intensity:—"I shall
drag the United States in. . . ."

This was a farsighted and correct conclusion. Churchill could not have imagined that it would take nineteen more months before the United States entered the war, but he had seen clearly, from his very first letter to President Roosevelt, that it was his first duty to nourish the president's sympathy for the Allied cause, and at the same time to use every means to persuade the American public that Britain would fight to the end, and that it was in America's interest to support Britain—that its cause was *worth* supporting. He was particularly interested in the part that the British film industry could play to that end—in which my uncle Alex was already playing a leading role—Churchill was not too busy to read the early rough drafts of the script for *That Hamilton Woman* and add some patriotic flourishes of his own to it.

His task of convincing America that Britain would fight, and more important would win, was not made easier by the pessimism and isolationist views of the American ambassador to the Court of St. James, Joseph P. Kennedy. There was little or no trust or good feeling between the two men, and no more of Kennedy's old privileged position, when for two years he had felt free to drop by 10 Downing Street for a cozy chat with Neville Chamberlain. It rankled Kennedy that he was obliged to pass on Churchill's messages to the president, especially since Kennedy's *own* messages to the president and his advice were often ignored, or replied to with the president's trademark cheery blandness when Roosevelt disagreed with someone who thought himself close to him. When Kennedy wrote that he didn't think Britain had "a Chinaman's chance" of winning, the president simply ignored it. In his letters and his diary Kennedy constantly refers to Churchill's drinking—Kennedy was himself a firm teetotaler although paradoxically the owner of a liquor company—and how "ill-conditioned" or "pasty" he looks, although those around Churchill all reflect the contrary, that he had never looked better or more energetic, as if crisis brought out the best in him, which was indeed the case. Like a nagging spinster aunt the ambassador never failed to remark on signs of Churchill's drinking, noting, "There was a tray with plenty of liquor on it alongside him and he was drinking a Scotch highball, which I felt was indeed not the first one he had drunk that night," or that there was a half-empty glass on his desk.

Ambassador Kennedy seems not to have been aware of the prime minister's lifelong habit of sipping a weak Scotch and soda throughout the day, at moments when a lesser man might have asked for coffee or tea, but there was nobody else who failed to recognize that drunk or sober a new and stronger personality was in charge. Churchill cabled President Roosevelt ("We are determined to persevere to the very end whatever the result of the great battle raging in France may be. . . ."), he paused to read the transcript of a telephone call from General Swayne, head of the British Military Mission to French GQG, speaking for security in the guarded English of a doctor about the situation of the French Army ("Patient is rather lower and depressed. . . . The lower part of the wound continues to heal, but, as I expected, the upper part has started to suppurate again. . . ."); on being told by Mrs. Churchill that the preacher at St. Martin-in-the-Fields had given a defeatist

Ambassador Joseph P. Kennedy, with his sons Joseph Jr. and John
(the future president).

sermon he recommended that the minister of information should have the offending clergyman "pilloried," he urged that Lord Gort fight his way south toward Amiens to make contact with the French, and finally, after endless drafts prepared on a special noiseless typewriter with large type, he spoke to the British people for the first time on the BBC and told them, at last, the alarming truth, in the first of his great war speeches.

A tremendous battle is raging in France and Flanders. The Germans, by a remarkable combination of air-bombing and heavily-armored tanks, have broken through the French defenses north of the Maginot Line and strong columns of their armored vehicles are ravaging the open country, which, for the first day or two, was without defenders. They have penetrated deeply and spread alarm and confusion in their track. Behind them there are now appearing Infantry in lorries and behind them again the large masses are moving forward. . . . Having received His Majesty's commission I have formed an Administration of men and women of every Party, and of almost every point of view. We have differed and quarrelled in the past, but now one bond unites us all. To wage war until victory is won and never to surrender ourselves to servitude and shame whatever the cost and the agony may be. If this is one of the most awe-striking periods in the long history of France and Britain it is also beyond all doubt the most sublime. Side by side . . . the British and French peoples have advanced to rescue not Europe only but mankind from the foulest and most soul-destroying tyranny which has ever darkened and stained the pages of history. Behind them gather a group of shattered states and bludgeoned races, the Czechs, the Poles, the Norwegians, the Danes, the Dutch, the Belgians—upon all of whom the long night of barbarism will descend unbroken by even a star of hope, unless we conquer—as conquer we must—as conquer we shall.

I remember staying up to hear that speech, and being impressed by the profound seriousness with which it was given—and listened to by those around me. Even my father seemed moved, and Nanny Low cried openly. My mother may have been at the theater, I do not remember her being there at any rate. We sat in the dining room, my father beneath the De Chirico that he bought in Paris before the war (he had once shared a studio with De Chirico in Paris), the dog at his feet, an old glass jam jar filled with brandy beside him—he hated such fanciness as brandy snifters and balloon glasses, and preferred to use his folding pocketknife instead of a table knife. At that age I could have had no real understanding then of what was at stake, let alone that the speech was only aimed in part at British listeners. It was aimed, and shrewdly aimed, at President Roosevelt, a kind of grand, almost symphonic reply to the doubts of Ambassador Kennedy, and at those in the Conservative Party and in Britain who, like Kennedy, still preferred Neville Chamberlain, and dreamed of appeasement and a separate peace. If we were going to go down, we would go down fighting, Churchill told us, and the enemy was not just the Germans but "the foulest and most soul-destroying tyranny" in history, as good a description of Nazi Germany as can be found to this day.

Over the next few days the bland optimism of the newspaper headlines would change radically to a tone of gravity backed up by harsh truths, which were now out in the open. Things were bad. They were going to get worse, *much* worse, and the French Army—as well as our own BEF—was in retreat. Although Churchill lavished praise on France, there were, for those who listened carefully to the speech, a number of hints that the battle for France was being lost and that we might have to fight on alone, and also several carefully phrased appeals for help from the United States.

These were followed a day later by a darker (and franker) personal message to the president, reemphasizing that the present government would never surrender, but pointing out that if "members of the present Administration were finished and others came in to parley amid the ruins, you must not be blind to the fact that the sole remaining bargaining counter with Germany would be the Fleet, and if this country was left by the United States to its fate, no one would have the right to blame those then responsible if they made the best terms they could for the surviving inhabitants. . . ."

This was indeed a blunter message than what "A Former Naval Person" had so far been sending the president, and a tone that President Roosevelt was not used to hearing either, very close to a threat in fact, and a good indication that at some level of his mind Churchill was already aware that Lord Gort was probably not going to cut his way southward to Amiens to join with the French, and that in the prime minister's own words "hard and heavy tidings were ahead." Churchill's moments of depression, "the black dog," as he called them, were not a part of his personality that was often on display, even to his own children (Mrs. Churchill was more familiar with these moods), but this was not one of them. It was among his remarkable qualities that he could look into the pit without blinking, or losing courage. He did not believe we would lose the war, but he would not conceal from his countrymen that it could happen, or disguise from them just how terrible the consequences would be.

For the first time it was clear to those who listened to Churchill's speech—and the whole country listened carefully—that all of the easy presumptions that had shored up appeasement, among them belief in the French Army, the legendary strength of the Maginot Line, the fighting qualities of the BEF, above all the hope that a deal of some kind might be made with Hitler at the last moment, were all swept away by his stark realism, and by the fact, now suddenly clear, that across the Channel a huge, historic battle was being fought—and would very likely be lost. It is no accident that J. R. R. Tolkien's *The Lord of the Rings* took on its length and dense sweep as an epic in that year, with its central vision of the Dark Lord Sauron's legions attacking an idyllic land not unlike Britain, as the apparently invincible armies of Hitler swept over

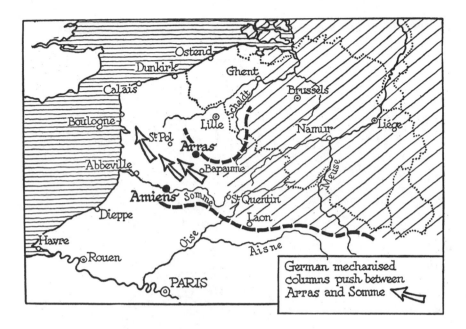

German mechanised columns push between Arras and Somme

one European country after another, taking familiar places that the British, the Belgians, and the French had fought and died for in the 1914–1918 war, ports that were well known to anyone who had ever traveled to "the Continent," and approached the English Channel itself, advancing swiftly toward the port city of Boulogne, where Napoleon himself had once stood, waiting for the moment to launch 200,000 men at England.

It is an indication of just how seriously Churchill viewed events that at nearly midnight of May 20, the day after his great speech to the nation and his personal message to Roosevelt, he perspicaciously told the War Cabinet that he thought as "a precautionary measure the Admiralty should assemble a large number of small vessels in readiness to proceed to ports and inlets on the French coast."

17

The Sharp End of the Stick

Gloria Swanson and her husband Henry de la Falaise,
marquis de La Coudraye.

THE 12TH (Prince of Wales Own) Lancers had been the first
Allied regiment to cross the Franco-Belgian frontier on May
10, 1940, and drive east through cheering crowds toward the Dyle
River, which their advance guard of armored cars reached that
night—the first step in General Gamelin's ill-fated Plan D.

Since then, the experience of the 12th Lancers mirrored that of
most of the BEF. They had, in the words of one trooper, been "bug-
gered about" for over a week, absorbing as an armored reconnaissance regiment the constant pressure of overwhelming stronger
enemy forces, bombed and machine-gunned remorselessly from

the air, and obliged to retreat from a line they thought they could have held into the vast chaos of a retreat from one line to the next. They fought to hold every stream, river, and canal along the way, of which there appeared to be hundreds, having been transformed overnight from the proud and dashing advance guard of the British Expeditionary Force into its beleaguered rear guard.

The 12th Lancers was an elite regiment that stood out even in an army full of regiments with long histories, many battle honors, and fiercely defended peculiarities of dress and behavior. Raised in 1697 as a regiment of "light dragoons"* intended to put down a Jacobite rebellion, the 12th Lancers not only fought the French in Egypt and at Waterloo but was honored by George III, who added "the Prince of Wales Own" to its name (after the future Prince Regent and George IV). Its cap badge became that of the three ostrich feathers bound with the Garter from the Prince of Wales's coat of arms, in addition to which its noncommissioned officers wore three coveted tiny silver ostrich feathers on their sleeves above their stripes. A "regular" regiment, the 12th Lancers surrendered their horses and converted to armored cars in 1928—a big change for a regiment a squadron of which had carried out the last full-scale lance charge in the history of the British Army, on August 28, 1914, at the Battle of Mons. Even in armored cars the officers of the 12th Lancers remained for the most part aristocrats or upper-class sportsmen at ease in the hunting field who prided themselves on their boldness, their stiff upper lip, and their almost feudal relationship with their troopers. Exchanging horses for armored cars had not altered the esprit de corps of the regiment, or its swagger.

Their Morris armored cars were far less well armored or armed than their German equivalents (as well as the French Panhard), basically an angular, clumsy-looking riveted armor-plate shell built on a fifteen-hundredweight truck chassis with an open-topped turret looking like an old-fashioned tin bathtub. It had

---

* "Light dragoons" evolved into hussar and lancer regiments and then were converted into light tank or armored car regiments.

Morris armored car.

a crew of three, a driver in a coffin-like armored box, with the commander and the gunner behind him seated side by side in the open turret, armed with a Bren light machine gun and the notoriously ineffective Boys antitank rifle. The Morris armored car had been designed with warfare against dissident desert tribes in Egypt, Iraq, and Afghanistan in mind, not for service in northern Europe against the German Army, and its armor plate would not stop anything much larger than a rifle bullet, but what the 12th Lancers lacked in sophisticated vehicles they made up for with espirt de corps.

General Georges had planned from before the war for a high level of integration between the British and French forces under his command. A Franco-British Military Mission of Liaison was set up with its headquarters at Arras, a prosperous and picturesque city in the Pas-de-Calais, close to the Belgian border. Selected English-speaking French officers were trained to accompany British fighting troops at the battalion level, not so much as interpreters merely, but rather as tactful facilitators intended to avoid

Belgian civilians fleeing.

conflict between British troops and French civilians and to act as the link between French units and British ones when needed. In some cases they rapidly became an integral part of the British unit they joined, despite wearing French uniform.

The liaison officer chosen for "A" Squadron of the 12th Lancers was James Henry Le Bailly de La Falaise, marquis de La Coudraye, who had joined the French Army while still underage in World War One and been awarded the Croix de Guerre, then went on between the wars to Hollywood, where he directed at least five films and married two major movie stars, first Gloria Swanson, then Constance Bennett. His marriage to Gloria Swanson turned him into something of a worldwide celebrity for a time, since it was the first marriage between a major movie star and a European aristocrat. Immensely handsome and courageous, a "man's man" to the core, but also notorious as a "ladies' man" on two continents (Lillian Gish gushed over the sight of him in a bathing suit on the beach at Malibu), Henry de La Falaise (as he was usually known to English speakers) was the perfect choice as liaison officer for the

12th Lancers.* The commanding officer of his squadron was "a high-strung polo player," a cool gambler, and a natural horseman, and the second-in-command was an earl—La Falaise must have fit right in from the first day.

Fortunately, along with charm, good looks, perfect manners, and guts, La Falaise had an eye for detail, and was in an ideal position to describe the battle as it unfolded. He was on leave in Paris on May 10, but he moved fast. By that evening he had reached Arras by rail, and he crossed into Belgium the next morning. He noted that the Belgian defenses against the French were formidable and difficult to remove once they suddenly became allies on May 10—the Belgians had played the "neutrality card" until the very last moment, perhaps even a moment *too* long. His journey toward the Dyle River to find his regiment was difficult, involving guile, good luck, and sheer determination. No rail traffic was moving east of Brussels, and La Falaise was basically a hitchhiker in a foreign uniform carrying his own kit toward the front line in search of the 12th Lancers, at a point when wild rumors of spies, German parachutists wearing Allied uniform or disguised as nuns, and "the fifth column" were rife.

Everybody's memories of the battle in Flanders contain incidents in which innocent civilians, or soldiers in the wrong place at the wrong time, were hastily executed in the panic that followed the German attack. "Better safe than sorry," was the general opinion in both the British and the French armies, and the safest thing was to shoot anyone who wasn't attached to a unit, or didn't have a good explanation for why he was on his own. A man alone on a battlefield is always at risk from his own side. Despite all this, La Falaise reached "the lovely green valley" of the Dyle safely in the late afternoon of May 11 (he seems to have been the only person to remark on its beauty), on the far side of which he at last rejoined

---

* His father won three Olympic gold medals for France as a fencer, and his niece would become the famous Loulou de La Falaise, fashion icon, much photographed beauty, and muse of the fashion designer Yves Saint Laurent.

his regiment, momentarily stunned by the ceaseless noise of artillery fire and bombs all around him.

When he was sent late that night to make contact with nearby French and Belgian units, his armored car was halted by "the flow of fleeing humanity . . . I can hear frantic screams when bombs plaster the road ahead . . . accompanied by the crash of nearby explosions and the bleating and mooing of the terrified farm animals."

The speed of the German advance was such that civilians suddenly found themselves engulfed in the combat zone and left their home or farm in panic—the first wave of a flood that within the next few weeks would put millions of people in Belgium and France on the road. The Germans contributed to the panic both as a matter of military policy—*Schrecklichkeit,* or sheer frightfulness, has always been the fallback position of Germany toward its enemies—and because the refugees unwittingly blocked the lines of communications of the Allied armies. The Germans bombed and machine-gunned the refugee columns mercilessly, which of course added to the panic, spreading fear far and wide and thus setting more people in motion. The burning of Belgian villages and the bombing of Belgian towns was carried out with the usual German thoroughness, reinforcing the impulse to flee. People set out with all the possessions they could carry, farmers even drove their own livestock before them (after all, they were a farmer's most important possession), while livestock left behind went unfed, unwatered, and unmilked, adding their cries of pain, complaint, and fear to the misery that was rapidly engulfing this peaceful, prosperous, rural corner of Western Europe.*

The fact that the Allies were withdrawing does not mean they

---

* Part of this was merely the immemorial cruelty of war, of course. The Allies too placed artillery batteries in orchards that had been lovingly tended for generations, parked tanks and armored cars in barns and stables to hide them from the German bombers, ransacked and looted abandoned homes, etc., but they did *not* deliberately bomb and strafe vast numbers of fleeing civilian men, women, and children or, at this stage of the war, target for bombing towns and cities of little or no military importance.

were not fighting. Gamelin's plan to hold a line on the Dyle quickly collapsed, partly because the Germans were moving too quickly to permit drawing a fixed line against them as he had intended, partly because he had not allowed for the overwhelming effect of German air superiority and the accuracy of the Stuka dive-bombers, nor for the collapse of Dutch resistance in only five days, but La Falaise's account of the next week of battle is a constant succession of intense firefights and soaring casualties, none of which seem to have dampened his spirits, or his uncanny ability to find freshly baked bread, wine, and cheese in the most unlikely places. By May 12 the 12th Lancers were about fifteen miles east of the Dyle River, the line on which the Allied armies were still assembling—and which, if they could hold it, would theoretically protect Brussels and the great port of Antwerp. They were about twenty miles southeast of historic Louvain, home of the famous university and its library, which the German Army had razed to the ground in August 1914, an act of vandalism that had shocked the world—and that the Germans were about to repeat.

In this tiny triangle of what is in any case, even for Europe, a small country, the Germans concentrated a devastating nonstop air assault, completely destroying countless small towns and villages. The Luftwaffe was virtually unopposed—the Belgians had no modern antiaircraft guns, the French and the British had not brought theirs forward yet, and the bulk of the RAF in France and what remained of the French Air Force was in action a hundred miles to the south, attempting to slow the German breakthrough from the Meuse to the west. The Ju 87 Stuka dive-bombers, with their slow speed and fixed undercarriage, were easy prey for British fighters, but in the absence of these—and aided by perfect weather—they flew in large formations and peeled off one by one to dive-bomb every target they could see, with remarkable precision.

"The Stuka was the sharpshooter among bombers," recalled one of the Stuka pilots, and British troops soon learned the importance of camouflaging every vehicle and gun, and of not concentrating at crossroads or in village squares. From a thousand yards up in good weather a Stuka pilot could see even the smallest sign of a potential target: puffs of dust raised by a vehicle on country roads or lanes, tracks of motorcycles and armored cars leading to cover in a wood or a farm, a carelessly placed cook stove, the barrel of an antitank gun sticking out of a hayrick leaving a telltale shadow, or a flash of sunlight from a pair of field glasses carelessly handled.

Soldiers eventually hardened to the infernal noise the dive-bombers made—in addition to the sirens below their wings, they had whistling fins on their bomb—and soon grew to accept the eerie sense of vulnerability that came from a sudden attack from the sky. A private of the 5th Border Regiment recalls jumping headlong into a filthy ditch for cover as he heard the noise of a Stuka diving, just beating a civilian to it as the bomb fell. When he stood up after the explosion, he saw an object rolling toward him across the road. "Who the hell is playing football at a time like this?" he thought, only to realize that what he was looking at was the civilian's head.

The first encounter of Allied troops with the enemy was usually the approach of a German advance guard of motorcycle troops coming down the road toward a bridge or village that was being held. Their motorcycle battalions were equipped with a high proportion of machines that had a sidecar for a gunner with a light machine gun. At the first sign of opposition the motorcycle troops dismounted and spread out under the cover of the light machine guns. If they could, they stormed the position, if not they sent a motorcycle messenger back to alert the tanks and armored cars behind them, with infantry in trucks and towed artillery behind *them.* If the opposition was more serious than they could overcome, air support was called in, either from Stukas or flights of twin-engine Heinkel 111 bombers, which flew straight and level and carried a heavier bomb load, enough to obliterate a small village. On both sides, casualties among motorcyclists were high—at a range of one or two hundred yards a man on a motorcycle is an easy target for a competent marksman, and standards of marksmanship in the British regular army were very high indeed. As for the British, almost every account of the fighting mentions dispatch riders lying dead or dying beside their machine, since the British relied on them to carry messages rather than on their relatively unreliable radios, and a man on a motorcycle presented a perfect target for the gunner of a low-flying Stuka or for German fighters.

Careful and detailed as Plan D was—and General Gamelin's staff had almost two years to perfect it—it still relied on wild overestimates of the tenacity and duration of Belgian and Dutch resistance, and on the belief that however quickly the Germans attacked initially they would sooner or later be stopped by a fixed line as in 1914–1918. The notion that Army Group B might get to central Belgium in strength before the Allied armies could even *prepare* a fixed line had been excluded from Gamelin's plan.

The experience of the 12th Lancers was typical of the bloody fighting that took place in the days that followed the German attack. The regiment moved well forward, nearly twenty-five miles east of the Dyle River, one troop holding "a small bridge on the River Gette, north of Tirelemont," with a Belgian division "fiercely engaged" on their left and a French *division légère méchanisée** (light armored division) heavily engaged on their right. The next day, La Falaise was ordered to drive forward with "the fighting lorry" (a truck carrying cans of gas and ammunition, a dangerous task) and after being machine-gunned by three Stukas firing from six hundred feet above him, managed to reach the point where one troop of the regiment's armored cars was holding a railway bridge across the Gette. The Germans were concealed in a line of trees about a hundred yards away, and had already managed to get a few machine guns across the stream, although not without suffering some casualties. "Three wrecked German motor cycles and six dead bodies [lay] sprawling on the mud thirty yards ahead," as La Falaise and his friend the

---

* These were *not* the equivalent of a German panzer division. They constituted basically infantry divisions in trucks, with elements of tank and armored car units attached to be used to support the infantry. Their purpose was *defensive*, not offensive; they were incapable of the kind of long, sweeping breakthrough being carried out by the divisions of Panzer Group Kleist to the south.

troop commander exchanged pleasantries under fire while watching German aircraft bomb a nearby village. By the evening the Belgian troops began to withdraw, and "loud explosions rock the earth as the Belgian ammunition dumps a mile away are blown up."

By nightfall the armored cars of the 12th Lancers were ordered to withdraw to the highway leading to Louvain. "An appalling sight greets us there. Enemy bombers have reduced this wide and lovely road to havoc and desolation. Trucks, large passenger buses, private cars, some still on fire, are strewn over it. One huge holiday bus has been blown up beside a wrecked house, its front wheels resting on what remains of the roof. It is still flaming like a gigantic pyre, casting a red glow on the pools of blood and the mutilated bodies which are lying about it."

The Belgians have come in for a bad press in history (and in the memoirs of British soldiers of every rank) since 1940 for fighting poorly and surrendering too quickly, but La Falaise captures in his narrative the terrible destruction caused by the German attack on a small, unprepared neutral country—a neutrality that had been solemnly reconfirmed by Germany as recently as October 1937. In

1940 as in 1914 Germany simply ignored Belgian neutrality, and rained death, destruction, and savage "reprisals" on the Belgian people, whose only offense was geographical: their country stood in the path of the German attack against France. The notion that both the Allied and the German war plan had transformed Belgium into the fighting ground for a major battle, and that every time the Allied forces "pulled back" or "withdrew" they were leaving part of Belgium to the untender mercy of the Germans was not one that was likely to inspire Belgian morale.

Later that night La Falaise reports more bad news—the two French DLMs to the south are falling back, taking (and possibly inflicting) heavy casualties, and the 12th Lancers are ordered to "retard" the enemy as long as possible. La Falaise takes shelter from a bombing attack in the cellar of a burned-out house, feels the presence of somebody beside him in the dark, turns on his flashlight and discovers "the mangled body of a woman, lying in a pool of coagulated blood a few inches from [him]. Her left leg is cut off from the thigh down. . . ." He stumbles over her leg as he leaves the cellar. At dawn he and the rest of the 12th Lancers stand in silent awe as wave after wave of German bombers methodically destroy Louvain again—rebuilt by innumerable donations from all over the world after the end of the First World War—the "ancient buildings fast becoming piles of stone and rubble . . . under a thick cloud of black smoke and dust."

By the evening of May 14 the 12th Lancers were back on the west bank of the River Dyle, only three days after they had crossed it, getting over the bridge just before the Royal Engineers blew it up, taking a platoon of German motorcycle scouts with it. In full keeping with the traditions of the British Army, La Falaise's friend Lord Frederick Cambridge (a member of the royal family, he being the nephew of Queen Mary, widow of the late King George V), a captain in the Coldstream Guards, sent him a bottle of "old brandy" by dispatch rider, with a note explaining that he was too busy to share it—Lord Frederick was fighting in the ruins of Louvain, where he would be killed the next day.

The following few days passed in an exhausted blur of bitter fighting, through one destroyed town after another. Caught up in the bitter, nonstop fighting around Brussels, La Falaise does not hear until May 16 about the German breakthrough farther south at Sedan, by which time he has been on his feet (and in his boots) for four days and nights, so the bad news scarcely makes an impact on him. On May 18 La Falaise learns that Brussels has fallen, and that the Allied armies are withdrawing to the Dendre River, with the 12th Lancers again forming part of the rear guard. Their fighting retreat takes them from the battleground of Waterloo to the sites of many of Marlborough's battles in the seventeenth century, and past some of the British Army's most terrible battles in World War One. It is as if this tiny patch of Belgium has been fought over for three centuries, and it is hardly possible to travel more than a few miles without seeing neat rows of British graves. Along the way the 12th Lancers continue to lose men and armored cars, pause to bury their dead, and move on.

La Falaise describes a typical moment, after a bombing attack:

A bright orange flame blinds me and a number of earsplitting explosions lift the car. . . . The armored car which was ten yards ahead of us, is on its side [now] in a deep gully. . . . For five minutes, we dig and push while another armored car skids and tugs at its bogged-down mate. . . . Our work is made more difficult by the constant attention that two bombers are showering on us in the shape of short bursts of machine-gun bullets. . . . My shirt and tunic are soaked with sweat from heat and fright. . . . Andrew, [the troop commander] who has worked twice as hard as any of us, finally straightens up and calls the whole thing off. All equipment and weapons are removed and the Major himself ends the life of the armored car with his own pistol, shooting the engine full of holes.

That night they "tear down the highway at full speed . . . passing bodies, wrecked cars and flaming farm houses," cross the Dendre River, and then drive on to lager for the night at Buissenal, about two-thirds of the way between Brussels and the Franco-Belgian border.

"The Major's voice giving orders to the squadron arouses me from my slumber," La Falaise writes, "I look at my watch. I have slept ten minutes!

> A small girl has just entered the kitchen. She has immense dark eyes, thick, curly, black hair and her skimpy pink dress is crumpled and soiled. She holds an infant in her arms and she begs for a little milk for the baby, her brother. I want to go back to sleep, but there is something so appealing in her quiet, assured, older-than-her-age tone of voice that I can't help watching her. Her right shoe is split open, her feet are swollen and sore and, while the milk is being made warm, she sits up very straight on a chair with the baby on her lap and tells me her story.
>
> She has walked all the way from Brussels, forty miles, in a day and a night. She is eleven years old. Her parents, German Jews, used to live near Berlin, but they had to flee when the Nazis came to power, and settled in Brussels. Soon they found jobs and things were beginning to look brighter. Then came the baby brother, the war, and the invasion. Once more they fled. She tells me that her mother and father are sick and that she has left them lying on some straw in a barn nearby.
>
> I can see that she has serenely taken upon her frail shoulders the whole responsibility for the family. She wants nothing for herself, only for her father, her mother, and the baby. Her only hope, her goal, is the frontier of France. She seems to feel that if she can get her family across the border they will be safe forever. She knows that they have over thirty miles to go, but she is a most amazing small person, in her absolute

certainty that the Allied troops are to stop the Germans—at least long enough for her to get to the border. I do not contradict her.

She asks me if I think it will be safe for her to lie down and rest for a few hours. "Because you see," she adds, "I am very tired, and my feet are very sore."

I promise her that I won't let her oversleep and will wake her up before we leave which will certainly be early in the morning.

The kind-hearted woman who owns the farm and who has overheard our conversation brings some hot water, a basin to bathe the child's feet and also gives her a pair of rubber sneakers to replace her worn-out shoes. Our cook makes sandwiches for her and her family, and, as the brave child leaves the kitchen, she thanks us with exquisite politeness and, with the dignity of a queen, solemnly steps out into the dark night holding her tiny baby brother in her tired, aching arms.

I follow her to the door and watch her as she crosses the courtyard and enters the straw-filled barn. As she walks away in the night, she suddenly seems to grow in stature and embody the spirit of her persecuted people as well as the undying determination of the human race to live on. And I suddenly feel ashamed of my weariness.

A radio operator brings us orders. We are to leave at 3.00 A.M., returning to the Dendre River to try to hold the heights above Lessines while our infantry withdraws.

There isn't an unoccupied square foot of flooring anywhere in the house on which to lie down and sleep; all the rooms are filled with refugees. So I roll up in my blanket under a damp pile of hay in the orchard."

La Falaise, perhaps because he is a European, has a sharper sense of what is in store for the young girl than his British fellow officers do. He knows that behind the German armies will be coming the Gestapo, the Sicherheitsdienst, and what Winston Churchill called "all the odious apparatus of Nazi rule,"* and that German-Jewish refugees, along with anti-Nazi Germans, will be among the first to be swept up and removed to concentration camps. He can do nothing for the young girl, he cannot take her, the baby, and her family in one of the 12th Lancers armored cars, and perhaps he has already guessed at some level what is likely to happen to them all once they are back in German hands. La Falaise is describing a tragedy within a larger tragedy, a tiny fragment, a sliver of the vast misery and suffering that is being unleashed on Western Europe. The frail Jewish girl in the pink dress holding her baby brother is both a symbolic and a real victim of French and British diplomacy in the thirties, of appeasement, of rearmament too long delayed, of American isolationism, of mistaken strategy and worse tactics. He sees her one last time, in a crowd of refugees pushing a baby carriage with one broken wheel toward France, surrounded by a vision of hell: "The road is a mess. Huge trees blasted by bombs, wrecked cars and transport buses riddled with bullet-holes bar it at several points. The bodies of disemboweled horses have been blown up on the embankments, and in several places men's bodies lie mangled and bloody in the dust. Straight ahead the smoke column rises ever blacker and thicker and bright red flames leap skyward over Tournai."

La Falaise is on his way in the staff car to scout the ruins of Tournai for the regiment, where he finds that every house is scorched and empty, the library is in flames, and the streets are blocked by live wires from overturned trolley cars, and by rubble. He cannot stop to speak with the little girl in the pink dress. There will be no Dunkirk for those like her.

By May 20 the 12th Lancers have crossed the frontier back into France only to learn that Arras, which just ten days ago was the headquarters of the British Expeditionary Force and of the Franco-

---

* House of Commons, June 4, 1940.

British Military Mission of Liaison, is already under attack by German tanks, and a plume of smoke rises from the city. Just a few miles from Arras, La Falaise's armored car is halted at a level crossing by a massive traffic jam caused by French artillery moving south while French infantry in trucks is moving north—a symptom of the collapse of the French command and control over the battle—and he discovers a dejected railway worker staring at a huge, overturned locomotive blocking the tracks. La Falaise asks why nobody is trying to clear the railway line. The railwayman "answers with a shrug: 'What the hell is the use? *Les Boches* have cut the line south of Arras.'"

For the first time, La Falaise realizes the full import of what has happened. "The long, steel cord which joined us to the heart of France," as he describes it, has been cut, the German breakthrough from the Meuse at Sedan has severed the connection between the French armies in the north and the bulk of the French Army to the west and south, leaving the BEF with no place to go but the sea, and stranding what remains of the Belgian Army in a tiny corner of northwestern Belgium.

Ordered to proceed toward Arras and see whether it is in German hands, La Falaise observes vast clouds thrown up by the long columns of refugees, French now, instead of Belgian, then realizes that the Germans are using the dust clouds to slip tanks in among the fleeing civilians and their cars, carts, and horses. The sound of a massive artillery barrage and bombing proves that Arras is still holding out, but then a German tank opens fire, punching a hole in one of the troop's armored cars, wounding one of its crew and killing another, and by the late afternoon the troop pauses, not far from Arras, to bury its dead in a "quiet pasture, surrounded by thick green hedges . . . reminiscent of an English landscape."

Settling down to defend a village for the night with some French armored cars of the 1st Cuirassiers,* La Falaise learns that the

---

* Cuirassiers were elite "heavy cavalry," wearing breastplates, brightly crested metal helmets, and thigh-high boots, like the Horse Guards in Britain, now converted to the "armored role" of tanks and armored cars.

French 1st DLM has experienced "staggering" losses, and over 80 percent of its tanks and armored cars have been destroyed. As for news from the world outside, the rumor is that General Gamelin and General Corap, commander of the French Ninth Army on the Meuse, have committed suicide. While nobody seems to believe this rumor, which was in fact untrue, the general feeling of the Cuirassiers officers is that they *ought* to have done so, given what a mess they have made of things.

By midnight they receive orders to take part in a last-ditch attempt to relieve Arras, which is visible in the dark as a vast, glowing fire on the horizon.

18

The Battle of Arras: "We May Be *foutu*"

Churchill, Lord Gort, and Pownall.

THERE IS NO way that the 12th Lancers could have known that their fate was being determined as part of a major discussion of strategy taking place between the War Cabinet in London, the French government, the Grand Quartier Général, and the headquarters of the British Expeditionary Force. Lieutenant-General Pownall, who recorded with satisfaction on May 20 that British infantry had repelled several German attacks around Arras "with the bayonet," also predicted that if a vigorous counterattack was not carried out successfully the next day, "we may be *foutu*."*

Pownall had already communicated this dire view of the BEF's situation through the proper channels to General Ironside, chief of the Imperial General Staff, who had presented it to the War Cabinet the day before, where it was vigorously opposed by the prime minister—perhaps explaining why Pownall, though he went on to fill many important staff posts during the rest of the war, never rose above the rank of lieutenant-general. Churchill insisted instead that the BEF "must fight its way southwards towards Amiens to make contact with the French," although how this was to be squared with the fact that two corps of the BEF were fighting tooth and nail to hold Arras, nearly fifty miles northeast of Amiens, or that German tanks were already reported to have arrived in Abbeville, at the mouth of the Somme River, well behind and to the right of the BEF, was not explained either by the prime minister or by General Ironside, who should have known better. It was all very well to argue, as Churchill did, against "the proposal to fall back on the Channel ports," but short of a miracle the BEF—together with what remained of the Belgian Army on its left and substantial remnants of the French First Army to its south—was about to be cut off on three sides with its back to the sea. As for the Channel ports, once the German panzer divisions reached Abbeville, they had only to turn east and roll them up one by one, first Boulogne, then Calais, then Dunkirk. The BEF would be lucky to reach one of them before the Germans did. In the event it was only by perhaps the biggest German mistake of the war that the BEF would reach Dunkirk, less than fifty miles away to the north.

Even the hint that the BEF might be hurled off toward Amiens dismayed the Belgians, who would either have to advance in tandem on the BEF's left, for which they had neither the vehicles nor the stomach (they would, after all, be moving *away* from their own

------

* *foutu* = fucked. General Pownall followed the delicate English tradition of putting obscenities into French in his diary.

country), or be left behind on their own, on the line of the Escaut River, which they could hardly hope to hold for long. Admiral of the Fleet Sir Roger Keyes, Churchill's personal liaison with the king of the Belgians, passed on the king's growing alarm and was sternly ordered to keep His Majesty in line. "Essential to secure our communications southward . . . ," Churchill cabled back to Keyes. "Use all your influence to persuade your friend [the king] to conform to our movements. . . . Belgian Army should keep hold of our seaward flank. No question of capitulation for anyone."

Looked at on a map, the "bulge" of the German armored thrust was less than thirty miles wide, so it is easy to see why it appeared possible, looking at a map in London, that a concerted attack eastward by the French Third Army toward Amiens and Bapaume, and by the BEF attacking southwest from Lens to join them, could meet in the middle, sever the German line of communications, and reconnect the Allied armies of the north with those farther west and south.

This was also the substance of the so-called Weygand Plan, which Weygand had adopted almost at once upon replacing General Gamelin as commander in chief on May 20. So urgently did General Weygand view the importance of this plan that he set off early the next morning to meet with the king of the Belgians, Lord Gort, and General Billotte in Ypres, against the advice of Premier Reynaud and Marshal Pétain, who feared for his safety. Communications between Paris and the armies of the north were by then almost completely cut off—the Germans had severed the telephone cable at Abbeville, and Weygand's original intention of making the journey by train and then by car had proved impossible, so that it was necessary to improvise an early morning military flight from Le Bourget airport to Béthune, with a fighter escort. None of that happened as planned; instead the journey was fraught with difficulty—a warning sign that the organization of the Allied armies and air forces was rapidly falling into chaos.

The commander in chief, after innumerable adventures, landed at a deserted military airfield accompanied only by his aide-de-camp. The telephone there had already been cut and there was no car to meet him.* He managed to commandeer a military truck and head out in search of a post office along "roads [which] were already encumbered by Belgian and French refugees, who were dragging along every sort of wheeled conveyance, loaded pell-mell with women and children and animals and all they had been able to save in haste from their homes." Despite the "disorder and panic" of fleeing Belgian soldiers who had abandoned their weapons and joined the civilian refugees blocking the roads, Weygand at last managed to reach a post office with a working telephone to pass on a message to General Billotte, and after sitting down at a country inn next to the airfield and ordering an omelet he flew on to Calais, where his aircraft managed to land just after the airfield had been bombed and the hangars destroyed.

He did not reach the ornate medieval Town Hall at Ypres until three in the afternoon, which means that the commander in chief of the Allied armies had by then been completely out of touch with events (and his own government) for over nine hours. Even a seventy-three-year-old man as spry as General Weygand must by then have been suffering from days of exhausting, risky, and uncomfortable air travel from Beirut to Ypres.

Learning at the Town Hall that the king was delayed by the crowds of civilians (and of his own soldiers) blocking the roads, Weygand took the opportunity to chat with members of the Belgian government waiting in the splendid Gothic lobby of the building (including M. Paul-Henri Spaak, minister of foreign affairs, and future secretary-general of NATO), and with his quick intelligence soon learned that the king and his government were at odds. The government was in agreement with the Weygand Plan; the king was reluctant to leave the small corner of Belgium he was in, or to order his army to do so. Once the king arrived, accompanied by General van Overstraeten, his Panglossian "military secre-

---

* His cars, each equipped with a siren and the flashing lights of the commander in chief, had been sent off by train during the night and were nearly captured by the Germans at Abbeville, another sign of growing dislocation.

tary," His Majesty made it clear to Weygand that the Belgian Army was in no state to cooperate with the French and British attack; indeed it was only with great reluctance that the king eventually agreed to draw his army back from the Escaut to the Lys River in order to cover the left flank of the BEF as it attacked. Weygand, like Lord Gort, actually wanted the Belgians to withdraw even farther back, to the Yser River, which would have given all three armies a straight line to defend close to the Franco-Belgian border, but the king believed that his army would disintegrate if it were ordered to retreat that far, giving up the important cities of Bruges and Ghent and all but a tiny sliver of Belgium. Conversation between Admiral Keyes and Weygand was strained. Weygand did not speak English, and Keyes's French was so halting that Weygand had great difficulty understanding him. The fact that no interpreter was present also points to the chaos surrounding the Allied commanders. If Weygand was going to communicate with General Lord Gort and Lieutenant-General Pownall, how was he to do so without an interpreter? But none had been provided.

In the event, this problem did not arise. The exhausted General Billotte finally arrived, the "fatigue and anxiety" on his face evident even to General Weygand, but there was no sign of General Lord Gort. Jean-Marie Charles Abrial, the pugnacious French admiral who was in command at Dunkirk, appeared with the news that the Calais airfield had been bombed again, and would soon be unusable. It was apparent by now there was some danger that the Allied commander in chief himself might soon be trapped in Flanders and find himself unable to return to Paris, so Weygand ordered his aircraft and its escort to fly back to Le Bourget at once, and accepted Admiral Abrial's offer of a motor torpedo boat to take him from Dunkirk to Le Havre.

Even this journey was not without incident. Dunkirk was already being heavily bombed, the pilings that lined the channel to the sea were on fire, and one of its oil storage tanks was sending thick black smoke into the air. To steer a course that was clear of mines the motor torpedo boat had to put in at Dover, then proceed from there to Cherbourg instead of Le Havre because a new minefield had been laid in the Seine estuary during the night. Weygand did not arrive in Cherbourg until five in the morning.

Weygand might have spared himself the exhausting trip from Paris to Ypres and back. He felt "a very lively regret at having failed to meet Lord Gort," with good reason, but Gort had not been informed of the meeting until late in the day, and even then with no mention of the time. He had been delayed during a visit to the front, where he had made the decision to withdraw the BEF from the Escaut River back to the French frontier, so it was left to General Billotte to explain General Weygand's plan to him.

Judging by Lieutenant-General Pownall's record of the meeting, Billotte did not put forward the idea of an attack against both sides of the German "bulge" as firmly as Weygand might have done, nor did Gort point out that he was about to begin an attack of his own south of Arras with two divisions of infantry and the last of the BEF's tanks.* Gort also does not seem to have made it clear that the BEF, with its supply lines to Le Havre and Cherbourg now cut, was reduced to three hundred rounds per gun, that its supply of small arms ammunition was running low, and that even at half rations there was only enough food left for four days—still less that the alternative to a victory at Arras was to fall back on Dunkirk and attempt to evacuate the army, the only Channel port left since the Germans had already taken Boulogne and German tanks surrounded Calais. Billotte may have been overwhelmed by the problems of the French First Army as well by his own new responsibilities toward the BEF and the Belgian Army—he had not issued any orders to Lord Gort for over four days, or even attempted to make contact with him, so he may not have been fully aware of the BEF's perilous position, or able

---

* This consisted of the remainder of two battalions of obsolete Mark I and Mark II "Matilda" Infantry tanks suffering badly from "track trouble," since they had to "waddle" all the way back from Brussels because of the striking Belgian railwaymen's refusal to load them onto flatcars. The "I" tanks had not been designed with road travel in mind.

to take in what Gort told him. Unless Pownall's notes are at fault, Billotte and Gort did not make much of an impression on each other at all. If Weygand and Gort had been able to meet, it might have made some difference to the course of events. Weygand, if nothing else, was energetic and realistic, and Gort was combative by nature, poor Billotte was neither.

What *does* come through clearly in Pownall's notes is the pessimism of the king of the Belgians, who pointed out sharply that once Gort had withdrawn the BEF from the Escaut, the Belgian Army would have no option but to fall back to the Lys River, like it or not. The king had already made it clear that "the Belgian Army existed solely for defence, it had neither tanks nor aircraft and was not trained or equipped for offensive warfare," something that neither the British nor the French government wanted to hear. In the absence of General Weygand, General Lord Gort had no idea that the Belgian government was already at odds with their King.

As for General Billotte, he had already given his opinion that the French First Army was "incapable of launching an attack, barely capable of defending itself," and it is unlikely that anything he heard from General Weygand or Lord Gort would have been likely to change his mind. What he thought of the results of the meeting at Ypres is impossible to know since his car was involved in an accident on the way back to his headquarters injuring him so severely that he never regained consciousness and died two days later.

Thus, what was probably the last chance for a concerted reaction to the German advance from the Allies had come and gone by the end of May 21. Broad and sweeping proposals for stopping the Germans would continue to be issued from London, and received with increasing skepticism and impatience by the French government, but the two principal commanders in the field had failed to meet and agree on a plan, and the BEF now had supplies left for only one more battle, at best.

It would change the course of history in the most unexpected way.

*   *   *

Although General von Manstein's plan for *Fall Gelb* had worked just as he had said it would, the rapid advance of the German panzer divisions to the Channel coast continued to cause anxiety, as well as dissension between General Guderian and everybody above him in the German chain of command. On May 20 General Halder noted the importance of turning Kleist's panzer group toward the south as soon as possible, a reflection that OKH (and possibly Hitler) were more concerned with developing a full-scale attack to defeat the French Army as a first priority, rather than dealing with the "pocket" containing the BEF, the French First Army, and the Belgian Army. To Guderian, every attempt to slow down the panzer divisions on their way to the sea was a mistake. Once he had reached Abbeville on May 20 and cut the BEF's main line of communications and supply, he was determined to turn east and cut off any possibility of its "retreat to the sea." Like a horse being pulled back by its own jockey just as it approaches the finish line in the lead, he sensed the magnitude of the victory that was just within his grasp.

Better than anyone, Guderian understood that the rapidity of the German armored attack had literally *paralyzed* the French Army—the mere approach of German tanks was enough to make whole regiments abandon their line and their weapons and retreat. On the German side, the fear that the tanks must slow down or stop to let the mass of the German infantry catch up with them was baseless—the tanks had achieved a psychological victory over the French that was out of all proportion to the number of tanks involved, or to the relative merits of French and German armored vehicles and each side's antitank weapons. The mere *idea* of the approach of German tanks, let alone their actual appearance on the battlefield, not only undermined the morale and the fighting spirit of French soldiers but was enough to unhinge their commanders, whose training and commitment to a defensive war left them unable to deal with one in which fixed lines no longer had any meaning. The paralysis that had gripped General Billotte already before his fatal accident had spread to other senior commanders, even to General Georges, who also seemed bewildered by the swift pace of events.

The truth of Napoleon's remark that "with victory comes the most dangerous moment," was about to be demonstrated again, in the form of the British counterattack at Arras, which took Major General Rommel, of all people, by surprise. Rommel had captured Cambrai without any great degree of difficulty, and no doubt expected to take Arras, about twenty miles northwest, without meeting much opposition. Instead he collided with what had been named Frankforce, after its commander Major-General Harold Franklyn, intended to relieve the German pressure on Arras, which had been for seven months the home of the headquarters of the BEF.

Only sixty-five miles from the English Channel, Arras was not only a good-sized city and a transportation hub but also "high ground" in an area noted for its flatness. As always in military matters this is relative, the rise on which Arras is built is not more than 123 feet above sea level, but that was sufficient to make Arras the focal point in May 1917 of a five-week battle that cost the British almost 160,000 casualties during the course of which the city was largely destroyed, and it was enough to attract the attention of Hitler in May 1940.

The Führer opened his working day at eleven every morning with a prolonged examination of the military maps, flanked on one side by the slavishly sycophantic General Keitel, chief of the OKW, and on the other by the stiff, no-nonsense General Halder, chief of the OKH,* no doubt biting his tongue; the latter's task was to translate Hitler's thoughts about the battle in France into the rigid language of operational orders, and when possible to provide

---

* The OKW was the high command of the German armed forces, the OKH the high command of the German Army. Keitel was a military bureaucrat, Halder the exacting high priest of the fabled German general staff.

Hitler helps himself to soup in the field.

a measure of stern professional caution and advice. On the need to seize the high ground at Arras, Hitler and Halder were not in disagreement—nor was Rommel.

Although Lord Gort does not get much credit for it, he was determined to hold on to Arras for the same reason that the Germans were determined to take it, and perhaps more important had come to understand that as the German armored divisions rushed ahead, the infantry divisions advanced in what resembled a relay race to defend their flanks. If he could find a gap between the tanks and the infantry, he might be able "to insert a wedge into the gap," cut off the German armored divisions, and destroy them. The place at which he chose to do this was Arras, which had already been holding out for four days against constant enemy attacks, but given the time pressure he could only put together "a scratch force" consisting of the 6th and 8th Battalions of the Durham Light Infantry and what remained of the 4th/7th Royal Tank Regiments—not more than two thousand men and seventy-four infantry tanks, of which only sixteen were Mark II infantry tanks with a gun powerful enough to engage the latest German tanks. Like the Mark I, the Mark II Matilda was slow, heavy, cumbersome, and prone to mechanical and track failure, but against its thick, three-inch armor the ordinary German 37 mm antitank rounds simply bounced off harmlessly, which had a disconcerting effect on German antitank gunners.

Rommel had managed to get within two miles of Arras on the night of May 20, as usual leading from the front, only to find that his motorized infantry was too far behind to support the tanks. He set off to find them in an armored car and discovered that a few tanks from a French light armored division had "infiltrated his line of communication." He managed to sort all this out during what remained of the night and the next morning, and even to bring up some of his artillery, but he was not able to resume his attack until about three o'clock in the afternoon of May 21, with the 7th Panzer Division advancing toward the east of Arras, supported by the motorized infantry division SS Totenkopf on its left.

The SS Death's Head Division was among the first of the Waffen SS units to see combat, but the SS troops had not yet acquired a reputation as "elite" soldiers, indeed their level of discipline, training, and armament was still considerably inferior to that of the best army divisions. They were there for political reasons, and through a complicated series of compromises fought under army command while still retaining their link to *SS Reichsführer* Heinrich Himmler.

Heinrich Himmler, with his daughter Gudrun.

Many of their older officers and NCOs were World War One veterans, but while the SS troops were eager to prove themselves in battle and were brave to a fault, at this point in the war they lacked the iron discipline* and steadiness of German Army regulars.

Rommel had "put his Armored Reconnaissance Battalion in between the Panzer Regiment, forming the spearhead, and the Rifle Regiments behind," in order to secure the road and prevent a dangerous gap from forming between the armor and the infantry, but despite this his infantry was once again slow to come up, and Rommel had to go back to "chase up" the infantry. This was exactly the kind of gap into which Lord Gort had hoped to drive a wedge.

Rommel was therefore not in the lead among his tanks, his preferred position in battle, when the first tanks of Frankforce appeared, exactly where they were supposed to, near the village of Wailly on the outskirts of Arras between the German tank force and the bulk of its infantry, almost catching Rommel and his aide-de-camp Lieutenant Most in the open as they attempted to sort out a traffic jam of infantry, and causing chaos among the scattered vehicles of the German infantry regiments. Rommel and Most managed to restore order and bring artillery to bear on the British tanks, running up and down under heavy fire to give each gun its target. The British attack was turned back, but Most was killed while standing beside Rommel, and only a couple of miles away the German antitank gunners, shaken by seeing their shells bounce off the Mark II Matildas, were overrun by British tanks, the line of German antitank guns and their gunners crushed by their tracks. During the confusion of the battle, the troopers of SS Totenkopf were pushed back in retreat, a humiliation that would soon have bitter consequences.

Rommel eventually managed to stop the British tank attack with his field artillery and the 88 mm antiaircraft guns that would remain the most formidable of German artillery weapons through-

---

* Sometimes referred to as *Kadavergehorsam*, i.e., the obedience of a corpse.

out the war, and by the early evening had managed to organize a tank attack against the rear and the flank of the British armored force. "During this operation the [25th] Panzer Regiment clashed with a superior force of enemy heavy and light tanks. . . ." Rommel wrote. "Fierce fighting flared up, tank against tank, an extremely heavy engagement. . . ." By nightfall fighting had ceased, for the moment the British and French still held Arras, but Frankforce had lost sixty of the eighty-eight British and French tanks engaged, thus depriving Lord Gort of most of his remaining armor.

The repercussions of the Battle of Arras, as it came to be called, were immediate. As the most dashing and self-confident of panzer commanders, Rommel was not accustomed to being stopped or slowed down. He attributed his problems before Arras on May 21 to having been attacked by five enemy divisions, not a mere two battalions of infantry, two below-strength British tank regiments, and a small number of French Somua tanks. What shocked him was the fact of the enemy attacking instead of retreating before his tanks, as well as the thick armor of the Mark II Matildas. As the news about his check at Arras made its way up the German chain of command, it reinforced the skepticism and doubt of more-senior commanders about Guderian's "race to the sea." Conventional wisdom had always been that the tanks must stop and wait until the infantry and artillery caught up with them, and Rommel had now demonstrated in the view of older and wiser heads the truth of this.

The fact that Guderian's panzer divisions had just taken Abbeville, effectively severing the BEF's line of communications, seemed less important than Lord Gort's attempt to separate Rommel's infantry from his tanks, and the fact that SS Totenkopf, supposed to be the toughest of the tough, had broken and run as the British tanks crushed the German antitank guns and their crews, came as a shock to the SS and party leadership.

A certain caution made its way back—Kleist passed his concerns up to General von Kluge, who passed them on to Colonel General

General Gerd von Rundstedt.

von Rundstedt, commander of Army Group A, and from there to General Halder and the Führer. The consensus was that the advance westward should be halted until the situation at Arras had been "cleared up." Even Halder, Guderian's fiercest supporter, notes with a degree of caution, "The decision will fall on the high ground of Arras," although Rommel had already shattered the British attempt to hold it.

Seldom has such a quick and triumphant victory produced such a moment of hesitation and caution in the victors. It led to one of the decisive mistakes of the war.

19

"Their Zest and Delight in Shooting Germans Was Most Entertaining"

British Bren Gun Carriers advancing as Belgian civilians flee.

"THE BATTLE OF Arras has been . . . a most gallant affair," General Pownall noted in his diary on May 22, while qualifying that statement a few lines further down. "We are now tactically in an impossible position," he wrote, an opinion that would not have been shared by the prime minister, had he known about it.

On the same day Churchill flew to Paris early in the morning to consult with the French government. The atmosphere was some-

German troops entering Ypres.

what less panicky there, now that it was clear the German armored columns were making for the Channel rather than for Paris. Churchill and Reynaud were driven to GQG at Vincennes, where General Weygand made an immediate good impression on Churchill, who found him "brisk, buoyant and incisive," despite Weygand's difficult twenty-four-hour journey to Ypres and back—despite also the gloom that tended to affect everyone who visited the sinister, ancient fortress where Henry V had died and the Duke of Enghien* was executed. At one moment, the prime minister looked out the window and saw a group of officers, presumably the remnants of Gamelin's staff, "pacing moodily up and down" in the courtyard. "C'est l'ancien régime," remarked one of Weygand's aides standing beside him.

Weygand, the *nouveau régime*, commanded respect not only by his spry appearance for a man of his age but by his energetic and fluently expressed plan of attack, which happened to coincide with the opinions of the prime minister. Weygand too believed that Boulogne, Calais, and Dunkirk could be held with the forces already there—although his visit to Calais and Dunkirk the day before should have made him more cautious on that subject—and that a full-scale British attack "in the Cambrai and Arras area and in the general direction of St. Quentin," covered by the Belgian Army to the east, should meet a French attack from the southwest and cut off the German armored divisions. The fact that the king of the Belgians had already expressed strong doubt that his army could do that—and that Lord Gort had just made an attack at Arras that had cost him most of his remaining tanks—was simply not mentioned. On the contrary, the prime minister returned to London invigorated by Weygand's performance, and sent Lord Gort an order that "the British Army and the French First Army should attack southwest towards Bapaume and Cambrai at the earliest moment—certainly tomorrow, with about eight Divisions—and with the Belgian Cavalry Corps on the right of the British."†

"Here are Winston's plans again," complained General Pownall after receiving this order. "Can nobody prevent him trying to con-

---

* Executed by Napoleon for treason, the duke remains famous for inspiring the immortal bon mot of Talleyrand when asked whether the execution was not a crime: "C'est pire qu'un crime, c'est une faute." (It's worse than a crime, it's a mistake.)

† This may have been an error on Churchill's part. Since the BEF was facing south and east, the Belgian Cavalry Corps would have been on its left, not its right. On the right of the BEF was Guderian's panzer corps, approaching the Channel ports.

duct operations himself as a kind of super Commander-in-Chief?" Pownall remarked that at this point the BEF's reserve consisted of "only one cavalry regiment," and not merely asked *where* the Belgian Cavalry Corps was but doubted (correctly) that it even *existed* for any practical military purpose.

The BEF was still holding a long front on the Escaut, Pownall wrote, "defensive posts [were] manned by many old people, the 'labor' Territorial divisions, R. E. [Royal Engineers] construction companies, anyone we can lay hold on thrown together. . . ." Many of these troops had not been issued rifles (they had been sent there to dig, not to fight), and those who had one had received no training in marksmanship. Supplies of small arms ammunition had now dropped so low that Lord Gort had urgently requested the RAF to drop SAA by air, which the RAF was unable to do because of German air superiority over the battlefield, and even on half rations the army was reduced to three days of food.

There was still no sign of an attack from the French Third Army from the Somme toward Arras and Cambrai intended to meet the BEF halfway, as Weygand had promised. Chief of the Imperial General Staff Tiny Ironside in London remarked in his diary that

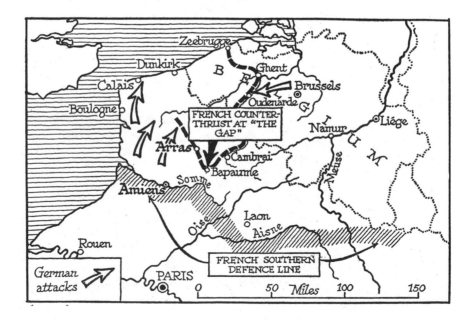

despite Weygand's energetic presentation of his plans, the French effort was "still all *projets*," implying elaborate, polished staff preparations for attacks that would never take place, a constant complaint that the British generals made about French staff work, which always seemed unconnected to the facts on the ground, as if faultless staff work were a reward in its own right.

"I am trying to square up this end to clear the Channel ports for Gort," Ironside added significantly, demonstrating the divergence between the prime minister's view of things and that of his chief military adviser. In Churchill's mind, the BEF was about to attack with eight divisions to meet up with a French attack; in that of Generals Ironside, Dill, Lord Gort, and Pownall the only hope of saving the BEF was to order a fighting retreat to Dunkirk and hope that the navy, aided by the RAF, could get at least *some* of the troops home to England, surely not *all* of them, and certainly without any of their equipment—tanks, armored cars, vehicles of every kind, guns, supplies, all of this would have to be destroyed or abandoned, nothing on this scale had ever happened in the history of the British Army, not even at the evacuation of Gallipoli in 1915, or the evacuation of Sir John Moore's army at Corunna from Spain in 1809 after his heroic death. "We buried him darkly at dead of night, the sods with our bayonets turning. . . ." One of the most famous poems in the English language—for some reason most boys used to memorize it in school—commemorated *that* defeat, but on May 22, 1940, nobody could anticipate that a British evacuation from Dunkirk would become an epic, even if it could be carried out, which seemed improbable.

By the next day the prime minister's "buoyant spirits" created by his brief trip to Paris had begun to subside. The minutes of the War Cabinet on the morning of May 23 reflect a grimmer note of reality. "The whole success of the plan agreed with the French [only the day before] depended on the French forces taking the offensive. At present they showed no sign of doing so." The prime minister, in the spirit of a man who has fallen head over heels in love and then discovered that the object of his affection hasn't done what she promised, quickly dictated a blistering telegram to Premier Reynaud, demanding that "French Commanders in the North and South and Belgian General Headquarters be given most stringent orders to carry this out and turn defeat into victory."

The chances of any of this being carried out were zero (it was received with a weary shrug in Paris), and some recognition of this apparently entered the prime minister's mind, since almost immediately after sending a scorcher to Reynaud he brought up the subject of making a "plan with the object of saving and bringing back to this country as many of our best troops and weapons with as little loss as possible."

A further grim note to that day took place at seven in the evening when Lord Gort gave what remained of the two British divisions in Arras the order to withdraw at once before they were surrounded, thus squeezing the BEF into a "pocket" less than fifty miles deep and thirty miles wide. To its south was the French First Army, now under the command of General Blanchard, only slightly less ineffectual than the unfortunate General Billotte; to its east was what remained of the Belgian Army; to the west, along the narrow Aa River and the Canal du Nord, neither of them a significant military obstacle, were the German panzer armies and the infantry trying to catch up with them.

Lord Gort may not have fully realized that by his timely decision to abandon Arras he would set off an angry row between the British and the French governments that would still be going on long after France had surrendered. Inadvertently, he had given Weygand one of the two excuses he needed for placing the blame for France's military disaster on the British—the withdrawal from Arras and the reluctance of the British to commit the bulk of the RAF fighter squadrons to France would become a constant refrain at every meeting between the two governments.

The former was a sensible decision given the absence of evidence that a French attack existed except as a *projet* on paper at

GQG; the latter would prove decisive during the Battle of Britain, which began two months later.

On the ground, fighting was intense, and bombing relentless, all the more terrifying as the noose around the BEF and the French First Army was pulled tighter, reducing the territory for both the armies and the civilians. The 12th Lancers had been ordered to make an attack toward Arras to help secure the withdrawal of the two British divisions there. Henry de La Falaise, with the 12th Lancers, described the chaos surrounding them on May 21: "The stampede of refugees has now become a matter of life and death for us. They must not be allowed to go on blocking the roads and impeding our movements. . . . Twice I have to pull out my revolver and threaten the peasants to make them turn back. These unfortunate people are frantic. They have fled southwards to escape the invader and have bumped right into him again. . . ."

He watched as German bombers, sixty of them at a time, saturated the area: "The earth rocks under incessant explosions and the atmosphere vibrates with the roaring of their motors." All around him were scenes of horror, dead refugees, dead and dying farm animals, British and French armored cars trying to make their way through the terrified mob, burning farms and villages. By evening the 12th Lancers were ordered to move northwest—their attack was canceled—with the even more dangerous job of finding just how far German tanks had reached.

Throughout the day on May 22 they were bombed, strafed, and shot at by German tanks. Two more of the armored cars were destroyed, several men killed, the commanding officer and one of the troop commanders wounded, the latter fatally. That night La Falaise bedded down on the floor in a deserted village café,

Barges on a Belgian canal.

with the sky illuminated by the city of Béthune in flames, kept awake by "tremendous" explosions as the Royal Engineers blew the bridges over the Aire Canal one by one.

An even closer view of the BEF in crisis was written by Arthur Gwynn-Browne, a lance-corporal in Field Security Personnel, attached to GHQ. Gwynn-Browne joined up in December 1939, at the age of thirty-five (an advanced age to join the army), after a career as a hotel manager. He had been educated at Malvern College, a mid-upscale English boarding school, and at Christ Church College, Oxford. He may have had some pretensions to being upper-class (Christ Church is the biggest and one of the most socially rarefied of the Oxford colleges, and he was for a time master of the Oxford Beagles),* but if so he dropped down the social scale sharply from there to provincial hotel keeping and obviously failed to get a commission when he joined the army, perhaps because the only sport he claimed to be interested in was tennis, rather than the obligatory rugby or cricket.

At some point between Oxford and the army he became a *devoté* of Gertrude Stein, the American-born modernist writer ("Rose is a rose is a rose is a rose") and cultural figure. In 1939, Field Security personnel were chosen for their ability to speak French, and were supposed to "assess civilian morale," "test the security of the Army's installations," and report on potential saboteurs and enemy propaganda. They were uniformed "snoopers," rather than apprentice James Bonds, and were equipped with a revolver and a motorcycle, making them rather independent of normal army routine and apt to be arrested themselves by the military police on suspicion of being an enemy agent.

Although Gwynn-Browne's attempt to write "Cubist" prose can

---

* He was up at the same time as W. H. Auden, Evelyn Waugh, and the aesthete Harold Acton (parodied as "Anthony Blanche" in Waugh's *Brideshead Revisited*), but there is no evidence that he knew them, although he calmly read Waugh's *Decline and Fall* while under shelling and bombardment at Dunkirk.

seem puzzling, he was that rarest of observers, a well-educated public school* Oxonian serving in the ranks. Since much of the time
his subunit was attached to General Headquarters, Gwynn-Browne
more or less followed its peregrinations as it retreated from one
château to another—at one point only hours before the town it
was in was taken by the Germans. At the time, the surest way of
telling where a British headquarters was located was by the number of motorcycles going back and forth to it—the shortcomings
of British wireless communication and the collapse of the Belgian
and Pas-de-Calais telephone systems made the dispatch rider, with
his leather gauntlets, knee-high buckled boots, and leather helmet
a necessary (and vulnerable, being a favorite target for low-flying
German fighter pilots) figure on or near the battlefield. The Field
Security personnel tended to mess with the DRs rather than with
the less sympathetic and more spit-and-polish military police.

Gwynn-Browne saw the retreating French and Belgian troops
go by in Avesnes mixed up with the refugees, "with their bicycles,
and bedding and bird-cages," and their broken-down cars, wheelbarrows, and weary horses. Gwynn-Browne even saw a steamroller
coming down the street at three miles an hour, pulling two large
farm wagons each full of at least thirty old people and children,
and "in the end one were two small dogs and attached to the end
wagon were two cows walking. . . . For four days and nights from
Belgium into France and across northern France at three miles
an hour in an open wagon under the black smoke of the smoking
chimney in a constant unchangeable shattering noise, this is how
these families had lived."

They were by now going nowhere, the battle was approaching
them faster than they could move from it, in fact they were moving
into it. The French soon grew hostile toward the Belgian refugees,
but Belgian or French they were a constant presence and could not
be ignored even by the generals since they "blocked the roads for
military movement," as General Pownall pointed out in vexation.

---

* In England, of course, "public schools" are actually private boarding
schools, and a basic class divider.

"Everywhere was refugees. Hundreds thousands and hundreds of thousands of refugees . . . helpless, motionless, listless, foodless. . . . I remember wondering so often about them why it was I could not feel some pity," Gwynn-Browne wrote, but neither did anyone else. There were too many of them to inspire pity, and even when a few of the oldest, the youngest, and the sickest were placed in cattle cars drawn up on the railway, they were left there on the filthy straw by the French without food or water (or a locomotive), then bombed by the Germans despite conspicuous markings of a red cross against a white background on the roof of each car.

The French troops retreating from the failed battle at Sedan were as miserable a sight as the refugees. "They had no arms and were saying that the struggle was hopeless. . . . They said that the Germans were invincible. . . . The streams of refugees were demoralizing enough but at least they kept the inhabitants occupied in attending to their needs. But seeing French soldiers just scattered and adrift was another matter. We found the people sitting in their shops and cafés, crying and hopeless, men as well as women."

Those drawing plans in London, and even in Paris, were unaware of the tidal waves of misery and defeat washing over an area small enough to begin with that grew smaller every day. The attack of Army Group B had driven the Allied armies in Belgium west to the French frontier and beyond into a part of the country with a bewildering mass of rivers, creeks, and canals, while Kleist's panzer divisions striking north and west from Sedan pressed them into a rapidly diminishing area, along with hundreds of thousands of civilian refugees from the east and the south unable now to move farther on or to return home without being caught up in the battle, and constantly under attack from the air. All war is hell, as General Sherman—and who would know better?—remarked, but the combination of military defeat and civilian anguish has seldom been as concentrated as this. Although there was a lot of firepower massed in a shrinking area, it was not being used effectively—General Pownall is probably correct that it would have been better to put the BEF, the French First Army, and the Belgians under the immediate command of Lord Gort, who was on the spot and eager to fight it out, rather than leaving it under the remote command of General Georges, who was neither, but to be fair the idea of putting French and Belgian troops under a British commander would have been a hard sell.

Gwynn-Browne caught the feel of it, when he found an obviously new and "huge French gun . . . stranded in a field, its crew indescribably dirty and about forty of them." An energetic commander in chief might have been able to pull all this scattered manpower and artillery together to some purpose, but no such person was appointed, so they remained three separate armies, each with its own strategy for survival, or surrender.

In one of those rare moments when the opinions of a lance-corporal and a lieutenant-general coincide, General Pownall paints a grim, but doubtless accurate, picture of the situation:

> This morning (at 9 a. m.) came news that a party of Germans, with some tanks, were coming at Hazebrouck where Brassard [the code name for GHQ] is situated. We ordered rear Brassard to shift to Cassel where (contrary to last evening's reports) there are in fact no Germans. But there are also no signal communications. . . . Our spirits rise and fall—sometimes, most of the time, the position seems perfectly hopeless and we are of course working out plans for withdrawal north-west; then the clouds lift a little and there seems just a chance of seeing it through. It's a wearing existence.

It was worse than wearing for those who were fighting from one river, canal, or ditch to the next—it was an intense and seemingly endless battle against heavy odds. Whatever the larger plans of GHQ or the War Cabinet were, nothing was communicated to the fighting troops but the need to keep on doing what soldiers have always done since the beginning of time. They did not get to see "the big picture," nor did they need to. They saw only what was in front of them, and apart from that were aware only of who was on either flank of them, and how reliable they might be. The Germans were not an abstraction on the map, or a nuisance like the refugees; they were the enemy at close range, and often the fighting was reduced to the closest kind, rifles, grenades, and the bayonet.

On May 21, the date of General Weygand's ill-fated fact-finding trip to Ypres, a private of the 2nd Royal Norfolk Regiment,* his company pinned down by enemy machine-gun fire near the Escaut River, close to Tournai, Belgium, a historic and oft-besieged city, saw his company sergeant-major, George Gristock, "crawling across this open ground on his elbows with his rifle in front of him. There were at least three other men behind him. They were moving towards a German machine-gun nest in front of them. . . . I saw him putting up his rifle and I heard him fire at least three shots. . . . I remember him reaching back, and throwing grenades." Gristock had taken command when his company commander was "hit in the guts, the back and the arm" and carried off on a car door ripped from its hinges since there were no stretchers. Gristock set off at once with three men to destroy the enemy machine gun that had wounded his captain and was inflicting serious casualties on the company. In the flat tone of the official *London Gazette*, in which all military promotions and decorations are recorded, "Company Sergeant-Major Gristock . . . was severely wounded in both legs, his right knee being badly smashed. He nevertheless gained his fire position, some twenty yards from the enemy machine-gun post . . . and by well-aimed rapid fire killed the machine-gun crew of four and put their gun out of action."

Gristock then managed to crawl back and secure his company's line despite his wounds, and was eventually evacuated back via the beach at Dunkirk to England, where he died shortly after surgery.

---

* The 2nd Royal Norfolk Regiment indicates the Second Battalion of the Royal Norfolk Regiment. When two numbers appear, e.g., 1st/5th Queen's, it means that the surviving elements of the First and Fifth Battalions, the Queen's Regiment, have been merged into one battalion for the time being.

For this "gallant action" he was awarded a posthumous Victoria Cross, one of only four awarded in the retreat to Dunkirk.

The official British war history, *The War in France and Flanders, 1939–1940,* is a chronicle of fierce and unrelenting hand-to-hand fighting to hold a perimeter around the BEF—whether it was going to attack toward the southwest and meet up with a major French attack from the Somme or (more likely) carry out a fighting retreat to the coast. This was a matter for the commander in chief to decide, as well as the War Cabinet and ultimately Winston Churchill, but whatever the decision, the survival of the BEF would depend on the ability of its fighting troops to hold back the enemy and thus prevent the disintegration of the BEF. Once an army begins to collapse into separated units and loses its will to fight, its surrender is certain, merely a matter of time—that process was already happening to the Belgian Army on the BEF's left, and there was considerable concern about the French First Army, to the south of the BEF, which was showing signs of fatal inertia at the top and weariness at the bottom. This was understandable— the French had borne the brunt of the fighting to the south, and taken heavy casualties, the Belgians had been pushed into a retreat that drove them out of their own country.

Now, on May 22, as the armies abandoned the Escaut and sought to reform along the line of the French frontier, the troops experienced "bitter and confused fighting" all day and long into the night—the 1st/6th Queens, for example, sustained four hundred casualties in two days (over 50 percent), the 1st Royal West Kents had to fight its way out at night, sacrificing most of one company, "thirty-four field guns were lost or destroyed," since "terrified refugees" blocked the roads that would have allowed the gun tractors to come up and tow them away.

Even privates could see that if the armies could not hold the Escault there was no good reason to suppose they could hold the Lys River, which for much of its length is quite narrow, but there was no dismay. A typical example was that of the 1st Royal Irish

Men of the Royal Irish Fusiliers preparing to defend a house—
note the bricks knocked out as firing points, or "loopholes."

Fusiliers, ordered to hold a line of nearly seven miles on the Canal
de La Bassée at Béthune, five miles south of the Lys, which would
give each company of just over one hundred riflemen almost a mile
to hold, an impossible task, indeed the British official history says
flatly, "A single battalion cannot defend seven miles." That, however, was their order, and they set out to do it.

Their approach to the canal was slowed by a "seemingly limitless
mass of piteous, weary, uprooted people," including "a demented
young mother whose ailing child had died on the roadside," children of all ages separated from their mother, and old men and
horses who had collapsed in the middle of the road, sights so lamentable that even hardened soldiers would have stopped to help if
they had not been ordered on firmly by their NCOs.

The canal itself, when they reached it, was narrow and had high
banks on either side, making it difficult to defend without heavy

digging, all the more so since their section of it was full of several hundred large canal boats that the Germans could make use of to cross over the canal even once the Royal Engineers had blown up all the bridges. In the end, the fusiliers had to send back for gas to set fire to the wooden barges and for explosives to blow up the steel ones, neither of which methods proved all that successful, since the canal was fairly shallow and the hulks merely settled on the bottom.

The fusiliers were too few to hold the Germans back for long, but they attracted a mixed force of retreating men and NCOs of the 4th/7th Dragoon Guards, the Argyll and Sutherland High-landers, the Royal Army Ordinance Corps, and two motorcycle companies of a French *division légère motorisée*, flotsam and jetsam from the battle raging only a few miles to the south of them. Some indication of the value of French troops, as opposed to their senior officers, is given in the account of Brigadier Guy H. Gough, DSO, MC, then the officer commanding the battalion:

> Later during [the] day survivors of French tanks and motor-ized units . . . trickled in in small numbers. Despite the fact that they had very few officers among them . . . [they] proved to be of a fine type, hardy, stouthearted to a degree and full of undampable cheerfulness. Their spirit of comradeship in moving to the hottest spots to help us, and in sharing with us anything from their weapons to their wine was worth going a very long way to meet. They were undaunted by the heavy casualties they suffered . . . and their zest and delight in shooting Germans was most entertaining.

These were not regulars like the fusiliers; they were French reservists, who often gave their position away by opening fire at too great a distance, and "suffered from a reckless disregard for con-cealment," two of the worst sins for a professional soldier, but it is interesting to note that when circumstances put French and British troops together they fought equally well, and were not discouraged by heavy casualties or the inability to speak each other's language.

This mixed batch of soldiers held their position for four days and nights of hard, continuous fighting against a much larger number of better-equipped Germans, despite unopposed German dive-bombing by day, heavy shelling by night, and constant German attempts to cross the canal. Only a handful lived to undertake the retreat to Dunkirk, but it was the stubborn resistance of men like these that not only preserved the BEF but was beginning to take its toll on the enemy.

The dogged defense of Arras (which Rommel had mistaken for a full-scale attack), the mounting German losses in men and tanks, and now the fierce, disciplined resistance of regular infantry, was finally beginning to alarm the OKH as news of it trickled in. Colonel Schmundt, Wehrmacht adjutant to the Führer, called insistently for news. The fact that Amiens and Abbeville were in German hands, or that Kleist's armored divisions were threatening Boulogne and Calais—all of these victories were beginning to be obscured by doubt and caution.

The painfully small number of British and French soldiers holding the line along the Lys River, like the 2nd Royal Irish Fusiliers, though they could not have known it and might not have cared, were about to make history.

Hitler arrives at the front.

PART THREE

Dunkirk

20

The Burghers of Calais

General Heinz Guderian.

I N LONDON A faint note of alarm had crept into the newspapers.
The Rt. Hon. Alfred Duff Cooper, DSO, MP,* Churchill's pick
as minister of information, did his best to put a cheery and optimistic face on things, egged on by Brendan Bracken, the prime
minister's parliamentary private secretary, but even the crudest
newspaper map showed a threatening picture as German forces

---

* Married to Lady Diana Cooper, a famous beauty, Duff Cooper became
a very successful ambassador to France and was raised to the peerage as
Lord Norwich. He was a hugely successful seducer of women, and his diaries, edited by his son, are fascinating and full of scandal. His biography of
Talleyrand is a classic.

Duff Cooper, as minister of information.

threatened Boulogne and besieged Calais. Although General Weygand got a very good press as the new commander in chief of Allied forces, and was reported—quite incorrectly—to be fighting at the head of the French Army ("WEYGAND TAKES COMMAND ON BATTLEFIELD," hailed the *Daily Mail*), there was still no sign of the promised major French attack from the Somme toward the encircled BEF, the French First Army, and the Belgian Army. "British Take Up New Line," the *Times* reported with its usual stoic calm, while Nanny Low's *Daily Mail* reported enemy armored columns destroyed or cut off under the enormous banner headline "GERMANS THROWN BACK." Still, all but the most credulous of readers could hardly help noticing the dissonance between reports from the war correspondents in the field and the blaring headlines on the front page of the more popular newspapers. The inside stories were notably more cautious, except for those from the Air Ministry, which were universally triumphant: hundreds of German aircraft shot down and German headquarters and supply dumps bombed to smithereens, as if the RAF were fighting a separate war—which the frontline troops believed was the case anyway, since they seldom saw any British fighters, and were attacked without letup by German Stukas.

My father greeted the morning and afternoon newspapers with his usual weary sigh. Korda family affection for Brendan Bracken and Duff Cooper did not prevent him, as a Central European, from recognizing propaganda when he saw it. Nanny Low must have sensed that things were going badly too, for she made me add the British Expeditionary Force to my prayers, and chose this moment to give me a small, leather-bound Collins Bible, a miniature "pocket" version of her own, about the size of a deck of cards with type so tiny that I can hardly read it now even with the aid of a strong magnifying glass. It was an expensive present, with gilt edges and woven gold braid end bands, printed on almost translucently thin paper, and shows few signs of wear to the black Morocco binding after accompanying me for seventy-five years. She signed the flyleaf and dated it: 1940.

Although I did not know it at the time, an almost equally impressive piece of printing was downstairs on my father's cluttered desk, a British passport, in those days a substantial, stiff document bound in gold-stamped imitation blue leather, proclaiming me a "British Subject by Birth." My previous travels, such as they were, had been as an addition to my mother's passport.

Now, without anyone's telling me, I had my own.

The bond between England and "the Channel ports" of France goes back to the twelfth century. All of them have been in English hands for long periods of history, and sometimes treated as English possessions. When Henry VIII's eldest daughter, Queen Mary (also known as Bloody Mary for her persecution of Protestants), was told that Calais had at last been taken by the French, she said, "When I am dead and opened, you will find 'Calais' written on my heart."

Until the postwar advent of cheap air travel, the British mostly

The White Cliffs of Dover.

entered France through the Channel ports of Boulogne, Calais, and Dunkirk. By the late nineteenth century all these ports had signs in English, English-style pubs for "day trippers," they were, at least in spirit, partly English, as well as a haven for those fleeing from England in debt or disgrace, like Nelson's beloved Lady Hamilton, who died in Calais, or Oscar Wilde after his release from prison. The Strait of Dover is less than twenty-one miles wide at its narrowest point—from Boulogne Napoleon had gazed longingly at the White Cliffs of Dover through his pocket telescope, from Dover Byron had "cast the dust of England from his feet."

This proprietorial feeling toward the Channel ports was reinforced by centuries of trade and shared, if unhappy, history—perhaps Rodin's most ambitious sculpture is his portrayal in bronze of *The Burghers of Calais*, commemorating King Edward III's demand in 1347 that its six richest citizens surrender themselves barefoot, each with a noose around his neck to be hanged in return for his sparing their city.* The desire to hold on to the Channel ports was instinctive, as well as strategic. So long as they were held, it was possible, at least in theory, to reinforce and supply

---

* The six men were pardoned at the urging of the queen.

The Burghers of Calais by Auguste Rodin.

the BEF and, if worse came to worst, to attempt to evacuate it. If they were lost, then the BEF was trapped.

None of these ports was ideal. Compared with Le Havre, Cherbourg, or Brest they were small, could only take a limited number of ships at a time, and even then not the larger ones, but by May 21, 1940, the bigger ports, with their huge depots of British weapons and supplies, were out of reach for the BEF, besides which the Channel ports seemed to many Britons like their only connection with the Continent, hence the famous joke about a headline in a British newspaper that read, "HEAVY FOG IN CHANNEL—CONTINENT CUT OFF."

By the twentieth century the French Channel ports were no longer the important commercial asset they had once been, but much British trade still moved as yet unmolested through the Strait of Dover. A good part of London's coal supply, needed for heating, electricity, and gas throughout the great city, still came by ship from Bristol through the narrow strait and up the Thames. It remained to be seen whether Britannia still "ruled the waves" in the global sense, but in the national mind the Strait of Dover *was* England. The country was still that "precious stone set in the silver sea / Which serves it in the office of a wall / Or as a moat defensive to a house / Against the envy of less happier lands." John of Gaunt's famous words of warning in Shakespeare's *Richard II* were quoted often in 1940, the Channel having lost none of its mystic and strategic importance since the old man's time. It was still England's "moat," and nobody mistook which "less happier" land was threatening it now.

Queen Elizabeth I, Henry VIII's second daughter, rode down to Tilbury in 1588, as bonfires were being lit from the Lizard to London to signal that the dreaded Spanish Armada had at last been sighted sailing for the Channel, to review her gathered army and proclaim one of the most defiant speeches in English history: "I know I have the body of a weak and feeble woman, but I have the heart and stomach of a king, and of a king of England too, and think foul scorn that Parma or Spain or any prince of Europe should dare to invade the borders of my realm." Feelings on the subject had not cooled down since that time, even though General Weygand dismissed the Channel rather snidely, though not inaccurately as "a pretty good anti-tank ditch."

It would have been unnatural for a government led by Winston Churchill *not* to fight for the Channel ports. He and Queens Mary and Elizabeth I would have been in agreement on that point despite the four centuries that separated them. Strategically, it might have made sense to concentrate what forces there were on *one* of them, probably Dunkirk because it was the closest to the BEF, but there was never any doubt that Churchill would prefer to fight for *all* of them. As early as May 21 the 2nd Welsh Guards and the 2nd Irish Guards, both part of the 20th Guards Brigade, were shipped overnight to Boulogne from Dover on two small passenger steamers, SS *Biarritz* and SS *Mona's Queen*, escorted by three destroyers. The 2nd Welsh Guards were still in training, in fact was in the *middle* of a training exercise in the pine forest near the staff college at Camberley when it received orders to "embus" for Dover. Twenty-four hours later the battalion was "fighting for their lives—and for the lives of many more"—in Boulogne, and thirty-six hours after their arrival in France those who had survived were home again.

German tanks were already close to Boulogne when they arrived, and the quay was packed with British, French, and Belgian soldiers, civilians and even German prisoners of war all waiting or hoping to be evacuated. One Welsh Guards officer noted, "In the midst of this very orderly crowd stood three or four men with led horses—the chargers of HRH the Duke of Gloucester* and the commander in chief, Lord Gort. I was sorry for the groom: he was obviously very tired and puzzled as to how he was ever going to get his chargers on a boat. Later I was told they were shot on the quayside."

This slightly grim note is altogether appropriate. The brigade's orders were to defend Boulogne "to the last man and the last round," but there was no way two battalions of infantry, even from the Brigade of Guards, could hold a whole city, in addition to which they rapidly learned that infantry, however well trained, could not defeat a determined attack by a large armored force. A British regiment of cruiser tanks and another battalion of infantry that were supposed to arrive from Calais to support the defense of Boulogne never turned up—they were already under siege in Calais—which made a prolonged defense even more problematic. A French infantry division was supposed to be blocking the German advance to the south of Boulogne, but there seems to have been very little communication between General Lanquetot, the French commander, and Brigadier W. A. F. L. Fox-Pitt, commanding the 20th Guards Brigade.

The 2nd Welsh Guards were expected to hold almost seven miles of a "defensive perimeter" northwest of the city of Boulogne,

---

* Major-General HRH Prince Henry, Duke of Gloucester, was a younger brother of King George VI, and at the time chief liaison officer of the BEF to the GQG. He had had a much hushed-up, but scandalous, affair, begun when he was on safari in Kenya, with Beryl Markham, the glamorous aviatrix (a major character as an adolescent in Isak Dinesen's *Out of Africa*, and author of *West with the Night*, a book much admired by Ernest Hemingway).

through which all the major roads to the city passed. Even with the
help of a mixed bag of French infantrymen, Royal Engineers, and
Auxiliary Military Pioneers (pick-and-shovel soldiers, not trained
infantrymen), this was an impossible task. The 2nd Welsh dug
themselves in as best they could forward on high ground, but the
Liane River separated them from the 2nd Irish Guards, so there
was no way for the two battalions to mount a coordinated defense.

Boulogne is a cramped and narrow port, overstuffed with history.
Its substantial walls were built in medieval times to protect it from
the English, and it contains the tallest column in France to mark
the place where Napoleon distributed eagles to the 200,000-man
"Army of England," which was camped in the hills around here in

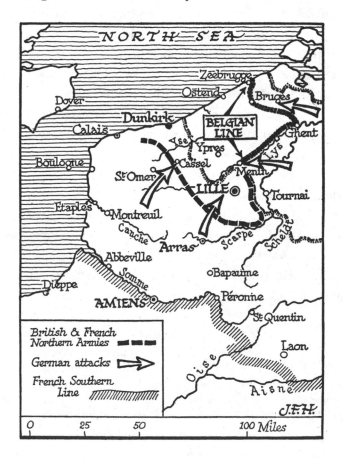

1803 and 1804 waiting to embark in wooden barges for the invasion of England that never took place. The ground rises sharply beyond the harbor and the roads to the "old walled town—known as the Haute Ville or 'the Citadel'—are steep." General Lanquetot took over the Citadel for his headquarters, to organize the defense of the city, apparently unaware that the Irish and the Welsh Guards were attempting to hold the high ground around it, or that his own division had been so badly shot up and scattered by German tanks and dive-bombers on its way to Boulogne that most of it would never arrive.

There were thus two separate battles at Boulogne, one by a small part of General Lanquetot's division at the Citadel, most of them the clerks, typists, and drivers of his headquarters, the other a failed British attempt to hold the high ground (2nd Welsh Guards) to the northwest and the area between the river and the sea (2nd Irish Guards) against the German 2nd Panzer Division (with the German 1st Armored Division in support). Because of the evacuation of the Rear General Headquarters of the BEF, part of a general plan to "get rid of useless mouths" from the Channel ports as soon as possible, Fox-Pitt had no radio communication with the UK, and no means to communicate with his two battalions or with General Lanquetot except by dispatch riders.

Not surprisingly the thinly spread British were constantly outflanked by German tanks, and as the Germans began to bring artillery and dive-bomber attacks to bear on them, they were obliged to undertake a fighting retreat with heavy losses step by step back into the city. By the evening of May 23 German tanks, infantry, and snipers had broken through into the city itself, and much of Boulogne had been destroyed. Although the harbor itself was now under fire from German artillery, mortars, and machine guns, the Royal Navy continued to send destroyers in to engage targets on shore and embark nonfighting troops. A French destroyer was sunk, and the captains of two British destroyers were each killed on their own bridge, though not before one of them, the captain of HMS *Keith*, had managed to pass the message to Brigadier Fox-Pitt that he was to embark what remained of his brigade rather than fight to the last man. Owing to the large number of wounded and "unattached men" it was some time before the fighting troops, who were now holding "a close perimeter" around the docks, could begin to board. Even so, 453 of them were left behind to become prisoners of war, which together with the dead and wounded counted for more than half the brigade's strength.

Perhaps almost as unfortunate was the fact that it had not been possible to inform General Lanquetot in the Citadel of the brigade's departure, so he woke up in the morning to find the British gone. The general and his headquarters staff fought on for another twenty-four hours before surrendering. This was yet another source of friction (and embarrassment) between the Allies, coming as it did on top of an angry claim by General Weygand that Lord Gort had abandoned Arras "without warning and without orders," which was passed on directly from M. Reynaud to Churchill, and which produced a brief, but distracting, flare-up until it became clear that since the French had not shown any sign of keeping their part of the bargain—an advance from the Somme to meet the Armies of the North halfway—Lord Gort had had no option but to give up Arras and make for the coast.

Edward Spears MP, whom the prime minister had selected to be his "personal representative" to M. Reynaud—once again Spears had been launched into the highest level of politics by his uncanny command of spoken French—was quickly flown to Paris in an RAF bomber to pour oil on these particular troubled waters, this time hastily promoted to the rank of major-general (he was only just able to get his new badges of rank sewn on his old World War One uniform, and even then left without time to acquire a general's cap), and the crisis passed with nothing worse than increased ill will and suspicion toward the British on the part of General Weygand.

That is not to deny that the capture of Boulogne was without serious consequences. The 2nd Welsh Guards and the 2nd Irish Guards had been ordered to hold Boulogne to the last round and the last man, and that order was then withdrawn. When it came to Calais, Churchill gave the same order to the troops holding it, at least in part to impress upon the French that the British meant business, and this time the troops would not be withdrawn.

Although the capture of Boulogne represented the triumph of the plan that General von Manstein had drawn up and that General Guderian had carried out so brilliantly, it produced no rejoicing on the German side. The panzer divisions had crossed the Ardennes unseen, then crossed the Meuse River and driven straight west to the Channel, all just as Manstein had promised, scything the French Army in two, isolating the BEF, and creating an anvil against which the hammer of Army Group B could crush the Belgian Army, all of it accomplished in less than two weeks, and with fairly minimal German losses. But Guderian was smarting over the fact that one of his panzer divisions had been held back by five hours by Kleist. Guderian had used 2nd Panzer and 1st Panzer to take Boulogne and isolate Calais, but the British resistance at both places was stronger than he had expected—the 20th Guards Brigade had apparently not fought in vain—and in any case it was Dunkirk that Guderian wanted. He believed he would have already have reached it had Kleist not interfered with him.

At a higher level, there was a strange combination of doubt and caution at the apparent success of the Kleist Panzer Group. To General Halder's fury, the Führer was still worried about the French Army to the south, no doubt because the bulk of the German infantry was still coming up slowly behind the armored "spearhead," inviting a counterattack. Halder's diary is studded with exclamation marks and snippy comments in parentheses about Hitler's concerns: (*"Pater noster!"*) ("That is the fault of interference at the top!"), as well as a brief comment about "the rather tense atmosphere" around Hitler, who did not share Halder's nerveless confidence in the staff work of the German Army. Hitler was displaying all the signs of a nervous crisis as he decided on his next move. A clue to his inner thoughts, however, may be found in Halder's diary entry for May 21: "Enemy No. 1 for us is France. We are seeking to arrive at an understanding with Britain on the basis of a division of the world."

This is not the kind of grandiose geopolitical thought that would have occurred to the orderly, practical military mind of General Halder, so he was clearly reporting a remark of Hitler's, without endorsing it. Evidently, the idea of "a regime change," as it would now be called, in which "the right people" in London would form a sensible government to replace Churchill and his cronies and make peace with Germany once France was defeated still lurked in Hitler's mind, doubtless reinforced by Göring and Ribbentrop whenever they could pry the Führer away from the map table.

It was clear enough to everyone that the next step—*Fall Rot*, or Case Red, as it was called—was to cross the Somme, cut off the French forces in and behind the Maginot Line and achieve a final victory over the French Army, and for this to be undertaken successfully the panzer divisions would have to play their part. One factor was the need to disentangle Army Group B from where it was, in Belgium and Holland, a huge task, but not a significant problem for the superbly trained staff officers of the OKH. The other was the question of whether the German tank crews, having fought their way from Sedan to the Channel, needed a rest, and of course the extent to which their losses could be replaced and their tanks serviced and repaired. Much like horses in the old days when a period of rest and shoeing was necessary after a long cavalry advance, the tanks were thought to need servicing. As everybody knows, cavalry troopers can be pushed much harder than their mounts; in the history of warfare it has always been so. Given the right leadership, men can handle starvation rations, lack of drinking water, lack of rest, but horses break down or die in similar conditions, nor can they be moved forward by patriotic speeches or martial music.

Guderian's notorious impatience and quick temper, as well as his idée fixe about the role of tanks, worked against him in this case. The harder he argued, the less anybody listened. He could have pointed out—after all, nobody knew better—that this had been carefully thought out. The tank crews were trained to service their tank at the end of each day before they fed themselves or rested, and every care had been taken to provide each panzer division with mobile service units that could repair the tanks, and if necessary replace the all-important tank tracks, but the comparison between horses and tanks was firmly, if unconsciously, imprinted at a much higher level than his. This caution was apparently passed on to General von Rundstedt, and imprinted itself on that otherwise superbly objective and professional military mind. He needed Kleist's armor for Case Red, and he did not want any of it wasted or damaged merely so Guderian could prove he could take all the Channel ports, besides which the lesson that Rundstedt had taken from the British fight at Arras, and now at Boulogne, was that British powers of resistance were more formidable than those of the French Army.

Rundstedt's mind was already fixed on the defeat of France, he did not want that to be jeopardized by dealing with the BEF, which was in any case retreating toward Dunkirk, taking it effectively off the field. His views were passed on to Hitler, where they added to the level of stress on and around the Führer.

21

"Fight It Out to the Bitter End"

Hitler at the map table; on the right, a visibly skeptical
General Halder.

THE ATTEMPT TO defend Boulogne was a sad failure. The attempt to defend Calais was a tragedy. Although shipping was still coming into Calais—including 350,000 rations for the BEF—the German 1st Panzer Division was already closing in on the town and seizing the main roads around it.

Late in the evening of May 23 the prime minister saw the king to warn him that if the attack promised by General Weygand "did not come off, he would have to order the BEF back to England," as the king confided to his diary. The king was stoic, but horrified: "The very thought of having to order this movement is appalling, as the loss of life will probably be immense."

Confusion haunted the reinforcement of Calais. The 30th Motor Brigade was ordered "to proceed to the relief of Boulogne" as rapidly as possible, then was diverted at the last minute to Calais when Boulogne fell. The brigade, under the command of Brigadier C. N. Nicholson, consisted of the 1st Prince Consort's Own Rifle Brigade, 2nd King's Royal Rifle Corps, 7th Queen Victoria's Rifles, plus the 3rd Royal Tank Regiment and a Royal Artillery anti-tank battery. This sounds like a more formidable force than it really was. The QVR was a motorcycle battalion that had been shipped without its machines, and many of its men were armed only with a revolver. Artillery, heavy machine guns, mortars, ammunition, and many other items had been so badly loaded that much of it remained unreachable below deck. The electricity supply to the docks of Calais had been interrupted and the French dockers were on strike, so it was only possible to unload the tanks of the 3rd RTR one by one using the ship's own derricks, a slow job that could not even begin until the deck had been cleared of thousands of gallons of gasoline in leaky tin cans. Complicating this process was the fact that each tank's gun had been removed and heavily greased, so time had to be spent stripping off the heavy preservative grease and "remounting" the gun. The captain of the 3rd RTR's ship tried to sail before unloading was completed and stayed only because he "was held at gunpoint" by a 3rd RTR officer.

Contradictory orders plagued the Calais garrison—such light

tanks and infantry as were ready were ordered first to proceed west to relieve Boulogne, but when it fell they were redirected east to escort a convoy full of rations to Dunkirk, only to find that the Germans had already blocked the road. By May 23 the British had been driven back to the walls of Calais, which having been built in the seventeenth century were now more of a historical curiosity than useful, and were effectively under siege by two armored divisions, with the bulk of 3rd RTR's tanks disabled or destroyed. By May 24 the Germans had artillery on the high ground surrounding Calais and the city was under constant shelling. Losses began to mount rapidly.

In the normal course of things the right decision would have been to evacuate the troops as soon possible, but Calais was not a normal town. In the first place, it was, more than any other French Channel port, deeply embedded in English history, and in the second, abandoning it would mean that two German panzer divisions would be free to invest Dunkirk, the last port remaining from which the BEF might be evacuated. A proposal from the navy to begin the evacuation of Calais was rejected on May 24 with a stiff note from the prime minister to General Hastings Ismay, his military adviser: "This is surely madness. The only effect of evacuating Calais would be to transfer the forces now blocking it to Dunkirk." This was followed by a longer and angrier note on the situation, again to Ismay. "I cannot understand the situation around Calais. The Germans are blocking all exits, and our regiment of Tanks is boxed up in the town because it cannot face the field guns planted on the outskirts. Yet I expect that the forces achieving this are very modest. Why, then, are they not attacked? . . . Surely Gort can spare a Brigade or two to clear his communications and to secure the supplies vital to his Army."

It was rare for Churchill to criticize Lord Gort, who was now in the difficult position of trying to move a quarter of a million men back toward the coast, and who in any case had no armored formation to spare for Calais. By the midafternoon Churchill had calmed down enough to listen to a fairly dispassionate statement on the situation at Calais to the War Cabinet from General Ironside. "German tanks had penetrated past the forts on the west side of Calais and had got between the town and the sea. The Brigadier . . . thought that it would be useless to dribble more infantry reinforcements into Calais."

The prime minister was under constant pressure from M. Reynaud to explain why Lord Gort had given up Arras, so he was loath to give up Calais as well. There was still no sign of the promised French attack to the northeast from the Somme, and in the meantime momentous great events were going on. The King of the Belgians was threatening to surrender, which would lay Lord Gort's left flank open to attack, General Weygand was already warning that he might have to give up Paris, and M. Reynaud was suggesting an approach to Mussolini, to seek out Hitler's terms for a negotiated peace. In the circumstances, Churchill did not feel that Calais could be given up as Boulogne had been.

By the night of May 26 he had made up his mind, as Ismay reported: "A telegram was sent to the commander at Calais, Brigadier Nicholson, telling him that his force would not be withdrawn, and that he must fight it out to the bitter end. . . . The decision affected us all very deeply, especially perhaps Churchill. He was unusually silent during dinner that evening, and he ate and drank with evident distaste. As we rose from the table, he said, 'I feel physically sick.' He has quoted these words in his memoirs, but he does not mention how sad he looked as he uttered them."

Churchill sent General Ironside, who was about to be replaced as CIGS by General Dill, a draft of the order he wanted sent to Brigadier Nicholson, as opposed to the previous rather lukewarm one, which made him ask whether there was "a streak of defeatist opinion in the General Staff." "Defence of Calais to the utmost is of the highest importance to our country and our Army now. . . . The eyes of the Empire are upon the defence of Calais, and His Majesty's Government are confident you and your gallant Regiment will perform an exploit worthy of the British name." In the end Churchill retired alone to send his own message to Brigadier Nicholson, emphasizing the most important point: "Evacuation will not (repeat not) take place, and craft required for above purpose are to return to Dover. . . ."

Calais was already in ruins from nonstop German artillery bombardment and from bombing; much of the city was on fire and darkened by smoke. The British had withdrawn to the area of the Citadel and the Old Town to shorten their line. The men were short of everything, not only food and ammunition, but even water since the water mains had burst, yet they fought on. The Germans were impressed and surprised—having reached Calais so quickly, they had not expected to have to fight this hard for it. It was also a demonstration, although too late, of what might have been accomplished had the French and the British fought together under a vigorous commander. In the words of the official British history, "The King's Royal Rifle Corps, and other detachments of the Queen Victoria's Rifles in the old town, fought grimly to hold the three main bridges into the town from the south. . . . A mixed British and French force held a key bastion and the French garrison in the Citadel fought off all attacks upon it though sustaining heavy casualties. Brigadier Nicholson established there a joint headquarters with the French commander."

Nicholson had already been offered one opportunity to surrender, when the Germans presented the mayor of Calais under a white flag with a German escort. Nicholson turned the offer down politely, remarking that if the Germans wanted Calais "they would have to fight for it." During the afternoon of May 25 "a flag of truce was brought in by a German officer, accompanied by a captured French captain and a Belgian soldier." Nicholson turned down this second demand for surrender, with great dignity and strict regard for military correctness:

"The answer is no as it is the British Army's duty to fight as well as it is the German's.

"The French captain and the Belgian soldier having not been blindfolded cannot be sent back. The Allied commander gives his word that they will be put under guard and will not be allowed to fight against the Germans."*

---

* This account is *in English* in the war diary of the German 10th Panzer Division, as quoted in Ellis, *The War in France and Flanders*, p. 167.

One senses a certain regret on the part of the Germans at Nicholson's refusal to surrender, but early the next morning heavy bombing further shattered the Old Town and separated the remaining British troops into small, isolated parties fighting separately amid the rubble. In the afternoon of May 26 the Germans finally managed to break into the Citadel and capture Brigadier Nicholson, and by evening the "fighting ceased and the noise of battle died away as darkness shrouded the scene of devastation and death."

Although the defense of Calais was later dismissed by General Guderian as heroic, but making no difference to the course of events, in fact the sacrifice of the 30th Brigade at Calais added to the hesitation and confusion of the German high command. The distance from Calais to Dunkirk is less than thirty miles, and once Calais had been taken there was no apparent reason why the two German armored divisions should not have continued on to take Dunkirk, which at this point had very little in the way of a defense. General Reinhardt's XXXXI Panzer Corps was even closer than the spearhead of Guderian's XIX Panzer Corps—less than twenty miles south of Dunkirk. Logically, the Germans could have—and should have—taken Dunkirk by May 27 or 28, and cut the BEF from any possibility of evacuation. As is so often the case, a historic victory was to be followed by a historic blunder.

"Victory has a hundred fathers, defeat is an orphan."* The blame for the BEF's escape from Dunkirk has been shifted from one person to another over the past seventy-five years, and not surprisingly most of the surviving German generals attributed it to Hitler, who was in no position after May 1945 to contradict them. In fact,

---

* Usually attributed to President John F. Kennedy, sometimes to Mussolini's son-in-law the Italian foreign minister Count Galeazzo Ciano, of all people, but it probably goes back to Roman times, if not earlier.

Hitler was reacting to the caution of his most senior generals—all except the dour and clear-sighted Halder, whom he disliked—rather than imposing his will on them. The dizzying success of Case Yellow so far had made them nervous, with the exception of Guderian, who as a mere corps commander had no influence on higher strategy, and whose passionate belief in the efficacy of armored warfare as he envisioned it struck many of his seniors as monomaniacal. The panzer divisions were not the answer to every problem, they felt, and the fact that Manstein and Guderian had been right about massing them in the Ardennes did nothing to endear them to older and wiser heads.

The impulse to halt the panzer divisions was not new. It had come up for the first time shortly after they had crossed the Meuse, as the German generals (and their Führer) looked toward the west with concern, searching for the first signs of the expected counterattack from the French Army that would separate the panzer divisions from the infantry coming up behind them more slowly, a replay of the Battle of the Marne that had stopped the Germans in September 1914 at the beginning of the First World War. It did not occur to them that France had no equivalent in 1940 of General Joseph Joffre, nor did it occur to either General Gamelin or his suc-

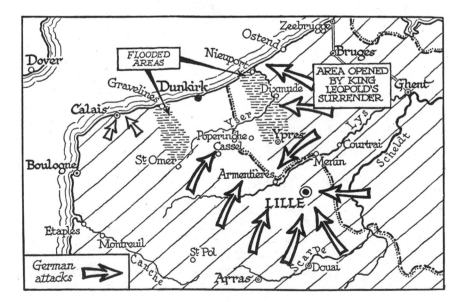

cessor General Weygand to replay his part. Another Joffre, a man of indomitable will, might have gathered all the divisions waiting behind the Maginot Line and boldly flung them against the Germans at the crucial point, but no such man existed. There would be no repetition of the heroic legend of "les taxis de la Marne," when the Paris taxicabs carried troops straight from the railway stations as they arrived to the front line. Neither psychologically nor militarily was the French Army in 1940 prepared to stage the massive attack on the exposed German left flank that the Germans feared.

The second halt in the advance of the armored divisions seems to have been caused by the unexpectedly stiff resistance of the British at Arras, which was briefly misread as a full-scale British counterattack. In both these cases Hitler was merely responding to Rundstedt's interpretation of the situation—Rundstedt, though the most implacable and levelheaded of Hitler's senior generals, still anticipated a French attack of thirty or forty divisions. He had known Gamelin before the war, and respected him; the idea that Gamelin was paralyzed and unable to act once the folly of his advance into Belgium was clear to him did not cross Rundstedt's mind.

The pause ordered after the Germans took Arras infuriated General Guderian, but did not seem unreasonable to the panzer troops themselves. General Rommel, commander of the 7th Panzer Division, wrote to his wife, Lucia, with his usual matter-of-fact professional calm about the violence of war: "A day or two without action has done a lot of good. The division has lost up to date 27 officers killed and 33 wounded, and 1,500 men dead and wounded. That's about 12 percent casualties. . . . Food, drink and sleep are all back to routine. Schraepler [his aide] is back already. His successor was killed a yard away from me."

The next rush forward took Guderian's panzer corps to Calais, and Reinhardt's to within easy reach of Dunkirk, only for them both to be halted again on May 24 by a surprising order that the panzer divisions were to stop along the line of "the Aire-St. Omer Canal," just short of Dunkirk. Various reasons have been given for this disastrous decision, which allowed the BEF to reach Dunkirk and begin evacuation, but as usual with Nazi Germany it seems to have been a mixture of the practical and the theoretical. Some historians believe that Hitler was concerned that Flanders, with its many canals and marshes (with which he was familiar from his service in the previous war), was unsuitable ground for tanks. This may have been so, but it would have been unusual for Hitler to override his generals' advice on a purely technical matter like this in 1940. (It became more common once he had lost confidence in them in 1942.)

General von Brauchitsch.

General Halder, while complaining as usual about the "unpleasant interview" and "painful wrangles" between the army commander in chief, Colonel General Walter von Brauchitsch, and the Führer on the subject, also notes that Hitler's intention was to fight the decisive battle in northern France, not in Flanders, for "political" reasons, and that "to camouflage this political move," the "halt order" for the panzer divisions was to be attributed to the problems of the terrain.

It is hard to see any sensible "political" advantage to this subterfuge, or indeed whom it was supposed to deceive, and Halder puts none forward, which may have been his way of saying that he did not believe a word of it. In any case, "political" did not have the same meaning in Nazi Germany as it did in Britain, France, or the United States, where politics implies an orderly process for reconciling different opinions. In the Third Reich there was no tolerance for different opinions; "politics" merely meant the elaborate political structure for putting Hitler's wishes into practical effect at every level, and for making the German people identify itself with them, and accept them with enthusiasm.

It is always difficult to penetrate the thought processes of Hitler—he was a past master at deceiving others, but he was also no slouch at deceiving himself—and he was quite able to keep two apparently conflicting motives in his mind at the same time. However, parsing Halder's notes carefully, it is apparent that Hitler wanted the panzer divisions halted, was tired of arguing about it, and used his ultimate weapon in arguments with his generals, the "political" motive. This was (and would remain) his trump card—the generals were not supposed to have any involvement in or insight into "politics," an area of expertise that the Führer reserved for himself. They had given all that up for good after the "Night of the Long Knives" in 1934, when every soldier took a personal oath of loyalty to the Führer. They could (and did) argue with Hitler about tactics, the terrain, even to a degree about strategy, but not about "politics," which in a one-party, one-man dictatorship meant everything that was not directly connected to the battlefield.

Somewhere at the back of his mind Hitler may still have believed that the British, or at least some of their major political figures,* would give in and that sparing their army might help to convince them of his good will—certainly several of his generals believed so—but at the same time he was aware that Rundstedt wanted to make sure the panzer divisions were intact and rested before undertaking Case Red, the "decisive battle" that would force the French Army to surrender.

Humanitarian aims never played any role in Hitler's decisions, and therefore did not prevent him from listening to Göring's claim that the Luftwaffe could annihilate the BEF on the beaches without the help of the panzer divisions, but how much faith he put in that is open to question, for he had already learned that even the most ambitious and well-planned of air campaigns is dependent on good weather. Given the subsequent bombing and shelling of Dunkirk and its beaches, sparing the BEF does not seem to have been one of Hitler's considerations, so the likelihood is that his

---

* These, we now know, included HRH the Duke of Windsor, Lord Halifax, and David Lloyd George. It cannot have been unknown to Hitler that Lord Halifax, the British foreign secretary, had already discussed with the Italian ambassador in London the notion of asking Mussolini to seek out what Hitler's peace terms might be.

major concern was to spare the panzer divisions for the big battle to come, rather than to fritter them away on the BEF, which was already beginning to evacuate.

Hitler is sometimes criticized for interfering too much in military decisions—though he did not interfere much more than Churchill—and sometimes for being "an armchair general," remote from his commanders in the field. This too is doubtful. On May 24 he went to Rundstedt's headquarters precisely to thrash out what the next move involving the panzer divisions should be, and heard Rundstedt out with a certain degree of patience. Although Rundstedt denied it after the war, there seems to be no doubt that at the time he urged caution on Hitler. For three fateful days the panzer divisions were halted, even though some of the tanks were so close to Dunkirk that Colonel Wilhelm Ritter von Thoma could see the beach. Whatever the mix of military and political considerations that was in Hitler's mind on May 24, the decision to halt the panzer divisions was—although it may not have seemed so at the time—a major turning point in the war, and a fatal one for Germany.

22

Flag Officer, Dover

Admiral Sir Bertram Ramsay surveys the channel from his
headquarters in the White Cliffs of Dover.

I N THE LONG history of Britain, the one thing that everybody
has always relied upon when all else failed is the steely professionalism of the Royal Navy. As early as May 23, when there was
still confidence in the appointment of General Weygand to succeed General Gamelin as Allied commander in chief, Churchill
had called for a plan to be made in case it became necessary to
withdraw the BEF from the French coast.

This was farsighted, but in fact the navy was ahead of the prime
minister. On May 15, only five days after the German attack on

France and the Low Countries, when it was still supposed that the Allied armies might defeat the Germans in Belgium in accordance with Gamelin's Plan D, a tiny announcement appeared in the *Times* under the innocuous headline "Motor-boat Census." The single paragraph in small print was buried on page three, between "Naval Promotions" and the death in Toronto of the anarchist Emma Goldman, and can have had little effect on anyone but those boat owners and yachtsmen who were assiduous readers of the *Times*: "The Admiralty has made an order requiring all owners or occupiers of self-propelled craft (including motor boats) in Britain between 30ft and 100ft in length used for their own pleasure or for fare-paying passengers for pleasure . . . to send particulars to the Admiralty within 14 days of yesterday."

This meant almost every small motorboat or motor yacht in England, in addition to such larger vessels as the familiar paddle-wheel sightseeing and pleasure steamers on the Thames, with their rows of varnished wooden seats. Ostensibly, this was a call-up for "minesweeping duties," but a skeptic might wonder how useful a thirty-foot motor yacht would be for dealing with a German naval mine.

*　　*　　*

Just as General von Manstein was the architect of the plan to cut off and defeat the BEF, the architect of the plan for saving it was then Vice-Admiral Bertram Ramsay. Ramsay was not a swashbuckling naval officer of the Horatio Hornblower school; he was a thoughtful technocrat and planner, and it is no accident that he would go on to become General Dwight D. Eisenhower's trusted planner for the naval forces used in the invasions of North Africa (1942), Sicily (1943), and Normandy (1944), and naval commander of the last two. Ramsay has been criticized for being impatient, "authoritarian," and "a stickler" for details, not uncommon traits among admirals, but he was also lucid, visionary, and not without savoir faire—after all, he ended up commanding American senior naval officers as well as his own, not an easy task given the clash of sensitivities and pride between the Royal Navy and the United States Navy.

Ramsay's interest in technology coincided with the Royal Navy's ambitious plans for modernization at the turn of the century. As a junior officer he had served on board the revolutionary HMS *Dreadnought*, the warship that at one stroke made the battleships of every fleet in the world obsolete in 1906 and did more than anything else to spark off the naval race between Imperial Germany and Great Britain. He went on from there to attend the Naval Signal School—wireless telegraphy was changing naval strategy overnight—then attended the prestigious Royal Naval War College, a new and ambitious institution, and a huge intellectual jump from the old tradition of learning naval leadership by experience on the deck of a warship. In the First World War Ramsay had the good fortune to command a monitor on the Dover Patrol, then a destroyer that took part in the failed second raid on Ostend in 1918 (commanded by Admiral Roger Keyes), thus ensuring that he knew the water, the tides, the ports, and the treacherous shallows of the English Channel like the back of his hand.

He rose steadily through the ranks at sea or in the Admiralty until 1935, when he was made chief of staff to the commander in chief of the Home Fleet, Admiral Sir Roger Backhouse. Although Ramsay and Backhouse were and remained friends, they clashed sharply over naval doctrine and Ramsay, by now a rear admiral, was moved to the Retired List in 1938 after refusing several postings. He spent his time in retirement working on a plan to "reactivate the Dover Patrol," and late in 1938 he was "coaxed" by his old friend Winston Churchill, whom he had known since 1903, to give up retirement and return to uniform as vice-admiral in command of Dover operations at the age of fifty-seven. He instantly shook things up.

Dover is a small but busy port, for the most part artificial, consisting of stone breakwaters that have been built up since the seventeenth century, and nestled by the famous White Cliffs.* In modern times the small town has grown to accommodate elaborate docks for the cross-Channel ferries and railroad ferries, a large fishing fleet (Dover sole), a yacht marina, a cargo area, and, by 1939, a substantial naval presence. Dover's small size belies its immense commercial importance—it represented the shortest and most convenient link between the United Kingdom and the Continent until the building of the Channel Tunnel—and its vital importance to the Royal Navy, for it overlooks the narrowest point in the Channel and commands the entrance to and the exit from the North Sea, still today the "busiest seaway in the world." More important to the Royal Navy, control of the Channel from Dover to Calais obligated German warships and submarines to go around the northernmost point of Scotland to enter the Atlantic or to run the gauntlet of British destroyers and minefields controlled by the flag officer commanding Dover.

If ever there was a serendipitous posting this was it—the Dover command might have been devised for Vice-Admiral Ramsay, or he

---

* Always the symbol of Britain's independence and sturdy separation from the Continent, the White Cliffs inspired one of Britain's most popular wartime songs, first sung by Vera Lynn: "(There'll be Bluebirds Over) The White Cliffs of Dover."

for it. Even though Britain was still at peace, he had hardly even settled in Dover Castle—the largest and the oldest castle in England, which includes among other historical wonders a lighthouse built during the Roman occupation of England—than he swept away two decades of neglect and immediately set about putting Dover on a war footing. He reopened the maze of tunnels that had been dug deep into the white chalk cliffs in anticipation of Napoleon's invasion and used them to store mines and fuel oil. He also rendered the harbor safe against submarines, and upgraded the primitive communications to create a modern underground operations room, with a broad semicircular table on which the coming and going of every ship in and out of the Channel could be marked and followed, similar to that which Air Chief Marshal Dowding had created for Fighter Command Headquarters at Bentley Priory.

Ramsay placed his own office in one of the tunnels in the cliffs, with a window looking out over the Channel from which, on the rare very clear day, he could see the coast of France, and began to gather a small flotilla of ships, some of them old pleasure steamers, to lay minefields and sweep for enemy mines. His was not a command of battleships, cruisers, and aircraft carriers—he had nothing bigger than destroyers, most of them old ones destined for the scrapheap, along with a miscellaneous collection of ships requisitioned from civilian owners, including a steamer of the Isle of Man Steam Packet Company that until recently had sailed between Liverpool and Douglas bearing "care-free holiday makers"—but it was still one of the most important commands in the Royal Navy. It was here, or near here, that the Germans would land if they ever attempted an invasion (Dover is less than twenty-one miles from France and only seventy-three miles by road from London), it was from here that many of the troops embarked for France, and it was from here that Ramsay would plan and carry out in extreme haste their return, in what came to be code-named Operation Dynamo.

It was as if in his orderly mind Ramsay had already factored in the possibility of their defeat, even as he was helping to organize the embarkation of the BEF to France in September 1939, not in any spirit of pessimism or from lack of confidence in the War Office or General Gamelin's war plan, neither of which was any concern of his, but as a natural element of naval professionalism. It was a consequence of Britain's supreme confidence in its naval power. "Britannia rules the waves," therefore its navy could take a British army anywhere it was needed, supply it—and evacuate that army if it became necessary, as had sometimes been the case before in British history. That is part of the meaning of "sea power." It was an eventuality that, even when unspoken lay in the back of every French mind—hence Premier Reynaud's complaint to General Spears at their first meeting that "British generals always made for the harbors" when things became difficult, a belief that lay behind the determination of the GQG in 1939 to keep the French First Army between the BEF and the sea as a precaution against just this possibility. However, it was part of every naval officer's training to prepare for the worst, and in Ramsay's case it was his duty to keep that precious twenty-one miles of sea clear of threats, whatever might happen on land. If the BEF needed supplies or reinforcements in an emergency, he could supply them; if it needed to be evacuated, he could do that too, and made his preparations so that he would not be taken by surprise.

The "eventuality" of rescuing the BEF was something Ramsay gave thought to long before Lord Gort at last made the decision to retreat to Dunkirk and attempt to evacuate his army. On May 15 Ramsay was already taking the first step toward putting every ship and motorboat in the United Kingdom under naval command; on May 19 he participated in a coldly realistic meeting at the War Office to consider, among other things, "the hazardous evacuation of very large forces." It was decided that if necessary "all available shipping should be placed at his disposal—naval or otherwise." There was still a week to go before Lord Gort made his decision, or Churchill embraced the idea of evacuation, but Admiral Ramsay had already been making his plans.

23

The Home Front

Vincent, Alexander, and Zoltan Korda.

T HE BRITISH PUBLIC was still at the time largely unaware of the scale of the catastrophe in France. For one thing, the French, however bloody-minded they might seem to many Britons, still benefited from their martial reputation in the First World War. The notion that they might be badly commanded, poorly led, and unwilling to fight had not as yet imprinted itself on the mind of the British public, still less on that of the prime minister. For assiduous readers of the *Times* it was clear enough that something had gone wrong, but only five days after the appearance of the ominous Admiralty announcement that all small ships and motorboats were to be registered, the *Times* still told its readers that "this great German offensive contains the seed of its own defeat," and found consolation in the appointment of General Weygand to lead the Allied armies, reminding readers that he had been Marshal Foch's chief of staff. After all, similar crises had taken place in the previous war, in 1914 when General Joffre stopped the German advance at the Marne, in 1916 when General Pétain held the Germans back at Verdun at the cost of more than half a million French casualties, and in 1918 when General Foch brought to a halt the *Kaiserschlacht*, the German Army's last great offensive, which nearly broke the Allied line at a cost of close to 850,000 British and French casualties (and nearly 700,000 German). "I will fight in front of Paris, I will fight in Paris, I will fight behind Paris," Foch had declared, and since Weygand had been his protégé and devoted follower, surely he would do the same? The powerful French counterattack on the exposed right wing of German Army B as it carried out its armored "scythe" to the sea was eagerly awaited by readers of the *Times* and also of the more popular newspapers.

In the meantime, had I been more astute (but I was, after all, not yet seven), I might have detected that other things were going on. It was then part of normal routine to be taken to tea at my grandparents' house in suburban Hendon on Sunday afternoons. My father, for reasons never explained to me, would not set foot in the Musgrove house, and my mother preferred to spend her Sundays in bed resting from her six nights and two matinees a week on the stage, so it was left to my nanny and myself to make this weekly pilgrimage to Hendon. My maternal grandfather, Octavius Musgrove, was a prosperous dentist who always dressed like an Edwardian gentleman, but it was my grandmother Annie who ruled the Musgrove household and exerted her formidable will on her husband, the Irish maid in her starched cap and apron, and the part-time gardener and chauffeur, since neither of my grandparents drove. "Ockie," as we called him, was from the north of England, and had a strong and undisguised Liverpool accent (recognizable to Americans from the early Beatles hits). My grandmother was also from Liverpool, but had long since refined her accent. She liked to say that *her* father was "in coal," but Ockie, when out of her hearing, would say, "Ay, 'e was in coal alright, 'e went from door to door with 'orse and cart shouting, 'Coal, coal!' " Dentistry, primitive as it was in England at the time (my grandfather's recommendation to all his patients was "'ave 'em all out, dear!" and his favorite tool was the forceps) had raised my grandfather to "professional" status, but he preserved a rich, northern sense of humor, a taste for the music hall, and an appreciation for spirits, wine, and tobacco in all their forms. He wore boldly checked suits, with the result that he looked like a successful bookie rather than a dentist, and a vest (waistcoat) in apricot- or plum-colored velvet, with gold buttons and a gold watch and chain, a gray bowler hat in the summer, and a black one in other seasons.

Hazy though class and regional differences in England were to my father, he had instantly understood how to subvert Ockie, whom he liked, and instituted their regular Saturday luncheon at Prunier on St. James's Street. They met after my father had attended the morning session of the art auctions at Christie's or Sotheby's. "Vincent is not such a bad chap," my grandfather would say reflectively, and my father felt the same about him. At Prunier they ate well, shared a good bottle of wine, and a glass or two of brandy afterwards. I imagine this luncheon was in part a reliable way my father had invented of irritating my grandmother without seeing her—he always referred to her, though never to Ockie, as "that bloody old voman."

What the two men found to talk about together over lunch was a mystery to most people, but my father enjoyed silence, and my grandfather Ockie was perhaps happy enough to get away from my grandmother's chatter and bossiness for a few hours. I accompanied my father a few times, and for the most part they ate in companionable silence. They had both fought, though on different sides, in the First World War, but they never spoke about that, or politics, or marriage in my hearing.

My grandmother represented respectability and tidiness, two

incomprehensible concepts to my father, who hated tidiness and lived in a chaos of his own making. He moved everywhere in a cloud of cigarette ashes, scattered scraps of paper with notes or sketches, discarded pencil stubs, and small change. He used a knotted-up polka-dot Sulka necktie to hold up his trousers, and wore his expensive bespoke Lobb shoes unshined, with the laces left untied for greater comfort. The Musgrove house represented everything my father disliked about England, from the crazy paving and the stone gnomes in the garden to the heavy cut-velvet upholstered furniture, the stained glass windows, the smell of furniture polish, and the neat antimacassars. Whenever the subject of the house in Hendon came up, he would say with a heartfelt sigh, "Poor Ockie."

My grandmother had not approved of my mother's marrying a Hungarian who at that time spoke little or no English, whose clothes (though admittedly expensive) looked as if he had slept in them, and who had no respect for English middle-class conventions, if indeed he had even noticed them.

A further complication to their relationship was that my grandmother was a classic "stage mother," who had pushed my mother onto the stage at an early age. This was a result of sibling rivalry between my grandmother Annie and her elder sister Maud Mary, who had not only pushed *her* daughter Madge Evans into show business as an infant, but all the way to Hollywood and a career as a child star and rival to Shirley Temple. (Madge would grow up to star in *Pennies from Heaven* with Bing Crosby.) Nothing could be better calculated to alienate my father than having to accept *two* ambitious stage mothers as relatives by marriage.

In any event, one of Ockie's neighbors owned a motor yacht, which he kept at Teddington, on the Thames, where it was moored with a lot of other small yachts in what would now be called a marina, but was then just a private boatyard, and he happened to drop in

Dutch schuyt, of which many were used at Dunkirk.

while we were at tea. I had been on the boat several times with my grandparents and knew her. She was painted white with neat blue trim and shiny varnished mahogany, a slow, broad-beamed and sturdy boat, about twenty-five feet long, what might be called "a cabin cruiser" in the United States, but there was nothing in the cabin except a small galley suitable for boiling a kettle, a table between upholstered benches, two bunks, and a pump toilet. The word "yacht" conjures up glamor, but there was nothing glamorous about her, and we only went on short cruises up and down the river, not far from the genteel neighborhoods of Bushy Park and

Strawberry Hill, and only in the very calmest of weather, with a wicker tea basket from Fortnum & Mason laid out under the blue-and-white striped awning in the stern. For these occasions Ockie wore white trousers, a striped blazer and a straw boater, and his neighbor sported a jaunty yachting cap as he stood at the helm and we chugged slowly and peacefully among the Thames barges, rowboats, and paddle-wheel steamers. I do not suppose the boat had ever sailed anywhere except the placid Thames upstream from the placid Teddington lock—it would be difficult to imagine her on the open sea, still less as a target for German aircraft, artillery, and torpedo boats.

The neighbor happened to mention over tea that he had been surprised to find a chief petty officer of the Royal Navy (roughly the equivalent of an army sergeant-major) holding a clipboard and examining his modest yacht the day before. He had obediently sent her particulars in to the Admiralty after reading the announcement in the *Times*, but had hardly expected a real live sailor to show up so soon, if at all. In those days everything was being registered and particulars taken down, not just boats, but cars, commercial vehicles, and motorcycles—government departments were intruding everywhere, inspecting cellars, enforcing rationing, requisitioning sporting arms, demanding to see the air raid shelter that was supposed to be built in people's back garden, stopping people who had left home without their gas mask. It was the age of the bureaucrat and the snooper, so registering his boat with the navy did not seem unusual.

Given the time it would take a postcard to reach the Admiralty from Hendon (those were still the days when the post was delivered overnight in London) that would place the date of the tea at my grandparents on Sunday, May 19—the beginning of the British "counterattack" at Arras and the last day of the French "attempt to stem the flood which broke the Meuse barrage," and which turned Kleist's armored group loose to make its advance to the sea. Churchill had been prime minister for only nine days at that date, and had as yet given no thought to evacuating the BEF from the beaches of Dunkirk or anywhere else.

"What's it all about, then?" Ockie's neighbor had asked the CPO as they stood on the dock beside his boat.

"No idea, sir," the CPO replied, with the stony politeness of non-commissioned officers of any service toward civilians.

"I can't see her as a minesweeper, which is what I hear they're looking for."

"Couldn't say, I'm sure," the CPO said, carefully writing down the particulars on his form. He gave the boat an appraising look. "She's got a nice shallow draft on her, though, I'll say that." He glanced out at the long row of motor yachts, gleaming mahogany speedboats, and sailboats of every size and shape, all neatly tied up. "A shallow draft is just the ticket," he said, putting a finger to the peak of his cap, not quite a salute, just a mark of respect, as he went off to look at the next boat.

"A shallow draft," mused Ockie's neighbor over his teacup. "Why on earth would they want that?" It was a good question. Boats like his were designed for cruising the river and the innumerable streams that fed into it, many of them quite shallow. A boat designed for the open sea usually has a deeper draft for better stability in rough water. That the Admiralty was already thinking of taking men off the beaches in shallow water had of course not yet occurred to anyone, let alone that they would have to evacuate nearly 400,000 of them. It would have been still harder to imagine that only ten days later Ockie's neighbor's yacht would be sailing the eighty-seven nautical miles of "Route Y" from Dover to Dunkirk, more than twice the length of the direct crossing "Route Z," but a course that Admiral Ramsay would be obliged to choose after the Germans took Calais, putting British ships and boats within the range of German guns on the shorter course. Stranger still, though considerably the worse for wear, she was delivered back by the navy, and stayed tied up at Teddington until after the war, since there was no gasoline for her. I saw her there myself, in 1947.

Although Hungary is a landlocked country, my father and his two brothers were "good sailors." None of them was ever seasick, even in storms that sent other passengers groaning to their beds on Channel or Atlantic crossings. On the other hand, my father would have had no interest in going up and down the Thames in my grandmother's company. He was, in fact, busy sorting out a naval problem of his own. *That Hamilton Woman* (it did not yet have that title, being still a screenplay in the making), the story of the love affair between Nelson and Lady Hamilton, would require the reenacting of the Battle of Trafalgar. This kind of thing is usually done by using small models, often with a matte shot to provide the sea in the foreground, but the result is never very convincing on the screen. Since the film was being made at Winston Churchill's suggestion. Alex was determined to make the naval scenes look as convincing as possible. "Special effects" and what was then called "trick photography" did not particularly interest him, but he was not unfamiliar with that kind of thing either. After all, *The Thief of Baghdad*, still being worked on, was a triumph of trick photography, perhaps even *the* triumph (it would win the Academy Awards for Special Effects and for Photography in 1940, as well as my father's Academy Award for Art Direction),* and as early as 1919 Alex had directed a futuristic Jules Verne science fiction novel on the Dalmatian seacoast as well as the biblical epic *Samson und Delila* in Vienna, which required sophisticated trick photography for the time, for the big scene in which Samson pulls the temple down on top of the Philistines.

Fortunately for Vincent he could draw on the advice of William Cameron Menzies, whom Alex had brought over to England from Hollywood to direct *Things to Come* and whom he brought back over despite the war to solve some of the many problems of *The Thief of Baghdad*. Jock Menzies was a difficult man and something of a genius—he was perhaps the man most responsible for pulling together the enormously complicated production of *Gone with the*

---

* By an odd coincidence *The Thief of Baghdad* was released on the same date as that other masterpiece of trick photography and imaginative filmmaking *The Wizard of Oz*. Odder still, neither one hurt the other at the box office— they were both huge hits.

Wind for David O. Selznick—and the first person in Hollywood to bear the title "production designer,"* but far from being rivals, he and my father had a deep professional respect for each other, and even a certain fondness.

The solution they came up with—helped by suggestions from Ned Mann, perhaps the most skillful designer of optical special effects in Hollywood—was to make the boats bigger, much bigger. Small model ships when photographed tend to move in an artificial straight line, drawn across on wires, but real sailing ships move with the waves, pitching, tossing, and heeling as they move. The solution was to build model ships of the line about the size of a dinghy, big enough to hold (and conceal) two prop men, who could furl and unfurl the sails, fire the guns and simulate damage by pulling down masts or spars.

Who came up with the idea of having the legs of prop men, encased in rubber fishing waders, stick down below the waterline of the dinghy so that they could walk it along with their feet on the bottom of a large, shallow tank, I do not know. Probably Menzies. Ned Mann came from Indiana, where he was unlikely to have been exposed to dry-fly fishing, still less my father, born on the vast plains of Hungary. In any case, the problem was solved, except for the fact that no such tank existed in England and that, in 1940, it was not possible to build a whole fleet of working model ships in a country gearing up at last (and possibly too late) for total war. The craftsmen who would have produced the model ships were busy making Fairmile motor torpedo boats or learning how to put their woodworking skills to the production of a revolutionary all-wood high-speed bomber, the de Havilland Mosquito.

By an odd coincidence the length of the model ships required for *That Hamilton Woman* was about fifteen feet—almost exactly

---

* An "art director" designs and decorates sets for a motion picture. Menzies (and later my father) as the "production designer" had a direct influence on the whole *look* of a film, often painting a series of panels showing each important scene in a film and how it would be lit and photographed. My father had started doing this for *The Private Life of Henry VIII* and would be responsible for much of the visual impact of *The Third Man*.

the length of the smallest of the "little ships" that would be used to evacuate troops from the beach at Dunkirk, the celebrated *Tamzine*, a clinker-built fishing boat from Margate with a sail and a small outboard motor, which is now preserved at the Imperial War Museum in London.

It must have seemed unlikely to my father that anything on this scale could be accomplished in England, in the spring of 1940, still less the many "retakes and added scenes" demanded by Alex for *The Thief of Baghdad*. For Alex filmmaking was a constant process of revision and second thoughts, whatever they cost—and the cost was enormous because the actors, their costumes, and the sets had to be reassembled for each scene, at great (and expensive) inconvenience to everyone.

In this case it was the money of the normally cautious Prudential Insurance Company, which had been investing in his films since the midthirties apparently without learning any lesson from its experience, and United Artists, of which Alex was a director and by a complicated series of transatlantic business maneuvers part owner. Alex not only had to find a way of *finishing* the film; it had to be a huge hit, and a good part of the responsibility for this rested on my father's shoulders.

It was a stressful time for the Kordas even without taking into account the events taking place on the other side of the Channel. About these, my uncle Alex was more pessimistic in private than he was in public. He knew and loved France, he had made films successfully there, France was one of the biggest overseas markets for his films (after the United States and, until 1933, Germany). The London Films office in Paris on the Champs-Elysées was even larger than his office in Rockefeller Center, and many of those who worked there worked for MI6 as well as Alex. France was, and would remain after 1945, a second home to him, as it did to my father, but he understood better than many people the deep ambivalence with which the French faced the war. He understood that *nobody* in France had wanted war and that everybody was determined not to repeat the carnage and destruction of the previous one—above all France was not an island and there was no Channel to separate the French from the Germans.

The British might defend themselves with their navy and their air force for a time, perhaps forever, the Americans and the Russians might sit the war out, but France would be engulfed if it lost the battle that was taking place in the last week of May 1940. Talking to his many friends in France, Alex drew his own conclusions about what was happening there, based on having lived in the Austro-Hungarian Empire as it faced defeat in 1918: a fatal combination of defeatism and light-headedness, such as one might feel going down the last sickening drop in a roller-coaster ride if there were no end in sight, and no way to stop or get off. The national motto might as well have been "Tout s'arrangera," a desperate belief that in the end reasonable people would make a deal, without taking into account that not only Hitler but the Nazi Party itself and perhaps the German nation was no longer reasonable.

Alex knew that, too. He had worked in Berlin in the 1920s, he had attended the frenzied first night of Brecht and Weil's *Die Dreigroschen Oper*, with jackbooted Brownshirts howling, throwing rocks and bottles, and trying to drown out the music with chants and curses, and he understood down to the marrow of his bones what was in store for everyone if the Germans won, yet he did not dislike the Germans, or think of Germany as an alien, foreign country— German was his second language, the years in Berlin had been, if not the happiest then certainly the most productive of his life. His friends included pro-Nazis like Leni Riefenstahl and Luftwaffe General Ernst Udet, on whom Carl Zuckmayer based his play and subsequent film *The Devil's General*, and also vehement anti-Nazis like Marlene Dietrich and Lotte Lenya. For him, my father, and my uncle Zoltan, Germany was not an abstraction; all three of them spoke German as well as they spoke English or French. They were fiercely opposed to Nazism, as they were to the fascism of Horthy's Hungary, but they remained sympathetic toward individual Ger-

Top left: General Udet, in flying clothes. *Top right:* Marlene Dietrich. *Bottom:* Leni Riefenstahl.

mans, unlike so many people in England who turned against German culture altogether.

The Kordas were not alone. A good part of the German film industry had moved to Paris, London, or Hollywood in the years since 1933, among them Otto Preminger and Billy Wilder, whose barber at the Adlon Hotel in Berlin, a Nazi Party member, had tipped him off to get out of Germany while shaving him in the morning. Wilder took his barber's advice seriously, and said he would go back up to his suite and pack. The barber shook his head sadly. "I wouldn't do that, Herr Wilder," he said, "I would go straight to the station."

Otto Preminger arrives in Los Angeles.

Germany had always played a huge role in film production and still loomed large in the mind of many people. When Preminger finally got to Los Angeles, he used to eat dinner sometimes at a Viennese restaurant on Santa Monica Boulevard called (of course) The Blue Danube. Sitting there at the bar one evening he heard a lot of the Hollywood Hungarians chattering away in Hungarian at a nearby table. Preminger got more and more annoyed, and finally he banged his glass down on the bar, turned around, and shouted at them, "Alright, you guys, knock it off, you're in America now—*talk German!*"

My father would have certainly understood that. Wherever he went, he remained a European. I remember him staring glumly at

French director
René Clair.

the *Times*. He was not as privy to inside information as his brother Alex was, but he was shrewd enough to tell the difference between propaganda and fact, besides which many of the friends he worked with were French filmmakers like Georges Périnal and René Clair. The French could tell from the license plates of refugees arriving in Paris by car just how badly things were going,* and with the ingrained cynicism that is part of the French national character they assumed that their government and their press were lying to them, and that however bad things looked, they were actually worse.

My mother, when she thought about the war at all, had the cheerful conviction that everything would work out well in the end because it always had for Britain, except for the war against the American colonies, and that was too long ago to matter. Far from being depressed, she was exhilarated. Even so staid a newspaper as the *Times* hailed the "hundreds" of enemy aircraft shot down by the RAF and by the Armée de l'Air (the latter had already virtually ceased to exist), and on May 27 headlined that "THE B. E. F. FRONT REMAINS INTACT," though it was already shattered, and praised the resistance of the Belgian Army, which was in fact laying down its arms and would surrender unconditionally the next day. Reading about these nonexistent triumphs of the Allied armies, my father shook his head sadly as he read one story and muttered, "This is all some nonsense of Brendan's."

He was right, of course. Brendan Bracken was Duff Cooper's

---

* There was a different two-number code for each *département* in France—"75," for example, stood for Paris, "06" for the Alpes-Maritimes—so it was possible to tell from the license plates of civilian refugees how much farther the Germans had advanced than the newspapers or the government admitted.

closest confidant, and with the shrewd judgment which he always had about the public's mood he was about to oversee a switch from overconfidence to frank realism, at just the right moment in time. The government was about to try a new and novel means of maintaining British morale, betting on the common sense of the British people when faced with disaster: to tell the truth.

24

"Presume Troops Know They Are Cutting Their Way Home to Blighty"

British troops prepare to defend a position.

O N MAY 25 Lord Gort, acting on his own, seems at last to have made the critical decision to evacuate the BEF. He started one of his divisions moving north toward the sea, instead of toward the south, where, it was painfully clear to him, the French attack from the Somme toward Cambrai, the so-called Weygand Plan, was never going to take place. At the same time, the Belgian forces on his left were inert or crumbling.

Gort was acutely conscious of the fact that the survival of the BEF was his first responsibility, and he had already begun the pro-

Remains of a British convoy after being attacked by Stuka
dive-bombers.

cess of "thinning out" the "useless mouths" of the army by evacuating them from Dunkirk—there was no further use for gunners[*]
without their guns, or for any of the numerous nonfighting troops
of a modern army (known officially as "Line of Communications
troops" or more colloquially as "odds and sods"), still less for the
numerous (and mostly unarmed) members of the RAF who had
been separated from their squadron or unit as the RAF tried
to withdraw from airfields and supply depots that could no longer be held.

With the fall of Calais and Boulogne the BEF had no port left
to go to except Dunkirk, and even that was by then reduced to a
wretched hell. Heavily and continually bombed, it no longer had
electricity, which put its cranes out of action, there was no water,

---

[*] In the British Army many formations do not use the rank "private." A private soldier in the Brigade of Guards is called a "guardsman," for instance;
in the cavalry (and armored forces) a "trooper"; in the Royal Artillery a "gunner"; in the Royal Engineers a "sapper"; in rifle regiments, a "rifleman"; in
fusilier regiments, a "fusilier"; etc.

and its streets were blocked with rubble and broken glass. "It is all a first-class mess-up," wrote General Pownall, "and events go slowly from bad to worse, like a Greek tragedy. . . ." For once Pownall was overoptimistic—events were not going from bad to worse "slowly," they were hurtling downhill very quickly indeed.

So little was heard from the Belgians on the British left that the 12th Lancers, "always most reliable," were sent off to look for them, but for all practical purposes the Belgians had simply stopped fighting, and the French First Army, in the words of one of its senior officers, "N'éxiste plus." As always, Henry de La Falaise accurately describes a day of bloody chaos as the 12th Lancers' armored cars advanced almost twenty-five miles in search of the Belgian Army despite constant bombing and machine-gunning from the air. They met up with a Belgian artillery supply unit, whose "terrified horses [were] milling around wildly, neighing with fear and running into the barbed wire fences as they try to get away," and masses of disorganized traffic and refugees in wagons blocking the roads. The only Belgian fighting troops the 12th Lancers encountered were in retreat, many without their weapons, but by then so was almost everybody else, except in rare places where the French made a gallant, but futile, stand against impossible odds. Once darkness fell, it took the 12th Lancers two hours to cover twenty miles—no one could use headlights, and every road, field, and village was blocked by trucks, fleeing civilians, artillery, and infantry, the total confusion of defeat. Eventually, they managed to report all this back to BEF headquarters, itself on the move, and were ordered to withdraw to the northwest.

Halting for a day to service their vehicles and clean their weapons—the mark of well-trained regulars—they received orders to move on and patrol the Loos Canal. La Falaise was shocked at the sight of the Furnes highway leading to it: "It recalls the paintings of Napoleon's retreat from Russia. Brand new trucks, tractors, guns of every caliber, line the ditches and fields. Millions of dollars worth of entirely new British equipment lies in the mud. . . . It is a horrible and disheartening sight." A British staff officer caught up in the retreat wrote later that he asked a French officer when the

German troops restring electric wires near Dunkirk using a
captured British vehicle.

French offensive would begin. The latter replied, "'Not yet, the
armies are *épuisées.*' Surely the Germans must be exhausted too,
the British officer suggested? 'But they are drunk* with success,
and we are sober with defeat,' the Frenchman said, 'and the drunk-
ard has the strength of seven men.'"

To be fair, most of the BEF had not yet been as hard-pressed
as the French and the Belgians, nor was their country (as was the
case with Belgium) or a significant part of it (as was the case with
France) already occupied by the Germans. Nobody in the BEF
had lost his home, his place of work, or his farm to the enemy.
To most of the Belgians, and a good many of the French, the war
was already lost, the future an uncertainty or a catastrophe—not
circumstances likely to provoke a determined last stand against an
enemy that had already proved itself superior in weapons, training,
zeal, and leadership.

It is worth noting that despite the grousing and complaining
about the Belgian Army from British soldiers of all ranks at the

* *Epuisé* means exhausted, but can also be a polite euphemism for drunk.

time (and from British historians ever since), Belgium fought for over two weeks with a poorly armed, led, and equipped conscript army against the full force of General von Bock's Army Group B. Militarily, there may not have been much to praise about the conduct or the morale of the Belgian Army, but it (together with the much maligned French First and Seventh Armies) slowed Bock down long enough to enable the BEF to reach Dunkirk more or less intact. Once an army has been pushed back out of its own country, its fighting spirit is in any case likely to collapse like a punctured soufflé and the Belgian Army was no exception. Then too, unlike the British, the Belgians and the French were not regular troops (or part-time volunteers, like the British Territorials), they were conscripts who were anxious to get home, and for whom the war was all but over. The German superiority in tank tactics and especially their sophisticated use of radio communication at every level to concentrate tanks, motorized infantry, artillery, and aircraft on a single point with devastating speed and power had overwhelmed conventional troops as well as their bewildered commanders.

Above all, the seemingly constant presence during daylight hours of Stuka dive-bombers attacking almost without opposition broke whatever fighting spirit was left among troops who had expected to wage war defensively from prepared positions (as in the First World War) and instead found themselves scattered along the roads among the refugees, and bombed day or night wherever they paused. A war of movement exposed not only the weaknesses in the Allied armies but the deficiencies and unwieldiness of their chain of command.

German control of the air had further demoralized them. Belgium's air force had been destroyed on the ground, France's air force had disintegrated almost at once, just as everybody in the know in French political circles had predicted it would, since it was equipped with inferior, outdated aircraft and had no modern integrated system of command and control.

Even in the BEF confidence in the Royal Air Force was plummeting. However superior British fighter aircraft were, all that the men on the ground saw was the unrelenting, uninterrupted attack of German bombers and dive-bombers. They seldom saw the "dog fights" going on high above them or appreciated the immensely high losses among the Battle or Blenheim bomber squadrons—on May 14, for example, forty out of seventy-one RAF aircraft sent to bomb German bridges over the Meuse were shot down, an unsustainable rate of loss. Given the exaggerated fear of "fifth columnists"* and German parachutists—in fact the whole German parachute force had been used to capture the vital Dutch and Belgian bridges on May 10—British airmen obliged to bail out were frequently treated as the enemy even by their own countrymen, and sometimes threatened with being shot by Belgian and French troops. It did not help matters that Luftwaffe and RAF uniforms and flying suits looked similar. Ironically, the RAF, which would achieve its moment of greatest glory only three months later in the Battle of Britain, had now reached a nadir of popularity among the troops such that the prime minister himself would feel obliged to deal with the matter—RAF personnel were being insulted and even "roughed up" by angry soldiers, thanks to the ubiquity of German aircraft.

La Falaise describes the common experience of a sudden attack by German aircraft in broad daylight: "Geysers of earth and tongues of flame leap into the sky. For three minutes or more, that seem endless, I cower under a wall holding my breath, my legs shaking, while houses to the right and left are smashed to the ground. Two hundred yards up the road a convoy of more than

---

* A phrase from the Spanish Civil War, when Fascist General Emilio Mola claimed that in addition to four columns of troops attacking Madrid he had "a fifth column" inside it. The notion of an elaborate organization of German troops in civilian clothes ("storm troopers" disguised as nuns was a favorite example) or German-sponsored civilian snipers and saboteurs was widespread in 1940, but there is very little concrete evidence that it really existed, although a good many unlucky people were summarily executed for belonging to it.

twenty ammunition trucks is hit repeatedly and blows up with a deafening explosion. Shells and men's bodies fly through the air. The ammunition cases keep on exploding an hour after the planes disappear, making it impossible for anyone to rescue the wounded."

Again and again one is struck by the fact that the Germans had spent nearly two decades thinking out every detail of the attack against France and the Low Countries with single-minded Teutonic efficiency. As airfields were captured, improvised teams of men quickly installed radio communication and erected repair facilities; as soon as they were done, the lumbering but reliable Ju 52 transport aircraft (the German equivalent of the Douglas DC-3 "Dakota," which would become ubiquitous in the same role after the United States entered the war) flew in specialists, fuel, and ammunition; thus the German air force leapfrogged directly behind the fighting troops, and was able to deliver aircraft like runners in a relay race. A squadron would attack, and while it was flying back to refuel and rearm, another would take its place, a constant, rolling delivery line of death and destruction.

British and French strategists (except for contrarians like Fuller and de Gaulle) had never anticipated this kind of efficiency, in which the aircraft were based right behind the front line and in constant radio communication with troops on the ground, so that a regimental commander could summon up waves of dive-bombers instead of waiting for artillery to be brought up. It had been considered impossible to supply aviation fuel to such advanced airfields, but the Germans simply flew it in and, what's more, had designed the twenty-liter stamped and welded steel "jerrycan," with its built-in pouring spout and leak-proof snap closure, which would soon be adopted by every army in the world, allowing them to move large quantities of fuel quickly, safely, and easily, at a time when everybody else was still using flimsy stamped tin containers that required a wrench and a funnel and leaked like a sieve.

Even somebody as practically minded as Churchill had supposed that German tanks would outrun their fuel supply quickly, without taking into account the mass production of the jerrycan—or the fact that Rommel moved so fast that he simply had his tanks stop and refuel at gas stations on the road, as if they were cars. It was not so much that every German weapon was superior as that each piece of their war machine, however small, fit into place like the pieces of a jigsaw puzzle, and that everything was built around the concept of movement. Whereas the French had put their money between the wars into the Maginot Line, as imposing and as firmly fixed in place as the Pyramids, the ultimate expression of defense, the Germans had instead built a functioning modern war machine—their mantra was mobility, its purpose was to attack.

On Sunday, May 26, General Lord Gort informed the secretary of state for war of his decision, with a certain degree of restraint: "At present we are strung out on immense front and great majority of force is in close contact with the enemy. There are not sufficient reserves with which to make a hole for a break. Some withdrawal essential. . . ." The word "Some" was a vast understatement. General Pownall commented to himself, more frankly, "Whether we ever get to the sea, how we get off the beach, how many of us survive is on the knees of the Gods. But it is the only thing to be done. We cannot stay here without being surrounded and there is no other direction in which to go."

By now, a note of caution and common sense had been sounded in the British War Cabinet too. The prime minister remarked, "It seemed from all the evidence available that we might have to face a situation in which the French were going to collapse, and that we must do our best to extricate the British Expeditionary Force from northern France."

It was a busy day for Churchill. To begin with, it had been declared a National Day of Prayer, a suggestion that the king had made three days before, and which rendered the prime minister's presence in Westminster Abbey necessary for ten minutes during the service—

the closest he could cut it. Churchill had not been enthusiastic about the king's idea, concerned that a day of national prayer might be seen as an admission of fear or defeatism by the enemy. He was not in any case an enthusiastic churchgoer—Churchill dutifully attended formal events that involved the church, weddings, funerals, christenings, and coronations, but observed of the Church of England that he "supported it from the outside, like a flying buttress." Like a former prime minister, Lord Melbourne, who had found the appointment of bishops one of the most burdensome duties of his office (and complained that they died only to annoy him), Churchill was without religious instincts,* and did not suppose that a church service, even one involving the king and the archbishop of Canterbury, would improve Britain's military situation. However, he had to go despite his grumbling, as Mrs. Churchill pointed out to him.

More on his mind that day was the fact that he had decided to replace the chief of the Imperial General Staff, General Sir Edmund Ironside, with General Sir John Dill, the vice-chief and a former corps commander of the BEF, an odd decision since Churchill rather liked Tiny Ironside and thought Dill was unimaginative and "a dinosaur." It may have been a reflection of the intense French dislike of Ironside, who had not bothered to disguise his contempt for the French generals, or of a growing expectation on Churchill's part that a German invasion of Britain would follow a French collapse and that Ironside, with his bluff, untactful nature, was the right man to knock heads together and improvise an effective defense. If so, he would be disappointed—Ironside rubbed his generals the wrong way in his new role as commander in chief, Home Forces, and Dill was not transformed by his promotion into the CIGS that the prime minister was looking for. Fortunately, the headlines about the German advance to the sea rather

---

* Churchill neatly summed up his religious beliefs himself: "I am prepared to meet my Maker. Whether my Maker is prepared for the ordeal of meeting me is another matter."

overshadowed the stories the next day about this hasty change in command.

Even bigger challenges faced Churchill early in the morning on May 26, starting with an alarming surprise: a telegram from Premier Reynaud that he was flying to London that day and "wished to meet with the Prime Minister alone, or perhaps with one other Minister present only," surely a sign that the French were already thinking about surrender. More depressing still was a message from Admiral Keyes that the king of the Belgians had decided "not to desert his army" and join his government in exile, and had written a personal letter to King George VI explaining his motives— king to king, as it were. A Belgian surrender, which was clearly imminent, would leave the left flank of the BEF wide open as it withdrew toward Dunkirk.

The message that Premier Reynaud flew to London to deliver to the prime minister personally over a hastily arranged lunch à deux at Churchill's flat in the Admiralty was not quite yet a counsel of despair, but it was not far from it. A week ago Reynaud had asked Marshal Pétain to return from Madrid, where he had been serving as French ambassador to Franco's Spain, and join the cabinet as deputy prime minister. The camel's nose was therefore already inside the tent—Pétain's pessimism, his vanity, his dislike of the British, above all his belief that the war had already been lost and should never have been begun in the first place had already affected the French government and undermined Reynaud's tenuous control of it. Reynaud's message reflected, however hard he tried to conceal it from Churchill, the rapid metastasis of French defeatism.

The message contained two separate parts, the first of which was to become the theme of every Franco-British meeting over the next two weeks: the French did not think that they could continue the war for much longer unless the British threw in all of Fighter Command at once—or unless the United States joined the war. The latter was of course beyond Churchill's control, and he strongly doubted that President Roosevelt could or would declare war against Germany, something he was in a good position to judge since he was in constant correspondence with the president and received frequent warnings on the subject from Ambassador Kennedy as well. As for the former, it would entail giving up any chance of defending Great Britain.

The fact that Fighter Command could not operate from make-shift airfields under German attack, and that it was dependent on a vastly complex system of radar observation and bombproofed, centralized communication was not discussed—radar was too secret to talk about, and in any case the prime minister himself had not yet fully understood the sheer complexity and sophistication of Britain's air defenses, of which the fighters themselves were only the most visible and glamorous part.

The second French request was for an immediate approach to Mussolini to prevent Italy from joining the war, in return for which Britain and France might offer to address some of Mussolini's demands in the Mediterranean—Reynaud rather vaguely alluded to the demilitarization of Suez, Gibraltar, and Malta, and to Italian claims to France's colony in Tunisia as possibilities for discussion. Churchill had a guarded respect for the man he called "the Italian lawgiver," whom he had met, but was not about to hand him control of the Mediterranean on a silver platter in return for a promise that Italy would stay out of the war.

It may seem odd, in view of the future performance of the Italian armed forces, that Mussolini's threat to enter the war was taken so seriously, but there was certainly something to be said for keeping Italy out of it. This would not only free up ten French divisions that were standing guard idly along the Franco-Italian border but, much more important, prevent the war from spreading to the Mediterranean when Allied forces were already stretched to (or beyond) the breaking point in northern France. Francophile though he was, the prime minister could hardly fail to notice that in the long tradition of Anglo-French diplomacy Reynaud was in effect proposing to buy peace with Italy in British coin—Suez, Malta, and Gibraltar.

Churchill disputed most of this, firmly but in good temper. He tried to raise Reynaud's spirits by saying that once the situation in northeastern France had been "cleared up," he thought the Germans would attack Britain next rather than break through the thinly held French line and go for Paris. Reynaud was not persuaded. It was "the dream of all Germans . . . to conquer Paris," he replied, correctly and with implacable French logic, and therefore "they would march on Paris."

Unfortunately no record of the conversation between the two prime ministers exists. Reynaud did not write about it until 1951, whereas Churchill came straight back from the lunch to tell the rest of the War Cabinet what had been said. That the War Cabinet resumed at 2 p.m. would seem to indicate that lunch was a hasty meal by Churchill's standards, and probably by those of Reynaud too. Sadly, it was a Sunday and Churchill's invaluable (and observant) young private secretary John Colville was away for the day in Oxford, flirting with Chief Conservative Whip Captain Margesson's daughter Gay—they dined together at the seventeenth-century pub and restaurant The Trout, by the Thames, still a wonderful restaurant even in my own days at Oxford—so we have no idea what kind of meal was served to Reynaud. In any event Churchill ended it by

John Collville.

asking Reynaud bluntly whether any peace terms had been offered to France, and Reynaud, surely with some embarrassment, replied evasively that none had been so far, but that he knew he could get an offer if he wanted one.

Churchill asked Halifax, Chamberlain, and Attlee to go over to the Admiralty and talk to Reynaud before he returned to Paris, but not before the crucial question came up that would dominate the next forty-eight hours politically. The minutes of the War Cabinet note rather modestly, "A short further discussion ensued on whether we should make any approach to Italy," without much detail. We know from the record that the prime minister "doubted whether anything would come of an approach to Italy," while the foreign secretary (Lord Halifax) "favoured this course" and thought that the last thing "Signor Mussolini" would want was "to see Herr Hitler dominating Europe."

This was a substantial difference of opinion, particularly since Halifax had already met with the Italian ambassador, Count Giuseppe Bastianini, to discuss not only the question of keeping Italy out of the war but the much bigger one of persuading Mussolini to ask Hitler what his terms for peace might be, or as Bastianini put it more diplomatically (as reported in the cautious words of Halifax) of not excluding "the possibility of some discussion of the wider problems of Europe in the event of the opportunity arising." Since Mussolini read and initialed Bastianini's report on the conversation, it was clear to him that Halifax was proposing that he repeat his bravura performance as the man who saved the world from war by sponsoring the Munich Conference in 1938, this time by bringing the warring parties to the conference table in May 1940.

Such a reprise would no doubt have appealed to Mussolini's colossal vanity, had he not already pledged to Hitler that he would join the war just as soon as the creaky stage machinery of the Italian armed forces could be moved into action of some sort—indeed *any* sort. Besides, Mussolini had already calculated that Germany was winning the war, had already as good as won it in fact, and that he would get a better share of the spoils if he came in as soon as possible on the German side—his only anxiety was that the French and the British might surrender *before* he could declare war, in which case Italy might get nothing, a concern made more acute by Hitler's apparent indifference to whether Italy joined in the war or not, and by the unmistakable hostility and contempt toward Italy of the German generals, who had no desire to add the Italian Army's logistical problems to their own.

One thing is certain, that Hitler already had learned from Rome that Halifax (and, he may have supposed, perhaps other members of the War Cabinet) was seeking a negotiated peace, "not merely an armistice but [a settlement that] would protect European peace for a century," to quote Bastianini's overinflated hopes. The same message was also reaching the Führer from Paris, via Rome, perhaps clouding his judgment momentarily.

Significantly, Churchill sent Halifax, Chamberlain, and Attlee off to the Admiralty with instructions to get Reynaud to have General Weygand *order* the BEF to march to the coast, so the French could not afterwards complain that they had not been informed, or that the British had let them down. Unlikely as it was that Weygand would oblige (or that the French would take any notice), Churchill told the secretary of state for war, Anthony Eden, to draft an order at once for General Gort to march to the coast and begin the evacuation of the BEF.

The War Cabinet resumed at 5 p.m. and Churchill was momentarily obliged to struggle against Halifax's desire to explore a negotiated peace, no doubt reinforced by his discussion with Premier Reynaud. The prime minister said "that we were in a different position from France. In the first place, we still had powers of resistance and attack, which they had not. In the second place, they would be likely to be offered decent terms by Germany, which we should not." He did not wish to be forced into "a weak position in which we went to Signor Mussolini and invited him to go to Herr Hitler and ask him to treat us nicely."

Halifax rejected this view. He thought it would be better to allow France "to try out the possibilities of European equilibrium," exactly the kind of diplomatic doubletalk that was likely to irritate Churchill. Halifax then remarked that he "would not like to see France subjected to the Gestapo."

Churchill dismissed this brusquely as unlikely.

Halifax replied that he was not so sure. He had not yet discovered that, unlike him, Churchill *enjoyed* arguing and that his opponent's arguments bounced off him like tennis balls aimed at a tank.

The line was now clearly drawn between them—there was a fissure in the War Cabinet, and Halifax felt obliged to put the argument *against* continuing the war to his fellow members of the War Cabinet. Unlike the prime minister, Halifax had taken full measure of Reynaud's report of the hopelessness of the French position, nor did he share Churchill's zest for battle or his experience on the battlefield of wringing victory from apparent defeat.

Churchill's reply was blunt and unambiguous. He thought it was best "to decide nothing until we saw how much of the Army we could re-embark from France." That operation, he thought, "might be a great failure." On the other hand, "our troops might fight magnificently and we might save a considerable portion of the Force." He ended the discussion—for the moment—with a flourish. "Herr Hitler," Churchill said, "thought he had the whip hand. The only thing to do was to show him that he could not conquer this country."

Admiration for the new prime minister was not yet universal. Sir Alexander Cadogan, permanent undersecretary at the Foreign Office, who attended the War Cabinet that afternoon, remarked in his diary that Churchill was "too rambling and romantic and sentimental and temperamental," a view that Halifax certainly shared, or at least with which he would have sympathized. "Old Neville still the best of the lot," Cadogan concluded, an opinion still shared by most Conservatives.

That evening Captain Claude Berkeley, a member of the prime minister's military staff, reported an impression different from that of Cadogan: "Reynaud was not impressive. The PM was terrific, hurling himself about, getting his staff into hopeless tangles by dashing across to Downing St without a word of warning, shouting that we would never give in, etc."

At 7 p.m. Churchill gave the crucial order to begin Operation Dynamo, Vice-Admiral Ramsay's plan for the evacuation of the BEF.

Late that night he sent a message to Lord Gort, whose army was moving in chaotic conditions and under constant attack toward Dunkirk, where the harbor was already being shelled by at least forty German guns. "At this solemn moment I cannot help sending you my good wishes. No one can tell how it may go. But anything is better than being cooped up and starved out. . . . Presume troops know they are cutting their way home to Blighty. Never was there such a spur for fighting. We shall give you all that the Navy and the Air Force can do."

25

Dynamo

Obergruppenführer Sepp Dietrich and Himmler.

AT 10 P.M. on Sunday, May 26, Vice-Admiral Sir Bertram Ramsay received the order from the Admiralty to commence Dynamo. Ramsay's mind was eminently practical—he had chosen Dynamo as the code name for the evacuation not because it connoted rapid movement or power but simply because his office in one of the tunnels of the White Cliffs of Dover was close to another containing the emergency generator. He set in motion his forces for Dynamo in the same practical spirit.

Although Churchill clung to the belief that Weygand's planned attack would actually take place until the last possible moment, the vice-admiral Dover had already long since concluded that evacuation might be necessary. On May 15, when the Germans had just crossed the Meuse and the BEF was still digging in at the Dyle line in Belgium, Ramsay had set in motion the "Census of [civilian] Motor-boats," the first essential step to gathering together every ship and boat that might be needed, and on May 19, in a meeting at the War Office, he brought up "the problem of the hazardous evacuation of very large forces."

Ramsay was not only farsighted; he was as a senior naval officer accustomed to making decisions on his own—the captain of a ship cannot always wait for orders or ask for them to be explained—and something of a buccaneer. The naval force he commanded as the vice-admiral Dover was small compared with the importance of his post, only eighteen destroyers and a mix of minesweepers, trawlers, "armed boarding vessels," and train ferries converted into minelayers, but he had used his destroyers daringly, slipping them into the port of Ijmuiden under the guns of the Germans to bring off the Dutch royal family and government, as well as all the Dutch gold reserve and a large stock of diamonds.

On May 24 Ramsay met with the vice-chief of the French Naval Staff, Admiral Auphan, and the *Amiral Nord*, Admiral Abrial. Both French admirals were, or pretended to be, shocked and angered by Ramsay's frank discussion of his plans for evacuating the BEF from Dunkirk. They had in mind defending Dunkirk as a kind of fortified bridgehead, supplied from England. Ramsay, with some difficulty, attempted to smooth their ruffled feathers, though he did not succeed in convincing Abrial, who would stay on to the very end in his underground headquarters at Dunkirk attempting to defend the city, while communicating as seldom as possible with his British allies—a fatal breach. Even among admirals, a notoriously tough bunch, Admiral Abrial was a tough nut to crack, and like most, if not all, French senior naval officers he regarded Britain as France's hereditary foe. The Germans were merely a coarse and unwelcome interruption in a naval rivalry that had been going on since the early eighteenth century.

It is worth noting that Ramsay was preparing for Dynamo and

discussing it with the French admirals a day *before* Lord Gort reluctantly reached his decision to retreat to the coast, and three days before Ramsay actually received the order to begin it. Photographs of him portray a calm, sturdy, realistic judge of events, feet spread as if he were on the bridge of his ship, unlikely to be swayed by rhetoric or windy emotion—in short, the perfect man for the job. It is some measure of Ramsay's organizational ability that within three days of the order to begin Dynamo he would put together a fleet consisting not only of warships but of almost everything that would float, including the lifeboats from ocean liners and freighters moored in the London docks, yachts, barges, paddle-wheel pleasure steamers, fishing trawlers, tugs, ferries, a London fireboat, and Dutch *schuits* (broad-beamed Dutch canal boats), a total of over eight hundred recorded vessels. He would also acquire a couple of hundred more privately owned vessels, among them *Sundowner*, a fifty-eight-foot yacht owned by Charles Lightoller, the retired second officer of RMS *Titanic*, who sailed her himself to the Dunkirk beaches aided by a crew consisting of his eldest son and a teenaged Sea Scout, and *Medway Queen*, a Thames paddle-wheel pleasure steamer, which made seven round-trips to the beaches, brought back seven thousand men, was credited with shooting down three enemy aircraft, and ended her career moored as a floating nightclub. Some of the bigger ferries that served the Isle of Man or the Channel Islands were diverted to Dunkirk with their white-jacketed stewards still ringing a little silver bell to announce that tea was being served in the saloon (for officers, rather than first-class passengers), or drinks and sandwiches.* Some of the larger ferries had been converted into hospital ships, painted white with conspicuous red crosses on the hull and funnel, but this did not protect them from being bombed or shelled by the Germans.

---

* Two hundred forty-three ships and boats are listed as having been sunk by German mines, torpedoes, gunfire, or bombing, but the actual number is probably far higher since many sinkings of private vessels went unrecorded. When a ship went down, the soldiers on board often went with her if they were below deck. When the destroyer HMS *Wakeful* was torpedoed, she took six hundred soldiers down with her, for instance.

Ramsay had already succeeded in getting 27,936 "non-fighting troops," as the official British war history calls them, out of Boulogne, Calais, and Dunkirk before Dynamo had even begun. Many of these were taken off the eastern mole of Dunkirk's outer harbor, a long stone-and-wood structure ending in a wooden jetty. Dunkirk was not then the modern port it has since become, nor was it a particularly convenient one from which to evacuate a large number of men. The entrance to the outer harbor was narrow, formed by two moles running out to sea at an angle of about forty-five degrees to each other like a giant funnel, its spout pointing out to sea, its wider end opening out as one approached the inner port, and leading to a longer and even narrower entrance to the docks themselves, which formed one side of the town.

At the best of times, it was a tricky port to enter, requiring an experienced pilot and a careful skipper; in bad weather—or under enemy bombing and shelling—it was a hazardous place to enter with even a moderate-sized ship, and would be made more so by the growing number of half-sunken shipwrecks. Once a ship entered the inner harbor and tied up to a wharf, she was immobilized— as a target for German dive-bombers it was like shooting fish in a barrel. It was easier and quicker to tie up in the outer harbor at the eastern mole, and much faster to get aweigh from there, but the eastern mole was narrow and precarious, almost three-quarters of a mile in length, limiting the flow of men toward the waiting ships. In addition, tides are big in the English Channel—the difference between low and high water can exceed fifteen feet at Dunkirk, which means that access to the ships often involved a long, steep, slippery gangplank, not easy for men who were exhausted and wet, having been under fire for days.

Ramsay learned a lot during the three days before Dynamo, none of it reassuring. The direct distance from Dover to Calais is only twenty-one miles, and the usual way of approaching Dunkirk was to steer directly south toward Calais then turn east for another twenty-five miles, running close inshore along the French coast to avoid the dangerous sandbanks (this was referred to as "Route Z"). With the fall of Calais, however, this course exposed Ramsay's ships to German artillery fire both coming and going, so he was forced to choose alternate courses. Following "Route Y" vessels sailed from Dover, Ramsgate, or Sheerness northward, clinging to the English shoreline, rounded the notorious Goodwin Sands, on which hundreds of ships large and small had come to grief over the years, turned due east toward Ostend, then southwest along the Belgian coastline to Dunkirk—a loop of some seventy-one miles, which had the further disadvantage of exposing ships to German submarines and E-boats in the North Sea, and of requiring precise navigation to avoid British minefields.

An alternative was "Route X," which reduced the distance to fifty-five miles, but followed a course that went *between* sandbanks and through a narrow swept channel in a minefield, and could only be used in daylight. Neither of these courses was difficult for naval ships, but required a degree of precision navigation greater than the average civilian vessel (or amateur sailor) was likely to possess.*

They also required the immediate preparation of a thousand specially prepared charts showing the new courses and, more difficult still, getting one of them into the hands of every captain or yachtsman sailing to Dunkirk, as well as precise sailing instructions from a naval officer. It was no longer possible to simply steer south by the compass until one saw Calais, then turn east along the coast to Dunkirk. Large or small, every vessel would be exposed to all the dangers of the sea, as well as the full fury of the Germans. Even for an island nation that still thought of itself as ruling the waves, this was a challenging undertaking.

---

* The new German magnetic mines posed an additional problem for Ramsay. Naval ships were equipped with a new and secret "degaussing" coil, which prevented the mine from being detonated by the ship's magnetic field, but there was no time to degauss every civilian vessel, and mines were to cause many of the sinkings during the Dunkirk evacuation. Ramsay set up five degaussing stations, but the crews of many of the smaller civilian vessels didn't know about them.

*   *   *

A further problem for Ramsay was the state of the troops themselves—as they arrived in Dunkirk, they abandoned their vehicles, blocking streets that were already filled with rubble from constant bombing, and producing chaos. Many of them had lost their officers, and some senior officers had already embarked, leaving behind what was in danger of becoming a disorderly mob. Order would be restored as fighting units began to move into Dunkirk, as a perimeter was set up, and as officers and the Royal Military Police began to separate those who could still fight from those who would be sent to the beaches. In the meantime the most important step Ramsay took was to send Captain W. G. Tennant of the Royal Navy, with a staff of 12 officers and 150 seamen on Monday, May 27, to take up his appointment as senior naval officer Dunkirk. Photographs of Tennant make it clear that he projected an aura of unmistakable command, and he must have been an instantly recognizable figure in his neat blue naval uniform and gold braid among the bedraggled crowd of khaki-clad soldiers. Tennant's staff, however, apparently decided that he needed some kind of symbol of his authority over the port and beaches of Dunkirk, so they fashioned the letters "S N O" out of silver paper from cigarette and chocolate packets and stuck them to his steel helmet with globs of pea soup.

Captain W. G. Tennant.

This seems to have been unnecessary. Tennant took in the situation immediately, and proceeded to apply his authority as SNO at once. Later he would write,

> As regards the bearing and behavior of the troops, British and French, prior to and during the embarkation, it must be recorded that the earlier parties were embarked off the beaches in a condition of complete disorganization.

> There appeared to be no military officers in charge of the troops. . . . It was soon realized that it was vitally necessary to dispatch naval officers in their unmistakable uniform with armed naval beach parties to take charge of the soldiers on shore immediately prior to embarkation. Great credit is due the naval officers and naval ratings for the restoration of some semblance of order. Later on, when troops of fighting formations reached the beaches, these difficulties disappeared.

This is in sharp contrast to the rosier view of the evacuation from Dunkirk in many histories, but accords with General Montgomery's opinion later that those who had been evacuated from Dunkirk should not have a special medal or a shoulder flash, since they had been involved in a defeat, not a victory. "I remember," Montgomery wrote, "the disgust of many like myself when we saw British soldiers walking about in London . . . with a colored embroidered patch on their sleeve with the title 'Dunkirk.' They thought they were heroes, and the civilian public thought so too. It was not understood that the British Army had suffered a crushing defeat. . . ."

By Monday, May 27, the bulk of the BEF, a quarter of a million men, and large numbers of the French Army, were all "falling back in hot battle," desperately fighting for survival against a better-armed and -led army of superior strength. Over the past few days there had been no moment of easy retreat. The only way to keep the BEF together was to fight every inch of the way. If the Germans could have broken through the hard shell of British resistance, the BEF might have been split piecemeal into isolated units, as the French had been after the German crossing of the Meuse. In that case the BEF might have collapsed, the Germans could have broken their way into Dunkirk, the last remaining port, and the entire BEF could then have been rounded up, or defeated as individual units or small groups of men making here and there an isolated last stand wherever the ground and their supply of ammunition made it possible. Nobody had a sense of "the big picture"—each soldier saw only the back of the man in front of him as he marched, or the men on either side of him as he stopped and fought.

Even for those at the top, there was no clear view of events. First of all there were three separate battles taking place, one on land, increasingly savage and bloody, one in the air, difficult to assess, and the last at sea. Then too, even at the very highest level, there was a certain degree of confusion and reluctance to face the facts. The British had only a vague idea of what the French were doing, or what they might still be capable of doing, still less of what the Belgians were doing, even though the Belgian Army was on the left flank of the BEF as it retreated. The fighting troops were exhausted, outnumbered, had been without rations for days, had been fiercely engaged with the enemy for nearly two weeks, and been bombed day and night. They were held together by those two old-fashioned, but vital, elements—discipline and loyalty to their own regiment, as has been the case since the mid-seventeenth century.

Celebration of the evacuation and immortalization of "the little ships" have tended to draw attention away from the savage fighting that preceded it. Hugh Sebag-Montefiore, in his magisterial account on the campaign, estimates that of the approximately 2,500 men in one brigade (his chosen example is 4 Brigade of 2nd Division of III Corps, consisting of 1st Battalion the Royal Scots, 2nd Battalion the Royal Norfolk Regiment, 1st/8th Battalion the Lancashire Fusiliers) only 650 made it back to England, which means that three-quarters of the brigade was killed, seriously wounded, or captured between May 10 and June 1, 1940—and there is no reason to suppose that 4 Brigade was unusual. This is a rate of loss comparable to that in the bloodiest battles of the First World War, or the American Civil War, and an indication of just how hard the fighting was during the retreat of the BEF to Dunkirk.

Although the German panzer divisions remained a major concern, the countryside between Lille and Dunkirk lent itself to the bitterest and most old-fashioned infantry warfare. The flat ground was intersected by a complex web of big and small rivers, canals, and ditches, and each bridge had to be fought over—or destroyed before the enemy could get to it. It was also a mass of small villages and farms, in which most of the buildings were solidly built out of local stone, ideal for mounting a defense, in a battle much of which was being fought at close range by rifle fire, machine-gun fire, grenades, and even the bayonet and the pistol, as well as by artillery and more modern weapons like tanks.

Accounts of it read like those of the fighting in the First World War. "They were closing in on all sides, mopping pockets up," one soldier recalled.

> The [German] infantry was bunched up behind the tanks. Following behind in bunches, using the shelter of the tank. . . . I found myself with a group of others being driven back towards the canal. I actually fired the Boys anti-tank rifle for the first time. It was a terrifying weapon. To even fire it, you had to hang on to it like grim death, because it would dislocate your shoulder if you didn't. I fired at a tank coming over the main bridge about 50 yards away, and I couldn't miss. It hit the tank—and knocked the paintwork off. That's all it done. It just bounced off, making a noise like a ping-pong ball. After that, an officer said, "Leave that blasted thing there, Doe, and get the hell out of it!"

The same soldier, Lance-Corporal Doe, also recalled looking down at a dead German and envying his superior equipment: "He had his jackboots on, a belt round his uniform, a canister at the side, but he wasn't lumbered down. He wasn't tied down with packs and equipment like we were. . . . We were not only outnumbered . . . but out-armed in every way."

One soldier remembered passing over the body of a British soldier cut in half by shell fire, the two halves connected only by the intestines; another, of the 9th Battalion, Durham Light Infantry, remembered trying to lift the body of a dead British soldier and finding that "when we lifted the top part of him, the bottom part stayed where it was. It was only the buttons on his battledress and his pants that were keeping his body together. . . . We took him and did with him what we did with all the others: we dug a hole in someone's garden and tipped them all in." The surprising thing is the toughness of these soldiers, many of whom were half-trained part-timers rather than hardened regulars.

The German superiority in armor was still important, particularly since the BEF had lost most of its much-smaller armored force defending Arras on May 21, but British infantry could still hold its own, and the Germans had to fight hard for every gain they made. Every war produces losses and casualties of course, but the German infantry had had a fairly easy time of it to this point. Once Army Group A had crossed the Meuse and broken through the ineffective French defenses, German losses were low, and the same was true for Army Group B, given the collapse of the Dutch Army and the rapid demoralization of the Belgian Army. By now the Germans were coming up against the hard core of British regular and Territorial infantry battalions, and they bitterly resented it.

May 27 was therefore marked by a serious incident that was to become all too familiar. The 3rd SS Division Totenkopf, originally formed from concentration camp guards, was part of the reserve of Army Group A and had already acquired an unsavory reputation in the ten days it had been fighting—among other things the division had refused to accept the surrender of French Moroccan troops and executed them out of hand instead, an example of orthodox Nazi racial fanaticism in the field that caused some senior German Army officers to raise a well-bred eyebrow. SS Totenkopf suffered from that familiar German combination of racial superiority coupled with a corrosive inferiority complex. They thought themselves superior to the rest of the German Army, but at the same time they knew they were looked down on as amateur soldiers and party hacks by many senior officers. They not only had a chip on their shoulder; they took heavier losses than were necessary, and were indecently quick to shoot civilians who got in their way or showed any degree of resentment.

The division's commander, SS Obergruppenführer Theodor Eicke, was a major figure in the SS, one of the creators of the Nazi concentration camp system and the infamous inspector of concentration camps, as well as the man who had executed the thuggish leader of the Nazi Brownshirts Ernst Röhm in his cell during "the Night of the Long Knives" in 1934, which among other things ensured the supremacy of the SS once and for all over the rest of the Nazi Party.

WAFFEN-SS

EINTRITT NACH VOLLENDETEM 17. LEBENSJAHR

AUSKUNFT: Ergänzungsstelle Südwest (V), Nebenstelle Strassburg, Elsassstrasse 10
sowie sämtliche SS- und Polizeidienststellen

Even in the Waffen SS, Eicke stood out for his brutality, and much to the German Army's dislike he and his troops thought of themselves as an elite force, entitled to despise and ignore the ordinary rules of war. They therefore felt particularly humiliated when they were beaten back and forced to retreat after the British counterattack at Arras on May 21, and suffered casualties during the following days that they regarded as excessive.

Thus they were in no mood for chivalrous behavior on the morning of May 27 when they came up against a British force consisting of companies from the 2nd Royal Norfolk Regiment, the 8th Lancashire Fusiliers, and the 1st Battalion, Royal Scots. The British, though badly outnumbered, fought hard—SS Totenkopf lost 4 officers and 150 men killed, and nearly 500 wounded—but they were eventually split up and cut off. Two companies of the Royal Norfolks dug in around a solid, ugly, two-story brick farmhouse near the unfortunately named village of Le Paradis, which they defended fiercely from before noon until after five in the afternoon, at which point they ran out of ammunition. They had been forced to abandon the farmhouse for a cow barn after the Germans brought up tanks and artillery to destroy it and what remained of the two companies, most of whom were wounded, came out with their hands up, and surrendered under a white flag once they could no longer fight.

The SS Totenkopf quickly demonstrated their contempt for the normal rules of warfare. The ninety-nine men were marched into a barn courtyard and machine-gunned. Any who showed signs of life were finished off with a pistol shot to the head or clubbed to death with a rifle butt, except for two men who although wounded miraculously survived under the pile of bodies, escaped during the night, and hid themselves in a pig sty, where they were discovered and cared for at great risk by a French farm family. They were finally captured by German Army soldiers and sent to a POW camp.

The SS officer who ordered the massacre, *SS Hauptsturmführer* Fritz Knöchlein, had already murdered about twenty men of the 1st Royal Scots that day, and hidden their bodies in a mass grave. At his trial after the war Knöchlein claimed that the Royal Norfolks had been using expanding or "Dum-Dum bullets," which are outlawed by the Hague Convention of 1899 and 1907, but that seems unlikely since all British small arms ammunition used in the Second World War was of the normal military full metal jacket pattern.[*]

On Tuesday, May 28, the next day, the 1st SS Division Leibstandarte Adolf Hitler, commanded by an even more notorious Nazi, Hitler's former chauffeur, bodyguard, and backstreet brawler SS Obergruppenführer Sepp Dietrich, massacred eighty officers and men of the 2nd Royal Warwickshire Regiment, the 4th Cheshire Regiment, the Royal Artillery, and some French soldiers, at Wormhoudt after they had run out of ammunition and surrendered.

---

[*] Knöchlein was found guilty and hanged in 1949.

Dietrich, who would rise to become the SS equivalent of a colonel general, was on close terms with the Führer, perhaps the only man who was permitted to refer to him, and even address him as "Adi," an affectionate diminutive of Adolf. He had made his name in the barroom fights and street violence that accompanied the Nazi Party's rise to power. He was not the man to restrain his officers and men from executing prisoners, and in fact men under his command would do so again in January 1945 when they murdered eighty-four Americans who had surrendered at Malmedy, Belgium, during the Battle of the Bulge, after four years of unrestrained war crimes on the eastern front.

Complaints about the massacres made their way up through the German Army chain of command at a leisurely pace, but when it came to discipline the Waffen SS reported to Himmler, not the OKH, and in any case Eicke and Dietrich were almost untouchable, so the two "incidents" were allowed to vanish into the vast paperwork of the German Army.

Even such imposing figures as Colonel General von Rundstedt knew when it was necessary to turn a blind eye.

26

"Fight It Out,
Here or Elsewhere"

British machine gunners in the streets of Dunkirk.

No NEWS OF these massacres reached Britain, of course, or even General Lord Gort's headquarters. Communications between units of the BEF had broken down, and communication between the BEF and London was reduced to faint and unreliable telephone calls. All that was known was that the army was falling back on Dunkirk.

In London no hint of the disagreement in the War Cabinet on

May 27 reached beyond the small circle of those who were close to its members. Churchill's private secretary John Colville was near enough to his new boss to note that "there are signs that Halifax is being defeatist," but even Churchill's old friend and confidant Lord Beaverbrook, owner of the *Daily Express* and the *Evening Standard*, who was certainly aware of everything that went on in the War Cabinet, was careful not to leak a word of what was going on. More people in Rome or Berlin knew of the rift between the prime minister and the foreign secretary than did people in London. Of course in Rome and Berlin they hoped that it was an old-fashioned "cabinet crisis," and that Halifax had weighty support in the War Cabinet, but in fact he had none—his doubts were personal and moral, or perhaps philosophical, and were not even shared by former prime minister Neville Chamberlain, now lord president of the council, whose detractors still spoke of him disparagingly as "Old Umbrella."

Chamberlain had reverted to the tough-minded, hard-nosed politician he had always been before being led down the garden path of appeasement, and showed little sympathy for Halifax's proposal to let the French find out what Hitler's terms might be for peace, preferably with honor if that were possible, and still less for giving in to French demands for more fighter aircraft and British troops. Possibly Chamberlain's experience of having Daladier as a partner during the Czech crisis—playing Sancho Panza to Chamberlain's Don Quixote—had soured him altogether on France, but he now appeared as the apostle of realpolitik. In any case he had never cared much for the French, even less for the Czechs, the Poles, or for that matter the Germans, whether as represented by Hitler or otherwise. He was mildly interested in foreign policy, but disliked foreigners, a very English point of view. Improbable as it seems, Chamberlain was now a full supporter of Churchill—he brutally dismissed French claims to have been deserted by the British, and disparaged French accounts of how hard they had fought. He offered little support to Halifax; indeed one has the impression that he had hardened within his carapace like certain sea animals. Certainly Hitler was mistaken if he supposed that a full-scale cabinet revolt was brewing—so far it only consisted of one man, battling for Churchill's soul, or his own. Still, that might have been enough, had Dynamo failed.

As yet, however, Dynamo had not even begun. The public had not been prepared for bad news—indeed the daily communiqué from the GQG in Vincennes remained improbably "cheerful" in tone and optimistic, in contrast to the real state of events, let alone the state of mind of General Weygand, Premier Reynaud, and the rest of the French government. The *Times* for May 28 passed on the official GQG view of events via the Ministry of Information with this headline: "B. E. F. FRONT REMAINS INTACT, COOPERATION WITH FRENCH TANKS," and repeated an old bromide of World War One, "The French, after twice repulsing the Germans at Valenciennes, have withdrawn to previously prepared positions," a euphemism older readers who had lived through the First World War would remember for "headlong retreat."

The more popular newspapers speculated that the Germans had already sacrificed nearly half a million men in suicidal attacks, possibly as many as 600,000, as well as most of their aircraft. In fact, the Germans suffered a total of about 150,000 casualties, of whom about 27,000 were killed, during the *entire campaign* from May 10 to the surrender of France, and the Luftwaffe more than made up its losses in aircraft. The gap between reality and the official French military communiqués had become so alarmingly wide that Minister of Information Duff Cooper was worried that the British public "were, at the moment, quite unprepared for the shock of realization of the true position." To that view Churchill sensibly replied that the announcement of the Belgian surrender "would go a long way to prepare the public for bad news."

In fact, most people in Britain were not nearly as misled as their leaders supposed them to be. They drew their own conclusions from the maps in the newspapers, which made it clear that the BEF was surrounded with its back to the sea, as well as from an instinctive mistrust of the French and, at least in southern England, from the sight of "small ships" and even small boats being gathered rapidly in familiar rivers and harbors.

The Ministry of Information was still combining patriotic propaganda with the kind of wildly improbable stories in the old Fleet Street manner so richly caricatured by Evelyn Waugh in *Scoop*, like that of a couple of unarmed Auxiliary Army Pioneers (pick-and-shovel men) who put two German tanks out of commission with their picks, then took the crews prisoner. Perhaps out of a sense of its own dignity the *Times* did not stoop to explain how to stop a tank with a pick, although the eminent literary critic Cyril Con-

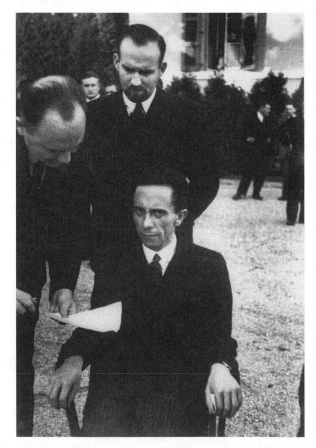

Dr. Joseph Goebbels, Reich minister of propaganda, having just been told that the person taking his photograph is Alfred Eisenstaedt, of *Life* magazine, a German Jew who had emigrated to the United States.

nolly fiercely caricatured the story in "How to stop a tank": "If you are very close, insert a knitting-needle into the tank's most vulnerable spot, the back-ratchet."

Traces of this head-in-the-sand news policy would continue to surface in the press for some time, but eventually Churchill managed by his own gift for oratory and for dramatizing the historic moment to make the British public feel not only good but *heroic* about bad news,* something that Reich Propaganda Minister Joseph Goebbels never dared to try with the German public until it was too late.

At home in Hampstead my father looked increasingly grim, as well he might—a survivor of the collapse and surrender of the Austro-Hungarian Army in 1918, he recognized the signs of military disaster, however well disguised with *Schlag*,† better than most. The Austro-Hungarian Army in 1918 had "withdrawn to prepared positions" until it simply disintegrated, like the empire itself. At least its soldiers could march back home to Vienna, Budapest, or Prague, rather than to a beach. At the studio in Denham Vincent was surrounded by huge sets he had designed for films that could no longer be made there, and as his men were withdrawn into the armed forces or the weapons industry, the cavernous soundstages were silent and empty. Whatever his reluctance was, he must have known by then that he was going to have to fit into Alex's plans.

He was not, of course, about to share these with me. Like so many children in England at the time, most of them far less fortu-

* Like Lincoln, Churchill had a gift for uplifting oratory about grim news, perhaps borne out of his long relationship in war and peace with David Lloyd George. His first speech as prime minister struck exactly the right note: "I have nothing to offer but blood, toil, tears and sweat." He had an instinctive understanding of the fact that the British as a people dislike boasting, and pride themselves not on victory but on being able to "take it." The Ministry of Information and the press were slow to catch up with him.
† Whipped cream, without a frothy dollop of which no cup of coffee or dessert in Austria or Hungary is complete. It was a word often used in Hollywood in the days when many directors were Central European, meaning more sentiment or glamor, as in "Do it again, but this time with more *Schlag*."

nate than myself, I was about to be packed off in a hurry to places unknown. All over the country people were abandoning homes and families, children, pets, and cherished possessions, to undertake new and unexpected responsibilities, often in faraway places. Men younger than my father were "joining up"; indeed one of his assistants had already left to join the Royal Air Force. Men of my father's age and older of a certain class were being drawn away by one of the many mysterious organizations that had proliferated in London since the beginning of the war and were identified, if at all, only by odd initials like SIS or SOE.* My father had been eager to do his bit for his adopted country, and was interviewed for some hush-hush military job involving camouflage—which, as a painter and scene designer he would have been very good at—but the last question at his formal interview, put to him by a senior officer in uniform, was whether he would be willing to learn how to ride a motorcycle, to which he very sensibly said no.† My father was then forty-three years old, and anybody who had ever seen him struggle with a motorcar would have realized that there was no chance at all of his being able to ride a motorcycle. It may also be that my father's appearance, with his scuffed shoes, suit jacket with the buttons in the wrong buttonholes, and unpressed trousers, had something to do with it, or perhaps his thick Hungarian accent. It would have been hard to imagine him in British uniform crisply returning salutes.

In any event, Alex's needs, as always, took precedence over his own, even when it came to serving his country, so there was no chance of his getting into uniform. If Alex's films could not be made at Denham, then they would have to be moved to where they *could*

---

* SIS stands for Secret Intelligence Service, or MI6, and SOE for Special Operations Executive, intended to sow terror and subversion in German-occupied Europe.
† An alternative question was "What sports do you play?" to which the right answer was rugby and cricket. My father would have found this one equally difficult, since he played neither.

be made, and that was that. During April and May 1940 as the war began to escalate, Alex flew back and forth between London, New York, and Los Angeles at a time when this was neither safe and easy nor possible at all without a high government priority. He returned to London on May 17 via Tangier and soon met with his old friend Minister of Information Duff Cooper, who gave him Churchill's blessing for making *That Hamilton Woman* in Hollywood—a bold move intended to make it seem that the film was a big-budget American production, as opposed to just another British propaganda film. This was made more plausible by the fact that Olivier and Leigh were each just coming off a huge Hollywood success, he in *Wuthering Heights*, she in *Gone with the Wind*, and would have been treated as "bankable" stars by any Hollywood studio.

One might suppose that a man faced with the possible loss of the lion's share of the British Army followed by a German invasion would have other things on his mind than the making of a movie about Nelson and Lady Hamilton, but one of Churchill's most remarkable abilities was his determination to control every aspect of the war, down to the most minute details. Although business leaders are constantly advised to learn how to delegate, the four world leaders in the Second World War shared a passion for detail. Hitler reached the point where he was moving about mere battalions, Stalin spent hours reading through the lists of people condemned to be shot, initialing or countermanding every name with a sharp red crayon, and FDR had the memory of a computer when it came to politics.

Of them all, Churchill's interests were the most widespread, and from the very beginning of his prime ministership he sought to review and control every decision. When something drew his attention, he was unflagging in his determination to see it done the way he wanted it to be, from the dinginess of the Admiralty flag, which caught his eye, to the casting of Alex's film and the importance of launching it as an *American* film, not a British import. It was not just that propaganda, as Alex put it, needed "sugar-coating," in order to affect American public opinion; it also needed to sail under the American flag, not the Union Jack. Every effort was made to make *That Hamilton Woman* seem like a big Hollywood romantic drama, one that just happened to be about a British subject (so, after all, were *Wuthering Heights* and *Rebecca*).

My father had no particular desire to leave England for Hollywood, and anyway crossing the Atlantic for the moment was far more dangerous than being in London. Asked years later how he had felt about leaving for Hollywood at a time when many people expected an invasion, my father merely shrugged—he had done what Alex wanted him to do, and Alex had done what Winston Churchill wanted him to do, and that was that. When Alex and my father returned to Britain in 1942, they were briefly criticized for being "homing pigeons," as those who returned from Hollywood once the danger of invasion was over were called. (They included Laurence Olivier and Vivien Leigh, among many others, as well as Alfred Hitchcock.) My father, puzzled by their accusations, told a meeting of angry British filmmakers, "Please, vat is all this talk about 'homo-pigeons?'—at which point the meeting broke up in helpless laughter. Alex was knighted, the first film knighthood ever, and he and my father stayed on in London making films despite the bombing, the German "doodle-bugs," and the V-2s. Alex's house on Avenue Road was bombed, as was ours on Well Walk. My father never felt any degree of shame about leaving when he was told to. If asked about it in his old age, he would stare into space for a moment as if looking for Alex, then sigh and say, "Ah, vat the hell, all zat vas a long time ago."

Of course "all that" was still a long time before us on May 28, when the fate of the BEF was added to my nightly prayers, a sign that by then even Nanny Low, despite the best efforts of the Ministry of Information, understood that the BEF was in grave danger. I am guessing that several million other children in the United Kingdom also added the BEF to their nightly prayers about then. Even the sturdiest of optimists felt by now that it would take a miracle to save them—and, being British, assumed that God would provide one.

I know it was May 28 because that was my grandfather Ockie's birthday, in honor of which I was shepherded downstairs before going to bed to call him in Hendon and wish him a happy birthday—in those days it was an unusual thrill for a child of seven to make a telephone call, since the telephone was an instrument strictly for grown-ups, heavy and black, not at all like the bright, flimsy ones today. Ours sat on an antique side table in the hallway, and in the evenings my father was often obliged to take his glass of red wine out to the hall and stand there talking to one of his brothers in vehement Hungarian at great length. God only knows what the people who monitored overseas calls made of these long calls in Hungarian! Every so often one overheard a word or two in English, "dollars," "pounds," "Hollywood," and names of course: "Larry," "Vivien," "Ralph," "Orson," "Selznick," "Louis B. Mayer," and many more, sometimes even my own name, "Miki." Vincent made many calls to Los Angeles, a major undertaking in those days, to reach Zoli, the middle Korda brother, who had already made the trip to America with his wife and two small children. Afterwards my father would come back to the dining table, pour himself another glass of wine, and say, "Vat the bloody hell."

He never explained what the subject of the conversation had been—it was understood by everyone, even my mother, that anything said in Hungarian was none of our business, and also that asking about it would be pointless.

I duly wished my grandfather a happy birthday—he was always genial, kind, and slow-spoken, even on the telephone. Except for film people like my uncle Alex and my father (and theater people like my mother), most people tried to keep their telephone calls short in those days. Chattering on the telephone was considered wasteful and extravagant to begin with, and in any case the lines were supposed to be kept clear as much as possible for official use. But Ockie never hurried; he had the kind of warmth and old-fashioned courtesy that must have put all his patients at ease, even though he still used a foot-powered dentist's drill, and extracting forceps that looked like something that might be used on a horse, and he always sounded genuinely interested even in what a child of seven had to say, which not many people are.

Afterwards I was taken upstairs to the "nursery," where I had my supper, brushed my teeth, then got down on my knees to say my nightly prayers, over which Nanny Low usually presided sternly, arms crossed over her ample bosom, to make sure I went slowly and didn't leave out anything or anyone. This night, however, she surprised me by getting down on her "poor old knees" (as she always referred to them) beside me and told me to pray with her "for the safety of the British Army in France." Her own palms were pressed tightly together, and there were tears in her eyes behind her gold-rimmed pince-nez. She usually said her prayers long after I had said mine and gone to bed, and she had so far as I know no relatives in the BEF. It was nothing personal—it was as if the whole nation were, for a brief moment, united in anxious prayer or, for those who did not pray, in silent thought.

I did not picture in my mind our army on a beach. That idea had not as yet occurred to anyone except Admiral Ramsay—the idea was still to remove as many of them as possible from the port of Dunkirk, just as the German idea was to bomb the town and port day and night to prevent their evacuation. Getting fifty thousand of them out, Admiral Ramsay still thought, would be a triumph.

The next twenty-four hours would change that picture dramatically, to everyone's surprise.

Dunkirk was already a shambles. Bombing had shattered the town and set the inner docks on fire, as well as the numerous oil storage tanks of the big refinery to the west of the harbor, which would burn without letup for the next week, blackening the sky by day and producing a vast eerie orange glow, visible for miles, by night. Dunkirk already had "the stink of death. It was the stink of blood and cordite," according to one British soldier who passed through it. Those who were there never forgot the choking stench of burning fuel oil and the pall of dense oily smoke that blackened everything and

filled the lungs, mixed with the nauseating smell of decaying bodies
and burning gasoline and rubber as the British set fire to thousands
of vehicles to prevent their falling into enemy hands. (Even so, photographs of the German invasion of the Soviet Union a year later
show a surprising number of British Army Bedford lorries.)

The streets were full of rubble and broken glass, and there was
inevitably a certain amount of looting and indiscipline—many of
the troops had been on their feet, without sleep for three days or
more, under constant fire, and not a few had lost their officers. The
civilian population of Dunkirk had fled, or was dead or in hiding,
the contents of houses and shops blown into the streets. The water
plant had been destroyed, and such water as could be found was
contaminated by raw sewage—thirst, rather than hunger, was the
first thing that every survivor remembered.

Many of the rear guard had no idea of where they were retreating to, still less of the plan to get them home. They were in constant
contact with the enemy, marching by day, digging foxholes for the
night. Jack Pritchard, a guardsman of Number 4 Company, 1st Battalion, Grenadier Guards, describes what it was like for the troops:

> We found the roads in chaos, as constant shelling had brought
> down telephone and electricity poles. . . . We formed into col-
> umns of three and began to march. No-one was aware . . . of
> our destination. Hour after hour we marched. The journey
> continued, with only a few minutes break every hour, for the
> tired troops to relieve themselves, or to have a drink from
> their water bottles. . . . Men grew listless, and spoke very little,
> automatically marching in step. . . . Occasionally a guards-
> man would weave off to the flank, half asleep or suffering
> from dehydration. His weapons and ammunition would then
> be distributed among his comrades, and he would be placed
> in the centre rank between two of his comrades, who would
> steer him by his elbows in the required direction. No-one
> was allowed to fall out, or be left behind. . . . As the columns
> approached a bridge, there would be a flurry of activity by
> the sappers waiting there. The engineers would then deto-

nate the charges under the bridge, giving little time for the last Grenadier to find cover from the hail of bricks and debris which followed the explosion. The roads were littered with broken down and damaged vehicles, some were burnt out, and others . . . had simply run out of petrol. Refugees were everywhere . . . old people and invalids were just left sitting or lying in the shade of the trees, thoroughly exhausted, and unable to go any further. . . . We marched through all this desolation and despair, unable to help.

J. E. Bowman, then a Lance-Bombardier in the 22nd Field Regiment Royal Artillery, describes what it was like on May 28 as he too, with his beloved gun,* retreated without any idea of where he was going:

Obviously the whole front was becoming compressed and the roads more and more congested. . . . There was this village in which we hesitated and halted, running into the Hun, under shell fire and pointing the wrong way. Our infantry were busily engaged kicking open doors, lobbing grenades through windows and protecting each other as they darted from cover to cover. . . . Through debris, past sagging walls and burning interiors we edged along. . . . Through a broken window I glimpsed a body hanging by the neck. Summary justice was meted out in these parts. We crept along, up a corridor with enemy troops very close on one side, and not very far on the other.

Private Gordon Spring of the 2nd/5th Royal Leicestershire Regiment described a typical moment of the retreat.

We got to this barn and dead tired fell asleep in the hayloft. When I woke up there were Germans below us. We had

---

* A "gun" always means an artillery piece, in this case "a 25-pounder Mark Two" (the standard field artillery piece of the British Army in World War Two and the Korean War), *never* a pistol, rifle, or machine gun.

to wait for dark, jump and leg it. We came across another building. I did have a Thompson [sub]machine gun with me. We approached it warily. Nothing there. We'd just turned around to leave and shots rang out. My sergeant was dead. In anger I rushed back blasting away with [it]. I shot three of the bastards, but then needed to get away myself. No shots followed me.

On Tuesday, May 28, the entire BEF, as well as several French divisions, was converging painfully on Dunkirk from three directions, constantly machine-gunned and bombed from the sky, a sweltering mass of over 400,000 men, some in vehicles of every description, most on foot, many of them in fierce close combat with the enemy, with the "sappers" (Royal Engineers) blowing up bridge after bridge over rivers and canals, often just as the Germans reached them.

Ahead of them was the glow and black smoke cloud of Dunkirk—they only had to get there.

Although there was no way the soldiers could know it, the British War Cabinet was still dealing with the politely expressed doubts of Lord Halifax about the wisdom of continuing the war. That afternoon the prime minister made a dignified statement to the House that "the Belgian Army [had] ceased to resist the enemy's will" and surrendered. He had been dissuaded at the last minute from heaping scorn on the king of the Belgians, and went on to speak perhaps his finest words on the war: "Meanwhile, the House should prepare itself for hard and heavy tidings. I have only to add that nothing which may happen in this battle can in any way relieve us of our duty to defend the world cause to which we have vowed ourselves; nor should it destroy our confidence in our power to make our way, as on former occasions in our history, through disaster and through grief to the ultimate defeat of our enemies."

Churchill had not yet acquired the affection of his own party—

there were still louder cheers for Chamberlain than for the new prime minister. Their hearts were still with Chamberlain, not him. Applause had been surprisingly tepid and perfunctory in the House when he spoke of "blood, toil, tears and sweat."

On the other hand, Churchill had, as if by instinct, found the right phrases to appeal to the public. They were prepared to suffer through "disaster" and "grief" so long as their government was willing to fight, and Churchill's natural bellicosity caught the national mood, even if it did not appeal to many of his own party.

The division between the old and the new showed up when the War Cabinet met on May 28. Halifax had Sir Robert Vansittart, perhaps the most determined anti-appeaser in the Foreign Office, find out exactly what the Italian government had in mind. This was an odd choice for the task since Vansittart was vehemently opposed to the dictators, and to Halifax's patient search for peace as well, and the choice may have been intended to put Vansittart in his place. In any case, he brought back from the Italian Embassy the message that what Mussolini expected was a "clear indication" that Great Britain wanted his mediation. The prime minister instantly pounced on this. "The French," he said, "were trying to get us on to the slippery slope." There was some rather testy discussion about the French approach to Mussolini, and about Reynaud's hopes for an Allied appeal to President Roosevelt. Arthur Greenwood, the (Labour) minister without portfolio, echoing Churchill, dismissed the latter suggestion bluntly: "M. Reynaud was too much inclined to hawk round appeals. This was another attempt to run out."

As recorded in the minutes, Halifax eventually staked out his position clearly: "He still did not see what there was in the French suggestion of trying out the possibilities of mediation which the Prime Minister felt was so wrong."

Churchill staked out *his* ground: "The nations which went down fighting rose again, but those which surrendered tamely were finished."

It is possible that Halifax would have carried this argument to the point of resigning, thus causing a cabinet crisis, but fortunately

Churchill was obliged to end the War Cabinet to attend a meeting of the full cabinet, which had been arranged most providentially "earlier in the day."

There he made a much more impassioned impromptu speech of nearly one thousand words, telling the cabinet very frankly of the disastrous military events of the past few days, and ending with the conclusion that he had not so far been willing to present to Lord Halifax.

> It was idle to think that if we tried to make peace now, we should get better terms from Germany than if we went on and fought it out. The Germans would demand our fleet— that would be called "disarmament"—our naval bases, and much else. We should become a slave state, though a British government which would be Hitler's puppet would be set up—"under Mosley* or some such person." And where

Sir Oswald Mosley, Bt.

---

* Sir Oswald Mosley, Bt., was leader of the British Union of Fascists, and was imprisoned during much of the war together with his wife, Diana, one of the Mitford sisters. The Führer had been a witness at their marriage in the Berlin home of Reich Propaganda Minister Dr. Joseph Goebbels.

should we be at the end of all that? On the other side, we had immense reserves and advantages. Therefore, he said, "We shall go on and we shall fight it out, here or elsewhere, and if at last the long story is to end, it were better it should end, not through surrender, but only when we are rolling sense-less on the ground."

These were the words he had been unwilling to address directly to Halifax, and they produced first a murmur of assent, and then a rare explosion of passion seldom experienced in British politics among the twenty-five members of all three major parties in the cabinet—the members of the War Cabinet did not attend the meeting, rather a pity, although it was just the kind of theatricality that Halifax deplored, noting, "It does drive me to despair when [Winston] works himself up into a passion of emotion when he ought to make his brain think and reason." But Churchill was as moved by his own words as his audience was, the mark of a born orator. "Quite a number seemed to jump up and come running to my chair, shouting and patting me on the back," Churchill recalled later, a feeling that he thought was almost universal, "a white glow," as he described it fulsomely, "overpowering, sublime . . . ran through our Island from end to end."

The "white glow" did not extend to Halifax when the War Cabinet resumed about the time that I was saying my prayers, but it had stiffened Churchill's resolve in the meantime. The cabinet had spontaneously and emphatically backed his position against Halifax's search for peace terms. Halifax was no coward—he had sought active service in the First World War despite having been born without a left hand, a defect he nearly always managed to hide, and he would have been as willing as Churchill to die choking on his own blood if needs be, but he did not think that a fight to the finish was necessary if Hitler's peace terms were to prove acceptable. There was not much chance they *would* be, of course—he knew that; after all he had met Hitler—but he thought it was prudent and logical to find out before Britain was bombed or invaded.

But Churchill's determination to fight on was reinforced now by the knowledge that he had the backing of the full cabinet—not only that, their applause and admiration—and he ended the argument between himself and Halifax abruptly about the time that I fell asleep in Hampstead. He would not join the French in making an appeal to Mussolini, or allow Halifax to continue his exploration of that possibility. When Halifax brought up once again Reynaud's proposal for an Allied appeal to President Roosevelt, the prime minister put an end to that too. He thought that "an appeal to the United States would be altogether premature. If we made a bold stand against Germany, that would command their admiration and respect; but a groveling appeal, if made now, would have the worst possible effect."

Late that night, the prime minister called Premier Reynaud in Paris to give him the news personally, and exhorted him to remember that "we may yet save ourselves from the fate of Denmark or Poland." It was in vain. Reynaud was looking toward the Somme and the Seine, where French resistance was crumbling, Churchill toward the beaches of Dunkirk, where the BEF was beginning to mass.

That day, May 28, Admiral Ramsay's ships took 5,390 men off the beaches to the east of Dunkirk, and 11,874 from Dunkirk harbor. Even Captain Tennant, the senior naval officer in Dunkirk, thought that the evacuation could not be continued for more than another thirty-six hours, and that the chances were "100 to 1 against being able to bring a large proportion of the troops back." Nobody, least of all the Germans, could have guessed the evacuation would go on for another full week, or that 338,226 troops would be brought home.

27

Holding the Line

The beach at Dunkirk.

IRONICALLY, BY May 28 the German generals were becoming aware that they had made a major mistake. Admittedly much of this would come out in the form of being wise after the event, expressed to Allied interrogators after they had surrendered, during which almost to a man they cast the entire blame on Hitler.

The argument that the area around Dunkirk was not "good panzer country" was true enough, but had the Germans neverthe-less committed the three armored divisions close to it on May 26 or 27, it is hard to imagine they would not have broken through the perimeter defense of Dunkirk and exposed the beach and the shore to direct fire. As a result a reasonably successful evacuation might have been turned into a bloodbath. As would so often be the case later in the war, Göring had promised more than he could deliver: the decision to rely on the Luftwaffe to finish off the BEF was a mistake—the combination of bad weather and thick black smoke over Dunkirk greatly diminished the accuracy of the air attacks, and the sand dunes of the beaches tended to absorb bomb explosions rather than to produce lethal bomb splinters.

Even General Halder, usually an acerbic commentator on military decisions other than his own, merely remarks to his diary with a certain degree of schadenfreude that "the British are streaming back to the coast and trying to get across the sea in anything that floats. *La Débâcle.*"*

In this case, however, Halder was wrong. The evacuation of the BEF at Dunkirk was not a downfall; it would prove a salvation. Had the Germans been in a position to slaughter the BEF or compel its surrender, the polite disagreement between Halifax and Churchill in the War Cabinet might have taken a very different turn, but the arrival of "anything that floats" was about to change disaster into a victory of sorts—and to demonstrate, as so often in British history, the advantages of being a seafaring nation and of living on an island.

The initial days of Operation Dynamo were not an unqualified success. *Mona's Isle*, a former pleasure steamer of the Isle of Man Steam Packet Company, managed to berth in Dunkirk's battered inner harbor and take off 1,420 troops, but was shelled on her way home, one shell disabling her rudder, then was "machine-gunned from the air" by German fighter aircraft, which killed 23 men and wounded 60. That and the heavy bombing of the town and inner harbor led Captain Tennant to advise Dover that shipping should concentrate on the beaches to the east of Dunkirk and the outer

---

* Halder is presumably referring to Emile Zola's novel about the French defeat of 1870.

(or eastern) mole. Use of the beaches would require a multitude of small boats to carry troops out to ships waiting in deeper water, while the outer mole had never been intended for ships to tie up to—it was essentially a narrow breakwater, a long stone jetty the last few hundred yards of which consisted of a fragile wooden exten-

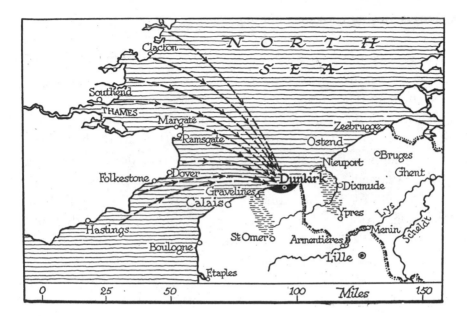

The Isle of Man steamer S.S. *Mona's Queen* goes down after hitting
a mine at Dunkirk, and opposite, in her peacetime role.

sion. A kind of ramshackle boardwalk had been built for most of its length, just wide enough for four or five people to walk abreast, but in places it was missing whole sections. The eastern mole was a good place to fish from, but not necessarily one from which to evacuate more than 100,000 men under fire.

It was Tennant's genius to see that it could be done, and to start the movement of men down the beach to the east of the harbor from Nieuport Bains toward the eastern mole, along a stretch of dunes sparsely covered with grass almost twenty miles in length on May 28. At first, his concern was to take off "line of communications troops" (the "useless mouths") and the wounded, but as units of the fighting troops began to converge on the beach, Lord Gort, who placed his headquarters that night at La Panne, a modest beach resort about ten miles east of Dunkirk harbor, soon realized that getting the fighting units back to Britain was a more urgent priority than sending the wounded and line of communications troops home. It was a harsh, but sensible, military decision. Although not put into practice universally or with any kind of draconic precision on the beaches, it was more easily enforced as troops lined up neatly to file onto the eastern mole. If there is

The beach at La Panne.

one thing the British are good at it is queuing, as the troops were to prove (with some exceptions) over the next few days.

By May 28 the BEF and at least three divisions of French troops had been driven back to what was called "the canal line," forming a purse-shaped pocket that followed the Canal de Bergues from Dunkirk east to Furnes, then the Canal de Furnes northeast to the sea at Nieuport Bains. At its widest point the pocket was only six miles deep. The ground to the west of Dunkirk was held by one loosely spread French division, and from there the German front line was less than five miles from the center of Dunkirk—all evacuations would therefore have to take place from the Dunkirk eastern mole and from the beaches to the east of the port. Because the focus of attention since the war has always been on the "little ships" and the beaches, the hard, unrelenting fighting of those British and French troops who were holding the perimeter, without whose sacrifice no evacuation could have taken place at all, is seldom given its due. The relatively slow pace at which the Germans were able to compress the perimeter is an indication of just how hard the fighting was. Even deprived of the panzer divisions that would have dealt the BEF the coup de grâce, the Germans had an immense superiority in numbers and equipment, and no inclination to slacken off now that they were in sight of their goal.

Each of the many bridges across the canals was the scene of fierce fighting. A British war correspondent in Nieuport describes how one "gallant sapper," discovering that the fuse to the charges laid by the Belgians to destroy a bridge had been placed on the wrong side of the bank, ran back across it under fire, lit the fuse, then swam back across the canal as the bridge exploded.* The Germans themselves were astonished at the ferocity and skill of the British defense, although in many places British troops were beginning to run short of small arms ammunition—in some units soldiers were issued only five rounds—a case of the organization

---

* This sounds like a propaganda story, but in Charles More's *The Road to Dunkirk* the sapper, Lance-Corporal Hourigan, is named and the incident described in detail.

collapsing, since the area surrounding Dunkirk was full of abandoned trucks, many of them loaded with ammunition. Clearly, if the Germans could break through the relatively thin line holding the eastern flank of the perimeter, they would be able to roll up the scattered and poorly armed mass of British forces on the beach waiting for evacuation, but at no point did they ever manage to break that thin line. They forced it back relentlessly for five days, but it continued to hold to the very end, when the perimeter consisted of nothing more than the eastern mole, a few streets, and a few miles of open beach—a remarkable feat of arms. A thoughtful German Army report issued on the battle, *Der englische Soldat*, reflects a certain admiration for the British soldier, particularly when it came to defense: "He bears his own wounds with stoical calm. He did not complain of hardships. *In battle he was tough and dogged* . . . a fighter of high value. . . . In defense the Englishman *took any punishment that came his way*" (italics in the original).

The Germans set a high store on careful infiltration by small groups and sniping, intended to break the enemy's will, and they were good at both, which probably explains why so many of the British troops believed they were being shot at from behind or from the flanks by renegade "fifth column" civilians, and also the high number of civilians shot out of hand for looking suspicious, or for replying in Flemish (often mistaken for German), or simply for being in the wrong place at the wrong time.

One artillery battery was so harassed by sniping that a gunner took to the lower branches of a tree to reply with a Boys antitank gun, a heavy weapon of amazing awkwardness that looked like a complicated piece of plumbing and was normally carried by two men. "Mouthing a string of indecipherable Gaelic curses, with the word 'bastard' frequently interpolated . . . at his one and only shot, L—— was propelled from the tree by the powerful recoil and was brought to the ground, shaken but with no limbs broken."

What sustained the troops on the perimeter, which the German report fails to mention, was above all a sense of humor and ironclad, old-fashioned loyalty to their own regiment or branch of service: among them the Black Watch, the South Lancashire

Regiment, the Royal Irish Fusiliers, the East Surrey Regiment, the Duke of Cornwall's Light Infantry, the Coldstream Guards, and the Grenadier Guards; these and others were among the finest and oldest regiments of the regular British Army, not to speak of the batteries of the Royal Artillery, which kept up a steady shelling of the enemy despite heavy losses until they ran out of ammunition or were ordered to blow up their own guns. Many of the infantry regiments still retained fierce local loyalty, for example, the 2nd/5th (Territorial) Battalion of the Leicestershire Regiment. The regiment, whose nickname was "the Tigers" because of the Indian tiger on their cap badge and buttons, dated back to 1688 and was recruited almost entirely from the city of Leicester—soldiers and noncommissioned officers knew each other and had roots in the city or its suburbs, creating bonds that were unlikely to break even in the most extreme circumstances. The officers came from the same area, were simply of a different class. The Black Watch too was a regiment with strong local roots, still recruited from the same area of the Scottish Highlands, and fiercely devoted to the regiment's long history, customs, and traditions, including its famous black-and-green kilt, the pattern and color of which has been borrowed by manufacturers of shirts, dressing gowns, and Scottish souvenirs all over the world.

As the fighting troops pulled back under German pressure, all of them remarked on the squalor and chaos of the roads jammed with refugees, Belgian and French troops, many of whom had thrown away their weapons and abandoned vehicles of every description. One officer of the Royal Irish Fusiliers reported being overrun by a horsed regiment of French cavalry, which "pushed us with extreme selfishness into the ditch," and commented disapprovingly on the "anachronistic appearance of this unit with its carbines and its sabres," while to their other side British gunners "bore themselves in a pleasantly business-like way," firing at the enemy in textbook fashion as if they were firing a salute at the king's birthday.

The fairest assessment of May 28 is that those troops in contact with the enemy were holding out magnificently under increasingly difficult conditions, while those who had reached the beach between Nieuport and Dunkirk were suffering from lack of organization and control, caused in some cases by officers taking the first chance they could to get on a boat, leaving their men behind. Fighting troops, as they approached the evacuation area, were shocked. "The scene on the beaches was indescribable," wrote Jack Pritchard of the 1st Battalion Grenadier Guards. "Long columns of troops stretched far into the sea. . . . All kinds of debris littered the foreshore. Haversacks, rifle, bayonets, thousands of sealed tins of Players cigarettes, tinned foods and discarded clothing, stretched as far as the eyes could see. . . . Here and there lay a dead horse, some stinking to high heaven, with their feet in the air, and their distended stomachs seemingly ready to burst. Others were being mutilated by Frenchmen, who were cutting steaks from the hindquarters of the unfortunate animals."

"In the roadside fields," as the official history describes it, "burning equipment and abandoned stores heightened the appearance of disintegration. But through the formless texture of the scene the British divisions which had been fighting by day and retiring at night wove a firmer thread; marching doggedly, tired and often hungry, shocked by all the crowding and confusion but too preoccupied to bother much, they moved imperturbably through a crumbling world, upheld by discipline and the traditions of their Service."

That Captain Tennant, in the highest traditions of *his* Service, managed to get nearly 18,000 men off the beaches and the eastern mole on May 28 was a kind of miracle. By that night the evacuation fleet had grown to "3 hospital carriers, 7 personnel steamers and 2 destroyers" operating from the eastern mole in Dunkirk Harbor, and a strange mixed fleet operating over more than twelve miles of open beach to the east of Dunkirk around Bray consisting of: "some twenty destroyers, 19 paddle and fleet [mine] sweepers, 17 drifters, 20 to 40 shoots, 5 coasters, 12 motor-boats, 2 tugs, and 28 pulling cutters (or row boats) and lifeboats." The Dutch schuyts, like the coasters, motorboats, and tugs, could get closer in to the beach than the destroyers and minesweepers, but it was realized at once that the critical factor would be the oared "pulling cutters" and lifeboats that could actually approach the beach close enough to pick up men as they waded into the water to waist or shoulder level, then take them out to the larger ships waiting offshore—although if they ran aground it took a tremendous effort to slide them back into the water again, or they had to wait under bombing or machine-gunning for the rising tide to refloat them.

More small boats were desperately needed, as well as men experienced in handling them; in the meantime the boats from the destroyers were used, but there were constant problems as "they were rushed and swamped by the soldiers." Order was eventually restored during the day, and by nightfall the boats from two of the destroyers had carried off nearly one thousand men "during continuous bombing attacks." This was a hopeful sign, but Tennant was still not optimistic about the chances of evacuating more than a fraction of the BEF. The surf on the beaches complicated the task of getting men into the boats without capsizing them; as for the eastern mole, tying ships up to it in the daylight hours made them a sitting target for German dive-bombers.

The German Army seems, for once, to have been caught napping, or perhaps it was simply not prepared for the stout resistance of a foe they thought had already been defeated. The ubiquitous 12th Lancers, now reduced to five armored cars and "a fighting lorry," was thrown again into the thick of the fighting around Nieuport to secure the eastern flank of the perimeter, where the canal line met the sea. Henry de La Falaise describes a bold attack on a German motorized detachment late on May 28, in what he calls with his usual light touch "a lively encounter," during which many Germans were killed.

By the end of the day, he recalls, the 12th Lancers were "holding the bridge at Furnes," with "intense machine-gunning and artillery fire all along the front. The gun fire is especially sharp and spectacular. . . ." After a "forlorn hope" defense of a bridge at Nieuport, during the course of which the 12th Lancers were relentlessly bombed and shelled, what remained of them would be withdrawn to a new position within six miles of Dunkirk, only eighteen days after they had crossed the Belgian frontier at dawn as the leading unit of the Allied attack.

28

"The Little Ships"

A S THE TROOPS defending the perimeter were pulled back, they all experienced a sense of defeat, together with the shock of seeing the crowded beaches for the first time. Early on Wednesday, May 29, Henry de La Falaise records his first sight of his regiment's destination: "Overturned trucks, equipment, broken cases with thousands of unopened cans spilled out, heaps of cigarette packages and clothing are strewn everywhere in the mire. As the day lightens, we can see many freshly-dug graves and bloated horses left putrifying in the fields. Long lines of worn-out troops trudge wearily on amidst the wreckage."

Now within sight of the dense black cloud of smoke over the town of Dunkirk, he writes, "The moment we all dreaded has finally arrived." The remaining armored cars of the 12th Lancers are stripped of their weapons, backed into a muddy canal, and blown up. Afterwards the men gather in an open field and start a large bonfire, into which they throw all their kit and their personal equipment, and are soon under "strong and savage air attack." There is no place to shelter. Dozens of abandoned French artillery horses gallop aimlessly in terror as the bombs fall. "The din is terrific. . . . I have taken refuge in a shallow ditch. To quiet my nerves more than anything else, I, too, am shooting [at the German dive-bombers] with a borrowed rifle."

Not far away Gunner Bowman and his sergeant-major went about the drastic, "shameful" task of destroying their gun. "The procedure," Bowman wrote, quoting the toneless flat prose of the gun's manual, which every gunner knew by heart, "is set out in the *Gun Drill for Q. F.* [quick-firing] *25pr.* in Appendix IV under 'Disablement.' 'The extent of the disablement ordered will depend on the time available and the probability of recapture. To destroy the gun, place an HE [high-explosive] shell in the muzzle. Load with HE. Fire the gun from under cover by means of a length of rope or telephone wire attached to the firing lever.' "

This drill was almost the unthinkable for a gunner. Neither the sergeant-major nor Bowman was able to look back on the wreckage they had created, nor to speak. "There was firing all around us. Shell bursts, mortar fire and bullets from light weapons were closing in. It really was time to go." In silence they mounted their quad truck* and made for the beach.

The day had not started on a high note for anyone. At 10 Downing Street the prime minister began it by sending a stern message to his cabinet ministers and all senior officials: "In these dark days the Prime Minister would be grateful if all his colleagues in the Government, as well as high officials, would maintain a high morale

---

* The Morris "Quad" was the four-wheel-drive vehicle used to tow the limber and the gun.

in their circles, not minimizing the gravity of events, but showing confidence in our ability and inflexible resolve to continue the war until we have broken the will of the enemy to bring all Europe under his domination. . . ."

In Berlin, in perfect spring weather, General Halder fumed that the British were being allowed "to get away to England right under our noses," no doubt a dig at Göring's promise that the Luftwaffe could destroy the BEF at Dunkirk all by itself. In Paris the GQG continued to calmly release daily communiqués that totally contradicted the reality of General Weygand's growing defeatism and the government's search for a way to negotiate an armistice without alienating its British ally: "The French and the British troops that are fighting in Northern France are maintaining with a heroism worthy of their traditions a struggle of exceptional intensity. . . . Nothing important to report on the rest of the front."

Despite the chaos and improvisation on the beach, Captain Tennant's naval shore party had by then managed to set up a kind of order, while "the little boats" that were so desperately needed began to make their way to Dunkirk, some manned by naval crews, some by civilians. One soldier of the 2nd/5th Leicesters managed to scrounge a lift from a party of sappers, until they were stopped by an MP and told "to dump the truck in a field," where there were already hundreds of them—the roads into Dunkirk were choked with abandoned vehicles of every kind. Recognized as an infantryman, he was sent back to fight in the rear guard (unlike some, he had evidently retained his rifle, bayonet, and ammunition pouches), "then told to get into town and down to the docks." Getting into town was an ordeal—"it was in ruins . . . and still being bombed and shelled." An officer of the same regiment wrote that the chaos in the center of Dunkirk was "indescribable." "No one knew what was happening and the town was being heavily shelled and bombed. Someone said they thought we were being evacuated so we made for the beach. There were thousands of men in long queues. We met some people with food and about 9.00am we had a breakfast of chocolate and tinned asparagus."

*   *   *

As the BEF concentrated on Dunkirk, troops of all kinds massed there, the "odds and sods" of every unit. That extremely odd member of Field Security Personnel Lance-Corporal Arthur Gwynn-Browne, possibly the only admirer of Gertrude Stein's prose at Dunkirk, arrived there with his unit on the night of May 26. His surrealist vision, idiosyncratic *faux naïveté*, and curiously detached point of view, at once terrified and coldly objective, makes his description of Dunkirk unique. The men of Gwynn-Browne's FSP unit parked their motorcycles meticulously, with the precision beloved of the British Army, within a hundred yards of the burning oil tanks in Dunkirk Harbor. Their next order was to destroy them with hatchets. Having done so, they watched "great black bunches of smoke and rubble bursting up . . . from Dunkirk" for some time, under a lurid sky. Then they were told to take what food they could and go to the beach. Gwynn-Browne took packets of biscuits and a tin of milk. "Everybody was destroying everything," he writes, adding, "It was not exhilarating."

Dunkirk was still less so.

> We joined the stream of troops and walked on into town. We came to a wide open cobbled space by the docks and there we sat down. . . . A short way off a warehouse was blazing. There was a continuous crackle coming from it. It was a store for small arms ammunition. . . . We walked through more streets. They were full of broken tiles and brick ends. We passed some groups of burnt out searchlights and smashed up A. A. guns. . . . We crunched glass under foot. The shops stood deserted, their contents strewn higgledy piggledy on the cobbles and pavements. We reached a big open space of sand dunes. It was dotted with troops. We sat down in the sand.

Even less literary souls than Lance-Corporal Gwynn-Browne found the sight of Dunkirk hallucinating, like a real-life three-

Guernica by Pablo Picasso.

dimensional version of Picasso's *Guernica*. Gunner Bowman experienced "a brilliant flame and tremendous crash," then recovered to find himself in a kind of erotic nightmare, "sprawled out alongside what looked like a naked woman." He stood up to see more naked women, "some with fragments of flimsy clothing attached." He had been blown through the glass window of a ladies underwear shop, the figures were mannequins dressed in samples.

Over the years "the Spirit of Dunkirk" has largely erased the reality of it—the sight of Dunkirk in the last days of May appalled everyone, even hardened soldiers. The air was dense with burning oil, "which stung the eyes and burnt the throat," choking everyone and covering everything with greasy black soot, the sea was covered in oil slick and floating debris from sinking ships, unburied bodies lay everywhere on the streets and beaches, and the smell from broken sewage pipes and the burning rubber from thousands of vehicles that were being destroyed "assaulted the senses." One writer compared it "to a scene from Dante's *Inferno*," and went on to add,

> Drink was freely available from a dozen or more smashed cafes, and there had been much looting. The chief memory for many who passed through the wreckage of the town . . .

was of the copious quantity of free cigarettes. Thousands upon thousands of cartons were available from bombed warehouses, and the bedraggled survivors filled their pockets. Drunken soldiers occupied cellars and doorways, a mass of British, French and Senegalese,* some of them lying in the road in their stupor, surrounded by vomit. British soldiers were seen staggering through the streets wearing women's hats and other apparel looted from abandoned shops."

Photographs taken by the Germans after they captured Dunkirk show a shocking chaos of abandoned British guns and heavy equipment, dead British soldiers lying amid the rubble, endless piles of abandoned clothing and small arms, dead horses, the town itself a picture of desolation and annihilation, hardly a house standing with a roof and windows intact, the harbor and the foreshore dotted with sunken ships and overturned boats, the waves and each incoming tide bringing in the flotsam and jetsam of an army, pools of sodden clothing, wooden duckboards, discarded tins and cans, endless man-made driftwood. War has seldom produced a more desolate sight, bringing to mind the Duke of Wellington's famous remark about Waterloo, "Nothing except a battle lost can be half as melancholy as a battle won."

Although liquor was plentiful for those who cared to risk prowling through the town's rubble to find it despite constant air raids, most of the soldiers suffered worst from raging thirst—the water works had been bombed, taps produced nothing, many men had long since emptied their water bottle, some still more unwisely had filled it with liquor filched during the retreat. One of the first tasks of the navy was to bring in water, which was, however, impossible to distribute on beaches that were packed with thirsty men who were being bombed and machine-gunned. Food was a problem too, except for scavengers who prowled through the ruins of grocery shops and the immense stores of abandoned NAAFI goods.

---

* The French had brought in large numbers of colonial troops, notably from Algeria and Senegal.

One soldier remembers hacking away at a huge lump of corned beef covered in diesel oil, another of opening a carton of jars only to find that they contained caviar, presumably destined for some senior officer's mess, a torment for a man suffering from acute thirst. The ruins of Dunkirk's warehouses contained immense masses of foodstuffs in bulk, meat, rice, flour, but there was nothing to cook them in, and no organized attempt to put together a functioning open-air cookhouse on the beach.

All the same, for others the grim horror of the town was relieved by their first sight of the beach and of the open sea beyond. Robert Holding, 4th Battalion Royal Sussex Regiment, passed through "the eerie ghost town . . . lit by a fiery red glow from the burning dock area," to confront an "extraordinary" sight:

> There before me, lit to an almost daylight brilliance by a large passenger ship that blazed from end to end . . . was a long sandy beach that stretched as far as the eye could see. . . . It was the men that riveted my attention. They lay in their hundreds, huddled along the edge of the dunes or in long columns stretching down to the sea. Most of them were sleeping the sleep of sheer exhaustion—many were sleeping their final sleep. I wandered around for a while, trying to find someone that I knew. Unsuccessful, I made my way to the dunes to find a place to sleep.

On May 27 and May 28 "the bulk of the evacuation effort was focussed on the beach [to the east of Dunkirk]. However, the process of embarking men into whalers at the water's edge, rowing them out to [naval] ships that they then boarded by scramble nets, while the whalers returned to the shore for more men, was painfully slow—" many of the whalers and small boats could take only ten or fifteen men at a time out to the larger ships offshore—the more modern destroyers could take up to a thousand men once they were loaded, packed shoulder-to-shoulder like sardines in a can above and below deck, although the crowded deck gravely inhib-

Ramsay at Dover.

ited the use of the destroyer's guns. Waiting while the boats were rowed back and forth was not only slow but dangerous. The naval ships, some of them irreplaceable destroyers, were constantly bombed (or attacked by German submarines and E-boats) as they waited offshore in shallow water to load up. On May 28 alone the Royal Navy lost two destroyers, HMS *Wakeful* and HMS *Grafton*, off the beaches, together with all the troops that were on board them. *Wakeful* was cut in half by a torpedo and went down in fifteen seconds. By Wednesday, May 29, Admiral Ramsay, following Captain Tennant's advice, had decided to concentrate the evacuation on the eastern mole of Dunkirk harbor—there, makeshift and precarious as it was, ships could tie up and the process of loading them could be better controlled and above all speeded up. Not that the mole was safe either, *Mona's Queen*, a modern 3,000-ton liner of the Isle of Man Steam Packet Company loaded with canisters of water, hit a German mine as she approached the eastern mole and went down in minutes, taking fourteen of her crew with her. The Isle of Man Steam Packet Company lost three of its ships that day.

In fact the two contradictory processes would continue to the last. In the end more than half the number of men evacuated were embarked from the eastern mole of Dunkirk harbor by destroyers, while only a mile or two away a fantastic array of lifeboats, motorboats, yachts, whalers, and dinghies brought men off the beach to an equally improvised fleet of passenger liners, fishing trawlers, cross-Channel ferries, and the like waiting offshore. To this day the romantic legend of Dunkirk centers on the "little ships" and the beach, but Captain Tennant, as senior naval officer Dunkirk, strove to rectify that view of events shortly after the event. "The destroyers put up by far the finest show of any of the forces concerned with the evacuation," he wrote. "After them I would put the personnel ships [he means passenger steamers], closely followed by some of the officers and men of the beach parties, who worked waist deep in water getting men away until they practically dropped in their tracks." This was not always an easy or pretty process, either. Small boats approaching the beach were often swamped or even capsized by soldiers struggling to board them, having waded out until they were chest deep in the surf—some hardy souls even stripped down to swim out to the boats, carrying their boots around their neck knotted by the laces.

By the twenty-ninth the first of the famous "little ships" were arriving to take men off the beach and out to bigger ships waiting farther offshore, or in some cases all the way back to the English Channel ports. Known as the Côte d'Opale, or Opal Coast, probably an attempt to compete with the more glamorous Mediterranean Côte d'Azure, the beach stretching from the east mole or breakwater of Dunkirk harbor to Nieuport is the longest in Europe—over twenty miles—and the widest, hence its popularity as a tourist destination, then and now. Even in the late nineteenth century the wide, flat, firm beach was famous as a place to race "land yachts," as it still is today. Although there are a number of modest summer resort towns along the beach—starting from west to east Malo-les-Bains, with its casino, Bray-Dunes, La Panne, and Nieuport—none of them has a port. La Panne was the final headquarters of the BEF in May 1940, and had been the headquarters of King Albert I during the First World War, since it was on the last small part of

Belgian soil not occupied by the Germans from 1914 to 1918. The water off the beach is shallow even at high tide, and behind it there is a strip of sand dunes topped with spiky tufts of beach grass, and cut by drainage ditches. Behind the dunes, in the careful way of Belgium and northern France, agriculture and husbandry begin at exactly the line where the sand ends, so not a square inch of arable land is wasted. By May 29 over two hundred thousand men were massed on the beach and dunes, with more arriving all the time. They could look out toward the sea at the passenger liners, ferries, and fishing vessels waiting for them, but there was no way to *get* them there. Ships lowered their own boats to row back and forth, but it was an agonizingly slow procedure. Clearly, the only way to get the men off the beach was to bring in boats with a shallow draft in large numbers, just as Admiral Ramsay had foreseen.

The Admiralty's initial approach to recruiting civilian sailors was, perhaps deliberately, low-key. During the BBC evening news a matter-of-fact announcement, one of several, was read in the cool, mid-upper-class voice of the BBC: "The Admiralty want men experienced in marine internal combustion engines for service on yachts and motorboats. Others who have had charge of motorboats and have good knowledge of coastal navigation are needed as uncertified second hands. Applications should be made to the nearest Registrar, Royal Naval Reserve, or to the Fishery Officer."

This was something less than an urgent or thrilling call to arms, but it had a major impact on the small world of boat owners and amateur sailors. Much like the Admiralty's earlier request for registering small boats and yachts, it would have been easy to overlook in the shadow of more sensational news, but there existed, in fact, a kind of "bucket shop" at the Admiralty known as the Small Vessels Pool, which was responsible for the normally humdrum job of providing auxiliary ships to the Royal Navy as needed. They moved at once to respond to Admiral Ramsay's urgent requests for small boats and the people to man them. Consisting of fewer than a dozen, the staff of the Small Vessels Pool was overwhelmed

with offers of boats and volunteers to man them, but they organized themselves quickly, and with remarkable efficiency. Armed
with a list of those who had offered their boat, they set out immediately to examine small boats "at places like Teddington, Kingston, Hampton Wick, Ranelagh, Chiswick and everywhere at the
anchorages of the Thames yacht clubs," as well as in other ports
and harbors of the south coast, and to get in direct touch with
the owners.

At first, the process of finding the crews had about it something
reminiscent of the Royal Navy's infamous eighteenth- and early
nineteenth-century press-gang, which brutally impressed likely-
looking civilians from seaside towns by force to serve on His Majesty's ships. John Osborne,* who worked at the Royal Primrose Soap
Factory in East London and took a ferry across the Thames to get
there and home, was an enthusiastic amateur sailor, a devoted follower of the national passion for "messing about in boats," in the
immortal phrase from Kenneth Grahame's *The Wind in the Willows*,
who had volunteered for the Royal Navy the day after war broke
out, only to be told that volunteers would be enlisted as cooks,
which he did not fancy. He then learned that possession of "a
Yacht Master's (Coastal) Certificate" might qualify him to join the
Royal Navy as a midshipman, and enrolled at Captain O. M. Watts's
famous Navigation School in Albemarle Street, London, to study
for this certificate. Osborne was surprised when he was told one
afternoon that all students should report to the Port of London
Authority Building, near the Tower of London, that evening; sup-
posing that he was to be interviewed about a Royal Navy Volunteer
Reserve Commission, he went home and put on his best suit before
reporting to the PLA building.

There was no such interview. Instead, he found himself part of
a large crowd that was brusquely instructed to "Pay attention!" A
naval officer then told them "a secret, and probably dangerous,

---

* This is based on Mr. Osborne's account, prepared for the BBC's WW2
People's War homepage, 10/15/14, www.bbc.co.uk/history/ww2peopleswar/
user/39/u1497339.shtml.

operation was being mounted, which called for the short-term services of anyone, of any age, with some knowledge of small boats and
their handling." Those who did not choose to withdraw (nobody
did) were allowed to contact their family, then taken by bus to Tilbury, a port on the north bank of the mouth of the Thames, where
they were issued a steel helmet and signed on as "Merchant Service
Deckhands."

"I was in a party who were then taken to the quayside where,
alongside, was a large number of ships' lifeboats, the traditional
type carried by all ocean-going passenger liners pre-war, each at
least 30 ft long," Osborne recalled.

> We were determined to man these lifeboats in crews of about
> seven hands in each. . . . The lifeboats with their crews on
> board, were then formed into "trots" (a trot is a line of small
> boats secured one behind, or astern of, the other, ready for
> towing) of four or five boats, and taken in tow by a tug. . . .
> The tug towed trots alongside each other, so the helmsman
> [of each boat] had to steer in order to keep clear of the boats
> in the line alongside, and avoid collision when under way.
>
> By this time it was quite late in the evening and it was
> dark when we set off, so we were told, for Southend pier. . . .
> We arrived there . . . and were issued with basic provisions of
> bread and tinned meat."

The boats were then towed to Ramsgate, the crews were given their
orders, and they were finally towed by zigzag course through the
minefields across the Channel to Dunkirk beach.

What Osborne saw there under a pall of smoke was an incredible array of boats:

> barges, train ferries, car ferries, passenger ferries, RAF
> launches, fishing smacks, tugs, motor powered lifeboats,
> oar propelled lifeboats, eel-boats, picket boats, seaplane ten-
> ders . . . yachts and pleasure vessels of all kinds, some very

expensive craft, some modest DIY conversion of ship's lifeboats . . . Thames River excursion launches with rows of slat-
ted seats and even a Thames River fire float."

"Our tug," Osborne writes,

was able to get quite close before we were cast off and left
to our own devices to row to the beach and pick up some
soldiers who were patiently waiting by their thousands, continually under bomb and shell fire. Six of the crew rowed,
an oar each and one steered. The troops were very well disciplined, just waiting in long columns, hoping to be taken
off. . . . We were able to get right to the sandy beach and took
on board 30 soldiers. . . . We rowed away from the shore and
took our "passengers" to the nearest craft lying off shore that
we could find, a tug, a trawler, anything that could risk coming so close.

Osborne and his crew made more trips than he could count—
at one point the lifeboat ran aground and he was obliged to get
into the water up to his neck in his best "interview suit," all of
the time surrounded by "ships being sunk and survivors rescued,"
bombs falling and shellfire. He spent three days and nights doing
this until he and his boat were finally returned to Ramsgate by a
tug. There the Royal Navy efficiently signed him off, he was paid
five pounds as compensation for the damage to his best suit, and
returned to Tower Bridge by launch.

Osborne finally managed to join the Royal Navy as an ordinary seaman, was then commissioned as a temporary sub-lieutenant in the
Royal Navy Volunteer Reserve and saw action at sea from 1941 to
the end of the war. His well-organized and calm account of what he
did at Dunkirk typifies the experience of thousands of those who
manned the boats and vessels of the evacuation; also typically, he

was back at work and his afterwork lectures on navigation the day after the evacuation ended as if nothing had happened, and with nothing to show for it but his ruined suit.

Those who had registered their boats were called at home, among them Charles H. Lightoller, the sixty-six-year-old former second officer of the *Titanic*, who was swept overboard as she went down. Commander Lightoller was famous for construing the customary "Women and children first" as "Women and children *only*," low-ering some of the ship's lifeboats half empty rather than let men aboard. Lightoller received a call from the Admiralty to come down to his fifty-eight-foot motor yacht *Sundowner* at once. He was met there by a naval officer who asked him to take the boat around to Ramsgate, where a naval crew would take her on to Dunkirk. This was to underestimate Lightoller, a tough customer who had maintained order and decorum on the *Titanic* with his revolver as she sank and rescued thirty survivors from the water in a flimsy, folding canvas raft, ordered them to sway back and forth in time with the waves during the night, both to keep warm and to balance the raft, then went on to be awarded the DSC in World War One for engaging a German zeppelin.

Interviewed on the BBC about Dunkirk ten years later, Lightoller still sounds in 1950 like a formidable and crisply no-nonsense fig-ure. He told the naval officer that he "had another guess coming," and that he and his eldest son would take *Sundowner* to Dunkirk themselves. In the event, he added an eighteen-year-old Sea Scout to his crew, and the three of them took her down the Thames to Gravesend, Southend, and eventually Ramsgate. The other motor vessels gathered there seemed to Lightoller too slow, so he "pushed off" on his own. The interviewer asked whether he was attacked on the way over.

Lightoller matter-of-factly replied that he had been. "Yes, we had lots of fun on the way," he said without irony, "the first one was [when] a couple of enemy bombers had a shot at it, and fortunately . . . H. M. S. *Worcester* [a W-class destroyer] was just passing us at the time, and she drove them off. But then we had lots of other escapes from bombing and machine-gunning until we got over to the other side." Lightoller paused to pick out of the sea the crew of another motor cruiser that was "well on fire" and shortly exploded, then entered Dunkirk harbor, which was being shelled and bombed, and went on board the *Worcester* to tell the captain that he "could take off a few men." " 'He said, how many?' Well, I once had twenty-one on board, I didn't tell him that, I told him, 'Oh, about one-hundred,' and he said, 'Right, take them,' and they started to pour on board." A naval rating was counting them, and when they got to fifty down below, Lightoller asked whether it was getting a bit crowded. His son shouted up, "Oh, plenty of room yet," and they finally got one hundred thirty men on board, packed in like sardines in a can, seventy-five below and the rest on deck. "She was getting pretty tender," Lightoller recalled, "so I called a halt and cast off, and started on my way back."

Sundowner was attacked several times on the way home, but, Lightoller explained, "she's very quick on the helm," despite her load. Every time a German fighter aircraft dived low to machine-gun him, he "put the helm over hard . . . and dodged him." Zigzagging every time a fighter came in to machine-gun *Sundowner*, Lightoller managed to get his boat and his passengers back unharmed. "Got back to Ramsgate, went alongside, they started to pile off then, and the Chief Petty Officer was tallying them ashore, and as the last ones went over the side his remark stays in my mind: 'My God, mate, where did you put them all?' "

The master of a Thames tugboat reflected on Dunkirk for the BBC years later, "At 8:50 p.m. we were hailed by the S.S. *Prague* to tow her clear of the eastern arm [of the harbor]. She was loaded with troops . . . and having great difficulty in getting clear. We took hold of her at 9:00 p.m. and towed her out into the roads." Having done this, the tugboat returned to the harbor under heavy shelling, and was hailed by a destroyer moored alongside the mole "to assist him because of the dense smoke caused by the fires on the quayside." The tug pulled the destroyer clear, then went back to load up with men, despite a heavy barrage and shrapnel, and steamed away with them to Dover. "There was no mistaking Dunkirk from a distance for fairyland," the tugboat master recalled.

Hundreds of similar feats in Dunkirk harbor and on the beach enabled 47,310 men to return to Britain on May 29, more than three times the number on the previous day, and gave hope that a far greater number of the BEF might be evacuated than had been anticipated. German reaction at sea to the evacuation was still somewhat hampered—the English Channel from Dunkirk to Dover is shallow, with many treacherous shoals and sandbanks, not an ideal hunting ground for U-boats, and the German E-boats (fast motor torpedo boats) operating from newly occupied ports in Holland met with fierce resistance—but the bombing and machine-gunning from the air took a frightful toll on the boats and ships. Still, the day's results enabled the prime minister to express the hope at the War Cabinet that men might be evacuated at the rate of two thousand an hour. This did not necessarily comfort those who still had doubts about him. Sir Alexander Cadogan, permanent undersecretary of state for foreign affairs, noted in his diary, "News unpleasant. We have got off 40,000 men. . . . But the end will be awful. A horrible discussion of what instructions to send to Gort. WSC [Churchill] rather theatrically bulldoggish. Opposed by NC and H [Neville Chamberlain and Halifax] and yielded to a reasonable extent. Fear relations will become rather strained. That is Winston's fault—theatricality."

The instructions to General Lord Gort were constantly being revised, since it was recognized by everyone that Gort would prefer to remain with those of his troops who could not be saved rather than to be evacuated himself, and at the same time that the capture of the British commander in chief would mean handing the Germans an unnecessary propaganda coup. In the end, Churchill was persuaded, much against his instinct, to send a rather bland hortatory message to Gort, marked "Personal," leaving it up to him to decide who should surrender and when, and ending with a typical Churchillian flourish: "His Majesty's Government are sure that the repute of the British Army is safe in your hands." This was clearly a concession to Chamberlain and Halifax. The prime minister continued to mull over Gort's instructions for the next twenty-four hours—he was still enough of an old soldier himself to understand that Gort would need (and obey) precise orders, but he was not yet certain what they should be.

His mood must have improved that evening. He was "in great form" at dinner, and afterwards composed a gracious and comradely mes-

Sir Alexander Cadogan.

sage to Premier Reynaud assuring him that French troops would "share in evacuation to the fullest possible extent," and attempting to calm French anxieties about the removal of British heavy equipment south of Amiens. "This is only to get into order and meet impending shock, and we shall shortly send you new scheme for reinforcement of our troops in France."

Finally, he paid a late-night visit to the War Room at the Admiralty, where he and Mrs. Churchill were still living until the Chamberlains moved out of 10 Downing Street. While he was examining the maps, Captain Richard Pim, RNVR, who was "in charge" of the Map Room, came up to him and asked "for four days leave to enable me to give a hand in the evacuation." Later he would write, "Mr. Churchill not only approved my request, but said, and I remember his words, 'God bless you; I wish I were going with you myself."

29

"The Best Mug of Tea I Have Ever Had in My Life"

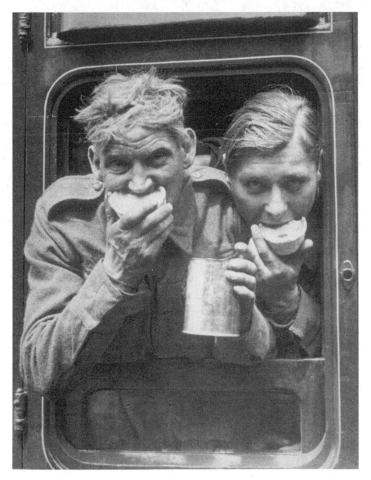

Home again!

B Y THURSDAY, May 30, it was clear enough to everybody that the BEF was struggling to get home and that the German hold on Dunkirk was tightening with every hour. There was, of course, no equivalent to people crowded around a television set, as they would be today, watching events as they took place in a kind of national communion, nor of "embedded" correspondents reporting independently on what was happening in "real time." News was carefully filtered and released a day later, much of it still untrue, or at least tidied up.

German losses were wildly exaggerated, and many tales were told of the Germans' marching like obedient automatons into withering fire, and of scores of German aircraft being shot down by a handful of British fighter planes. The official French communiqué of the day was even more divorced from reality: "The French and British troops that are fighting in Northern France are maintaining with a heroism worthy of their traditions a struggle of exceptional intensity. . . . The French Navy, in defending their ports and lines of communication, is lending them powerful support. Under the command of Admiral Abrial, with a very large number of ships, it is engaged in supplying the fortified camp of Dunkirk. . . ."

In fact, the doughty *Admiral Nord,* Vice-Admiral Jean-Marie Abrial, commander of French naval forces in the north, was in a state of barely concealed fury at the British. Sequestered at his fortified headquarters in Bastion 32 of the old Dunkirk fortifications (which had been built to protect Dunkirk from the British), Abrial had not been informed of the British decision to evacuate the fighting troops of the BEF, not just "the tail." *His* intention was to defend the town of Dunkirk "to the last man," and his attitude toward the British was one of bristling hostility at their departure, only barely concealed by ironic Gallic politeness. Not surprisingly he would go on to become a major figure in the collaborationist government of Marshal Pétain.

Perhaps because of Abrial's attitude toward the British, there was almost no communication between General Lord Gort at La Panne and Admiral Abrial in Dunkirk, a distance of about ten miles, as if they were fighting two entirely separate battles. Lord Gort disliked scenes and arguments with the French, and was certain to get both at Bastion 32. Abrial and his staff had been outraged by British demands to demolish the bridges over the canals in Dunkirk, and seem to have ignored the vast fleet of naval vessels and small boats gathering off Dunkirk, even though the mole and the beach to the east of Dunkirk were perfectly visible from Bastion 32, had he chosen to come out of it.

Gort's irascible chief of staff, Lieutenant-General Pownall, to whom Gort delegated a good deal of the irritating business of talking common sense to the French, expressed his feelings vehemently in his diary: "I suppose they [the French commanders] think we are tiresome, pig-headed people, but their slackness, lack of self-discipline, and 'temperament' is, to us, just appalling and we can't compete." Pownall was particularly incensed by the French taste for grandiose patriotic rhetoric, unaccompanied by any realistic plan. "The Admiral's boast that he would hold on till kingdom come was nonsense. The French formations there . . . are quite useless. Any holding that may be done will be done by us." Admiral Abrial would later sum up his own opinion of British behavior at Dunkirk with his own, eloquently expressed bias: "The British never took part in the struggle as faithful and loyal fighting comrades—but only, and on occasion not without bravery, for their own personal ends . . . the evacuation of British personnel."

The British government had already expressed its intention to evacuate as much of the BEF as it could, together with what remained of the French First Army, but either this message did not reach the French commanders on the spot, or they simply did not wish to hear it and were in any case determined to pin as much of the blame for a military disaster as they could on the British.

Needless to say, none of this was reflected in the newspapers. At Well Walk in Hampstead my mother, who like many middle-class English children had been educated at a French convent school despite being Protestant—she had taught me the multiplication table in French to the tune of "La Marseillaise" repeated over and over again—retained a firm belief in the greatness of the French Army. They had stopped the Germans at the Marne in 1914, they would stop them now on the Seine, if not before, and her confidence in General Weygand was unshaken. This was common throughout Britain, and rose right to the top, since Winston Churchill, who by now should have known better, still had faith in the French genius for warfare. Churchill's confidence in his old friend and luncheon companion General Georges was slightly shaken, but he still believed that the Napoleonic touch would soon appear, although those few who were permitted to approach General Weygand, the Allied commander in chief, whose routine of quiet mealtimes without any military "shop talk," followed by a healthy stroll on the gravel paths outside his office after lunch and dinner, saw no trace of it appearing as yet. Only those who were in direct contact with the French Army doubted its ability to recover. My father retained from his service in the Austro-Hungarian Army a profound lack of respect for the generals of every army, and complete lack of confidence in the truth of any military communiqué.[*]

Whatever confidence the prime minister had in the French Army was surely somewhat shaken by the arrival in London of Lieutenant-General Pownall, accompanied by Captain the Earl of Munster, Lord Gort's aide-de-camp, via a "Thames tripper steamer" to Margate under "heavy air attack." Pownall was not the man to sugarcoat the situation or to be overawed even by the prime minister. A more timid soul than Pownall might have felt that he was like a prisoner in the dock called before a meeting with Churchill in the center chair like a judge, attended by the service ministers and the chiefs of staff, like a jury. Pownall declined to be

---

[*] An exception to this was General Édouard ("Eddie") Corniglion-Molinier, film producer, bon vivant, pioneer aviator, war hero, member of the French Resistance, and eventually prominent Gaullist political figure, who played much the same role for the Korda family in France since the 1930s that Brendan Bracken did in Britain.

"pinned down" about casualties, and when told by the prime minister of "the importance of embarking French as well as English," he replied that if "the French did not produce resources of their own for embarkation this meant that every Frenchman embarked meant one more Englishman lost."

Pownall noted in his diary, with some satisfaction, that this was "an inconvenient truth which he [Churchill] did not gladly hear," and congratulated himself on putting it to Churchill "straight enough." It is worth noting that telling Churchill what he didn't want to hear was not necessarily a good personal strategy. Despite his widely acknowledged competence Pownall was never advanced to a higher rank for the rest of his career—he seems to have lacked the right personality to "click" with that of the prime minister. Interesting as Pownall's diaries are, they do not show any evidence of charm, tact, or a sense of humor, still less of the ability to hold his tongue in the face of wrath, some or all of which were necessary to deal with Churchill. Pownall emphasized the need for more small boats—he had seen for himself how exhausted the rowers were as he was taken out from the beach to the *Royal Eagle*—and

Thames pleasure steamer heading for Dunkirk.

reported frankly on the difficulties between the British and Admiral Abrial. During the discussion on this subject, it became clear that there was in fact no common policy on evacuation between the French and the British governments, which does much to explain Abrial's hostility.

Pownall managed to convince everybody at last of the importance of taking off the fighting elements of the BEF, instead of just the "tail," and above all confronted Churchill with the need to provide Lord Gort with a specific order about when to come home, since otherwise he would certainly choose to remain with his men. After the meeting Pownall went to Buckingham Palace to tell his story to the king, then back to the War Office, where he seems to have been the first to point out that while the RAF had been "working all out," those standing on the beach at Dunkirk had not seen the airmen and were complaining so bitterly that soldiers sometimes refused to let airmen into the boats.

Whatever else Pownall's visit did, it prompted Churchill to follow his first instinct and give Lord Gort a firm order. "Report every three hours through La Panne. If we can still communicate we shall give you an order to return to England with such Officers as you may choose at the moment when we deem your Command so reduced that it can be handed over to a Corps Commander. You should now nominate this Commander. . . . This is in accordance with correct military procedure, and no personal discretion is left to you in the matter. . . . The Cabinet have approved this telegram." If one of the marks of leadership is to write or dictate a clear order, Churchill certainly had this most precious ability. There is not the slightest ambiguity in his message to Gort—although Churchill never rose above the rank of lieutenant in the British Army, it could have been written by Wellington or Grant.

He was less successful at dealing with the French, who were still pleading for more British fighter planes and infantry divisions. In contrast to his resounding communiqués, General Weygand had told Major-General Spears, Churchill's personal representative to

Premier Reynaud, "Nous sommes à la limite." The fate of the northern armies, including the BEF, was no longer the first concern of the French—they now faced an enemy that was vastly superior in numbers, and had shown itself to be superior in equipment, fighting techniques, and, perhaps most important of all, fighting spirit along the line of the Somme, the Aisne, and the Maginot Line, a front almost five hundred miles long from the sea to the Swiss border. Although Premier Reynaud was far from communicating his thoughts to his British ally, he was already considering the possibility of forming a "national redoubt" in Brittany and of sending half a million men of military age to North Africa for training. The question was no longer whether the north could be held—it was already lost—but whether, once the Germans had recovered their second wind, Paris could be held.

For those approaching Dunkirk, these larger issues were not a concern. Despite the confusion, the chaos, and the bloodshed on the beach, many of the British derived a strong sense of comfort from their first sight of the sea. From here it was only thirty miles to England, and for an island race the sea appears as a friend, not an enemy. Unfortunately, there was still a serious lack of organization on the beach—General Gort and his staff considered it to be their job to get the BEF *to* the beach, after which the navy would take over; the navy considered its job to be taking the troops home, so nobody had given much thought to organizing the efficient evacuation of some 400,000 men. The process of improvising on the spot an evacuation of this size was necessarily makeshift, rough-and-ready, and on occasion brutal, particularly since the days and nights of retreat and the separation of many men from their own unit, with its familiar faces, its officers and NCOs, and its esprit de corps, led to a certain decline in discipline. Some officers used their rank to get into the boats first, and in the circumstances cohesion and respect for rank and orders tend to deteriorate rapidly, replaced by the spirit of *sauve qui peut*, every man for himself.

This was much less true of the evacuation from the eastern

mole, which was only five feet wide and nearly a mile long and on which Captain Tennant's men could maintain order more firmly, but on the miles of open beach the troops tended to form up in untidy lines themselves, until they reached the water. This was in part because the habit of queuing in an orderly way was a well-known national obsession. The queues were sometimes broken when German fighter aircraft flew low and machine-gunned the beach, or when German bombers and dive-bombers dropped bombs, but as soon as they were gone the lines reformed and most men retuned to their original place, except for the dead who were quickly buried in the sand, and those badly wounded who needed to be carried to the nearest medical post. Stretchers were in short supply, as well as the men to carry them, and only the fittest could wade out to the boats, sometimes chest or neck deep in rolling surf, and then try and climb into a rolling, overloaded small boat. The seriously wounded who could be moved were mostly evacuated from the eastern mole by stretcher onto small passenger liners converted into hospital ships. First impressions of the beach were almost always misleading. Bombs and canon shells were less dangerous than the Germans (or the troops on the beach) expected—the sand tended to bury a bomb or a shell before it exploded, muffling the effect and preventing the spray of hot metal splinters that were the most dangerous side effects of an explosion, unless of course you were unlucky enough to receive a direct hit. On the other hand, "strafing" by low-flying fighter planes caused many more casualties where men were standing in line or bunched up—small-caliber machine-gun fire was deadly.

Captain Henry de La Falaise, the French liaison officer to the 12th Lancers, arrived on the beach midmorning on May 30, after the regiment had abandoned and destroyed their remaining armored cars. Trying to cross the bridge leading to La Panne, he encountered a momentary difficulty: British officers and military policemen were preventing French troops from crossing the bridge, and it was only after his commanding officer and his troop commander linked their arms through his and insisted he was part of their regiment that he was allowed to proceed. French troops were being sent farther west along the beach to the small resort towns of Bray-Dunes and Malo-les-Bains, where for the time being they were not being removed by boat. It was "a good two mile walk before reaching La Panne," writes La Falaise, "which, we can see, and hear, is being blasted by artillery fire as well as bombed from the air. It [the road] is jammed with abandoned trucks which are being emptied of their contents by hundreds of stragglers in French uniform who are camped gypsy-fashion around fires in the neighboring dunes. Some of them are drunk."

At first La Falaise was embarrassed by this lack of discipline among his countrymen, until he realized that these were older men from the reserves who were not going to be evacuated by the British and knew they were going to be facing German captivity. It was now *he* who was embarrassed as they watched him enviously, marching down the road with the British to what they regarded as safety. La Falaise went through the ruins of La Panne, in peacetime a pleasant little beach resort, and at the end of a narrow street, "we smell the tang of a salty breeze and a few minutes later, beyond a narrow stretch of yellow sand . . . the glorious sight of the splashing surf and beyond, stretching to the end of the horizon, the dark green waves over which we may be borne to England. . . ."

This was a common reaction to the sight, but actually *getting* to England was, for La Falaise like thousands of others, a long, dangerous, and exhausting experience. He describes how tarpaulins were laid down on the beach under constant artillery fire allowing vehicles to be driven over the sand at low tide to form a makeshift jetty, but by midafternoon there were still no boats in sight, and the destroyers were several miles out to sea, exchanging shellfire with German artillery, which was now less than four miles away from La Panne. Tons of explosives came roaring over the beach in both directions, shells occasionally falling short and landing in the sand or the shallow water. In the afternoon a full-scale German bombing raid rained bombs down on La Panne. "The noise and the commotion," La Falaise writes, "are so great that I feel my legs shaking under me and my heart pounding in my chest." It was not until the early evening that the destroyers moved inshore and began to take off soldiers in their own boats, but they were quickly filled, and La Falaise ended the day still on the beach drinking that traditional English restorative in difficult situations—a hot mug of tea.

One problem that affected the embarkation was the lack of any effective communication between the ships and the beach, or of any reliable direct communication between Dunkirk and Dover. Few wireless sets had survived the rigors of the long retreat, and as rear-echelon troops were evacuated before the "fighting" troops, the number of signalers was quickly reduced—even at the best of times radio equipment was not the strong point of the British Army in 1940 in contrast to the Germans. The day before there had been a costly error when Admiral Ramsay received a message from BEF headquarters in La Panne—transmitted from there to the War Office and then on to the Admiralty until it finally reached Ramsay in Dover—mistakenly warning that Dunkirk harbor "had been blocked by damaged ships." Another roundabout wireless message from Captain Tennant was mistakenly decoded as meaning that it was now "impossible . . . to embark more troops" from the harbor. Losses among the destroyers prompted the Admiralty to withdraw the more modern ones from Ramsay, leaving him with only fifteen older ones, most of them World War One veterans. All this probably explains the confusion and the absence of boats in some places on May 30, which La Falaise and others commented on. The result was that more men were embarked from the beach than from the harbor, the only day of the evacuation of which this was true, and that the total for the day was 53,823, well short of what Ramsay had hoped for.

*   *   *

Even for those who succeeded in getting away it was not an easy day. Fred Clapham, of the Durham Light Infantry, recorded his experience, which was typical:

> We went down to the beach again and could see a couple of lines of men standing from the beach out into the sea, with the most seaward men up to their necks in water. Enquiring, we were told that they were waiting their turn for a boat to pick them up and take them out to a ship, and we had better get to the end of the queue. Can you imagine standing in single file, in water, being periodically shelled and machine-gunned, and waiting for a boat!? . . .
>
> Along the water's edge there was a continuous line of flotsam and rubbish washed ashore from the sunken ships. Bits of boat, lifebelts, broken tables, chairs, tins, cans, etc etc. We came across two halves of a canoe, and would you imagine it still had two perfectly good paddles floating alongside it. Nearby was also a floating ship's raft. So we took off all our heavy gear, rifles, packs, ammunition, tin hats, boots and piled them in the centre of the raft which was about 5 feet long by 3 feet wide, and took a paddle each and pulled off to sea in the direction of the nearest ship.

Unfortunately, the swell tipped over Private Clapham's raft, and he and his "mate" had to swim back to shore, soaked and coated with diesel oil. There they waited until a naval boat rowed in to the beach, at which point a sailor told him to go around to the bow of the boat and hold it steady while other men boarded it, which he did, with the oily water occasionally breaking over his head. When the sailors began to row the boat away from the beach, Clapham shouted out, "Hey! what about me?" The boat paused long enough for one of the crew to haul him on board, then they rowed out to where its parent ship waited, the minesweeper *Albury*, and Clapham was given "the best mug of tea I have ever had in my life. Real navy stuff. Hot, strong, sweet and with a generous ration of rum to boot." He was allowed to strip off his uniform and dry it in the engine room, and "was in uniform when we landed at Margate to a hero's welcome." Of his battalion of 800 men only 250 eventually returned to England. He was a lucky man.

All war is luck and chance of course, but the evacuation of the BEF was something more like a lottery on a large scale. Some people went to the beach, fell into the right line, were taken aboard a ship with a minimum of drama, and disembarked a few hours later at Dover; others waited for hours or days on the beach, or in the reeking ruins of Dunkirk, waded out to sea, and were nearly drowned before reaching a ship, only to have it sunk from under them by a mine, a torpedo, or a bomb. Some were maimed or killed on the beach—and not a few on the narrow eastern mole, which was exposed to constant shelling and bombing—others merely spent a few hours of grim, dismal waiting, punctuated by moments of terror and surrounded by sights of the wounded and dead from which it was impossible to avert one's eyes.

A lot of men made the crossing packed shoulder to shoulder on deck and exposed to machine-gunning by German aircraft, while others crowded below decks in foul-smelling darkness on board a fishing trawler. Some of the Channel Island and Isle of Man passenger liners and ferries had been pressed into service with their peacetime routines still miraculously intact. One soaked, exhausted, and thirsty officer was met by a steward in a white jacket, asked him for a beer, and was told very politely that he could not be served it until the ship was beyond the three-mile limit; another was taken to the first-class salon, to the tinkle of bells and silverware, and served tea on a silver tray, along with a plate of tea sandwiches neatly arranged on a starched napkin with the bread crusts carefully cut off.

Despite the relatively small number of French personnel taken off in the first few days, it is often possible to see French officers and soldiers mixed in with the British in photographs of the ships as they docked in England, and in one case a French nurse in an elegant cape, carrying a leather satchel slung over one shoulder that looks as if it had been bought on the rue du Faubourg Saint-Honoré in Paris. Luck had everything to do with it—the military police tried to stop vehicles approaching the beach, but French drivers ignored them and careened onto the beach or into the streets of Dunkirk; sergeants and Captain Tennant's men tried to assemble people in neat lines, according to their own view of priorities, but some made their own way onto boats anyway.

Brian Bishop, a soldier, was "roped in by a naval officer to help carry wounded on stretchers alongside the mole to the ships tied alongside. The mole had been bombed in several places and across the gaps gangplanks had been placed. It was difficult carrying stretchers along it and then having to lift them shoulder height across the gangplanks. . . ." Bishop and his fellow soldiers were strafed—there was no protection on the mole and nowhere to take cover, so they were open targets. At one point, an officer examined his stretcher case and said briskly, "He's dead, tip him out and fetch another." Late in the afternoon a naval officer helped him load a stretcher case onto the paddle-wheel pleasure steamer *Medway Queen*,[*] formerly of the New Medway Steam Packet Company, Rochester, Kent, and in a moment of unexpected kindness suddenly said, "Jump aboard, this is your last chance." Although the ship was bombed and machine-gunned on the way home ("it was standing room only and no life-jackets," wrote another passenger on her, Dick Cobley), Bishop was landed in Dover at midnight, and greeted by a young girl holding a tray of sandwiches. In an age when almost everyone smoked, the one thing most of the troops remember is being able to pick up hundreds of packets of ciga-

---

[*] *Medway Queen* eventually took off more than seven thousand men in seven trips, became known as "the Heroine of Dunkirk," and is now restored and preserved, moored at Gillingham Pier, on the river Medway.

Waiting at home for the troops to return—
the "NAAFI girls" with tea.

rettes from NAAFI stores littered on the beach and in the streets of Dunkirk.

Tales of NCOs and officers maintaining discipline and order at gunpoint are common among survivors, and no doubt they did, but it is worth noting that many of the troops were still armed— those who lost their weapon mostly did so in the surf as they tried to board a boat, or were ordered to chuck it into the sea as they boarded a ship—and that threatening a bunch of armed men with a pistol is a risky thing to do. Tales of men being shot because they broke into a queue or tried to force their way on board a ship are rife but must be taken with a grain of salt, and there is no mention of summary executions in the casualty lists, perhaps not surprisingly. A certain number of men lost their nerve under the constant bombing and shelling—it was called "shell shock" in the previous war—but for the most part those in charge seem to have tried to find a place for them, and their fellow soldiers seem to have been sympathetic, rather than judgmental.

*   *   *

Winston Churchill reviewed the evacuation that evening with the service ministers and the chiefs of staff. "860 vessels of all kinds were at work," he reported, from yachts, lifeboats and fishing vessels to destroyers, passenger liners, and ferries. The total number of troops brought off had by then reached about 120,000, of whom only 6,000 were French—a matter of deep concern to the prime minister, who had made plans to fly to Paris the next day for a meeting of the Supreme War Council, accompanied by the lord privy seal, Clement Attlee, the leader of the Labour Party, and the chief of the Imperial General Staff, General Sir John Dill.

There were sure to be French complaints about this.

30

"Arm in Arm"

ARLY IN THE morning of Friday, May 31, Churchill and his
party left for Paris in two de Havilland Flamingos, escorted by
nine Hurricanes. Popular with neither its crews nor its passengers,
the Flamingo was slow, cramped, noisy, and prone to ground accidents, and in this case the journey was protracted by a long roundabout route over the Jersey Islands (soon to become the only part
of the United Kingdom occupied by the Germans, for five long
years), then due east to Villacoublay, a French Air Force field close
to Versailles, in order to avoid enemy fighters. Churchill does not
seem to have cared or noticed—action, risk, danger, movement
always cheered him up and got his juices flowing. He was still, at

heart, the same young man who had participated in the last major cavalry charge of the British Army in 1898 at Omdurman in the Sudan with the 21st Lancers, Mauser C-96 automatic pistol in hand (a present from his mother, Lady Randolph Churchill), shooting dervishes at a gallop as they appeared before him.

He paused for lunch at the elegant British Embassy in Paris (whatever the crisis, Churchill was not a man who ever skipped a meal, or hurried one, if he could avoid it), but once the meeting of "the Supreme Allied War Council" began, it quickly became apparent that the small number of French troops who had been evacuated so far from Dunkirk was not the chief concern of the French. They wanted more British troops, and above all more British fighter squadrons, neither of which the prime minister was in a position to provide. The truth is that the French War Cabinet had already written off the battle in the north, although nobody had as yet bothered to tell Admiral Abrial in Dunkirk of the fact. With the prescience of the damned they were waiting for the German armies to attack southwest, cutting off the Maginot Line and rendering it useless, and isolating Paris, which they correctly anticipated would fall like a ripe piece of fruit. The last days or hours of the "bridgehead" at Dunkirk was by now the least of their concerns. Even the news that Lord Gort would be ordered to leave that night, now that his command was reduced to the strength of a corps, did not make much of an impression on them, any more than did Churchill's announcement that henceforth fighting troops would be brought off before the wounded, since the most urgent need was to reform and rearm those "who were vital for continuing the struggle."

Churchill's robust presence seems to have momentarily reanimated Premier Reynaud, but did not win over most of those present, possibly because he insisted on speaking in execrable French throughout the meeting. When Admiral Darlan, the commander in chief of the French Navy, proposed sending a message to Admiral Abrial in Dunkirk that when the troops holding the perimeter were obliged to withdraw, British troops should be embarked first, the prime minister intervened, and with a vivid gesture locked his arms together in front of his chest. "Non, bras dessus, bras dessous" (arm in arm), he said vehemently, and promised that the French would be gotten off first from now on.

The presence of Marshal Pétain, now deputy premier, put a damper on the proceedings. Major-General Hastings Ismay, Churchill's chief staff officer and military adviser, trenchantly described the atmosphere of the meeting: "As we were standing around the table . . . a dejected-looking old man in plain clothes shuffled towards me, stretched out his hand and said, 'Pétain.' It was hard to believe that this was the great Marshal of France whose name was associated with the epic of Verdun. . . . He now looked senile, uninspiring and defeatist." Captain Berkeley, a member of the War Cabinet military staff and a fluent French speaker (whose gift does not seem to have been required), remarked that Pétain "looks his 84 years." Berkeley also remarked that Churchill's favorite, Major-General Spears, was "muscling in on a very high plain," causing tremendous indignation among the French. (Berkeley may have been among those who thought that Spears's ability as a French linguist was less than his reputation among his fellow British.) "An agreeable person but, it seems, a ruffian," Berkeley commented. "I hear sad accounts of Desmond Morton, Prof. Lindemann and Brendan Bracken* also. PM does like glib imposters!"

At the conclusion of the long meeting—it appeared even to Churchill, who was not always sensitive to the feelings of others, that Pétain's attitude throughout "was detached and sombre"—Spears challenged the old man face-to-face about what would happen if France sought a separate peace. "I suppose you understand, *M. le Maréchal*, that that would mean blockade?" Pétain did not reply, his

---

* Desmond Morton was Churchill's adviser on secret intelligence and Professor Lindemann (later Lord Cherwell) was Churchill's adviser on scientific matters. They, along with Bracken, were thought to be overbearing, impatient with minds less quick than their own, and a bad influence on Churchill.

icy blue eyes reflecting nothing, least of all his feelings about a British temporary major-general addressing a marshal of France this way, but someone else among the French smoothly remarked that in the event that "a modification of foreign policy," a wonderfully tactful French phrase, was forced upon France, a British blockade of French ports "would perhaps be inevitable." Spears then spoke directly to Pétain, pointing out sharply that it would mean not only blockade "but *bombardment* of all French ports in German hands."

The unthinkable had been spoken. Pétain said nothing—it was as if he had not heard Spears speak to him—but after the departure of the British he turned to Reynaud and said, "And now *your* ally threatens us!" The British were now Reynaud's ally, not France's, and the full meaning of it was unmistakable—that Reynaud could no longer rely on his own cabinet.

Despite all this, Churchill's spirits were buoyed. He insisted on "tramping through the tall grass in the flurry of propellers with his cigar like a pennant," to review the nine Hurricanes of his fighter escort. He had reason to be pleased, for the number of troops being returned was rising sharply—over 68,000 would be brought home by the end of the day on May 31, bringing the total so far to 194,620. More than half the BEF was home.

For those on the beach at Dunkirk, however, it did not seem like a triumph. By now Dunkirk Harbor was almost blocked by the wrecks of ships the Germans had sunk, there were great gaps in the eastern mole, and the foreshore of the beach was littered with wreckage and sunken boats and ships. By noon on May 31 the destroyers that had been waiting offshore along the beach had to withdraw farther out to sea as they came under fire from German heavy artillery, 155 mm and heavier. "Each time the destroyers put to sea, gloom settles along the beaches, everyone wears a long face," wrote Henry de La Falaise. Remarkably, the 12th Lancers had not only been kept together but retained their weapons and their kit. After nine hours in the dunes and on the beach under heavy bombing and artillery fire, the colonel arrived in a small car salvaged from the beach, and the regiment was ordered to follow him toward Dunkirk, almost ten miles away. La Falaise's squadron was placed in arrow formation. "The Major walks along unflinchingly. He is shouldering parts of the kits of many exhausted men and has not once slackened his pace or ducked to dodge bombs and bullets." The thick sand slowed the men down, and it was early evening before they reached the outskirts of Malo-les-Bains, after seven miles of marching under fire. "When we reach [the colonel] he tells us that we have now come to the end of the road and must take to water. We are going to embark!"

Longboats and launches were coming toward them, and the sailors signaled the troopers to come out as far as they could into the water. "The wind is rising and there is quite a swell as everyone wades out into the cold sea. We are soon shoulder deep." Together with the senior officers of the regiment, La Falaise helped to get the men into the launches without capsizing them, then tried to make it to a nearby dredger that was coming inshore. "A heavy swell which washes over my head makes me lose the haversack I was holding above the water. In this I had put a dry shirt, a sweater, some valued personal belongings and my gas mask. I try in vain to recover it, but it sinks to the bottom like a stone, waterlogged." A launch floated near him, but he did not have the strength to climb into it, weighed down by his heavy soaked uniform, his riding boots, and his steel helmet. He dropped his helmet and his revolver into the sea and tried again, at the end of his strength now, then "four strong arms" hauled him into the launch. "All I can hear is the roaring of the German motors sweeping over us, the screaming of the bombs and the loud explosions." Another French officer helped him extract a treasured flask of brandy from his pocket, and they shared it as the bombs fell all around them.

Two hours later La Falaise was "sitting stark naked on a heap of coal in the engine room of the dredger," with his uniform hung in front of the furnace to dry, still shaking from the cold, while the damaged dredger drifted since, as a stoker told him cheerfully, she was off course and lost in a minefield. A passing minesweeper hailed the dredger and gave her master a new course, and La

Falaise, with what remained of his adoptive regiment, proceeded toward Dover and the White Cliffs at a stately two knots, since the German bombs had loosened some of the bow plates. Wearing his dried uniform, another man's dirty boots in his face, La Falaise fell fast asleep in the crowded wheelhouse for the first time in days, the war behind him for the moment.

The beach presented an extraordinary spectacle from the sea. "Almost the whole ten miles of beach was black from sand dunes to waterline with tens of thousands of men. In places they stood up to their knees and waists in water. . . . It seemed impossible we should ever get more than a fraction of all these men away. . . ." The great need was "pulling" boats. (In the Royal Navy oarsmen "pull"; only in civilian boats do they "row.") The day before had seen the arrival in numbers of the vast and strangely assorted fleet of small boats that was required to get men off the beach and farther offshore where the larger ships waited (it was also the day when the Channel Islands passenger ship *Dinard*, converted into a hospital ship, made it out of Dunkirk harbor under shellfire, earning for her peacetime stewardess, the fifty-nine-year-old Mrs. A. Goodrich, the only Mention in Dispatches awarded to a woman during the evacuation).

May 31 also presented the rescuers and the rescued with a new and serious problem: bad weather, "a fresh northerly breeze blowing and at once a heavy sea." Of course the word "breeze" connotes something different for a sailor than for a landsman, still more a "fresh" breeze. It produced mountainous surf, which broached and capsized many small boats and forced others onto the beach, where they had to be abandoned as the tide fell—both soldiers and "pullers" were by now too exhausted to drag them a hundred yards or more to where water was deep enough to float them as the tide ran out. By now a whole armada of "little ships" was at work, including the lifeboats of every port in southern England, the "floating fire-engine" of the London Fire Brigade *Massey Shaw*, a fleet of Thames sailing barges (many of which were lost, and one of which, *Lady Rosebery*, carried the youngest seaman to be killed

Nurses returning to Dover.

at Dunkirk, J. E. Atkins, aged fifteen), "old cutter-rigged cockle boats of the Thames Estuary," the War Department's launches, and five Royal Air Force motorboats (fast seaplane tenders of the kind T. E. Lawrence had served on in his last years in the RAF as Aircraftman Shaw), two of which were sunk. The names of the motor yachts, most of them captained by their owner, with the help of a civilian crew (including several teenagers and at least one woman), evoke a whole different peacetime world of summer day cruising on the rivers of southern England: *Golden Spray, Gipsy King, Rose Marie,*

Count Dracula (a former World War One German navy launch), *Blue Bird, Folkestone Belle, Gertrude, Grace Darling IV, Madame Sans Gêne* (!), *Miss Modesty, Our Maggie, Pudge,* numerous *Skylarks, White Lady,* and *Yola,* to name only a few. Gaily painted and varnished, with gleaming brass, they were bombed and machine-gunned like every other vessel, and the Admiralty's list of civilian vessels at Dunkirk is full of private motorboats bluntly described as "lost," by my count sixty-nine, one of them only eighteen feet long, two of them rowboats, one of them described with blunt naval stoicism as "Mined & sunk with all hands." This amounts to a loss of about 10 percent of the total number of privately owned ships and boats.

There had never been such a brave and bizarre fleet as that collected from the motor yacht owners of England, who included numerous doctors, a typographical designer, a scenery designer, and a pub keeper (the Gloucester Arms at Kingston). Several were owned by celebrities, like *Blue Bird of Chelsea,* the fifty-two-foot motor yacht built for Sir Malcolm Campbell, the famous world speed record holder (his land speed record was over 300 mph, set in 1935, and his water speed record was 141.740 mph, set in 1939). The oldest skipper was over seventy, many of the seamen were mere boys, and the actor Laurence Olivier's brother, Gerard, not only sailed to Dunkirk but won a Distinguished Service Medal there. By May 31 the number of boats operating off the beach was so great that one skipper compared it to Piccadilly Circus at rush hour. The navy helped with charts, good advice, supplies of gasoline, water, and food and arranged for most of the hundreds of motorboats to be towed across the Channel and through the minefields, but the civilians were often treated with gruff no-nonsense commands by the professionals—one bewildered motor yacht owner entering Dunkirk harbor asked where to go (the harbor was strictly reserved for bigger ships) and was crisply told from the bridge of a destroyer, "Get out of the bloody harbor!"

On Friday May 31 the stream of yachts, fishing vessels, and small boats being towed by tugs and drifters made a continuous stream over five miles long, one that the Germans bombed and machine-gunned from the air all the way across. "The bombs dropped out of a cloudless sky," one yachtsman recalled. "Some came down in steep dives. . . . One came low, machine-gunning a tug and its towed lifeboats. Then came another. We knew it was coming our way. It was crazy to sit there, goggle-eyed and helpless, just waiting for it, but there seemed singularly little else to do. The seconds were hours. 'Wait for it and duck!' shouted someone above the roar of the engines. 'Now! and bale like bloody hell if he hits the boat.' We ducked. The rat-a-tat of the bullets sprayed around the stern boats of our little fleet. . . ."

The number of people brought off the beach by the small boats and yachts was extraordinary. Dr. Basil Smith's yacht *Constant Nymph*, for example, brought off over nine hundred men, an amazing feat for a twenty-foot motor yacht. Dr. Smith skippered his boat himself, with a crew of two Royal Navy stokers-in-training. It took him three days to get to Dunkirk, because of endless naval formalities, but once there he and his crew worked the beach for nearly twenty-four hours nonstop, with nothing to eat or drink, in constant danger of being hit by a bomb or swamped. Dr. Smith and his crew were ordered to hand his boat over to a naval petty officer and some naval ratings, but the petty officer soon got into trouble with *Constant Nymph*, the wind and waves having increased, and Smith and his two stokers had to give up their "tea and bread and butter and jam" on board HMS *Laudania* (a Dutch freighter taken over and armed by the Royal Navy) to take her over again. By the end of the day *Constant Nymph*'s engine was giving out—a constant problem with motor yachts was that people tended to put them up for the winter and not get around to servicing the engine until the summer, which in England means July and August—so Dr. Smith was obliged to turn his beloved *Constant Nymph* over to a naval drifter that was said to have mechanics on board, and return to England on the *Laudania*. Dr. Smith, who would be awarded the Distinguished Service Medal for his services at Dunkirk, was a jaunty and self-confident man. As he boarded the *Laudania* and got his pipe going to his liking, an old soldier wearing the 1914–

1918 ribbon saw him and remarked that he had thought this was "a young man's war." "Well, you're no bloody chicken!" Smith replied, somewhat ruffled, but when he saw his face in a mirror with several days' growth of beard, he thought he looked like a tramp. On the way home, he watched as the crew attempted unsuccessfully to blow up a drifting mine, and after she moored at Margate, the navy sent him home to Ramsgate in a taxi. Since *Constant Nymph* does not appear on any of the Admiralty lists of vessels lost at Dunkirk, he may have been eventually reunited with his yacht.

The vessels that did such heroic service on May 31—and the days before and after—were all sailed with reckless courage by soldiers and civilians alike. They included such oddities as "*Falcon II*, a sailing clipper of 1898, which had spent its working life bringing Port from Portugal to England," surely one of the oldest boats at Dunkirk, a sailing barge named *Ethel Maud* built in 1889, and *Chalmondsleigh*, the motor yacht of the famed comedian and showman Tommy Trinder,* a favorite of the Royal Family. The Germans bombed everything that floated mercilessly, but fortunately few targets are harder to hit from the air than a moving vessel, and their bombing of Dunkirk itself was hampered by the dense clouds of black smoke from the burning oil tanks.

On shore in Dunkirk a tense binational drama took place on May 31, when Major-General the Hon. H. R. L. G. Alexander, on whom command of the BEF had descended with the departure of Lord Gort, paid a visit to Admiral Abrial in his bastion. Either because he had not been informed that the remaining British divisions were to be evacuated rather than participating in a last-ditch

---

* The yacht's name was pronounced "Chumley." Trinder loved to make fun of the English upper-class tradition of names that were pronounced altogether differently from the way they were spelled, and would introduce himself as "Trinder, that's spelled T-R-I-N-D-E-R, pronounced Chumley."

General Alexander.

defense of Dunkirk, or because he knew but was determined to make General Alexander squirm, Abrial insisted that General Lord Gort had promised him three British divisions to defend Dunkirk. Abrial could hardly have chosen a better target for his sarcasm than General Alexander, the future field marshal and 1st Earl of Tunis, an Englishman who presented the perfect image of an English gentleman as perceived by the French, better even than that famous hero of Pierre Daninos's bestselling book *Les Carnets du major Thompson*, who would typify to a later generation of French everything they ridiculed (and secretly admired) about the English. Like Churchill, Alexander was educated at Harrow, but unlike Churchill, who had been miserable there and did not become sentimental about Harrow until old age, Alexander as schoolboy had been something of a legendary cricket hero in what has been described as "the greatest cricket match of all time," played between Harrow and Eton in 1910. Having chosen soldiering as a career rather than art, his first choice, Alexander went on to Sandhurst, was commissioned in the Irish Guards, and became a much decorated hero of World War One, winning the DSO, the MC, and the Légion d'Honneur, as well as the admiration of Rudyard Kipling, whose only son had been killed as an officer in the Irish Guards. Alexander was tall, handsome, wore a carefully trimmed military mustache, was always perfectly dressed and groomed whatever the conditions—the very picture of what a guards officer should look like. Unlike his colleague Major-General Montgomery (the future field marshal the Viscount Montgomery of Alamein), Alexander was also modest, well-mannered to a fault, and horrified of being thought brainy or pushy. It would have been hard to find an officer in the British Army less suited than General Alexander to breaking to the prickly admiral the news (if it *was* news, about which there is much doubt) that the BEF was going, rather than staying on to defend Dunkirk hand in hand with the French.

It fell to Alexander to tell Abrial and French General Fagalde, "Lord Gort has not told me to hold a sector of the Dunkirk bridgehead with French troops; he has told me that all English troops are to be evacuated." Abrial and Fagalde felt (or pretended to feel) incredulity. Since the only record of the discussion was taken by the French, it inevitably bears a strong Anglophobic tone, noting that Alexander spoke "without conviction" and seemed embarrassed. Abrial spoke disparagingly of the British offer to evacuate French troops: "The 5,000 places which the English Navy has put at our disposal for the last two nights are insufficient to evacuate the 100,000 Frenchmen who are defending Dunkirk." This was a gross exaggeration. There were at most 70,000 French soldiers left in the Dunkirk perimeter, and many of them were in the dunes and on the beach, trying to get away, hardly defending anything. Alexander replied that he was sorry, that all those who did *not* leave would be captured by the Germans, and that "everything that can be saved will be saved." At this point a French naval officer, *Capitaine de Frégate* (Commander) de Laperouse, made exactly the kind of grand statement that never fails to irritate the British about the French: "No, General, it is still possible to save honour."

The record then notes that General Alexander stared at the table in front of him, wiped his forehead and pretended he did not understand. Any French patriotic statement that featured "honor," "glory," or "the flag" was likely to produce among the British by this time a sharp counterreaction. Upon Alexander it produced a polite, but stubborn, determination to keep on repeating the order that Lord Gort had given him. He let the flood of inflated French rhetoric flow over him until Admiral Abrial finally said that the only way to resolve matters was to go and see Lord Gort at La Panne, at which point Alexander was forced to admit that Gort had already left for Dover at 4 p.m. Whoever was taking notes wrote down, at this point, "Long silence—disappointment." Abrial dug the knife in a little deeper, determined to have the last word. "Since we cannot count on English co-operation, General," he said,

"I will fulfil my mission using French troops. We French have a mission which is to fight to the last man to save as many soldiers as possible from Dunkirk. Until we have achieved this goal, we will remain at our posts."

Others reported that when Alexander was told that he should place three of his divisions so as to support the French resistance he had laughed and said, "You must be joking!" but this does not sound like Alexander. As for Abrial, far from fighting personally to the last, he was evacuated, received in audience by King George VI, returned to France to become an important figure in Pétain's collaborationist government, then condemned to ten years of forced labor in prison after the war. The French taste for passionate patriotic rhetoric (and for having the last word, historically speaking) and the British preference for the stiff upper lip and steely avoidance of public demonstrations of emotion had hardly ever been in sharper contrast—each nation lived up to the other's unflattering stereotype.

Despite these age-old differences of national character, each of the allies did more than the other had expected. If a substantial number of French units had not fought on to protect Dunkirk Harbor from May 31 to June 3, the evacuation would have had to be cut off. And in the end, the British would take off about 140,000 French soldiers, as compared with 198,000 of their own. Of the 140,000 only 3,000 would eventually choose to join de Gaulle's Free French forces; the rest were repatriated to France to rejoin the battle and mostly ended up in German prisoner-of-war camps for the remainder of the war.

31

"We Are Going to Beat Them"

Back to Blighty! (Note gas masks.)

SATURDAY, JUNE 1, did not signify the end of Britain's dis-agreements with France, but the relative success of the evacu-ation to that date *did* at least bring to an end the prime minister's reluctance to deal with pro-peace arguments from within the War Cabinet. He had been reluctant to release the French to seek out German peace terms, and more reluctant still to join them, but felt he could push Lord Halifax only so far. Now almost half of the fighting strength of the BEF was back in England, over three times the number that even the optimists had predicted a few days ago—admittedly without its equipment, its artillery, in many cases even its rifles and boots, but the men could be rearmed. Churchill's nimble mind was already turning toward the hundreds of thousands of rifles France had ordered from the United States but which had not yet been shipped, and which he could divert to Britain. The United States still had hundreds of thousands of brand-new rifles in storage from World War One, and in those days the government armories and the arms manufacturers of Massachusetts and Connecticut set standards in the mass production of weapons that were the envy of the world. Arms could be provided—the important thing was that the trained regulars, commissioned and noncommissioned, those indispensable professionals without whom the army could not be rebuilt, were coming home or already there. The sense of dread was giving way not to optimism but to a glimmer of confidence in the island's power to resist what would have to be, after all, a hastily German improvised invasion.

Early in the morning of June 1 the prime minister replied to two of the many notes and papers on his bedside table with the firmness that would henceforth be his hallmark. To a suggestion from the Foreign Office (always foremost among government departments in pessimism under Halifax) that if worse came to worst the prime minister should consider making "the most secret plans" to evacuate the royal family to some part of the British Empire, together with the crown jewels and the coronation chair, Churchill replied bluntly, "I believe we shall make them rue the day they try to invade our island. No such discussion can be permitted."

There was no hint of shilly-shallying about his words, still less for the director of the National Gallery, Kenneth Clark, the future life peer and television documentary star of *Civilization*, who had proposed to send the masterpieces of the collection to "a safe haven" in Canada for the duration: "No. Bury them in caves and cellars. None must go. We are going to beat them."

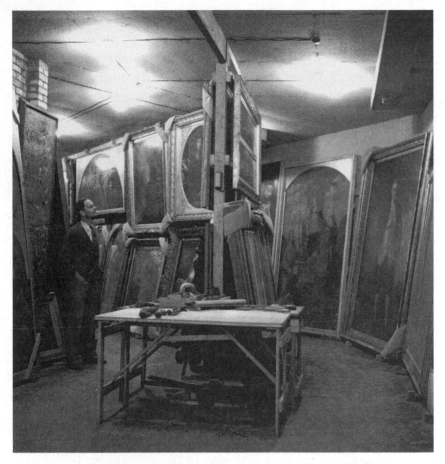

Kenneth Clark surveys the masterpieces of the National Gallery
removed for safekeeping.

*   *   *

From the port and beach of Dunkirk that would have seemed an
unlikely proposition. Dunkirk was now besieged, and the Germans
were nibbling away at the slender stretch of beach the British still
held. To those trapped there under the pall of oily smoke, exposed
to constant shelling and attacks from the air, it presented the nightmare picture of a defeated army, in no position to "beat" anyone.
Major-General Alexander, now in command of what remained of
the BEF, about twenty thousand troops, made his way to Admiral

Abrial's headquarters early in the morning for yet another baffling and fruitless conversation. Nothing illustrates better the confusion of French strategy and politics than Abrial's position at Dunkirk. The French had placed a senior naval officer in command at each of the major ports. With perfect Cartesian logic as the French First Army and the BEF retreated to Dunkirk, they therefore came under the command of Admiral Abrial, at least in his own mind. This resulted in a land battle commanded by an admiral. It has to be said in Abrial's favor that he was made of sterner stuff than most of the French generals in and around Dunkirk, but as an admiral who never came out of his bastion in Dunkirk harbor, he was not in a position to lead a land battle, nor did he attempt to communicate with the commander of the BEF, which would soon be forced to evacuate La Panne, and with it the last direct telephone line to London.

One result was that General Alexander had no idea that there were still nearly seventy thousand French troops in and around Dunkirk with more arriving every day, some of whom (but by no means all) were fighting hard to hold back the Germans, while Abrial was unaware of the heavy losses the British had already sustained in naval and commercial shipping, not to speak of smaller vessels and boats. The meeting between Abrial and Alexander on June 1 was therefore like a dialogue of the deaf, made even more difficult by the gaping differences between them. Abrial supposed he had authority over Alexander, and resumed his habit of making grandiose patriotic statements. At this point, the words *gloire, honneur,* and *drapeau* tended to make British generals roll their eyes.

For his part, Alexander, the most reserved, polite (and solidly realistic) of generals, remained unmoved by Abrial's rhetoric. "He considered the salvation of three of the best divisions in the British Army more important than amity with the French, whose fortunes already seemed to him beyond repair."

It is perhaps a pity that Alexander did not speak French better (he would have to take French lessons after the war when he was appointed governor general of Canada), but the message he had for Abrial was in any case not one the admiral wanted to hear—the

Royal Navy did not think the evacuation could be continued past the night of June 1–2, and Alexander's orders were to get as many of his men out by then, not to fight a last-ditch battle alongside the French.

Abrial was not comforted by Alexander's promise that French soldiers would be evacuated on what Anthony Eden, secretary of state for war, described as "a 50-50 basis," a reaction to Churchill's somewhat rash promise to Premier Reynaud to leave "bras dessus, bras dessous." This was partly because Abrial still thought it was his job to defend Dunkirk, partly because the French forces repeatedly failed to liase with the British senior naval officer. Over the next few days many ships continued to make the dangerous crossing to pick up French troops only to find there were none there at the appointed time. Still, Alexander did his best to obey his orders: over the next three days during which he was in command of the BEF, he would evacuate 20,000 more British troops and over 98,000 French, a far better proportion than the promised "50-50." Owing largely to poor discipline and lack of liaison, however, many of the French troops "missed the ships, and the ships missed the men," causing ill will both among the waiting sailors and the French.

Alexander was not exaggerating—losses of vessels of all kinds had reached so high a level that by June 1 evacuation was possible only in the hours of darkness. The perimeter was reduced to the point where German guns could reach not only everywhere on the beach and in the harbor but all the approaches by sea to Dunkirk. Despite the heroic efforts of Fighter Command, which were for the most part out of sight of the troops on the ground and the sailors, and despite mounting German losses in aircraft, the Luftwaffe appeared to control the sky during the daylight hours, bombing and machine-gunning vessels of every size and kind.

The bombing was relentless and effective, and it made no attempt to spare hospital ships, although they were clearly marked as such under the Geneva Convention—indeed at one point a message en clair was sent to the German authorities emphasizing that ships bearing the wounded were unarmed and painted white, but the only effect was to redouble German air attacks on them. The hospital ships went back and forth despite being bombed to the very end. The wear and tear on vessels of every kind and their crews mounted under the constant attacks. A direct hit was not needed to put a vessel out of action—the blast effects of a near miss sprung plates and rivets, or sheered steam lines and oil lines, putting countless ships out of action and littering the narrow approaches to Dunkirk with floating wrecks, adding to the dangers of navigation.

By now the British press was finally reporting on the Dunkirk evacuation wth relative frankness. The *Times* report was in fact remarkably accurate:

> A withdrawal from a hostile coast while still engaged with an enemy is one of the most difficult of all operations of war. . . . The Navy's difficulties have been by no means light. The Flanders coast is one of shallow waters, narrow channels from which all lights and most aids to navigation have perforce been removed, and strong tide streams by which any ship even temporarily disabled is liable to be swept ashore. To add to these difficulties, ships off the coast and in the ports have been subjected to continuous and intense air bombing. . . .

The piece marks a significant change from the Ministry of Information's previous policy of manufacturing good news for home consumption and downplaying disasters, and also the first step in the transformation of Dunkirk from a humiliating military defeat into a proud national epic even as it was taking place. "Grin and bear it" might have been the new motto for Britain, in which the ability "to take it," rather than any significant victory, became a source of national pride, and even of optimism.

The news reflected a dramatic change in British sensibility. Even "human interest" stories made no effort to spare the reader from the reality of what was happening, like that of the fifteen Red Cross nurses, "who by some mischance had got wet through by the capsizing of the little boat in which they were at first on their way to embark." Taken on board by a minesweeper, "they were tired out and shivering, so they were at once put to bed between warm blankets." The next morning, when they reached a British port, "they were presented with their uniforms, washed, pressed, and ironed by a member of the minesweeper's crew who fancied himself as a laundryman. They landed fit for immediate inspection by [even] the most dragon-like of matrons." (In those days a nurse's uniform was a mass of knife-edged, starched creases.) No attempt was made to disguise the unpleasant truth that everyone was in full flight, or that the nurses had been rescued from a capsized small boat. It was a story that would have been vigorously censored only a few days before, like those of the special trains carrying thousands of "tired and battle-stained troops" from the Channel ports to be returned to their regiment and rearmed. Without disguising the scope of the German victory, the press was at last reflecting the truth: the bulk of the BEF had escaped and was home. Britain, unlike Holland, Belgium, and soon France, would be accorded a breathing space, a time for the German generals and their Führer to contemplate the gray, choppy waters of the English Channel and try to decide whether to cross it or not.

Hitler was ambivalent on the subject of invasion. His mind was still set on the conquest of France, which seemed a bigger challenge than it turned out to be. The generals, particularly Halder and Guderian, complained that "the enemy are getting away to England right under our noses," forgetting that only a few days before they had decided that the area around Dunkirk was poor tank country, with its many canals, sandy dunes, and marshes, but Hitler himself did not seem disturbed. Some of those closest to him thought that he was moved by higher geopolitical ambitions, envisaging a world that would be ruled by Germany and Britain, and that sparing the BEF would be a shrewder move than destroying it, others that he was waiting for a peace offer from London, perhaps the final ripple from Halifax's démarche with the Italian ambassador on May 27. The notion that a political crisis in Britain might place "the right people" in power and bring about peace talks was not, in fact, all that far-fetched. Had Chamberlain still been in office as prime minister, or had Halifax succeeded him, that is no doubt exactly what would have happened. But Churchill was by now firmly in power, and the notion of a fight to the finish was becoming fixed not only in his but in the British mind, even among those who until only a few days earlier had been in favor of joining the French in asking for terms.

The trains and railway stations crowded with exhausted and disheveled soldiers who had been evacuated from Dunkirk *raised* British spirits, rather than depressing them. Ambassador Kennedy, still the most persistent of appeasers and defeatists, might cable Washington that things "could not be worse," that in his opinion the Germans would be willing to make peace, "on their own terms, but terms that would be a great deal better than they would be if the war continues," and urge the British government to ship its gold and securities to Canada at once, but these were no longer opinions that were being listened to in 10 Downing Street, nor even in the White House at this point. Churchill did not need a propaganda minister like Joseph Goebbels—he was his own best propagandist, and his instinct that the British would rally when their backs were to the wall was proved correct. The good news that the Führer expected to hear from London never came, and the "right people," far from taking power, would soon be dispersed, among them Lord Halifax to Washington as British ambassador, Sir Samuel Hoare to Madrid as British ambassador, and the Duke of Windsor to the Bahamas as governor. It was the most British of coups, in which those who had favored peace talks with Germany were simply shuffled off the stage far from Westminster to important jobs on the periphery of power, where they were to remain for the rest of the war. Henceforth Churchill would never need to worry about criticism for having chosen to fight on—the example of France would serve as a constant reminder of what surrender would entail.

Throughout the day of June 1 French troops camped out as best they could in the high, rolling sand dunes behind the beach at Dunkirk—the town of Dunkirk was now a death trap—in the absence of any organized plan for their evacuation. The rear guard of the BEF continued to march west toward the port, some of it in good order, as befits fighting troops. General Alexander remarked on his disgust at seeing the number of weapons that had been abandoned on the beach—he had not yet realized that many naval officers were ordering troops to leave their weapons behind—and his pride at watching battalions of the Foot Guards marching toward Dunkirk in step, as if they were on parade. He himself had reached the beach on a bicycle, having abandoned his staff car and set it on fire, together with his kit, so that he carried only his revolver, his field glasses, and his briefcase. With the practicality that had always marked his career, Alexander had his "divisional engineers [drive] their lorries on to the beaches at low tide and bridge them with a superstructure of planks to make a pier. Thus, when the tide came in, small rowing-boats could take off six or eight soldiers to small ships or other craft waiting to receive them. The plan was that every boat-load taken off would have someone detailed to row it back for the next consignment. I was not very pleased with the response."

Alexander was displeased that not many men wanted to row a boat back to the beach once they had reached a ship, and thus many boats were simply abandoned, compounded by the fact that few landsmen were skilled at handling them in rough water and strong tides. Alexander pointed out correctly that the only way to get large numbers of troops off efficiently was from the mole, "where complete units were embarked onto destroyers, corvettes or ferries" under the command of their own officers. It was possible to take more than a thousand men on a destroyer, many of them in good order and still carrying their rifles—there are photographs of huge stacks of rifles being collected at Dover—and by June 1 the mole, though under constant gunfire, was the principal means of evacuation.

Many soldiers still tried to embark from the beach, rather than make the long trudge through the sand to Dunkirk, which was still under constant bombing and bombardment. Unless they were ordered to do otherwise, their first instinct was to get onto anything that floated, or promised to float. Even the mole offered no security. Bombs had destroyed many stretches of it, and the gaps had been covered with precarious planks. It was no easy task to walk along it single file under fire, and many preferred to take their chances on one of the many boats that had washed up on shore, or had been stranded by the tide, often improvising oars out of whatever flotsam and jetsam they could find. One soldier remembers that "the beach was filled with masses of troops mostly under no command, with equipment of all kinds strewn everywhere." Another, Clifford Holman, remembers his "mate" lying down on the beach after days of marching under fire while he went off to find out what was happening, only to be told that it was now "every man for himself." Holman went back to find his mate sitting upright in a shallow trench, dead. He hailed a passing Royal Army Medical Corps officer to tell him his mate "was dead with no marks." The officer paused briefly to say, "It happens, soldier," then took the dead man's identity tags, and said, "You bury him, if you wish." Holman joined a group of men on a Bren Gun Carrier (a small, lightly armored tracked vehicle then popular with the British Army) and tried to run it as far out to sea as they could. When it stalled, they swam back to the beach and found an abandoned rowboat, but no oars. They improvised oars, squeezed into it, thirteen men in all, paddling and bailing with their helmets until they reached a barge, at which point their boat capsized and they were pulled aboard, and arrived fourteen hours later in Ramsgate.

There were hundreds, indeed thousands of such stories, of men who by sheer perseverance managed to get off the beach, rather than join the immense queues at the mole. One soldier remembers swimming a hundred yards out to sea to haul in an abandoned row-boat and rigging an improvised sail, another of boarding a vessel only to be trapped on board her when she was bombed and caught fire, and plunging into the sea half naked to float there until a passing boat saw him and threw him a line. The basic thread to all such stories was the deep desire to get back to Britain whatever the difficulties and danger, and the belief that anything would be better than to be captured by the Germans, which, from the stories of those who were, was certainly true.*

Across the years, Saturday, June 1, 1940 sticks in my mind, since I remember that my mother, with some of her actress friends, went to one of the London railway stations that day to help pass out tea, sandwiches, "buns," and cigarettes to the returning troops. As a result I heard from her what was happening—perhaps because as a glamorous West End star they felt they could talk more freely to her than to women in uniform, more likely because she was simply good at drawing people out. At any rate she came home with a clearer view of the retreat and the evacuation of the BEF than most people had at the time.

Insufficient attention has been paid to the success of the immense and hastily improvised plan to provide trains at a

---

* Most films about Allied prisoners of war in German hands deal with officers or aircrew and present a glamorized picture of what it was like to be a POW. The Geneva Convention allows "other ranks" (i.e., not officers) to be put to any work not directly related to war production. Many of the British soldiers captured at Dunkirk were beaten, marched under horrendous conditions through France, Holland, and Belgium, then shipped in cattle cars to POW camps in occupied Poland and put to work in salt mines or the equivalent on starvation rations for five years.

moment's notice for several hundred thousand men, almost as remarkable a feat as the mobilization of nearly a thousand ships. Hundreds of passenger trains (one source lists a total of 569 trains, carrying a total of over 330,000 men) had to be provided, moving over already overcrowded lines to comparatively small railway stations on the southeast coast of England, then routed to take the men to places where they could be housed, fed, reclothed, and redeployed. This required close cooperation between the director of movements at the War Office and the traffic departments of the major railway companies (in those days, before the postwar Labour government nationalized the railways and created British Railways, there were four major railway companies), and a complex plan had to be developed overnight to prevent this huge number of trains from getting snarled up, or stopping all other railway traffic throughout the country. Very few of the trains were routed through London, not from any desire to hide the evacuation from the capital, but because the main London stations were not the most direct route to the north and west. Some of the trains, from the LM&S (London, Midlands and Scottish) Railway, were routed through Kensington Station (Addison Road), and that is probably where my mother and her fellow actresses passed out tea and buns.

She was not alone. The trains stopped at stations all over southeastern England, and although there was no direct order to do so, they were met everywhere by uniformed members of the Women's Volunteer Service and the Red Cross, as well as by civilians of all ages bearing everything from bottles of beer to dry socks—no triumphant army could have been greeted with more enthusiasm or on a greater scale. It was like a national party, starting at Dover, where "the ladies meeting us as we disembarked gave each man five Woodbines [a cheap brand of cigarette] and a bar of chocolate and an apple." As if the tradition of British reserve had momentarily broken down, young women leaned into the windows of railway carriages to kiss total strangers. Others handed in telegraph forms and postcards so that soldiers could inform their families they were still alive. In some places people popped open champagne bottles and passed them around. It was as if the British had won the war rather than been driven out of the Continent. Joan Launders, then an "English schoolgirl, complete with panama hat and blazer," passed out bouquets of flowers to soldiers as the trains halted in a Kent village station not far from her school, and helped distribute egg sandwiches to the troops from trestle tables on the platform.

The troops, she remembered, "were very mixed. Some cheerful, some so sound asleep we didn't rouse them, others just sitting with blank staring faces. Poor men. Various nationalities too. I spoke to Frenchmen . . . and one colored man in baggy white trousers, red waistcoat and a strange hat who came from heaven knows where. . . .* Some were wrapped only in blankets. Others were quite spruce but all had the strained look around the eyes that shows when anyone has been through a hard time."

Authority, discipline, and class consciousness were all abandoned for a brief moment. The vast mob of men, some of them still armed, got into trains and made their way willy-nilly, virtually without orders, to wherever their train took them. Nobody deserted, many got off their train when it stopped at a local station to telephone their family or their girlfriend, and not a few were taken in by total strangers and given a bath, a chance to shave, and a meal before boarding the next train.

They presented an unusual spectacle. Mrs. Anne Hine, who was on holiday in Blackpool remembers "the hush that fell over the promenade" as a column of soldiers came out of the station. "That was not an uncommon sight in Blackpool because the town was then full of troops but these were different. They were dressed in assortment of odd uniforms, some had no caps and I remember clearly that some had no boots and their faces were drawn and tired. . . . I stood to watch them pass with tears streaming down my face."

---

* Probably from the French colonial troops, perhaps a Zouave or a Sénégalais Tirailleur.

Tears streamed down my mother's face too, as she told me about her day at the station, although she emphasized how "cheerful" the soldiers had been. The wounded had been hard for her to take; many had been hastily patched up on the beach or in Dunkirk before being evacuated, and although the most seriously wounded had been left to the mercy of the Germans, together with the RAMC personnel looking after them, some of the walking and stretcher-borne wounded were in terrible condition. All of them cheered up at the sight of actresses and showgirls passing out tea and food. "Oh, they were so brave," my mother said with an effort at gaiety. My father, who had seen similar scenes in 1917 and 1918 as the Austro-Hungarian Army struggled toward defeat, nodded darkly. The railway stations in Vienna and Budapest in 1918 had been full of brave cheerful wounded men, but that had not saved Austro-Hungary from defeat. Still, as my mother would have pointed out, Austro-Hungary was not an island.

32

The Dunkirk Spirit

Some of the "little ships" of Dunkirk being towed home.

ALTHOUGH ADMIRAL RAMSAY was doubtful about continuing the evacuation beyond the night of June 1–2, and General Alexander still more so, it would be continued, incredibly, for two more days, by that point largely to take off as many French troops as possible. Most of those in the know politically, and all of the British generals, had by now written off the possibility of the French Army being able to hold a line against the Germans, with the significant exception of the prime minister, whose stubborn belief in the French will to fight continued, despite the warning signs of collapse. For the moment that line was intended to be on the Somme and Oise fronts, but even General Weygand, the French commander in chief, did not pretend that it could be held for long, if at all—and with good reason, since it was merely an imaginary line drawn on the map rather than a solid, well-prepared defensive line, and only signified the French government's hope to hold on to Paris, provided that the British could produce a minimum of three more divisions and that "the maximum British air strength," as Weygand put it, was sent to France at once. These demands produced an agonizing discussion in the British War Cabinet about the

possibility that France might be forced to make a separate peace and that Britian would be left alone, to face the Germans. "This would mean the establishment in France of a Government friendly to the Nazis. . . . We might eventually be faced with a French Government, not merely out of the war, but actually hostile to us."

The notion that France might not only surrender but even change sides was so daunting that it must have been with some relief that Churchill ended the meeting and went off to deal with the perennial problem of the debts of his son, Randolph. Randolph Churchill had inherited many aspects of his father's personality, but lacked the genius, the fierce ambition, and the disciplined work habits. Churchill himself had always lived far beyond his means, run up gambling debts (father and son both had a fatal weakness for casinos), persistently failed to pay his bills, and drunk more than was good for him, but Randolph's character was further spoiled by rudeness, poor judgment, and an inflated view of his own importance; nor did he have the moments of charm, wit, and sentimentality that sometimes won over even Churchill's bitterest political enemies.

The next two weeks would see the French tragedy played out to its fatal conclusion, with the fall of Paris on June 14 and the French surrender three days later. The British could not strip Fighter Command of the aircraft that would shortly be needed in the Battle of Britain, nor was it possible to reequip the men who had been evacuated from Dunkirk and form them into new divisions in time to help France. French appeals to President Roosevelt merely produced vague offers of moral support, while British and French appeals to Mussolini not to join the war had no effect on the Duce, who was determined to enter it in time to share in the pickings. In the meantime, if the French were to be kept in the war at all, the evacuation, however difficult, had to continue. By now it could only be carried out from Dunkirk harbor by night, and even then the risk to ships was enormous—"it was clear that the rate of loss could not continue." German artillery was now in reach of all the approaches to Dunkirk, and eight of the big personnel-carrying ferries had already been sunk, as well as six destroyers. The outer port was by now itself a danger for all ships; it was littered with wrecks and wreckage, and the innumerable cut lines and cables would often wind themselves around propellers, immobilizing the vessel. Destroyers and vessels of a similar or larger size could only leave the port by backing out astern through the narrow opening in the breakwaters, a challenging maneuver in the dark, let alone under artillery fire. The destroyers themselves were vulnerable—to get a thousand men on board one, everything that was not immediately necessary, like mess tables "and all possible moveable gear," had to be thrown overboard and the watertight doors that normally sealed off each compartment of the ship opened to make room for more men, thus a hit from a single bomb or a shell could flood the whole ship and sink her. Under these conditions it was agonizing for the captain of a vessel to wait in the harbor when troops failed to turn up because of a failure of communications or, in the case of the French, fatal disorganization.

By dawn on Sunday, June 2, most of the British troops had been evacuated—by then consisting of the rear guard who had been fighting hard without interruption for three days to hold what remained of the beach and the eastern side of the town. From the ships the sound and flash of nearby rifle and machine-gun fire remained constant throughout the night, indicating that the enemy was now closing in on the port. Naval officers went ashore in the dark to urge the troops along to the breakwater, one of them making his way through the gutted, ravaged streets around the port playing "a set of bagpipes as a summons to the weary men."

As the French troops being evacuated began to outnumber the British, the inevitable language problems and national differences began to make themselves felt. To quote A. D. Divine, DSM, who was there, "It was impossible to explain to inland Frenchmen the intricacies of small-boat handling on a failing tide. Among certain units discipline had broken down, and it was equally hard without an absolute command of the language to stop them from rushing the boats and settling them firmly in the sand. It was impossible to stop late-comers jumping into overloaded boats. There were not a few cases of small craft that left the beach and sank as soon as they reached deep water and the tumultuous wash of the destroyers." It should be noted, in all fairness, that many British naval officers and yachtsmen made the same complaint about British soldiers on the beach, and that members of the fighting formations disparaged the behavior of line of communication on troops. There was in any case much tighter discipline on the mole than on the beach, where men had to wade out to sea and struggle to get on a boat. Despite all these difficulties, however, nearly 27,000 people were evacuated on June 2 alone.

Still, it was not enough. In order to move the French troops off it was necessary to continue evacuating even after dawn on Monday, June 3, many of them lifted from the beach in small boats, yachts, and fishing vessels. Admiral Ramsay had intended to end the evacuation during the night of June 2, but when he learned that elements of the French rear guard were still covering "the retirement of the British rearguard," he overruled himself. "We cannot leave our allies in the lurch," he wrote, "and I must call on all officers and men detailed for further evacuation tonight, and let the world see that we never let down an ally."

Complaints that British warships had waited under fire on the night of June 2 to take off French troops, but because these never arrived were obliged to go back to Dover empty, made their way up to Churchill, who telegraphed Premier Reynaud in Paris, urging him "to make every effort in co-operation with us to evacuate their men as quickly as possible." By now, the last three thousand of the British rear guard had already been embarked, Major-General Alexander and Captain Tennant, the senior naval officer, made a tour of the harbor and the beaches in a fast motorboat to make sure that nobody who could reply in English was left, then returned to the mole to board a destroyer for home in the early hours of the morning.

*   *   *

Despite the peril to ships and boats Admiral Ramsay made a last major effort on the night of June 3–4, taking off a further 26,175 men for a grand total of 338,226, of whom 139,921 were French. The last ship to leave was the destroyer HMS *Shikari*, at 3:40 in the morning of Tuesday, June 4, with German infantry firing only a few streets away from where she was moored. Most of the remaining French troops were by now totally out of ammunition.

General Alexander, when he reported to Anthony Eden, secretary of state for war, received his congratulations, but replied, with what his biographer Nigel Nicolson describes as "engaging modesty," "We were not hard pressed, you know." Certainly "engaging modesty" would be a hallmark of Alexander's throughout his long career, during much of which his good manners and modesty were always contrasted, as they still are by historians, with Montgomery's brash boastfulness, but in fact Alexander was right. The Germans could have pressed much harder—a couple of panzer divisions could have broken through to the beach and the harbor and prevented the evacuation altogether by May 31, but the Germans were already looking toward June 5, the date set by Hitler for Case Red, the advance of nine armies, consisting of 140 divisions (including all the panzer divisions), intended "to annihilate the allied forces still remaining in France. . . . Operational enemy reserves in considerable numbers need no longer be expected. It will therefore be possible first to break down under heavy assault the hastily constructed enemy front south of the Somme and the Aisne and then, by rapid, deep penetration, to prevent the enemy from carrying out an ordered retreat or from forming a defense line in [the] rear."

Against this formidable force, now rested and fresh, the French could assemble only forty-three divisions, some of them still in the process of formation, many of them depleted, tired, and beset with poor morale, plus the thirteen immobilized "fortress divisions" of the Maginot Line, which were as useless in the coming battle as toy

Destroyed French heavy tank.

soldiers, three badly depleted armored divisions, three useless cavalry divisions, one British infantry division—the 51st (Highland) Division—a detached British brigade, and the much reduced British 1st Armored Division.

Had the Allied commander in chief been a general of genius rather than the timid and defeatist Weygand, and had the British been willing to risk their whole air force, the outcome would still have been the same: a swift and catastrophic French defeat. Even the evacuation from Dunkirk of nearly 140,000 French soldiers would have no effect on the battle—except for the few who would eventually join de Gaulle, they were shipped back to France just in time for the French surrender, and so spent the rest of the war as prisoners in German camps, contributing their number to the nearly two million French POWs held by the Germans—equivalent to about 10 percent of the adult male population of France.

It should be borne in mind that despite French claims that the British abandoned their ally, a charge that only intensified after the surrender by Vichy propaganda, the reality is that almost half of those evacuated from Dunkirk were French. On June 3 Churchill addressed what Hugh Dalton, minister of economic warfare, called "a squash of ministers," by which he meant the much larger full cabinet, as opposed to the War Cabinet, and spoke with great frankness, as recorded by Dalton.

> He had thought of nothing but the dead, wounded, and long dreary processions making their way to prison camps and starvation in Germany. The French? They will ask us for help and we must give them more than we can spare, which will still not be all they ask. We must not denude this island. "We've got the men away but we've lost the luggage." The French insisted on the post of honour at the end, and so "after a seemly wrangle we brought the Cameron Highlanders away. Otherwise they were to have stayed and died at the end." The PM wants to be able to say to the House tomorrow, "If I wavered for a moment, all my colleagues in the Government would turn and rend me." No one raised any objection to this.

Churchill voiced his thoughts more fully to the assembled ministers than to the War Cabinet. There was still plenty of waverers in his own party and at least one in the War Cabinet, but even to them the return of the BEF from Dunkirk demonstrated that neither Hitler nor the German War Command was infallible, and that though the German Army was formidable it was not, perhaps, unstoppable, as well as the indisputable fact that the Royal Air Force had proved itself at least the equal of the Luftwaffe and that the Royal Navy's supremacy and resourcefulness remained undiminished. So long as the fight was at sea or in the air, Britain still had a chance to survive, and no German invasion was likely to succeed without German command of the sea and the air over the Channel. There was, in fact, a glimmer of hope, however small and

Three of the armada of "little ships."

faint, even if France collapsed, which the prime minister was not as yet willing concede.

The "squash of ministers" may have been a rehearsal for what was to come the next day—one of Churchill's most famous speeches, certainly the one containing the most memorable (and often remembered) of lines. It is a curious blend of realism and exhortation, as if he wanted to encourage people and at the same time caution them against assigning to Dunkirk "the attributes of a victory."

"Wars are not won by evacuations," he warned them, and in a speech of nearly four thousand words, lasting over half an hour, he related with remarkable frankness the story of the debacle that had fallen upon the BEF and the French First Army, rising at the end to that most defiant of perorations:

Even though large tracts of Europe and many old and famous States have fallen or may fall into the grip of the Gestapo and all the odious apparatus of Nazi rule, we shall not flag or fail. We shall go on to the end, we shall fight in France, we shall fight on the seas and the oceans, we shall fight with growing confidence and growing strength in the air, we shall defend our Island, whatever the cost may be, we shall fight on the beaches, we shall fight on the landing grounds, we shall fight in the fields, and in the streets, we shall fight in the hills; we shall never surrender, and even if, which I do not for a moment believe, this Island or a large part of it were subjugated and starving, then our Empire beyond the seas, armed and guarded by the British Fleet, would carry on the struggle, until, in God's good time, the New World, with all its power and might, steps forth to the rescue of the old.

Here, in a nutshell, was his strategy, just as he had explained to his son Randolph—to struggle and survive at all costs and however long it might take until events brought the United States into the war, even if Britain was alone. Here too was his message to the British people—that they must prepare themselves for the possibility of French surrender (without in any way letting France "off the hook"), and for the long, hard, lonely fight that he had predicted in his short speech of May 13.

His old friend Josiah Wedgwood wrote to him on June 4, "That was worth 1,000 guns & the speech of 1,000 years," and it was scarcely an exaggeration. Churchill had turned words into weapons, and in the days ahead those words would do more than anything else to sustain the British cause, at home and in the United States.

The novelist Vita Sackville-West wrote to her husband that the speech "sent shivers (not of fear) down my spine," and even today there are still people alive who feel the same way. Yet few people actually *heard* him give it. The words were read aloud by an announcer on the BBC that night—Churchill did not get around to recording the speech in his own voice until 1949, and even then, that recording does not do justice to his delivery of it in the House of Commons, the majestic voice, the dramatic pauses that made listeners wait spellbound for the end of a phrase or a sentence, the deep descent of his voice to emphasize the last word of a sentence or paragraph. "One feels the whole massive backing of power and resolve behind [his words] like a great fortress," Sackville-West wrote: "they are never words for words' sake." They were not accidental. Churchill's speeches were carefully composed by him, typed in the form of blank verse on a typewriter with special large type, and carefully memorized and rehearsed until he was word perfect.

Many who heard him in the House felt the same emotion as Vita Sackville-West, while others noted that the cheers and applause from his own side of the House were still by no means equal to those that Chamberlain had received on his return from Munich. Churchill controlled the Conservative Party—the preeminent appeaser and former fervent supporter of Neville Chamberlain, chief whip David Margesson, enforced party discipline—but he did not yet have its heart.

That would come a month later, not for one of his great war speeches, but ironically for his announcement on July 4, 1940, that a British fleet had opened fire on the French fleet anchored at Mers el-Kebir in Morocco to ensure that these warships would not be turned over to the Germans or the Italians. The House at last greeted Churchill, who stood with tears streaming down his face, with heartfelt applause and cheers at the fact that Britain had at last acted with the bold, decisive use of force of a great power in what Churchill described with sorrow as "this melancholy action." He would later describe it as a "hateful decision, the most unnatural and painful in which I have ever been concerned," but however repugnant it was to have sunk an ally's ships it carried a message heard clearly in Berlin and, more important still, in Washington— that Britain would henceforth follow in the spirit of Palmerston's famous declaration that it had no permanent friends, only permanent interests, and would act with unapologetic ruthlessness in the defense of those interests, whether toward friend or foe.

*   *   *

It should not be supposed that the whole country was infused with courage from top to bottom, nor that everyone's spirits were buoyed by the evacuation from Dunkirk. "The Spirit of Dunkirk" came later, *much* later, as did the adoption of Churchill as the embodiment of defiance and victory. At the time, there were still plenty of people whose reaction to Dunkirk was ambivalent—it was a great relief that the majority of the BEF was home safe and sound (if without their weapons), but at the same time many people still feared a German invasion. It would take the Battle of Britain, from July 1940 to the end of September, to lay that fear to rest, but then came the Blitz, the German mass bombing of London and many other cities.

"Mass Observation," organized under the Ministry of Information and soon known after Minister of Information Duff Cooper as "Cooper's Snoopers," carried out what would now be called "opinion polls" on a mass basis, as well as secretly reading huge volumes of people's mail, and the conclusions were alarming—fear of an invasion was widespread, as well as resentment that the government was not telling the truth about how bad things were. This is partly because Britain remained largely unchanged since before the war—class consciousness, poverty, the sense that "the wrong people," toffs, nobs, the rich, and the well educated were still in charge and as selfish and incompetent as ever, all these things were *intensified* by the war, not ended by it.

The huge difference in pay, comfort, accommodations, and respect in the armed services between commissioned officers and "other ranks" mirrored the same class rivalry that continued to thrive in British private life despite appeals to "national unity." It had only been fourteen years since the "General Strike" in support of the miners had brought the country to a halt and exposed the bedrock of class distinction. "Working class" people in 1940 suspected that "the upper class" continued to dine well at their clubs and restaurants, and to evade most of the deprivations and irritations imposed by the government on the public, and they were not wrong. People who had country homes, or estates in the country, were able to get eggs and meat far beyond the scale laid down by rationing, and expensive restaurants continued to thrive for those who could attend them. Even the Blitz, when it finally began, seemed to recognize English class distinctions, since the area most heavily bombed at first was the East End of London, impoverished and working class. This was deliberate—the Germans hoped to stir up working-class discontent against the British government—but also accidental, since the great Port of London was a strategic target and easy for German airmen to find.

The spirit of wartime unity between the rich and the poor was not altogether a fiction, but it was nothing like as strong as it became portrayed later on in British propaganda, let alone in films and eventually television. Titles, accent, inherited wealth, a childhood and youth spent at the "right" schools and in what came to be known later as "Oxbridge," still determined who got fed the best, who got a commission instead of serving "in the ranks," and whose children were evacuated to the safety of Canada or the United States. British class warfare was ever so slightly suspended during the war, but by no means eliminated.*

Dunkirk fit into the British war narrative so well that it became myth even as it was going on. The fact that many officers at first got off the beach or the mole without their men was suppressed, along with the incompetence that had sent the BEF to France so poorly equipped for modern war or the political stupidity that had put the BEF under the command of General Gamelin in the first place. It was, however, the "little ships" that captured the minds of most people, with yachtsmen and Sea Scouts performing miracles, rather than the reality, which was that good planning by the Royal Navy was responsible for taking off the lion's share of those who were evacuated. The deeply ingrained modern English preference for amateurs over professionals had something to do with this, and there was also a populist appeal in the notion that ordinary peo-

---

* Clive Ponting's much reviled history of 1940 is a compendium of such class differences, and how they continued to flourish in wartime.

ple, without rank or professional training, could play such a large role by simply sailing across the Channel and "pitching in." "The Dunkirk Spirit," somewhat sentimentalized, is still a potent factor in the way the British think of themselves, and of the difference between them and Continental nations.

All the same, not everyone was cheered by it, or regarded Dunkirk as a triumph. In May of 2016 a letter to the *Times* described feelings that were not uncommon in 1940.

> Sir, seventy-six years ago this week the German army pushed out troops back to Dunkirk, where despite all odds most were rescued. As an 11-year-old I joined a crowd looking over the bridge at St. John's station in Bedford. The platform was full of soldiers sitting on the ground, huddled together, 200 or more. Some had no boots, many without tunics, some wrapped in blankets, many were bandaged up. Moving among them were Women's Voluntary Service members handing out drinks. The most memorable thing was the silence. These men had just been lifted from the beaches and were exhausted.
>
> I went home and told my mother who cried out, "What will become of us?" Then she clutched me hard and burst into tears. I was too young to understand that invasion was probably imminent. Those were desperate days.

33

At Sea

The "little ships."

I DON'T REMEMBER FEELING any fear at home myself, but then I was approaching seven, not an eleven-year-old. My mother was congenitally unafraid—she was moved to tears by the plight and the courage of the soldiers returning from Dunkirk, but not at all afraid of invasion, which I am sure she never imagined would take place. As for my father, he was too busy to be afraid, his mind was on his work. Nothing short of the arrival of a German tank outside the door of our house in Well Walk, Hampstead, would have deflected his attention from the films Alex was planning.

Well Walk, Hampstead.

Perhaps one of the reasons for the calm with which the British faced the defeat of their army and the possible invasion of their island was the perfect weather. Most, if not all, the photographs of the Dunkirk evacuation and the return home of the troops were taken in black-and-white, and as seen in newsprint they look bleak and gray, but late May and early June are the loveliest months in a country not famed for its good weather.* The fact is, the weather was beautiful; everywhere the flowers were in bloom and the trees in full leaf. Our garden at home had never looked prettier (whose job it was to keep it that way I do not remember), even I remember it. Looking at photographs of the time one might conclude that the whole nation was in a state of fear and collapse, but such was not the case. Flower shows, garden parties, and the neat, tidy merrymaking in London's parks (and nearby Hampstead Heath) went on as usual. Children sailed their boats, people walked their dogs, or rode, or fed the ducks—life went on as usual. Only an occasional glimpse of reality, like my mother's at the railway station, shattered the illusion that it was just another perfect early summer. If the Germans' intention was to terrify the British, they failed. They read and listened to the news with attention, but did not have the sinking feeling of collapse that pervaded France—that is the advantage of the Channel. The Germans had reached it, with catastrophic consequences for the allies, but could they cross it? The British are never more irritatingly secure of themselves than when they are alone, looking out at the chaos in Europe across the gray, choppy waters of the Channel.

In those days of course it was not possible to stay "glued to the television set" for days during major historical crises, as it is today, or even to the radio, but my father read the morning papers, the afternoon papers, and the evening papers, and even my mother glanced at the headlines—the theater generally absorbed most of her attention, and people were still going to it, eager to forget what was happening for a few hours of entertainment. The theater and the cinemas never did better business.

My father spent most of his days at the studio, but he was now working at his drawing board. Some of his sketches he brought

---

* Since George II the sovereign's birthday has been officially celebrated early in June no matter what date he or she was born, since the chances of good weather for parades, garden parties, and grand ceremonies like the Trooping of the Color are better than at any other time of the year. The early summer of 1940 was exceptionally nice, although exhausted men standing up to their neck in seawater at Dunkirk were unlikely to notice it.

home in a big artist's portfolio, to refine at night—some of them were in brilliant color, not the usual black-and-white, and while I did not know it, they were for new sets for *The Thief of Baghdad*, the Technicolor extravaganza that had been languishing since the outbreak of war, but whose completion was vital for Alex's survival.

By then my father must have known that it could not be completed in England. Alex's wartime flights back and forth to America had been increasing in frequency—not that anybody mentioned that to me, so far as I knew he was still living in his mansion on Avenue Road. Certainly by May he had already decided that *The Thief of Baghdad* could only be completed in Hollywood, and it had already been made clear to him that his second most important task was to complete *That Hamilton Woman* as quickly as possible. California held no particular attraction for Alex; even when he lived there in the late twenties, he had hated everything about it, from the avocados and swimming pools to the studio moguls. Like a buccaneer, he had returned there from time to time on swashbuckling raids that brought him to a seat on the board of United Artists or deals that made it easier to distribute his pictures in the United States—he was at once the equal of the studio heads in Hollywood and their rival, determined to create a motion picture industry in Britain that could compete with them on equal terms.

In Charles Drazin's superbly detailed biography of Alex much is made of his close connections with the British Secret Service and his friendship with Winston Churchill, and both those things, apart from taste, sophistication, culture, and a certain weary grandeur, set him apart from the other Hollywood film moguls.

Certainly he was eager to rejoin Merle again. They had only been married for a few months, before she left for Hollywood, shortly after the outbreak of war, and made it clear that she preferred to remain there, but the main reason for his return there was his conviction that British "propaganda" films, if they were to have any influence on Americans, must seem to be American products, and not imitations of ham-handed, boastful propaganda films from Germany, which nobody wanted to play, or see. His job was not to convince Americans that Britain could fight but to produce in America a certain sympathy for Britain and for the British cause. This conviction was shared by Churchill and Duff Cooper, "both of whom," to quote Drazin, "nudged him towards the Hollywood option as not only the best way of serving his own but also Britain's interests."

Those most famous of lovers, Laurence Olivier and Vivien Leigh, both of them under contract to Alex, were already in Hollywood, thus the pieces were set in place for the making of *That Hamilton Woman*; financing for it was deftly aided with the help of His Majesty's Government, so Alex set off for America once again with a brief to make the story of Nelson and Lady Hamilton into what would appear to be a star-studded, lavish Hollywood historical drama. Apart from the stars themselves, one of the most important of those pieces was my father, whose job it was to endow it with the look of a glossy Hollywood production—it was to be a quintessentially English story, although produced, directed, and art-directed by Hungarians, and masquerading as an American picture.

Even as I was having the newspaper stories about Dunkirk read aloud to me by Nanny Low, arrangements were being made to ship me to America. These coincided with the peak of the British government's controversial plan to evacuate children just in case the Germans *did* manage to invade. This scheme had been hatched when Chamberlain was prime minister, under the then current belief that the war would begin with gigantic air raids that would destroy London and other urban centers. Once placed in the hands of the bureaucrats, it quickly grew beyond anybody's expectations, and would ultimately lead to the evacuation of nearly three and a half million people—an immense, confused, and poorly supervised social movement on a scale better suited to one of the totalitarian countries than to Britain. Complaints about it from families whose children were taken away from them were equaled only by the complaints from those who were ordered to take them in.

The prime minister, perhaps understandably, does not seem to have been aware of the scale of the exodus, or of the number of children who were being sent overseas, a relatively small (and privileged) fraction of the total. In reply to a question in the House of Commons on the subject, Churchill replied, "I must frankly admit that the full bearings of this question were not appreciated by His Majesty's Government at the time it was first raised. It was not foreseen that the mild countenance given to the plan would lead to a movement of such dimensions, and that a crop of alarmist and depressing rumors would follow at its tail, detrimental to the interests of National Defense."

Nothing, however, could stop or slow down a plan that had already been so firmly implanted by the civil service on such a broad scale. Churchill did not disguise his dislike of the schemes for evacuating. In reply to a question about whether he would like to send a message to the prime minister of Canada to be hand delivered by one of the evacuated children, he replied rather testily, "I certainly do not propose to send a message by the senior child to Mr. Mackenzie King, or by the junior child either. . . . I entirely deprecate any stampede from this country at the present time."

I would have agreed with him, but my own opinion was not of course sought.

Looking back on it, I now realize that my mother was strongly against leaving for the United States, and that my father's insistence on moving us all was very likely the first, and perhaps the most important, of the disagreements that would lead them to divorce after my father returned to England in 1941. In her case, she remained so ashamed of leaving England in 1940 that she could not bring herself to go back even for a visit for several decades after the war. She remained as unmistakably English as ever, but transplanted reluctantly to America. In my father's case, the matter was very simple—what Alex wanted, he would always do, and that was that. Alex's formidably efficient secretary Miss Fisher was already in Los Angeles, and had rented a house on North Rodeo Drive in Beverly Hills for us before my father had even told my mother of our impending move.

The departure of children then was controlled by numerous regulations as a part of the general scheme to evacuate children from urban centers, but in practice it was limited only by the difficulty of finding passage on board a ship, and of securing an entry visa into the United States, easy enough to obtain in those days for families that had relatives or friends there. The wealthy and the well connected had little difficulty in evacuating their children, and over seventeen thousand were sent overseas by their parents in the six months after June 1940, not an inconsiderable number considering the limited number of passenger ships crossing the Atlantic in wartime. Their number included the future historians

Sir Martin Gilbert, Sir Alistair Horne, and John Julius Norwich, Duff Cooper's[*] son. That indefatigable gossip and diarist Chips Channon MP sent his son, Paul, to America in 1940 and described "a queue of Rolls-Royces and liveried servants and mountains of trunks" on the platform of Euston Station as Paul departed in a train full of children, but this may merely be a dig at Duff Cooper, the fierce opponent of Chamberlain and appeasement, nevertheless taking the opportunity of sending his son to safety.[†] At the time no particular shame was attached to sending your children to safety if you could afford it, nor did I feel any when I was bundled off from drab, smoky Euston Station to Liverpool, in the summer of 1940, still wearing my gas mask on a strap around my shoulder, as well as a package on a string around my neck containing my passport, my pocket Bible and travel documents, to board the SS *Duchess of Richmond*, along with hundreds of other children, bound for Montreal. What I remember best was the grayness of everything. The ship was painted wartime gray, the sea was gray, most of the interior had been painted a dull, flat gray too, covering up what had doubtless been elaborate woodwork and decorations. The portholes were covered over to prevent any light from attracting a U-boat, and the atmosphere was anything but cheerful, what between seasickness and homesickness. I do not think there was any child on board who would not have preferred to go home, but given the natural curiosity of children there was a certain excitement when, in the end, we came in sight of Canada, unpromising as its shoreline looked. Other than that the journey remains a blur, perhaps fortunately.

The spirit of Dunkirk, now ingrained in the British consciousness, did not emerge immediately or take hold as completely as is now

---

[*] Duff Cooper was to become Viscount Norwich in 1952.
[†] Paul Channon, then five, managed to reach Rhinebeck, New York, where he went to a tea party given by Helen Astor, which President Roosevelt attended. As the president left, Paul shouted, "I hope you beat Mr. Wilkie!" The president remarked, "He's beginning his political career young!"

supposed. If a cabinet minister like Duff Cooper could send his son abroad after Dunkirk without causing comment, it is a fair conclusion that many people still remained anxious about the possibility of a German invasion, despite the national habit of putting a brave face on things. The contrarian Clive Ponting points out that the "Children's Overseas Reception Board," a hastily contrived scheme to arrange for the evacuation of children to the Dominions, received over 210,000 applications between June and July 1940, when it was abruptly terminated because of the sinking of two passenger ships bearing evacuated children across the Atlantic—certainly an indicator of some degree of pessimism in the upper classes about Britain's chances. Not until the Battle of Britain had been won in the autumn of 1940 did people begin to believe that whatever else Hitler might have up his sleeve, a German invasion was no longer likely.

King George VI spoke for the whole nation when he wrote to his mother Queen Mary after the fall of France, "Personally, I feel happier now that we have no allies to be polite to and to pamper." Dunkirk is not unrelated to the emotions of those who demanded "Brexit," the British exit from the European Union in 2016. There was a national sense of relief in 1940 at leaving the Continent and withdrawing behind the White Cliffs of Dover.

Some might question whether Britain could win the war without allies, but most felt that the French had been a troublesome ally from scratch, having failed to show the right spirit from the very beginning of the German attack on May 10, even though French casualties far outweighed those of the British (and, for that matter, the Germans) in the battles of June 1940: over 90,000 French dead, 200,000 seriously wounded, and 2,000,000 sent to hard labor and starvation rations in Germany for five years as prisoners of war.

The transformation of a calamitous defeat into a legendary victory was one of the singular British triumphs of the war, one that would sustain the people through the next four years, during which they were overshadowed by their two more powerful allies, the Soviet Union and the United States, and for over seventy years thereafter, and doubtless will continue to do so whenever they look across the Channel toward the Continent, for Britain never suffered invasion, occupation, or the marching away of millions of men into captivity. Despite the horrors of five more years of war Britain managed to stand alone until June of 1941, when Hitler attacked the Soviet Union, and December 1941, when Japan attacked the United States—surely Churchill's greatest achievement.

In that sense Dunkirk was, and remains, perhaps the greatest British victory of World War Two, that rarest of historical events, a military defeat with a happy ending.

Acknowledgments

First and foremost I want to thank my late wife Margaret for suggesting the idea, as opposed to my writing another long biography. I am grateful, too, to Lynn Nesbit for bringing *Alone* to a safe harbor. I want to thank Robert Weil for his personal enthusiasm and optimism, Marie Pantojan for her care and support, and Dawn Lafferty for all her hard work and support on the home front.

Mike Hill's help was, as always, invaluable, and I am also indebted to Peter Metcalfe for his assiduous research in the United Kingdom, without which I could never have written the book, to Rebecca Karamehmedovic for her photo research, and to Pat Holl for her work in procuring permissions.

As always, any errors are mine alone.

Notes

Chapter 1: To the Brink

6   **"How horrible, how fantastic"**: Robert Self, *Neville Chamberlain* (London: Hutchinson, 2006), 41.

9   **"masterful, confident"**: Keith Feiling, *The Life of Neville Chamberlain* (London: Macmillan, 1946), 303.

10   **"Let no man say that too high"**: *New York Times*, Sept. 30, 1938.

10   **"the commonest little dog"**: Martin Gilbert and Richard Gott, *The Appeasers* (Boston: Houghton Mifflin, 1963), 146.

12   **"a good Lord Mayor of Birmingham"**: Self, *Neville Chamberlain*, 4.

16   **"I must confess"**: Feiling, *The Life of Neville Chamberlain*, 403.

Chapter 2: The Failure of Diplomacy

32   **"whether there was 'any serious danger'"**: Martin Gilbert and Richard Gott, *The Appeasers* (Boston: Houghton Mifflin, 1963), 245.

32   **"not in itself a grave one"**: Ibid., 244.

33   **"the conversion of the entire German economy"**: Adolf Hitler, *Hitler's War Directives, 1939–1945*, ed. H. R. Trevor-Roper (London: Sidgwick & Jackson, 1964), 7.

33   **"If we are not careful"**: Gilbert and Gott, *The Appeasers*, 249.

34   **"no belief in [Russia's] ability"**: Ibid., 240.

35   **"'Not that anymore'"**: Count Galeazzo Ciano, *The Ciano Diaries, 1939–1943: The Complete Unabridged Diaries of Count Galeazzo Ciano, Italian Minister for Foreign Affairs, 1936–1943*, ed. Hugh Gibson (Garden City, NY: Simon Publications, 2001), 118–19; William L. Shirer, *The Rise and Fall of the Third Reich: A History of Nazi Germany* (New York: Touchstone, 1981), 509.

38   **"that he accepts the British Empire"**: Gilbert and Gott, *The Appeasers*, 271.

39   **"fulsome, obsequious and deferential"**: William Manchester, *The Last Lion: Winston Spencer Churchill*, vol. 2, *Alone 1932–1940* (Boston: Little, Brown, 1988), 509; R. J. Minney, *The Private Papers of Hore-Belisha* (London: Collins, 1960), 220.

39   **"a great schoolboy"**: John Toland, *Adolf Hitler* (Garden City, NY: Doubleday, 1976), 423; Andrew Roberts, *The Holy Fox: The Life of Lord Halifax* (London: Head of Zeus, 2014), 101.

41   **"if he wanted war"**: Gilbert and Gott, *The Appeasers*, 284.

42   **"as the culimination of his work"**: Andrew Roberts, *Eminent Churchillians* (London: Phoenix, 1995), 16–17; John Lukacs, *Five Days in London, May 1940* (New Haven, CT: Yale University Press, 1999), 64, n. 32; ibid., 128.

43   **To the dismay of the Poles**: Gilbert and Gott, *The Appeasers*, 306.

43   **"courteous and polite"**: Ibid., 307.

Chapter 3: "Speak for England!"

47   **"If the German Government should agree"**: *Times* (London), Sept. 4, 1939, p. 4; Martin Gilbert and Richard Gott, *The Appeasers* (Boston: Houghton Mifflin, 1963), 316.

50   **"without informing the Duce"**: Count Galeazzo Ciano, *The Ciano Diaries, 1939–1943: The Complete Unabridged Diaries of Count Galeazzo Ciano, Italian Minister for Foreign Affairs, 1936–1943*, ed. Hugh Gibson (Garden City, NY: Simon Publications, 2001), 137.

50   **"Henderson was announced"**: Paul Schmidt, *Hitler's Interpreter*, ed. R. H. C. Steed (New York: Macmillan, 1951), 157–58.

Chapter 4: The Phoney War

55   **"Is Hitler trying to bore us"**: Richard Carreño, *Lord of Hosts: The Life of Sir Henry "Chips" Channon* (Philadelphia: Philabooks Press, 2016), 224.

58   **"My dear—the people one should"**: Noël Coward, *Future Indefinite* (London: Bloomsbury, 2014), 92.

61   **"History will be the judge"**: Quoted in John Charmley, "Churchill: The Gathering Storm," March 30, 2011, BBC History website, at http://www.bbc.co.uk/history/worldwars/wwtwo/churchill_gathering_storm_01.shtml.

62   **"So it was that I came again"**: Sir Winston Churchill, *The Gathering Storm*, vol. 1 of *The Second World War:* (Boston: Houghton Mifflin, 1948), 410.

65   **"By the 27th September the Royal Navy"**: Brian Bond and Michael Taylor, *The Battle for France and Flanders, 1940: Sixty Years On* (South Yorkshire: Leo Cooper, 2001), 129–30.

67   **"My dear Churchill"**: *Churchill and Roosevelt: The Complete Correspondence: Alliance Emerging*, vol. 1, *October 1933–November 1942*, ed. Warren F. Kimball (Princeton, NJ: Princeton University Press, 1984), 24.

72   **"a demonstration of motorized troops"**: Heinz Guderian, *Achtung-Panzer!*, trans. Christopher Duffy (London: Arms and Armour Press, 1992), 11–12.

73   **"Suitable terrain"**: Ibid., 181.

Chapter 5: Operation Pied Piper

77   *The Thief of Baghdad*: Charles Drazin, *Korda: Britain's Only Movie Mogul* (London: Sidgwick & Jackson, 2002), 201.

77   **What Alex did *not* tell**: Ibid., 213–19.

80   **"Many of the children"**: Harold Nicolson, *Diaries and Letters*, vol. 2, *1939–1945*, ed. Nigel Nicolson (London: Collins, 1967), 28.

80   **"separation from their parents"**: See Dwight Jon Zimmerman, "Operation Pied Piper: The Evacuation of English Children during World War II," Defense Media Network, Dec. 31, 2011, at http://www.defensemedianetwork.com/stories/operation-pied-piper-the-evacuation-of-english-children-during-world-war-ii/.

Chapter 6: Case Yellow

91   **"smooth, secretive, non-committal"**: Sir Edward Spears, *Assignment to Catastrophe*, vol. 1, *Prelude to Dunkirk July, 1939–May 1940* (New York: A. A. Wyn, 1954), 74.

91   **"wood strawberries"**: Ibid., 5.

93   **"The Allied advance would be so rapid"**: Ibid., 53.

98   **"a series of memoranda"**: Eric von Manstein, *Lost Victories: The War Memoirs of Hitler's Most Brilliant General* (Novato, CA: Presidio Press, 1994), 103.

98   **"the *main weight* of the attack"**: Ibid., 104.

102   **"surprisingly quick to grasp"**: Ibid., 120.

102   **"Hitler had a certain instinct"**: Ibid., 125.

Chapter 7: "Gad, Gentlemen, Here's to Our Greatest Victory of the War"

104   **"a schoolboy sense of humor"**: John Colville, *Man of Valour: The Life of Field Marshal the Viscount Gort* (London: Collins, 1972), 158.

104   **"Gort took pleasure"**: Ibid.

106   **"he must be careful how he deals"**: Ian R. Grimwood, *A Little Chit of a Fellow: A Biography of the Right Hon. Leslie Hore-Belisha* (Sussex, UK: Book Guild Publishing, 2006), 161.

106   **"a bad effect on the neutrals"**: Ibid., 165.

106   **Hore-Belisha was "summoned"**: Ibid.

107   **"Oliver Stanley will do well"**: Colville, *Man of Valour,* 165.

109   **"It all comes from allowing"**: Sir Henry Pownall, *Chief of Staff: The Diaries of Lieutenant-General Sir Henry Pownall,* vol. 1, *1933–1940,* ed. Brian Bond (Hamden, CT: Archon Books, 1973), 241.

110   **"absolutely filthy"**: Joshua Levine, *Forgotten Voices of Dunkirk* (London: Ebury Press, 2010), 80.

111   **"each battalion was allocated"**: See David Smurthwaite, Mark Nicholis, Linda Washington, et al., *Against All Odds: The British Army of 1939–1940* (London: National Army Museum, 1990), 80.

111   **"eye opener"**: Julian Thompson, *Dunkirk: Retreat to Victory* (New York: Arcade Publishing, 2011), 22–23.

113   **"that the subject of sex"**: Ibid., 23.

113   **"the magnitude of his blunder"**: Lord Alanbrooke, *War Diaries. 1939–1945* (Los Angeles: University of California Press, 2001), 18, 19.

113   **the Pioneers were "a tough crowd"**: Levine, *Forgotten Voices of Dunkirk,* 30.

Chapter 8: Hitler "Missed the Bus"

118   **"'Hullo. Why on earth'"**: Evelyn Waugh, *Put Out More Flags* (Boston: Little, Brown, 1945), 148.

120   **"I understand that it is the plan"**: Sir Henry Pownall, *Chief of Staff: The Diaries of Lieutenant-General Sir Henry Pownall,* vol. 1, *1933–1940,* ed. Brian Bond (Hamden, CT: Archon Books, 1973), 280–82.

121   **"one thing is certain"**: Sir Winston Churchill, *The Gathering Storm,* vol. 1 of *The Second World War* (Boston: Houghton Mifflin, 1948), 584.

121   **"This proved an ill-judged"**: Ibid., 585–86.

122   **"Within forty-eight hours all"**: Ibid., 591.

122   **"forestalled, surprised"**: Ibid., 601.

Chapter 9: "In the Name of God, Go"

125   **"a general feeling of apprehension"**: Harold Nicolson, *Diaries and Letters,* vol. 2, *1939–1945,* ed. Nigel Nicolson (London: Collins, 1967), 67.

125   **"To the House. It is packed"**: Ibid., 65–66.

125   **"dressed [as if] in deep mourning"**: Graham Stewart, *Burying Caesar: The Churchill-Chamberlain Rivalry* (Woodstock, NY: Overlook Press, 1999), 393.

126   **It was due to the influence of Mme de Portes**: Sir Edward Spears, *Assignment to Catastrophe,* vol. 1, *Prelude to Dunkirk July, 1939–May 1940* (New York: A. A. Wyn, 1954), 89–92.

127 **"the formlessness of our system"**: Sir Winston Churchill, *The Gathering Storm*, vol. 1 of *The Second World War* (Boston: Houghton Mifflin, 1948), 588.

127 **"six chiefs [and Deputy Chiefs]"**: Ibid., 642.

127 **"the day-to-day management"**: Ibid.

129 **Chamberlain made a "feeble"**: Nicolson, *Diaries and Letters*, 72.

130 **"absolutely devastating"**: Ibid, 73.

130 **"great gasp of astonishment"**: Ibid.

130 **"thunderous applause"**: Ibid.

131 **"his implacable sentences"**: Spears, *Assignment to Catastrophe*, 119.

133 **"a leer of triumph"**: Nicolson, *Diaries and Letters*, 74.

135 **"She was in black"**: Sir Henry Channon, *Chips: The Diaries of Sir Henry Channon*, ed. Robert Rhodes James (London: Phoenix, 1996), 245.

135 **"turned, picking his way"**: Spears, *Assignment to Catastrophe*, 129–30.

136 **"only a solitary little man"**: Channon, *Chips*, 247.

137 **"was almost entirely dependent"**: Ibid., 463.

138 **"either the Chancellorship of the Exchequer"**: Andrew Roberts, *The Holy Fox: The Life of Lord Halifax* (London: Head of Zeus, 2014), 266–67.

139 **"bright, sunny afternoon"**: Churchill, *The Gathering Storm*, 662.

140 **"in a more powerful position"**: Roberts, *The Holy Fox*, 269.

140 **"self-abnegation"**: Ibid., 268.

141 **"the duty would fall upon me"**: Churchill, *The Gathering Storm*, 663.

141 **"no communication with either"**: Ibid.

141 **"I think I shall be Prime Minister"**: Martin Gilbert, comp., *The Churchill War Papers*, vol. 1, *At the Admiralty, September 1939–May 1940* (New York: W. W. Norton, 1993), 1266.

142 **"We had had little or no sleep"**: Ibid., 1268.

143 **"haggard and worn"**: Ibid., 1281.

143 **"At about 4:45"**: John Colville, *The Fringes of Power: 10 Downing Street Diaries, 1939–1955* (New York: W. W. Norton, 1985), 121–22.

144 **" 'Then I knew' "**: Gilbert, *The Churchill War Papers*, 1281–82.

145 **"Tears came into his eyes"**; Ibid., 1284.

Chapter 10: "The Top of the Greasy Pole"

152 **the "definite undercurrent of despair"**: David Nasaw, *The Patriarch: The Remarkable Life and Turbulent Times of Joseph P. Kennedy* (New York: Penguin Press, 2012), 439.

153 **"a dictated peace with Hitler"**: Joseph P. Kennedy, *Hostage of Fortune: The Letters of Joseph P. Kennedy*, ed. Amanda Smith (New York: Viking Press, 2001), 433.

154 **"on a large front"**: *Times* (London), May 10, 1940.

155 **"wherever we went through a village"**: Joshua Levine, *Forgotten Voices of Dunkirk* (London: Ebury Press, 2010), 43.

155 **"News at present"**: Sir Henry Pownall, *Chief of Staff: The Diaries of Lieutenant-General Sir Henry Pownall*, vol. 1, *1933–1940*, ed. Brian Bond (Hamden, CT: Archon Books, 1973), 308.

156 **"little more than a wide stream"**: Alistair Horne, *To Lose a Battle: France 1940* (London: Penguin Group, 1990), 241.

158 **"pouring through the hole"**: Pownall, *Chief of Staff*, 309.

158 **"I could have wept"**: Horne, *To Lose a Battle*, 278–79.

159 **"As we were moving forward"**: Levine, *Forgotten Voices of Dunkirk*, 43–45.

162 **General Gamelin had set up at Montry**: Guy Chapman, *Why France Fell: The Defeat of the French Army in 1940* (New York: Holt, Rinehart and Winston, 1968), 84.

Chapter 11: Rommel Crosses the Meuse

164 **"Dearest Lu"**: Erwin Rommel, *The Rommel Papers*, ed. B. H. Liddell Hart (New York: Da Capo Press, 1953), 6.

166 **it was thought that the Führer**: Alistair Horne, *To Lose a Battle: France 1940* (London: Penguin Group, 1990), 320–22.

166 **The 7th Panzer was still in the process**: Ibid., 322.

168 **"I've come up for breath"**: Rommel, *The Rommel Papers*, 7.

169 **"Towards midday, groups of unsaddled"**: Horne, *To Lose a Battle*, 306–7.

169 **"an ancient weir"**: Ibid., 308–9.

171 **"and organized the fresh effort"**: Rommel, *The Rommel Papers*, 11.

172 **"a lively emotion"**: Horne, *To Lose a Battle*, 333.

172 **"*un pépin assez sérieux*"**: Ibid., 335.

174 **"of unimaginable chaos"**: Ibid., 362, quoting General Ruby.

Chapter 12: "We Are Beaten; We Have Lost the Battle"

176 **"Bad news from down south"**: Pownall, *Chief of Staff: The Diaries of Lieutenant-General Sir Henry Pownall*, vol. 1, *1933–1940*, ed. Brian Bond (Hamden, CT: Archon Books, 1973), 315.

177 **"a helplessly confused retreat"**: Erwin Rommel, *The Rommel Papers*, ed. B. H. Liddell Hart (New York: Da Capo Press, 1953), 14.

178 **"M. Reynaud was on the telephone"**: Sir Winton Churchill, *Their Finest Hour*, vol. 2 of *The Second World War* (Boston: Houghton Mifflin, 1949), 42.

178 **"he could no longer take"**: Alistair Horne, *To Lose a Battle: France 1940* (London: Penguin Group, 1990), 448.

179 **"the English didn't really like"**: Clare Boothe, *European Spring* (London: Hamish Hamilton, 1941), 160.

179 **"the drawing rooms of Paris"**: Ibid., 281.

Chapter 13: "The Mortal Gravity of the Hour"

191   **"venerable officials [pushed] wheelbarrows"**: Sir Winton Churchill, *Their Finest Hour*, vol. 2 of *The Second World War* (Boston: Houghton Mifflin, 1949), 46.

191   **"with unheard-of speed"**: Ibid.

193   **"If the French infantry could feel"**: Martin Gilbert, comp., *The Churchill War Papers*, vol. 2, *Never Surrender, May 1940–December 1940* (New York: W. W. Norton, 1995), 57.

193   **"This Army is in an indescribable disorder"**: Major General Sir Edward Spears, *Assignment to Catastrophe*, vol. 1, *Prelude to Dunkirk, July 1939–May 1940* (New York: A. A. Wyn, 1954), 146.

193   **"It was not reasonable that"**: Gilbert, *The Churchill War Papers*, 56.

Chapter 14: May 20, 1940: "A Pretty Fair Pig of a Day"

201   **"a long spell of dry weather"**: L. F. Ellis, *The War in France and Flanders, 1939–1940*, ed. J. R. M. Butler (Nashville, TN: Battery Press; London: Imperial War Museum, 1953), 69.

203   **"that British generals always made"**: Sir Edward Spears, *Assignment to Catastrophe*, vol. 1, *Prelude to Dunkirk, July 1939–May 1940* (New York: A. A. Wyn, 1954), 178–79.

206   **"barely alive—and what there is left"**: Ibid., 204.

206   **"If I had known the situation"**: Alistair Horne, *To Lose a Battle: France 1940* (London: Penguin Group, 1990), 556.

208   **Ironside lost his temper**: Sir Edmund Ironside, *Time Unguarded: The Ironside Diaries, 1937–1940*, ed. Roderick Macleod and Denis Kelly (New York: David McKay, 1962), 321.

Chapter 15: "The Fatal Slope"

209   **"The whole art of war"**: David G. Chandler, *The Campaigns of Napoleon* (New York: Scribner, 1966), 147.

211   **"giving away the German victory"**: Florian K. Rothbrust, *Guderian's XIXth Panzer Corps and the Battle of France: Breakthrough in the Ardennes, May 1940* (Westport, CT: Praeger, 1990), 83.

211   **"suspend all westwar movements"**: Ibid., 84.

211   **"advance westwards unimpeded"**: Ibid., 87.

212   **"Hundreds upon hundreds of French troops"**: Erwin Rommel, *The Rommel Papers*, ed. B. H. Liddell Hart (New York: Da Capo Press, 1953), 22.

214   **"Our fate was sealed"**: Charles de Gaulle, *The Call to Honour, 1940–1942*, vol. 1 of *War Memoirs* (New York: Viking Press, 1955), 35–36.

215   **"Too proud for intrigue"**: Ibid., 72.

215   **"There, de Gaulle!":** Ibid., 37.
215   **"At the sight of those bewildered people":** Ibid., 39.

Chapter 16: "Hard and Heavy Tidings"

220   **"continued to agitate":** Clare Boothe, *European Spring* (London: Hamish Hamilton, 1941), 300.
221   **"I went up to my father's bedroom":** Martin Gilbert, comp., *The Churchill War Papers*, vol. 2, *Never Surrender, May 1940–December 1940* (New York: W. W. Norton, 1995), 70–71.
222   **"There was a tray with plenty of liquor":** Joseph P. Kennedy, *Hostage of Fortune: The Letters of Joseph P. Kennedy*, ed. Amanda Smith (New York: Viking Press, 2001), 426.
224   **"A tremendous battle is raging":** Gilbert, *The Churchill War Papers*, 84, 89, 90.
226   **"members of the present Administration":** Ibid., 93.
227   **"a precautionary measure":** Ibid., 96.

Chapter 17: The Sharp End of the Stick

233   **"the flow of fleeing humanity":** Henry de La Falaise, *Through Hell to Dunkirk* (Harrisburg, PA: Military Service Publishing Company, 1943), 21.
234   **"The Stuka was the sharpshooter":** Joshua Levine, *Forgotten Voices of Dunkirk* (London: Ebury Press, 2010), 74.
235   **"Who the hell is playing football":** Ibid., 73.
236   **"Three wrecked German motor cycles":** La Falaise, *Through Hell to Dunkirk*, 36.
237   **"An appalling sight greets us there":** Ibid., 40–42.
239   **"A bright orange flame blinds me":** Ibid., 90.
240   **"The Major's voice giving orders":** Ibid., 93–94.
242   **"The road is a mess":** Ibid., 101.
243   **"answers with a shrug":** Ibid., 105–6.
243   a **"quiet pasture":** Ibid., 108.

Chapter 18: The Battle of Arras: "We May Be *foutu*"

246   **"must fight its way southwards":** John Colville, *The Fringes of Power: 10 Downing Street Diaries, 1939–1955* (New York: W. W. Norton, 1985), 83.
247   **"Essential to secure our communications":** Martin Gilbert, comp., *The Churchill War Papers*, vol. 2, *Never Surrender, May 1940–December 1940* (New York: W. W. Norton, 1995), 101.
248   **"roads [which] were already encumbered":** Maxime Weygand,

Recalled to Service: The Memoirs of General Maxime Weygand of the Académie Francaise, trans. E. W. Dickes (London: Heinemann, 1952), 60.

251   **"the Belgian Army existed solely"**: L. F. Ellis, *The War in France and Flanders, 1939–1940*, ed. J. R. M. Butler (Nashville, TN: Battery Press; London: Imperial War Museum, 1996), 105.

251   **"incapable of launching an attack"**: Ibid., 108.

252   **"retreat to the sea"**: B. H. Liddell Hart, *The German Generals Talk* (New York: Harper Perennial, 2002), 131.

254   **"to insert a wedge into the gap"**: Ibid.

255   had **"infiltrated his line"**: Erwin Rommel, *The Rommel Papers*, ed. B. H. Liddell Hart (New York: Da Capo Press, 1953), 29.

256   **"put his Armored Reconnaissance Battalion"**: Ibid., 30.

256   **"Fierce fighting flared up"**: Ibid., 33.

258   Arras had been **"cleared up"**: Ibid., 34.

258   **"The decision will fall on the high ground"**: Franz Halder, *The Halder War Diary, 1939–1942*, ed. Charles Burdick and Hans-Adolf Jacobsen (Navato, CA: Presidio Press, 1988), 155.

Chapter 19: "Their Zest and Delight in
Shooting Germans Was Most Entertaining"

261   **"pacing moodily up and down"**: Martin Gilbert, comp., *The Churchill War Papers*, vol. 2, *Never Surrender, May 1940–December 1940* (New York: W. W. Norton, 1995), 110.

261   **"in the Cambrai and Arras area"**: Ibid., 112.

261   **"the British Army and the French"**: Ibid., 114.

261   **"Can nobody prevent him"**: Sir Henry Pownall, *Chief of Staff: The Diaries of Lieutenant-General Sir Henry Pownall*, vol. 1, *1933–1940*, ed. Brian Bond (Hamden, CT: Archon Books, 1974), 333.

262   **"defensive posts [were] manned"**: Ibid., 332.

263   **"I am trying to square up"**: Gilbert, *The Churchill War Papers*, 116.

264   **"French Commanders in the North"**: Ibid., 117.

264   a **"plan with the object of saving"**: Ibid., 118.

265   **"The stampede of refugees"**: Henry de La Falaise, *Through Hell to Dunkirk* (Harrisburg, PA: Military Service Publishing Company, 1943), 112.

265   **"The earth rocks under incessant"**: Ibid., 114.

266   **"assess civilian morale"**: Arthur Gwynn-Browne. *F.S.P.: An N.C.O.'s Description of His and Others' First Six Months of War, Jan. 1st–June 1st, 1940*, ed. N. H. Reeve (Bridgend, Wales: Seren, 2004), xvii.

267   **"in the end one were two small dogs"**: Ibid., 89.

268   **"Everywhere was refugees"**: Ibid.

268   **"They had no arms and were saying"**: Ibid., 86–87.

269   **"huge French gun"**: Ibid., 84.

269   **"This morning (at 9 a.m.)"**: Pownall, *Chief of Staff*, 337.

270   **"crawling across this open ground"**: Joshua Levine, *Forgotten Voices of Dunkirk* (London: Ebury Press, 2010), 81–82.

270   **"Company Sergeant-Major Gristock"**: *London Gazette*, Aug. 23, 1940.

271   **"bitter and confused fighting"**: L. F. Ellis, *The War in France and Flanders, 1939–1940*, ed. J. R. M. Butler (Nashville, TN: Battery Press; London: Imperial War Museum, 1996), 114.

271   **"thirty-four field guns"**: Ibid., 115.

272   **"seemingly limitless mass of piteous"**: Guy F. Gough, *Thirty Days to Dunkirk: The Royal Irish Fusiliers, May 1940* (Wrexham, Clwyd: Bridge Books, 1990), 47.

273   **"Later during [the] day survivors"**: Ibid., 60.

Chapter 20: The Burghers of Calais

282   **The 2nd Welsh Guards were still**: L. F. Ellis, *Welsh Guards at War, 1939–1946* (Aldershot: Gale and Polden, 1946), 96.

282   **"fighting for their lives"**: Ibid.

283   **"In the midst of this very orderly"**: Ibid., 97.

285   **"old walled town"**: L. F. Ellis, *The War in France and Flanders, 1939–1940*, ed. J. R. M. Butler (Nashville, TN: Battery Press; London: Imperial War Museum, 1996), 154.

287   **"Enemy No. 1 for us is France"**: Franz Halder, *The Halder War Diary, 1939–1942*, ed. Charles Burdick and Hans-Adolf Jacobsen (Navato, CA: Presidio Press, 1988), 156.

Chapter 21: "Fight It Out to the Bitter End"

291   **"The very thought of having to order"**: Martin Gilbert, comp., *The Churchill War Papers*, vol. 2, *Never Surrender, May 1940–December 1940* (New York: W. W. Norton, 1995), 126.

291   **"to proceed to the relief of Boulogne"**: L. F. Ellis, *The War in France and Flanders, 1939–1940*, ed. J. R. M. Butler (Nashville, TN: Battery Press; London: Imperial War Museum, 1953), 162.

292   **"This is surely madness"**: Gilbert, *The Churchill War Papers*, 138.

292   **"I cannot understand the situation"**: Ibid.

292   **"German tanks had penetrated"**: Ibid., 139.

293   **"A telegram was sent to the commander"**: Ibid., 160.

293   **"Defence of Calais to the utmost"**: Ibid., 149–50.

294   **"The King's Royal Rifle Corps"**: Ellis, *The War in France and Flanders*, 167.

295   **"fighting ceased and the noise of battle"**: Ibid., 168.

297   **"A day or two without action"**: Erwin Rommel, *The Rommel Papers*, ed. B. H. Liddell Hart (New York: Da Capo Press, 1953), 34.

300 **For three fateful days the panzer divisions**: B. H. Liddell Hart, *The German Generals Talk* (New York: Harper Perennial, 2002), 133.

Chapter 22: Flag Officer, Dover

302 **"The Admiralty has made an order"**: Sinclair McKay, *Dunkirk: From Disaster to Deliverance—Testimonies of the Last Survivors* (London: Aurum Press, 2014), 89.

305 **He reopened the maze of tunnels**: Ibid., 54–55.

305 **Ramsay placed his own office**: Ibid., 55.

305 **"care-free holiday makers"**: Ibid., 56.

306 **"British generals always made"**: Sir Edward Spears, *Assignment to Catastrophe*, vol. 1, *Prelude to Dunkirk, July 1939–May 1940* (New York: A. A. Wyn, 1954), 180.

306 **"the hazardous evacuation of very large"**: McKay, *Dunkirk*, 100.

306 **"all available shipping should be placed"**: Ibid.

Chapter 23: The Home Front

312 **"attempt to stem the flood"**: L. F. Ellis, *The War in France and Flanders, 1939–1940*, ed. J. R. M. Butler (Nashville, TN: Battery Press; London: Imperial War Museum, 1996), 103.

316 **"retakes and added scenes"**: Charles Drazin, *Korda: Britain's Only Movie Mogul* (London: Sidgwick & Jackson, 2002), 212.

Chapter 24: "Presume Troops Know They Are Cutting Their Way Home to Blighty"

324 **"It is all a first-class mess-up"**: Sir Henry Pownall, *Chief of Staff: The Diaries of Lieutenant-General Sir Henry Pownall*, vol. 1, *1933–1940*, ed. Brian Bond (Hamden, CT: Archon Books, 1973), 341.

324 **"terrified horses [were] milling around"**: Henry de La Falaise, *Through Hell to Dunkirk* (Harrisburg, PA: Military Service Publishing Company, 1943), 138.

324 **"It recalls the paintings of Napoleon's retreat"**: Ibid., 145.

325 **" 'Not yet, the armies are *épuisées* ' "**: *The Diary of a Staff Officer* (London: Methuen, 1941), 45.

327 **on May 14, for example**: Charles More, *The Road to Dunkirk: The British Expeditionary Force and the Battle of the Ypres-Comines Canal, 1940* (London: Frontline Books, 2013), 11.

327 **"Geysers of earth and tongues of flame"**: La Falaise, *Through Hell to Dunkirk*, 140.

329 **"At present we are strung out"**: Quoted in Pownall, *Chief of Staff*, 341.

329   **"Whether we ever get to the sea"**: Ibid.

329   **"It seemed from all the evidence"**: Martin Gilbert, comp., *The Churchill War Papers*, vol. 1, *Never Surrender, May 1940–December 1940* (New York: W. W. Norton, 1995), 152.

333   **"the dream of all Germans"**: Ibid., 155.

334   **"A short further discussion ensued"**: Ibid., 156.

334   **"doubted whether anything would come"**: Ibid.

334   **"the possibility of some discussion"**: John Lukacs, *Five Days in London, May 1940* (New Haven, CT: Yale University Press, 2001), 94.

335   **"not merely an armistice"**: Ibid.

335   **"that we were in a different"**: Gilbert, *The Churchill War Papers*, 157.

337   **Late that night he sent a message**: Ibid., 160.

337   **"At this solemn moment"**: Ibid., 161.

Chapter 25: Dynamo

339   **"Census of [civilian] Motor-boats"**: David Woodward, *Ramsay at War: The Fighting Life of Sir Betram Ramsay* (London: William Kimber, 1957), 20.

339   **"armed boarding vessels"**: Ibid., 14.

339   **Dutch royal family**: Ibid., 18.

339   **On May 24 Ramsay met with**: Ibid., 22.

343   **"S N O" out of silver**: Ibid., 24.

343   **"As regards the bearing and behavior"**: Ibid.

344   **"I remember," Montgomery wrote**: Nigel Hamilton, *The Full Monty: Montgomery of Alamein*, vol. 1, *1889–1942* (London: Penguin Press, 2001), 372–73.

344   **"falling back in hot battle"**: A. D. Divine, *Dunkirk* (New York: E. P. Dutton, 1948), 11.

346   **"They were closing in on all sides"**: Quoting Lance-Corporal Edward Doe, 2nd Battalion, King's Royal Rifle Corps, in Joshua Levine, *Forgotten Voices of Dunkirk* (London: Ebury Press, 2010), 119–20.

346   **"He had his jackboots on"**: Ibid., 122.

347   **"when we lifted the top part"**: Ibid., 130.

Chapter 26: "Fight It Out, Here or Elsewhere"

352   **"Old Umbrella"**: Baron Hugh Dalton, *The Second World War Diary of Hugh Dalton, 1940–1945*, ed. Ben Pimloff (London: Cape, 1996), 535.

353   **"were, at the moment, quite unprepared"**: Martin Gilbert, comp., *The Churchill War Papers*, vol. 2, *Never Surrender, May 1940–December 1940* (New York: W. W. Norton, 1995), 174.

354   **unarmed Auxiliary Army Pioneers**: *Times* (London), May 29, 1940.

355   **"If you are very close"**: *Parodies: An Anthology from Chaucer to Beerbohm—and After*, ed. Dwight Macdonald (New York: Random House, 1960), 385.

357   **He returned to London on May 17**: Charles Drazin, *Korda: Britain's Only Movie Mogul* (London: Sidgwick & Jackson, 2002), 232.

357   **"sugar-coating"**: Ibid., 236.

360   **"the stink of death"**: A. D. Divine, *Dunkirk* (New York: E. P. Dutton, 1948), 181.

361   **"We found the roads in chaos"**: Jack Pritchard, *Seven Years a Grenadier, 1939–1946* (Northamptonshire, UK: Forces & Corporate Publishing, 1999), 28–29.

362   **J. E. Bowman, then a Lance-Bombardier**: J. E. Bowman, *Three Stripes and a Gun: A Young Man's Journey towards Maturity* (Braunton, Devon: Merlin Books, 1987), 97.

362   **"We got to this barn"**: Matthew Richardson, *Tigers at Dunkirk: The Leicestershire Regiment and the Fall of France* (Barnsley, South Yorkshire: Pen & Sword Military, 2010), 58–59.

363   **"Meanwhile, the House should prepare itself"**: Gilbert, *The Churchill War Papers*, 179.

365   **"It was idle to think"**: John Lukacs, *Five Days in London, May 1940* (New Haven, CT: Yale University Press, 2001), 5.

367   **"100 to 1 against being able to bring"**: David Woodward, *Ramsay at War: The Fighting Life of Admiral Sir Bertram Ramsay* (London: William Kimber, 1957), 24.

Chapter 27: Holding the Line

369   **take off 1,420 troops**: L. F. Ellis, *The War in France and Flanders, 1939–1940*, ed. J. R. M. Butler (Nashville, TN: Battery Press; London: Imperial War Museum, 1996), 184.

373   **A British war correspondent in Nieuport**: Douglas Williams, *The New Contemptibles* (London: John Murray, 1940), 70.

374   **"Mouthing a string of indecipherable"**: J. E. Bowman, *Three Stripes and a Gun: A Young Man's Journey towards Maturity* (Braunton, Devon: Merlin Books, 1987), 98.

375   **"pushed us with extreme selfishness"**: Guy F. Gough, *Thirty Days to Dunkirk: The Royal Irish Fusiliers, May 1940* (Wrexham, Clwyd: Bridge Books, 1990), 152–53.

376   **"The scene on the beaches"**: Jack Pritchard, *Seven Years a Grenadier, 1939–1946* (Northamptonshire, UK: Forces & Corporate Publishing, 1999), 30.

376   **"In the roadside fields"**: Ellis, *The War in France and Flanders*, 210–11.

376   **By that night the evacuation fleet**: David Woodward, *Ramsay at War: The Fighting Life of Admiral Sir Bertram Ramsay* (London: William Kimber, 1957), 31.

377   **"they were rushed and swamped"**: Ibid.

377   **"a lively encounter"**: Henry de La Falaise, *Through Hell to Dunkirk* (Harrisburg, PA: Military Service Publishing Company, 1943), 147.

Chapter 28: "The Little Ships"

379   **"The moment we all dreaded"**: Henry de La Falaise, *Through Hell to Dunkirk* (Harrisburg, PA: Military Service Publishing Company, 1943), 150.

380   **"There was firing all around us"**: J. E. Bowman, *Three Stripes and a Gun: A Young Man's Journey towards Maturity* (Braunton, Devon: Merlin Books, 1987), 101.

380   **"In these dark days"**: Martin Gilbert, comp., *The Churchill War Papers*, vol. 2, *Never Surrender, May 1940–December 1940* (New York: W. W. Norton, 1995), 187.

381   **"The French and the British troops"**: *Times* (London), May 29, 1940.

381   **"then told to get into town"**: Matthew Richardson, *Tigers at Dunkirk: The Leicestershire Regiment and the Fall of France* (Barnsley, South Yorkshire: Pen & Sword Military, 2010), 66–67.

381   **"No one knew what was happening"**: Ibid., 67–68.

382   **"Everybody was destroying"**: Arthur Gwynn-Browne, *F.S.P: An N.C.O.'s Description of His and Others' First Six Months of War, January 1st–June 1st 1940*, ed. N. H. Reeve (Bridgend, Wales: Seren, 2004), 119.

382   **"We joined the stream of troops"**: Ibid., 120.

383   **"a brilliant flame and tremendous crash"**: Bowman, *Three Stripes and a Gun*, 102.

383   **"which stung the eyes"**: Richardson, *Tigers at Dunkirk*, 62.

383   **"to a scene from Dante's *Inferno*"**: Ibid.

383   **"Drink was freely available"**: Ibid.

385   **"the eerie ghost town"**: *Eyewitness War* (South Woodham Ferrers, Essex, UK: Colson House, 1995), 8–9.

385   **"the bulk of the evacuation effort"**: Richardson, *Tigers at Dunkirk*, 65.

387   **"The destroyers put up by far"**: David Woodward, *Ramsay at War: The Fighting Life of Admiral Sir Bertram Ramsay* (London: William Kimber, 1957), 28.

389   **"at places like Teddington"**: A. D. Divine, *Dunkirk* (New York: E. P. Dutton, 1948), 34.

390   **"barges, train ferries, car ferries"**: Norman Gelb, *Dunkirk: The Complete Story of the First Step in the Defeat of Hitler* (New York: William Morrow, 1989), 241.

392   he **"had another guess"**: BBC on-line World War II Archive, Dunkirk Evacuation, "How the 'Little Ships' Helped Rescue the Allied Troops," at http://www.bbc.co.uk/archive/dunkirk/14322.shtml.

394 **"News unpleasant. We have got"**: Sir Alex Cadogan, *The Diaries of Sir Alex Cadogan, O.M., 1938–1945,* ed. David Dilks (London: Cassell, 1971), 292; Gilbert, *The Churchill War Papers,* 191.

395 **"This is only to get into order"**: Gilbert, *The Churchill War Papers,* 191–92.

396 **"Mr. Churchill not only approved"**: Ibid., 193.

Chapter 29: "The Best Mug of Tea I Have Ever Had in My Life"

398 **"The French and British troops that"**: *Times* (London), May 30, 1940.

399 **"I suppose they [the French commanders]"**: Sir Henry Pownall, *Chief of Staff: The Diaries of Lieutenant-General Sir Henry Pownall,* vol. 1, *1933–1940,* ed. Brian Bond (Hamden, CT: Archon Books, 1973), 351.

399 **"The Admiral's boast that he would hold"**: Ibid., 354.

399 **"The British never took part"**: Sinclair McKay, *Dunkirk: From Disaster to Deliverance—Testimonies of the Last Survivors* (London: Aurum Press, 2014), 319.

400 **Pownall declined to be "pinned down"**: Pownall, *Chief of Staff,* 356.

402 **"Report every three hours"**: Martin Gilbert, comp., *The Churchill War Papers,* vol. 2, *Never Surrender, May 1940–December 1940* (New York: W. W. Norton, 1995), 200.

405 **"which, we can see, and hear"**: Henry de La Falaise, *Through Hell to Dunkirk* (Harrisburg, PA: Military Service Publishing Company, 1943), 154.

405 **"we smell the tang of a salty breeze"**: Ibid., 155.

406 **"The noise and the commotion"**: Ibid., 156.

406 **Dunkirk harbor "had been blocked"**: David Woodward, *Ramsay at War: The Fighting Life of Admiral Sir Bertram Ramsay* (London: William Kimber, 1957), 36.

407 **"the best mug of tea"**: Frank Shaw and Joan Shaw, comps., *We Remember Dunkirk: Over 100 Personal Accounts* (Hinckley, Leicestershire: n.p., 1990), 138–39.

409 **Brian Bishop, a soldier**: Ibid., 11.

411 **"860 vessels of all kinds"**: Gilbert, *The Churchill War Papers,* 203.

Chapter 30: "Arm in Arm"

413 **"who were vital for continuing"**: Martin Gilbert, comp., *The Churchill War Papers: Never Surrender,* vol. 2, *May 1940–December 1940* (New York: W. W. Norton, 1995), 211.

414 **"As we were standing around the table"**: Ibid., 206.

414 **"An agreeable person, but, it seems"**: Ibid., 205–6.

415 **"but *bombardment* of all French ports"**: Ibid., 219.

415   **"tramping through the tall grass"**: Ibid., 206.

415   **"Each time the destroyers put to sea"**: Henry de La Falaise, *Through Hell to Dunkirk* (Harrisburg, PA: Military Service Publishing Company, 1943), 160.

416   **"When we reach [the colonel]"**: Ibid., 161.

416   **"The wind is rising"**: Ibid., 162.

417   **"Almost the whole ten miles"**: A. D. Divine, *Dunkirk* (New York: E. P. Dutton, 1948), 117.

417   **"a fresh northerly breeze"**: Ibid., 145.

418   **"old cutter-rigged cockle boats"**: Ibid., 159.

420   **"The bombs dropped out"**: Ibid., 154.

421   **"The vessels that did such heroic service"**: "31st May 1940—Lovely on the Water," *The Dunkirk Project*, at https://thedunkirkproject.wordpress.com/the-dunkirk-project-2/the-dunkirk-project/31st-may-1940-lovely-on-the-water/.

424   **As for Abrial**: Hugh Sebag-Montefiore, *Dunkirk: Fight to the Last Man* (Cambridge, MA: Harvard University Press, 2006), 407–9.

Chapter 31: "We Are Going to Beat Them"

426   **"I believe we shall make them rue"**: Martin Gilbert, comp., *The Churchill War Papers*, vol. 2, *Never Surrender, May 1940–December 1940* (New York: W. W. Norton, 1995), 221.

426   **"No. Bury them in caves and cellars"**: Ibid., including n. 2.

428   **"He considered the salvation of three"**: Nigel Nicolson, *Alex: The Life of Field Marshal Earl Alexander of Tunis* (New York: Atheneum, 1973), 108.

429   **"missed the ships, and the ships missed"**: Ibid., 111.

429   **The bombing was relentless and effective**: A. D. Divine, *Dunkirk* (New York: E. P. Dutton, 1948), 214.

433   **"divisional engineers [drive] their lorries"**: Earl Alexander, *The Alexander Memoirs, 1940–1945* (New York: McGraw-Hill, 1962), 78.

434   **"the beach was filled with masses"**: Frank Shaw and Joan Shaw, comps., *We Remember Dunkirk: Over 100 Personal Accounts* (Hinckley, Leicestershire: n.p., 1990), 47.

436   **Hundreds of passenger trains**: Ashley Brown, *Dunkirk and the Great Western* (London: Great Western Railway Company, 1945), 33.

436   **"the ladies meeting us as we"**: Shaw and Shaw, *We Remember Dunkirk*, 121.

437   **"were very mixed"**: Ibid., 65.

437   **"the hush that fell over the promenade"**: Ibid., 68.

Chapter 32: The Dunkirk Spirit

441   **"This would mean the establishment"**: Martin Gilbert, comp., *The Churchill War Papers*, vol. 2, *Never Surrender, May 1940–December 1940* (New York: W. W. Norton, 1995), 230.

441   **"it was clear that the rate of loss"**: A. D. Divine, *Dunkirk* (New York: E. P. Dutton, 1948), 208.

442   **"a set of bagpipes as a summons"**: Ibid., 211.

442   **"It was impossible to explain"**: Ibid., 212.

443   **"We cannot leave our allies"**: Hugh Sebag-Montefiore, *Dunkirk: Fight to the Last Man* (Cambridge, MA: Harvard University Press, 2006), 448 and 634, n. 2.

444   **Most of the remaining French troops**: Divine, *Dunkirk*, 257.

444   **"We were not hard pressed"**: Nigel Nicolson, *Alex: The Life of Field Marshal Earl Alexander of Tunis* (New York: Atheneum, 1973), 114.

444   **"to annihilate the allied forces"**: L. F. Ellis, *The War in France and Flanders, 1939–1940*, ed. J. R. M. Butler (Nashville, TN: Battery Press; London: Imperial War Museum, 1996), 274.

446   **"He had thought of nothing"**: Gilbert, *The Churchill War Papers*, 238.

447   **"The attributes of a victory"**: Winston Churchill, *Never Give In!: The Best of Winston Churchill's Speeches*, selected by his grandson Winston S. Churchill (New York: Hyperion, 2003), 214; Gilbert, *The Churchill War Papers*, 243.

447   **"Wars are not won"**: Churchill, *Never Give In!*, 214; Gilbert, *The Churchill War Papers*, 243.

447   **"Even though large tracts of Europe"**: Churchill, *Never Give In!*, 218; Gilbert, *The Churchill War Papers*, 247.

448   **"That was worth 1,000 guns"**: Gilbert, *The Churchill War Papers*, 248.

448   **"sent shivers (not of fear) down my spine"**: Harold Nicolson, *Diaries and Letters*, vol. 2, *1939–1945*, ed. Nigel Nicolson (London: Collins, 1967), 90.

449   **"hateful decision, the most unnatural"**: Sir Winston Churchill, *Their Finest Hour*, vol. 2 of *The Second World War* (Boston: Houghton Mifflin, 1949), 232.

450   **"Mass Observation," organized under**: Clive Ponting, *1940: Myth and Reality* (Chicago: Elephant Paperbacks, 1993), 160–61.

452   **In May of 2016 a letter to the *Times***: Letter of David Housemen, *Times* (London), May 30, 2016.

Chapter 33: At Sea

457   **"both of whom nudged him towards the Hollywood option"**: Charles Drazin, *Korda: Britain's Only Movie Mogul* (London: Sidgwick & Jackson, 2002), 229.

458   **"I must frankly admit"**: Martin Gilbert, comp., *The Churchill War*

Papers, vol. 2, *Never Surrender, May 1940–December 1940* (New York: W. W. Norton, 1995), 542.

459   **"I certainly do not propose to send"**: Ibid., 546.

459   **The wealthy and the well connected**: Clive Ponting, *1940: Myth and Reality* (Chicago: Elephant Paperbacks, 1993), 148–49.

461   **Not until the Battle of Britain**: Ibid., 146–48.

461   **French casualties:** Alistair Horne, *To Lose a Battle: France 1940* (London: Penguin Group, 1990), 666–67.

Bibliography

Air Intelligence Liaison Officer. *The Diary of a Staff Officer*. London: Methuen, 1941.

Alanbrooke, Lord. *War Diaries, 1939–1945*. Los Angeles: University of California Press, 2001.

Alexander, Field Marshal Earl. *The Alexander Memoirs, 1940–1945*. New York: McGraw-Hill, 1962.

Amery, Leo. *The Empire at Bay: The Leo Amery Diaries, 1929–1945*. London: Hutchinson, 1988.

Anonymous. *Infantry Officer: A Personal Record*. London: B. T. Batsford, 1943.

Atkin, Ronald. *Pillar of Fire: Dunkirk 1940*. London: Sidgwick and Jackson, 1990.

Baedeker, Karl *Belgium and Holland*. London: Karl Baedeker, 1901.

Beaverbrook, Lord. *Politicians and the War, 1914–1916*. Hamden, CT: Archon Books, 1968.

———. *The Decline and Fall of Lloyd George*. London: Collins, 1963.

Beevor, Antony. *Ardennes 1944: Hitler's Last Gamble*. London: Viking, 2015.

Benoist-Méchin, J. *Sixty Days That Shook the West*. London: Jonathan Cape, 1963.

Bond, Brian. *The Battle for France and Flanders, 1940: Sixty Years On*. Edited by Michael Taylor. South Yorkshire: Leo Cooper, 2001.

———. *Britain, France and Belgium, 1939–1940*. London: Brassey's, 1990.

———. *France and Belgium, 1939–1940*. London: Davis-Poynter, 1975.

Boothe, Clare. *European Spring*. London: Hamish Hamilton, 1941.

Bowman, J. E. *Three Stripes and a Gun: A Young Man's Journey towards Maturity*. Braunton, Devon: Merlin Books, 1987.

Boyle, Andrew. *Poor, Dear Brendan: The Quest for Brendan Bracken*. London: Hutchinson, 1974.

Brown, Ashley. *Dunkirk and the Great Western*. London: Great Western Railway Company, 1945.

Brownlow, Donald Grey. *Panzer Baron: The Military Exploits of General Hasso von Manteuffel*. North Quincy, MA: Christopher Publishing House, 1975.

Cadogan, Sir Alex. *The Diaries of Sir Alex Cadogan, O.M., 1938–1945*. Edited by David Dilks. London: Cassell, 1971.

Carreño, Richard. *Lord of Hosts: The Life of Sir Henry "Chips" Channon*. Philadelphia: Philabooks Press, 2016.

Cartwright, Reginald. *Mercy and Murder: An American Ambulance Driver's Experiences in Finland, Norway and France*. London: Iliffe & Sons, 1941.

Cato. *Guilty Men*. London: Faber and Faber, 2010.

Chandler, David G. *The Campaigns of Napoleon*. New York: Scribner, 1966.

Channon, Sir Henry. *Chips: The Diaries of Sir Henry Channon*. Edited by Robert Rhodes James. London: Phoenix, 1996.

Chapman, Guy. *Why France Fell: The Defeat of the French Army in 1940*. New York: Holt, Rinehart and Winston, 1968.

Churchill, Sir Winston. *The Gathering Storm*. Vol. 1 of *The Second World War*. Boston: Houghton Mifflin, 1948.

———. *Never Give In!: The Best of Winston Churchill's Speeches*. Selected by his grandson Winston S. Churchill. New York: Hyperion, 2003.

———. *Their Finest Hour*. Vol. 2 of *The Second World War*. Boston: Houghton Mifflin, 1949.

Churchill, Sir Winston, and Emery Reves. *Winston Churchill and Emery Reves: Correspondence, 1937–1964*. Edited by Martin Gilbert. Austin: University of Texas Press, 1997.

Ciano, Count Galeazzo. *The Ciano Diaries, 1939–1943: The Complete Unabridged Diaries of Count Galeazzo Ciano, Italian Minister for Foreign Affairs, 1936–1943*. Edited by Hugh Gibson. Garden City, NY: Simon Publications, 2001.

Coad, Jonathan. *Dover Castle: A Frontline Fortress and Its Wartime Tunnels*. London: English Heritage, 2011.

Colville, John. *The Fringes of Power: 10 Downing Street Diaries, 1939–1955*. New York: W. W. Norton, 1985.

———. J. R. *Man of Valour: The Life of Field-Marshal the Viscount Gort*. London: Collins, 1972.

Cooper, Duff. *The Duff Cooper Diaries, 1915–1951*. Edited by John Julius Norwich. London: Weidenfeld & Nicolson, 2005.

Coward, Noël. *Future Indefinite*. London: Bloomsbury, 2014.

Curtis, James. *William Cameron Menzies: The Shape of Films to Come*. New York: Pantheon Books, 2015.

Dalton, Hugh. *Hugh Dalton Memoirs, 1931–1945: The Fateful Years*. London: Frederick Muller, 1957.

De Gaulle, Charles. *The Call to Honour, 1940–1942*. Vol. 1 of *War Memoirs*. New York: Viking Press, 1955.

———. *Salvation, 1944–1946*. Vol. 3 of *War Memoirs*. New York: Viking Press, 1960.

———. *Unity, 1942–1944*. Vol. 2 of *War Memoirs*. New York: Viking Press, 1959.

Divine, A. D. *Dunkirk*. New York: E. P. Dutton, 1948.

Drazin, Charles. *Korda: Britain's Only Movie Mogul*. London: Sidgwick & Jackson, 2002.

Dutourd, Jean. *Les taxis de la Marne*. Paris: Gallimard, 1956.

Ellis, L. F. *The War in France and Flanders, 1939–1940.* Edited by J. R. M. Butler. Nashville, TN: Battery Press; London: Imperial War Museum, 1996.

———. *Welsh Guards at War,* 1939–1946. Aldershot: Gale and Polden, 1946.

Eyewitness War. South Woodham Ferrers, Essex, UK: Colson House, 1995.

Feiling, Keith. *The Life of Neville Chamberlain.* London: Macmillian, 1946.

Fowler, Will. *France, Holland and Belgium, 1940–1941.* Hersham, Surrey: Ian Allan Publishing, 2002.

Franklyn, Sir Harold E. *The Story of One Green Howard in the Dunkirk Campaign.* Richmond, Yorkshire: Green Howards, 1966.

Fraser, David. *And We Shall Shock Them: The British Army in the Second World War.* London: Book Club Associates, 1983.

Gelb, Norman. *Dunkirk: The Complete Story of the First Step in the Defeat of Hitler.* New York: William Morrow, 1989.

Gilbert, Martin, comp. *The Churchill War Papers.* Vol. 1, *At the Admiralty, September 1939–May 1940.* New York: W. W. Norton, 1993.

———, comp. *The Churchill War Papers.* Vol. 2, *Never Surrender, May 1940–December 1940.* New York: W. W. Norton, 1995.

Gilbert, Martin, and Richard Gott. *The Appeasers.* Boston: Houghton Mifflin, 1963.

Gough, Guy F. *Thirty Days to Dunkirk: The Royal Irish Fusiliers, May 1940.* Wrexham, Clwyd: Bridge Books, 1990.

Goutard, Adolphe. *The Battle of France, 1940.* Translated by A. R. P. Burgess. New York: Ives Washburn, 1959.

Graham, Stewart. *Burying Caesar: The Churchill-Chamberlain Rivalry.* Woodstock, NY: Overlook Press, 2001.

Grimshaw, Geoffrey. *British Pleasure Steamers, 1920–1939.* London: Richard Tilling, 1945.

Grimwood, Ian R. *A Little Chit of a Fellow: A Biography of the Right Hon. Leslie Hore-Belisha.* Sussex, UK: Book Guild Publishing, 2006.

Guderian, Heinz. *Achtung-Panzer!* Translated by Christopher Duffy. Strand, London: Arms & Armour Press, 1992.

Gwynn-Browne, Arthur. *F.S.P.: An N.C.O.'s Description of His and Others' First Six Months of War January 1st–June 1st 1940.* Edited by N. H. Reeve. Bridgend, Wales: Seren, 2004.

———. *Gone for a Burton.* London: Chatto & Windus, 1945.

Halder, Franz. *The Halder War Diary, 1939–1942.* Edited by Charles Burdick and Hans-Adolf Jacobsen. Navato, CA: Presidio Press, 1988.

Hamilton, Nigel. *The Full Monty.* Vol. 1, *Montgomery of Alamein, 1889–1942.* London: Penguin Press, 2001.

Hay, Ian. *The Battle of Flanders: The Army at War.* London: His Majesty's Stationery Office, 1941.

Hinsley, F. H. *British Intelligence in the Second World War.* New York: Cambridge University Press, 1993.

Hitler, Adolf. *Hitler's War Directives, 1939–1945.* Edited by H. R. Trevor-Roper. London: Sidgwick & Jackson, 1964.

Horne, Alistair. *To Lose a Battle: France 1940.* London: Penguin Group, 1990.

Horrabin, J. F. *Horrabin's Atlas-History of the Second Great War.* Vol. 1, *September 1939 to January 1940.* London: Thomas Nelson, 1940.

Ironside, Sir Edmund. *Time Unguarded: The Ironside Diaries, 1937–1940.* Edited by Roderick Macleod and Denis Kelly. New York: David McKay, 1962.

Ismay, General Lord. *The Memoirs of General Lord Ismay.* New York: Viking Press, 1960.

Jackson, Robert. *Dunkirk: The British Evacuation, 1940.* London: Cassell Military Paperbacks, 2002.

Karslake, Basil. *1940: The Last Act: The Story of the British Forces in France after Dunkirk.* Hamden, CT: Archon Books, 1979.

Kennedy, Joseph P. *Hostage of Fortune: The Letters of Joseph P. Kennedy.* Edited by Amanda Smith. New York: Viking Press, 2001.

Keyes, Lord. *The Keyes Papers: Selections from the Private and Official Correspondence of Admiral of the Fleet Baron Keyes of Zeebrugge.* Vol. 3, *1939–1945.* Edited by Paul G. Halpern. London: Allen & Unwin for the Navy Records Society, 1981.

La Falaise, Henry de. *Through Hell to Dunkirk.* Harrisburg, PA: Military Service Publishing Company, 1943.

Langstaff, C. K. *Diary of a Driver—With the R.A.S.C. in Britain and in France, 1939–1940.* London: Epworth Press, 1943.

Levine, Joshua. *Forgotten Voices of Dunkirk.* London: Ebury Press, 2010.

Liddell Hart, B. H. *The German Generals Talk.* New York: Harper Perennial, 2002.

Linklater, Eric. *The Defence of Calais.* London: His Majesty's Stationery Office, 1941.

———. *The Highland Division.* London: His Majesty's Stationery Office, 1942.

Longden, Sean. *Dunkirk: The Men They Left Behind.* London: Constable & Robinson, 2009.

Lord, Walter. *The Miracle of Dunkirk.* New York: Viking Press, 1982.

Lukacs, John. *Five Days in London, May 1940.* New Haven, CT: Yale University Press, 2001.

Macdonald, Dwight, ed. *Parodies: An Anthology from Chaucer to Beerbohm—and After.* New York: Random House, 1960.

Macintyre, Ben. *A Spy among Friends: Kim Philby and the Great Betrayal.* New York: Crown, 2014.

Maisky, Ivan. *The Maisky Diaries: Red Ambassador to the Court of St. James's, 1932–1943.* Edited by Gabriel Gorodetsky, translated by Tatiana Sorokina and Oliver Ready. New Haven, CT: Yale University Press, 2015.

Manchester, William. *The Last Lion: Winston Spencer Churchill.* Vol. 2, *Alone, 1932–1940.* Boston: Little, Brown, 1988.

Manstein, Eric von. *Lost Victories: The War Memoirs of Hitler's Most Brilliant General.* Foreword by B. H. Liddell Hart. Novato, CA: Presidio Press, 1994.

Mattingly, Garrett. *The Defeat of the Spanish Armada*. Boston: Houghton Mifflin, 1984.

Maupassant, Guy de. *The Necklace and Other Stories*. Translated by Sandra Smith. New York: Liveright, 2015.

McDonough, Frank. *Hitler, Chamberlain and Appeasement*. Cambridge: Cambridge University Press, 2002.

McKay, Sinclair. *Dunkirk: From Disaster to Deliverance—Testimonies of the Last Survivors*. London: Aurum Press, 2014.

Mepham, C. R. *From Belgium to Dunkirk*. London: Arthur H. Stockwell, 1943.

Michelin. *Le Guide Michelin 2014: Hotels & Restaurants*. Boulogne: Michelin, 2014.

Minney, R. J. *The Private Papers of Hore-Belisha*. London: Collins, 1960.

More, Charles. *The Road to Dunkirk: The British Expeditionary Force and the Battle of the Ypres-Comines Canal, 1940*. London: Frontline Books, 2013.

Narracott, A. H. *War News Had Wings: A Record of the R.A.F. in France*. London: Frederick Muller, 1941.

Nasaw, David. *The Patriarch: The Remarkable Life and Turbulent Times of Joseph P. Kennedy*. New York: Penguin Press, 2012.

Nicolson, Harold. *Diaries and Letters*. Vol. 2, *1930–1939*. Edited by Nigel Nicolson. London: Collins, 1967.

Osgood, Samuel M. *The Fall of France, 1940: Causes and Responsibilities*. 2nd ed. Lexington, MA: D. C. Heath, 1972.

Overy, Richard. *Britain at War: From the Invasion of Poland to the Surrender of Japan, 1939–1945*. London: Carlton Books, in association with IWM, 2014.

Ponting, Clive. *1940: Myth and Reality*. Chicago: Elephant Paperbacks, 1993.

Pownall, Sir Henry. *Chief of Staff: The Diaries of Lieutenant-General Sir Henry Pownall*. Edited by Brian Bond. 2 vols. Hamden, CT: Archon Books, 1973–74.

Prior, Robin. *When Britain Saved the West: The Story of 1940*. New Haven, CT: Yale University Press, 2015.

Pritchard, Jack. *Seven Years a Grenadier, 1939–1946*. Northamptonshire, UK: Forces & Corporate Publishing, 1999.

Reynaud, Paul. *In the Thick of the Fight, 1930–1945*. New York: Simon and Schuster, 1955.

Richardson, Matthew. *Tigers at Dunkirk: The Leicestershire Regiment and the Fall of France*. Barnsley, South Yorkshire: Pen & Sword Military, 2010.

Roberts, Andrew. *Eminent Churchillians*. London: Phoenix, 1995.

———. *The Holy Fox: The Life of Lord Halifax*. London: Head of Zeus, 2014.

Rommel, Erwin. *The Rommel Papers*. Edited by B. H. Liddell Hart. New York: Da Capo Press, 1953.

Roosevelt, Franklin D., and Winston Churchill. *Roosevelt and Churchill: Their Secret Wartime Correspondence*. Edited by Francis L. Loewenheim, Harold D. Langley, and Manfred Jonas. New York: Saturday Review Press, E. P. Dutton, 1975.

Rossiter, Mike. *I Fought at Dunkirk*. London: Bantam Press, 2012.

Rothbrust, Florian K. *Guderian's XIXth Panzer Corps and The Battle of France: Breakthrough in the Ardennes, May 1940.* Westport, CT: Praeger, 1990.

Rowe, Vivian. *The Great Wall of France: The Life and Death of the Maginot Line.* New York: C. P. Putnam's Sons, 1961

Ryan, Cornelius. *The Last Battle: The Classic History of the Battle for Berlin.* New York: Simon and Schuster Paperbacks, 1994.

Schmidt, Paul. *Hitler's Interpreter.* Edited by R. H. C. Steed. New York: Macmillian, 1951.

Schneider, Wolfgang. *Panzer Tactics: German Small-Unit Armor Tactics in World War II.* Mechanicsburg, PA: Stackpole Books, 2000.

Sebag-Montefiore, Hugh. *Dunkirk: Fight to the Last Man.* Cambridge, MA: Harvard University Press, 2006.

Self, Robert. *Neville Chamberlain.* London: Hutchinson, 2006.

Shaw, Frank., and Joan Shaw, comps. *We Remember Dunkirk: Over 100 Personal Accounts.* Hinckley, Leicestershire: n.p., 1990.

Shirer, William L. *Berlin Diary: The Journal of a Foreign Correspondent, 1934–1941.* New York: Galahad Books, 1995.

———. *The Rise and Fall of the Third Reich: A History of Nazi Germany.* New York: Touchstone, 1981.

Smurthwaite, David, Mark Nicholis, Linda Washington, et al. *Against All Odds: The British Army of 1939–1940.* London: National Army Museum, 1990.

Spears, Sir Edward. *Assignment to Catastrophe.* Vol. 1, *Prelude to Dunkirk, July 1939–May 1940.* New York: A. A. Wyn, 1954.

———. *Assignment to Catastrophe.* Vol. 2, *The Fall of France, June 1940.* New York: A. A. Wyn, 1955.

———. *Liaison, 1914: A Narrative of the Great Retreat.* London: William Heinemann Ltd., 1931

Stewart, Geoffrey. *Dunkirk and the Fall of France: Campaign Chronicles.* Edited by Christopher Summerville. Barnsley, South Yorkshire: Pen & Sword Military, 2008.

Stewart, Graham. *Burying Caesar: The Churchill-Chamberlain Rivalry.* Woodstock, NY: Overlook Press, 1999.

Taylor, A. J. P. *The Origins of the Second World War.* New York: Simon and Schuster, 2005.

Thompson, Julian. *Dunkirk: Retreat to Victory.* New York: Arcade Publishing, 2008.

Toland, John. *Adolf Hitler.* Garden City, NY: Doubleday, 1976.

Trevor-Roper, Hugh. *The Secret World: Behind the Curtain of British Intelligence in WWII and the Cold War.* Edited by Edward Harrison. London: I. B. Tauris, 2014.

Tuchman, Barbara W. *The Guns of August, The Proud Tower.* New York: Library of America, 2012.

Waugh, Evelyn. *Men at Arms.* Boston: Little, Brown, 1952.

———. *Put Out More Flags.* Boston: Little, Brown, 1945.

Weygand, Maxime. *Recalled to Service: The Memoirs of General Maxime*

Weygand of the Académie Française. Translated by E. W. Dickes. London: Heinemann, 1952.

Wheeler-Bennett, John W. *The Nemesis of Power: The German Army in Politics, 1918–1945.* London: Macmillan, 1954.

Williams, Douglas. *The New Contemptibles.* London: John Murray, 1940.

Wilson, A. N. *Victoria: A Life.* New York: Penguin Press, 2014.

Woodward, David. *Ramsay at War: The Fighting Life of Admiral Sir Bertram Ramsay.* London: William Kimber, 1957.

Young, G. M. *Stanley Baldwin.* London: Rupert Hart-Davis, 1952.

List of Illustrations

Index

Page numbers in *italics* refer to illustrations and maps.

About the Author

Michael Korda was born in London in 1933 and has lived in the United States since 1958. He was educated at Le Rosey, in Switzerland, did his military service in the Royal Air Force, and then attended Magdalen College, Oxford. In 1956, he drove to Budapest with three friends to deliver medical supplies to the insurgents, for which he was made a Commander of the Order of Merit of the Republic of Hungary in 2006.

After working briefly for CBS TV in New York City, Korda joined Simon and Schuster as an assistant editor in 1958, and subsequently became managing editor, executive editor, and editor in chief. Over nearly five decades his authors have included presidents Carter, Reagan, and Nixon; Charles de Gaulle; Dr. Henry Kissinger; Mayor Ed Koch; the Duchess of York; such stars as Cher, Kirk Douglas, and Shelley Winters; such media figures as Phil Donahue and Larry King; historians such as David McCullough, Richard Rhodes, Michael Beschloss, and Cornelius Ryan; novelists Larry McMurtry, Jacqueline Susann, Jackie Collins, Mary Higgins Clark, James Leo Herlihy, Susan Howatch, James Lee Burke, and Stephen Hunter; and such theater figures as Tennessee Williams, John Gielgud, and Laurence Olivier. Korda is now editor in chief emeritus of Simon and Schuster.

His books include the #1 bestseller *Power*, the best-selling novels *Queenie* and *The Fortune*, a widely acclaimed book about his family, *Charmed Lives*, and, more recently, *Hero: The Life and Legend of Lawrence of Arabia*, *With Wings Like Eagles: A History of the Battle of Britain*, *Ike: An American Hero*, *Country Matters*, *Another Life*, *Horse People*, *Ulysses S. Grant*, *Journey to a Revolution*, and *Clouds of Glory: The Life and Legend of Robert E. Lee*.